Big Picture Workshop (BigPicture 2023)

Singapore
7 December 2023

ISBN: 978-1-7138-9046-1

Printed from e-media with permission by:

Curran Associates, Inc.
57 Morehouse Lane
Red Hook, NY 12571

Some format issues inherent in the e-media version may also appear in this print version.

Printed with permission by Curran Associates, Inc. (2024)

For permission requests, please contact the Association for Computational Linguistics at the address below.

Association for Computational Linguistics
209 N. Eighth Street
Stroudsburg, Pennsylvania 18360

Phone: 1-570-476-8006
Fax: 1-570-476-0860

acl@aclweb.org

Additional copies of this publication are available from:

Curran Associates, Inc.
57 Morehouse Lane
Red Hook, NY 12571 USA
Phone: 845-758-0400
Fax: 845-758-2633
Email: curran@proceedings.com
Web: www.proceedings.com

BigPicture 2023

The Big Picture Workshop

Proceedings of the Workshop

December 7, 2023

The BigPicture organizers gratefully acknowledge the support from the following sponsors.

Gold

amazon | science

Google

Silver

Introduction

Welcome to the Proceedings of the first iteration of the Big Picture Workshop (The Big Picture: Crafting a Research Narrative). The workshop is hosted at EMNLP 2023, in Singapore, on December 7, 2023.

The Big Picture Workshop provides a dedicated venue for exploring and distilling broader NLP research narratives. All research exists within a larger context, and progress is made by standing on the shoulders of giants: building on the foundations laid by earlier researchers. In light of rapid publication rates and concise paper formats, it has become increasingly difficult, however, to recognize the larger story to which a paper is connected. The Big Picture Workshop invites researchers to reflect on how their individual contributions fit within the overall research landscape and what stories they are telling with their bodies of research. The goals of the workshop are to enhance communication and understanding between different lines of work, highlight how works connect and build on each other, generate insights that are difficult to glean without combining and reconciling different research narratives, encourage broader collaboration and awareness of prior work in the NLP community, and facilitate understanding of trajectories and insights within the field of NLP.

We received 12 submissions, of which we accepted 10 for presentation at the workshop. Those 10 accepted papers are contained in this volume. We also accepted for presentation two additional papers to be included in Findings of EMNLP 2023.

The workshop schedule features one standard invited talk, and three special invited presentations designed to foster live engagement between different lines of related work. In these special presentations, two to three invited presenters speak on their individual lines of work and the connections between them, followed by a moderated discussion further exploring the overall narrative that emerges from these works in aggregate. In addition to invited presentations, the workshop features one Best Paper session, one in-person poster session, and one virtual poster session.

We extend heartfelt thanks to our program committee, our participants, and all authors who submitted papers for consideration—your engagement has been critical to the success of the workshop. We also thank Amazon, Google, and Hugging Face for generous sponsorship. Finally, we thank the EMNLP 2023 organizers for their hard work and support.

The Big Picture Workshop Organizers,

Yanai Elazar, Allyson Ettinger, Nora Kassner, Sebastian Ruder, Noah Smith

Organizing Committee

Program Chairs

Yanai Elazar, Allen Institute for AI & University of Washington, USA
Allyson Ettinger, Allen Institute for AI
Nora Kassner, Google DeepMind, United Kingdom
Sebastian Ruder, Google DeepMind, Germany
Noah A. Smith, Allen Institute for AI & University of Washington, USA

Program Committee

Reviewers

David Ifeoluwa Adelani, Jacob Andreas, Maria Antoniak, Akari Asai

Jonathan Berant, Ben Bogin

Eunsol Choi

Philipp Dufter, Greg Durrett

Matthias Gallé

Valentin Hofmann

Alankar Jain

Tal Linzen

Kyle Mahowald, Gaurav Mishra

Hao Peng, Jonas Pfeiffer, Barbara Plank

Machel Reid, Paul Roit

Ori Shapira, Vered Shwartz, Anders Søgaard

Ivan Vulić, Yogarshi Vyas

Adina Williams

Keynote Talk: The Vision Thing: Finding and Pursuing your Research Passion

Raymond J. Mooney
UT Austin
2023-12-07 09:15:00 – Room: **Virgo 1 & 2**

Abstract: A key contribution to being a successful researcher in natural language processing, as in any area, is having a clear overarching vision of what your body of research is trying to accomplish. Using my own 40-year career as an example, I will attempt to provide general advice on formulating and pursuing a coherent research vision. In particular, I will focus on formulating a unique, personal objective that exploits your specific talents, knowledge, and passions, and that is distinct from the current popular trends in the field. I will also focus on formulating a vision that bridges existing fields of study to produce an overarching agenda that unifies previously disparate ideas.

Bio: Raymond J. Mooney is a Professor in the Department of Computer Science at the University of Texas at Austin. He received his Ph.D. in 1988 from the University of Illinois at Urbana/Champaign. He is an author of over 200 published research papers, primarily in the areas of machine learning and natural language processing. He was the President of the International Machine Learning Society from 2008-2011, program co-chair for AAAI 2006, general chair for HLT-EMNLP 2005, and co-chair for ICML 1990. He is a Fellow of AAAI, ACM, and ACL and the recipient of the Classic Paper award from AAAI-19 and best paper awards from AAAI-96, KDD-04, ICML-05 and ACL-07.

Keynote Talk: Is Attention = Explanationand the Role of Interpretability in NLP

Sarah Wiegreffe
AI2 & UW
2023-12-07 11:00:00 – Room: **Virgo 1 & 2**

Abstract: Attention mechanisms have become a core component of neural models in Natural Language Processing over the past decade. These mechanisms not only deliver substantial performance improvements but also claim to offer insights into the models' inner workings. In this talk, we will highlight a series of contributions we have made that provided a critical perspective on the role of attention as a faithful explanation for model predictions, and sparked a larger conversation on the overarching goals of interpretability methods in NLP. We'll contrast our methodological approaches and findings to highlight that there is no one-size-fits-all answer to the question "Is attention explanation?". Finally, we'll explore the role of attention as an explanation mechanism in today's NLP landscape.

Bio: Sarah Wiegreffe is a postdoctoral researcher at the Allen Institute for AI (AI2), working on the Aristo project. She also holds a courtesy appointment in the Allen School of Computer Science and Engineering at the University of Washington. Her research focuses on understanding how language models make predictions in an effort to make them more transparent to human users. She received her PhD from Georgia Tech in 2022 advised by Professor Mark Riedl, during which time she interned at Google and AI2 and won the AI2 outstanding intern award. She frequently serves on conference program committees, receiving outstanding area chair award at ACL 2023.

Keynote Talk: Is Attention = Explanationand the Role of Interpretability in NLP

Sarthak Jain
AWS AI Labs
2023-12-07 11:00:00 – Room: **Virgo 1 & 2**

Abstract: Attention mechanisms have become a core component of neural models in Natural Language Processing over the past decade. These mechanisms not only deliver substantial performance improvements but also claim to offer insights into the models' inner workings. In this talk, we will highlight a series of contributions we have made that provided a critical perspective on the role of attention as a faithful explanation for model predictions, and sparked a larger conversation on the overarching goals of interpretability methods in NLP. We'll contrast our methodological approaches and findings to highlight that there is no one-size-fits-all answer to the question "Is attention explanation?". Finally, we'll explore the role of attention as an explanation mechanism in today's NLP landscape.

Bio: Sarthak Jain is an Applied Scientist working on generative AI models at AWS. He received his PhD in 2022 from Northeastern University, where he was advised by Byron Wallace. Before this, he completed his BTech in Computer Engineering from Delhi Technological University. His current research interests include the interpretability and analysis of deep learning models.

Keynote Talk: On the Outcomes of Scientific Disagreements of Machine Morality

Liwei Jiang
University of Washington
2023-12-07 13:30:00 – Room: **Virgo 1 & 2**

Abstract: Disagreements and conflict are vital for driving scholarly progress, social and scientific alike. In research, we often identify gaps in others' and our own work, to present new ideas that remedy them. Disagreements are often small in nature: We disagree on methods rather than the research programme itself. In this talk, we discuss a disagreement of a different nature: namely one in which the substance of the disagreement is the existence of the task itself. We reflect on the experience of the conflict, how it was resolved, and what outcomes it has had.
In particular, Liwei will share her current interdisciplinary research journey on AI + humanity sparked by the Delphi experience. She will introduce Value Kaleidoscope—a novel computational system aiming to model potentially conflicting, pluralistic human values interwoven in human decision-making. Finally, she will talk about an exciting co-evolution opportunity unfolding between frontier AI technology and humanity fields.
Zeerak will go over ongoing work that considers the foundations and limits of machine learning and NLP with regard to ethically appropriate work. Specifically, they will discuss the use of the distributional hypothesis, and what particular visions of our societies it offers, and how machine learning seeks to construct our future in the vision of the past.

Bio: Liwei Jiang is a Ph.D. student in the Paul G. Allen School of Computer Science and Engineering at the University of Washington, specializing in Artificial Intelligence (AI) and Natural Language Processing (NLP). She is intrigued to tackle real-world needs with AI and understand the charms, mysteries, and peculiarities of humans. Thus, Her current research focuses on the co-evolution of AI and humanity: how to build better AI by taking inspiration from humans and how to gain valuable insights into humans by advancing AI. She has published at many NLP and AI venues (e.g., ACL, EMNLP, NAACL, NeurIPS, AAAI). Her work has been featured in many media outlets, including the New York Times, Wired, the Guardian, the Verge, IEEE Spectrum, and Nature Outlook. She works as a student researcher at Allen Institute for Artificial Intelligence (AI2).

Keynote Talk: On the Outcomes of Scientific Disagreements of Machine Morality

Zeerak Talat
Mohamed Bin Zayed University of Artificial Intelligence
2023-12-07 13:30:00 – Room: **Virgo 1 & 2**

Abstract: Disagreements and conflict are vital for driving scholarly progress, social and scientific alike. In research, we often identify gaps in others' and our own work, to present new ideas that remedy them. Disagreements are often small in nature: We disagree on methods rather than the research programme itself. In this talk, we discuss a disagreement of a different nature: namely one in which the substance of the disagreement is the existence of the task itself. We reflect on the experience of the conflict, how it was resolved, and what outcomes it has had.
In particular, Liwei will share her current interdisciplinary research journey on AI + humanity sparked by the Delphi experience. She will introduce Value Kaleidoscope—a novel computational system aiming to model potentially conflicting, pluralistic human values interwoven in human decision-making. Finally, she will talk about an exciting co-evolution opportunity unfolding between frontier AI technology and humanity fields.
Zeerak will go over ongoing work that considers the foundations and limits of machine learning and NLP with regard to ethically appropriate work. Specifically, they will discuss the use of the distributional hypothesis, and what particular visions of our societies it offers, and how machine learning seeks to construct our future in the vision of the past.

Bio: Zeerak Talat (formerly known as Zeerak Waseem) is a Research Fellow at Mohamed Bin Zayed University of Artificial Intelligence. Zeerak holds a Ph.D. in Computer Science from the University of Sheffield, with a focus on natural language processing. Zeerak's work examines the assumptions that underpin NLP and machine learning (ML) technologies. Drawing on research from anthropology, discard studies, science and technology studies, and media studies, their work seeks to consider NLP and ML technologies through the lens of content moderation technologies to understand how they can cause harm to individuals and societies.

Keynote Talk: The Role of Demonstrations: What In-Context Learning actually does

Sewon Min
University of Washington
2023-12-07 16:00:00 – Room: **Virgo 1 & 2**

Abstract: In-Context Learning (ICL) enables a language model (LM) to learn a new correlation between inputs and outputs during inference, without explicit gradient updates. In this talk, we show a series of work centered around the research question: whether or not the correctness of demonstrations is needed for good performance of ICL. Through a series of experiments and analyses, we delve into the nuances of this relationship across various experimental setups, models (plain LMs or instruction-tuned ones), and tasks (classification or generation). Our findings contribute to a broader understanding of how LMs engage in in-context learning, shedding light on what new correlations they can or cannot learn, and leading to a new line of research in discovering unexpected behaviors of LMs.

Bio: Sewon Min is a final year Ph.D. candidate at the University of Washington, advised by Luke Zettlemoyer and Hannaneh Hajishirzi. Her research is in language modeling, focusing on new dimensions in modeling, scaling, and efficiency, and their extensions for information-seeking, legality, and privacy. She co-instructed and co-organized multiple tutorials and workshops at ACL, EMNLP, NAACL and NeurIPS. She is a recipient of the J.P. Morgan Fellowship, and was at Meta AI, Google Research, and Salesforce Research.

Keynote Talk: The Role of Demonstrations: What In-Context Learning actually does

Junyeob Kim
Seoul National University
2023-12-07 16:00:00 – Room: **Virgo 1 & 2**

Abstract: In-Context Learning (ICL) enables a language model (LM) to learn a new correlation between inputs and outputs during inference, without explicit gradient updates. In this talk, we show a series of work centered around the research question: whether or not the correctness of demonstrations is needed for good performance of ICL. Through a series of experiments and analyses, we delve into the nuances of this relationship across various experimental setups, models (plain LMs or instruction-tuned ones), and tasks (classification or generation). Our findings contribute to a broader understanding of how LMs engage in in-context learning, shedding light on what new correlations they can or cannot learn, and leading to a new line of research in discovering unexpected behaviors of LMs.

Bio: Sewon Min is a final year Ph.D. candidate at the University of Washington, advised by Luke Zettlemoyer and Hannaneh Hajishirzi. Her research is in language modeling, focusing on new dimensions in modeling, scaling, and efficiency, and their extensions for information-seeking, legality, and privacy. She co-instructed and co-organized multiple tutorials and workshops at ACL, EMNLP, NAACL and NeurIPS. She is a recipient of the J.P. Morgan Fellowship, and was at Meta AI, Google Research, and Salesforce Research.

Keynote Talk: The Role of Demonstrations: What In-Context Learning actually does

Kang Min Yoo
NAVER Cloud, NAVER AI Lab
2023-12-07 16:00:00 – Room: **Virgo 1 & 2**

Abstract: In-Context Learning (ICL) enables a language model (LM) to learn a new correlation between inputs and outputs during inference, without explicit gradient updates. In this talk, we show a series of work centered around the research question: whether or not the correctness of demonstrations is needed for good performance of ICL. Through a series of experiments and analyses, we delve into the nuances of this relationship across various experimental setups, models (plain LMs or instruction-tuned ones), and tasks (classification or generation). Our findings contribute to a broader understanding of how LMs engage in in-context learning, shedding light on what new correlations they can or cannot learn, and leading to a new line of research in discovering unexpected behaviors of LMs.

Bio: Kang Min Yoo is actively engaged in the fields of artificial intelligence and computational linguistics. He currently holds key roles as a Research and Applied Scientist at NAVER Cloud and as a Visiting Professor at Seoul National University's AI Institute. With an Integrated M.S. and Ph.D. in Computer Science from Seoul National University, his primary areas of expertise include large language models and natural language processing. At NAVER Cloud, he has spearheaded projects focused on developing Korean-centric LLM-based chat agents and the HyperT5 Seq2Seq HyperCLOVA. Additionally, Kang Min Yoo contributes to the academic community through his roles as an area chair and program committee member.

Table of Contents

Program

Thursday, December 7, 2023

10:05 - 09:15 *Break*

09:00 - 09:15 *Opening Remarks*

09:15 - 10:05 *The Vision Thing:Finding and Pursuing your Research Passion*

10:05 - 10:30 *Talk*

The Case for Scalable, Data-Driven Theory: A Paradigm for Scientific Progress in NLP
Julian Michael

11:00 - 10:30 *Break*

11:00 - 12:00 *Is Attention = Explanationand the Role of Interpretability in NLP*

12:00 - 13:30 *Lunch Break*

11:00 - 12:00 *From Machine Morality to Pluralistic Human Values:When AI Interfaces with Humanity*

14:30 - 15:30 *Poster Session*

Where are We in Event-centric Emotion Analysis? Bridging Emotion Role Labeling and Appraisal-based Approaches
Roman Klinger

Working Towards Digital Documentation of Uralic Languages With Open-Source Tools and Modern NLP Methods
Mika Hämäläinen, Jack Rueter, Khalid Alnajjar and Niko Tapio Partanen

Computational Narrative Understanding: A Big Picture Analysis
Andrew Piper

Thesis Distillation: Investigating The Impact of Bias in NLP Models on Hate Speech Detection
Fatma Elsafoury

Thursday, December 7, 2023 (continued)

Large Language Models as SocioTechnical Systems
Kaustubh Dhole

Towards Low-resource Language Generation with Limited Supervision
Kaushal Kumar Maurya and Maunendra Sankar Desarkar

Transformers as Graph-to-Graph Models
James Henderson, Alireza Mohammadshahi, Andrei Catalin Coman and Lesly Miculicich

It's MBR All the Way Down: Modern Generation Techniques Through the Lens of Minimum Bayes Risk
Amanda Bertsch, Alex Xie, Graham Neubig and Matthew R. Gormley

Analyzing Pre-trained and Fine-tuned Language Models
Marius Mosbach

15:30 - 16:00 *Break*

16:00 - 17:00 *The Role of Demonstrations:What In-Context Learning actually does*

17:00 - 17:15 *Closing Remarks*

Where are We in Event-centric Emotion Analysis? Bridging Emotion Role Labeling and Appraisal-based Approaches

Roman Klinger
Institut für Maschinelle Sprachverarbeitung
University of Stuttgart, Germany
roman.klinger@ims.uni-stuttgart.de

Abstract

The term emotion analysis in text subsumes various natural language processing tasks which have in common the goal to enable computers to understand emotions. Most popular is emotion classification in which one or multiple emotions are assigned to a predefined textual unit. While such setting is appropriate for identifying the reader's or author's emotion, emotion role labeling adds the perspective of mentioned entities and extracts text spans that correspond to the emotion cause. The underlying emotion theories agree on one important point; that an emotion is caused by some internal or external event and comprises several subcomponents, including the subjective feeling and a cognitive evaluation. We therefore argue that emotions and events are related in two ways. (1) Emotions are events; and this perspective is the fundament in natural language processing for emotion role labeling. (2) Emotions are caused by events; a perspective that is made explicit with research how to incorporate psychological appraisal theories in NLP models to interpret events. These two research directions, role labeling and (event-focused) emotion classification, have by and large been tackled separately. In this paper, we contextualize both perspectives and discuss open research questions.

1 Introduction

> "Communication is an exchange of facts, ideas, opinions, or emotions by two or more persons. The exchange is successful only when mutual understanding results." (Newman et al., 1967, p. 219)

The development of computational models in natural language processing aims at supporting communication between computers and humans; with language understanding research focusing on enabling the computer to comprehend the meaning of text. Sometimes, understanding facts is sufficient, for instance when scientific text is analyzed to automatically augment a database (Li et al., 2016; Trouillon et al., 2017). Factual statements can also comprise explicit reports of emotions or sentiments, such as "They were sad.", and in such cases, the analysis of subjective language blends with information extraction (Wiebe et al., 2004).

Emotion analysis, however, goes beyond such analysis of propositional statements. To better understand what emotion analysis models are expected to do, it is worth reviewing emotion theories in psychology. There are many of them, with varying purposes and approaches, but most of them, if not all, agree on the aspect that *emotions are caused by some event* and come with a change of various subsystems, such as a change in motivation, a subjective perception, an expression, and bodily symptoms. Another component is the evaluation of the causing event, sometimes even considered to constitute the emotion (Scarantino, 2016).

The *emotion also corresponds to an event itself*, embedded in a context of other events, people, and objects. All components of such emotion events (cause, stances towards other involved people, opinions about objects) may be described along an explicit mention of an emotion name. Any subset of them may appear in text, and may or may not be sufficient to reliably assign an emotion representation to the text author, a mentioned entity, or to a reader (Casel et al., 2021; Cortal et al., 2023).

This complexity has led to a set of various emotion analysis tasks in NLP, which we exemplify in an integrated manner in Figure 1. The most popular task is emotion prediction, either representing the writer's or the reader's emotion as a category, as valence/arousal values, or as appraisal vector (at the bottom of Figure 1, we will describe the underlying psychological theories in §2.1). Adding the task of cause detection bridges to the role labeling setup (visualized in more completeness at the top). Here, the emotion event is represented by the token span that represents the emotion experiencer, the cue, and the cause. *Emotion prediction focuses on*

Proceedings of the the Big Picture Workshop, pages 1–17
December 7, 2023

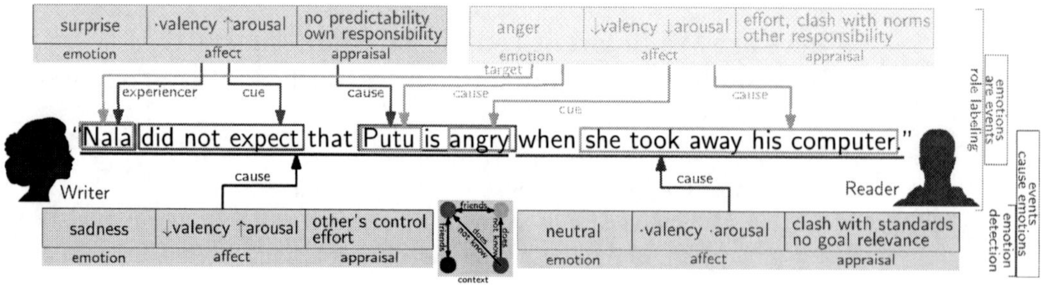

Figure 1: Integrated Visualization of Research Tasks in Emotion Analysis

understanding from text how events cause emotions, while role labeling focuses on understanding how emotions are represented as events themselves.

sWe now introduce the background to emotion analysis, including psychological theories, related tasks, and use cases (§2). Based on that, we consolidate recent research on the interpretation of events to infer an emotion and on emotion role labeling (§3.1–3.2). We then point out existing efforts on bridging both fields (§3.3) and, based on this, develop a list of open research questions (§4). We show a visualization how various NLP tasks and research areas are connected to emotion analysis in Figure 8 in the Appendix.

2 Related Work

2.1 Emotion Theories in Psychology

Before we can discuss emotion analysis, we need to introduce what an emotion is. The term typically refers to some feeling, some sensation, that is defined following various perspectives. Scarantino (2016) provides an overview of various emotion theories and differentiates between a *motivation tradition*, a *feeling tradition*, and an *evaluative tradition*.

2.1.1 Categorical Models of Basic Emotions

The motivation tradition includes theories that are popular in NLP such as the basic emotions proposed by Ekman (1992) and Plutchik (2001). They differ in how they define what makes an emotion basic: Ekman proposes a list of properties, including an automatic appraisal, quick onset, brief duration, and distinctive universal signals. According to him, non-basic emotions do not exist but are rather emotional plots, moods, or personality traits. Plutchik defines basic emotions based on their function, and non basic-emotions are gradations and mixtures. The set of basic emotions according to Ekman is commonly understood to correspond to joy, anger, disgust, fear, sadness, and surprise. However, in fact, the set is larger and there are even emotions for which it is not yet known if they could be considered basic (e.g., relief, guilt, or love, Ekman and Cordaro, 2011). The basic emotions according to Plutchik include anticipation and trust in addition. In NLP, such theories mostly serve as a source for label sets for which some evidence exists that they should be distinguishable, also in textual analysis. A study that uses a comparably large set of emotions is Demszky et al. (2020), while many other resource creation and modeling attempts focus on subsets (Alm et al., 2005; Strapparava and Mihalcea, 2007; Schuff et al., 2017; Li et al., 2017; Mohammad, 2012, i.a.).

2.1.2 Dimensional Models of Affect

An alternative to representing emotions as categorical labels is to place them in a (continuous) vector space, in which the dimensions correspond to some other meaning. The most popular one is the valence/arousal space, in which emotions are situated according to their subjective perception of a level of activation (arousal) and how positive the experience is (valence). This concept stems from the feeling tradition mentioned above and corresponds to affect (Posner et al., 2005). It also plays an important role in constructionist theories, which aim at explaining how the objectively measurable variables of valence and arousal may be linked by cognitive processes to emotion categorizations (Feldman Barrett, 2017). While we are not aware of any applications of the constructionist theories in NLP, emotion analysis has been formulated as valence/arousal regression (Buechel and Hahn, 2017; Preoţiuc-Pietro et al., 2016, i.a.). Valence and arousal predictions are related to, but not the same as, emotion intensity regression (Mohammad and Bravo-Marquez, 2017).

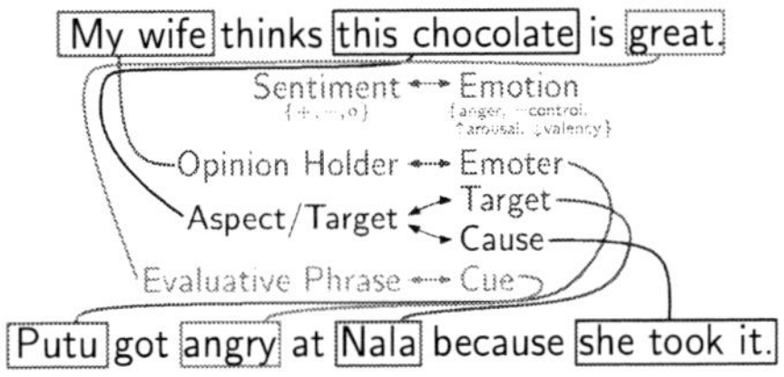

Figure 2: Comparison of structured sentiment analysis and emotion role labeling.

2.1.3 Appraisals

Affect is not the only so-called dimensional model to represent emotions. More recently, the concept of appraisals that represents the cognitive dimension of emotions, i.e., the cognitive evaluation of the event regarding the impact on the self, found attention in NLP. The set of appraisals that can explain emotions is not fixed and depends on the theory and the domain. It often includes variables that describe if an event can be expected to increase a required effort (likely to be high for anger or fear) or how much responsibility the experiencer of the emotion holds (high for feeling pride or guilt). Smith and Ellsworth (1985) showed that a comparably small set of 6 appraisal variables can characterize differences between 15 emotion categories. Scherer et al. (2001) describes a multi-step process of appraisal evaluations as one part of the emotion – their emotion component process model also reflects on additional emotion components, namely the bodily reaction, the expression, the motivational aspect, and the subjective feeling. Appraisal theories led to a set of knowledge bases and models that link events to emotions (Balahur et al., 2012; Cambria et al., 2022; Shaikh et al., 2009; Udochukwu and He, 2015), but only recently, resources and models have been proposed which make appraisal variables explicit (Stranisci et al., 2022; Hofmann et al., 2020, 2021; Troiano et al., 2022, 2023b; Wegge et al., 2022). This paper discusses work on appraisal theories to interpret events regarding the potentially resulting emotion in §3.1.

2.2 Tasks Related to Emotion Analysis

Emotion analysis is a task grounded in various previous research fields, from which we discuss sentiment analysis and personality profiling.

2.2.1 Sentiment Analysis

Sometimes, sentiment analysis is considered a simplified version of emotion analysis in which multiple emotion categories are conflated into two (positive or negative, sometimes distinguishing multiple levels of intensity, Kiritchenko et al. (2016)). We would like to argue that the tasks differ in more than the number of labels. Sentiment analysis is often equated to classifying the text into a more unspecific connotation of being positive or negative (Liu, 2012). Commonly, the sentiment of the text author is analyzed, which renders the task to be overlapping with opinion mining (Pang and Lee, 2008; Barnes et al., 2017). Emotion analysis is hardly ever about detecting the opinion regarding a product; while that is a common focus in sentiment analysis (Pontiki et al., 2014).

A more powerful approach to sentiment analysis is to not only detect if the author expresses something positive, but also to detect opinion holders, evaluated targets/aspects, and the phrase that describes the evaluation (Barnes et al., 2022; Pontiki et al., 2015, 2016; Klinger and Cimiano, 2013). The tasks of such "sentiment role labeling" and "emotion role labeling" do, however, barely match (see Figure 2):

(1) The *opinion holder* in sentiment analysis is a person that expresses an opinion, regarding some object, service, or person. This commonly follows a cognitive evaluation, likely to be a conscious process rather than an unbidden reaction. We would therefore not call the person experiencing an emotion a "holder" but rather an *emotion experiencer*, or *feeler*, or an *emoter* (to make the difference between an emotion and a feeling explicit).

(2) The *aspect/target* in sentiment analysis might correspond to two things in emotion analysis. It can be a *target*, I can be angry *at* someone, who is not solely the *cause* of that emotion. I can be angry at a friend, because she did eat my emergency supply of chocolate. But I cannot be *sad at* somebody. In emotion analysis, we care more about the *stimulus* or *cause* of an emotion. Sometimes, targets and causes are conflated.

(3) The *evaluative, subjective phrase* in sentiment analysis corresponds to emotion words (*cue* in Figure 1).

It is noteworthy that evaluative statements in sentiment also express an appraisal of something but the overlap with appraisal theories in emotion analysis is minimal – the evaluation of a product in sentiment analysis is often expressed explicitly. On the contrary, appraisal-based emotion analysis fo-

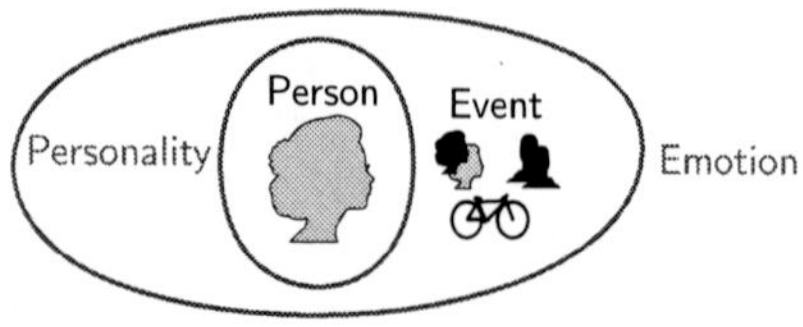

Figure 3: Comparison of personality detection and emotion analysis.

cuses on inferring the internal appraisal processes of a person purely from an event description. We refer the interested reader to Martin and White (2005) for a comprehensive analysis of the language used to describe evaluations.

2.2.2 Personality Profiling

Sometimes the task of personality analysis is seen to be similar to emotion analysis, because both an emotion and the personality are based on a person. Personality is, however, a function that depends only on the person, while an emotion depends on the person in interaction with a situation (see Figure 3). Therefore, personality is a stable trait, while emotions are states that change more flexibly (Geiser et al., 2017). The most prominent model that found application in NLP is the OCEAN/Big-Five model (Goldberg, 1999; Roccas et al., 2002), comprising openness to experience, conscientiousness, extraversion, agreeableness, and neuroticism (Pizzolli and Strapparava, 2019; Lynn et al., 2020; Kreuter et al., 2022; Golbeck et al., 2011). An alternative is HEXACO, adding the dimension of honesty (Lee and Ashton, 2018), which did, however, lead to less attention in NLP (Sinha et al., 2015). Early work in personality analysis based on linguistic features was based, similar to sentiment or emotion analysis, on word-counting approaches (Pennebaker and King, 1999). The Myers–Briggs Type Indicator (MBTI, Myers, 1998) received attention in NLP, partially because of a straight-forward way to collect data with hash-tag-based self-supervision (Plank and Hovy, 2015; Verhoeven et al., 2016). This model has weaknesses regarding reliability and validity (Boyle, 1995; Randall et al., 2017) which affect the robustness of NLP models (Stajner and Yenikent, 2021).

2.3 Use-Cases of Emotion Analysis

Every kind of text in which an interpretation of the emotional connotation is of value constitutes a potential use case for emotion modeling. This includes the analysis of social media (Mohammad et al., 2018; Klinger et al., 2018; Wang et al., 2012, i.a.), of news articles (Bostan et al., 2020, i.a.), of figurative language (Chauhan et al., 2020; Dankers et al., 2019, i.a.), of abusive language (Rajamanickam et al., 2020; Plaza-del Arco et al., 2022, i.a.) of literature (Kim and Klinger, 2018; Alm and Sproat, 2005; Dodds et al., 2011; Kim et al., 2017, i.a.), of clinically relevant disorders (Islam et al., 2018; Pestian et al., 2012, i.a.), or the support of customer agents (Labat et al., 2022).

Each domain implicitly defines which subtasks are relevant. For news headlines, the author's emotion is least interesting while estimating the (intended) impact on the reader is important, for instance to understand reactions in the society and intentional use to manipulate readers (Caiani and Di Cocco, 2023). For hate speech detection or other social media analysis tasks, the author's emotion is central. In literature, an interesting aspect is to understand which emotion is attributed to fictional characters (Kim and Klinger, 2019b; Hoorn and Konijn, 2003).

Each domain also comes with particular challenges, stemming from varying task formulations: News headlines are short and highly contextualized in the outlet, the time of publication, and the reader's stance towards topics (Schaffer, 1995). Social media comes in informal language (Kern et al., 2016). Literature often requires interpretations of longer text spans (Kuhn, 2019). Each of these applications therefore comes with design choices:

- What is the emotion perspective?
  (reader, writer, entities)
- What is the unit of analysis?
  (headline, tweet, paragraph, n sentences)
- Is text classification of predefined units sufficient or does a model need to assign emotions to automatically detected segments in the text?
- What are the variables to be predicted and the possible value domain?
  (emotion categories, appraisals, affect, spans of different kind)

So far, models have mostly been developed for specific use-cases, where such constraints can be clearly identified. This has, however, an impact on the generalizability of models. We will now discuss the two perspectives of *events that cause emotions* as an interpretation of emotion analysis as text classification of predefined textual units (§3.1) and of *events as emotions*, the case of emotion role labeling (§3.2). After that, we explain the efforts

Relevance	Implication	Coping	Normative Significance
Novelty • suddenness • familiarity • predictability • attention • att. removal Intrinsic Pleasantness • pleasant • unpleasant Goal Relevance • goal-related	Causality: agent • own responsib. • other's respons. • situational resp. Goal conduciveness • goal support Outcome probability • consequence anticipation Urgency • response urgency	Control • own control • others' control • chance control Adjustment • anticipated acceptance • effort	Internal standards compatibility • clash with own standards External standards compatibility • clash with norms

Figure 4: Variables used by Troiano et al. (2023b) to analyze text according to combined dimensions proposed by Scherer et al. (2001) and Smith and Ellsworth (1985).

to bring these two directions together (§3.3) and we build on top of this consolidation to point out important future research directions (§4).

3 The Link between Emotions and Events

3.1 Events cause Emotions: Appraisals

3.1.1 Traditional Emotion Analysis Systems

Most emotion analysis systems were, before the deep learning revolution in NLP, feature-based, and features often stemmed from manually created lexicons (Mohammad and Turney, 2013) and included manually designed features for the task (Štajner and Klinger, 2023; Aman and Szpakowicz, 2007). Since the state of the art for the development of text analysis systems is transfer learning by fine-tuning pretrained large language models (such as BERT, Devlin et al., 2019), the phenomenon-specific model development focuses on exploiting properties of the concept. One example is DeepMoji, which adapts transfer learning to the analysis of subjective language and identifies a particularly useful pretraining task, namely the prediction of emojis (Felbo et al., 2017). Another strain of research aims at developing models that aggregate multiple emotion theories (Buechel et al., 2021).

3.1.2 Event Interpretation

We focus on the aspect of emotions that they are caused by events. Interpreting events is challenging, because event descriptions often lack an explicit emotion mention (Troiano et al., 2023a). Such textual instances are considered "implicit" regarding their emotion (Udochukwu and He, 2015; Klinger et al., 2018): The challenge to be solved is to link "non-emotional" events to the emotion that they might cause. Balahur et al. (2012) tackled this by listing action units in an ontology, based on semantic parsing of large amounts of text. Cambria et al. (2022) developed a logics-based resource to associate events with their emotion interpretation.

3.1.3 Incorporating Appraisal Variables in Text Analysis Models

These attempts, however, do not model appraisal variables explicitly as a link between cognitive evaluations of events and emotions. There is also not only one appraisal theory, and depending on the theory, the computational modeling is realized in differing ways. Based on the OCC model (an appraisal theory that provides a decision tree of appraisal variables to characterize emotions, Steunebrink et al., 2009), both Shaikh et al. (2009) and Udochukwu and He (2015) develop methods to extract atomic variable values from text that are the building blocks for appraisal-based interpretations. An example appraisal variable is if an event is directed towards the self, for which they use semantic and syntactic parsers. Other such variables include the valence of events, the attitude towards objects, or the moral evaluation of people's behaviours – all detected with polarity lexicons. These variables are then put together with logical rules, such as `If Direction = 'Self' and Tense = 'Future' and Overall Polarity = 'Positive' and Event Polarity = 'Positive', then Emotion = 'Hope'` (Udochukwu and He, 2015). The advantage of this approach is that it makes the appraisal-based interpretation explicit; however, it does not allow for reasoning under uncertainty, partially because these studies do not build on top of manually assigned appraisal variables to text.

3.1.4 Appraisal-Annotated Corpora

To understand the link better between appraisals in text and emotions, Hofmann et al. (2020) manually annotated autobiographical event reports (Troiano et al., 2019) for the appraisal dimensions identified by Smith and Ellsworth (1985): does the writer want to devote attention, were they certain about what was happening, did they have to expend mental or physical effort to deal with the situation, did they find the event pleasant, were they responsible for the situation, could they control the situation, and did they find that the situation could not be changed by anyone? They found that the annotation replicates the links to emotions as found in original studies (Hofmann et al., 2021, Fig. 1). Further, they showed that appraisals can reliably be detected, but they did not manage to develop a model that predicts emotions better with the help

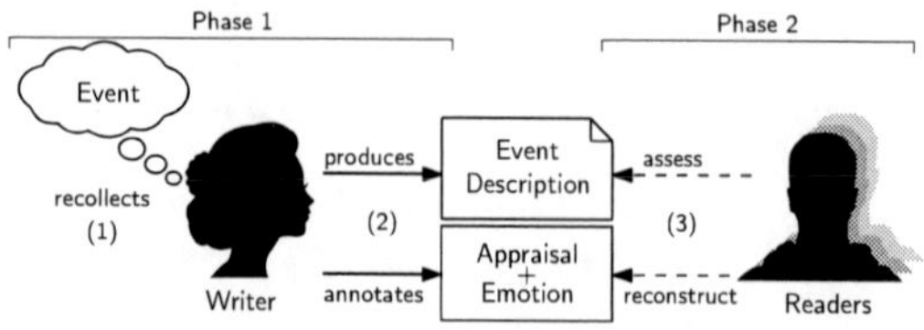

Figure 5: The study design that lead to the crowd-enVENT data set (Troiano et al., 2023b).

of appraisals than without. Hence, they proposed a new way of modeling emotions in text, but did not succeed to develop a multi-emotion model.

3.1.5 Appraisal Annotations by Event Experiencers

To understand better if this inferiority of a joint model might be a result of an imperfect noisy appraisal annotation, and to create a larger corpus, Troiano et al. (2023b) setup the experiment depicted in Figure 5 (replicating Troiano et al. (2019), but with appraisal variables). They asked crowd-workers to describe an event that caused a specific emotion and to then assign appraisal values (this time following the sequential approach by Scherer et al., 2001, with 21 variables, Figure 4) how they perceived the respective situation (Phase 1). They then asked other people to read the texts and reconstruct the emotion and appraisal (Phase 2). Unsurprisingly, the readers sometimes misinterpreted an event. For instance "I put together a funeral service for my Aunt" is mostly interpreted as something sad, while the original author was actually proud about it. These differences in interpretation can also be seen in the appraisal variables – Appraisals explain the differences in the event evaluation: The interpretation as being sad comes with evaluations as not being in control, while the interpretation to cause pride comes with being in control.

3.1.6 Emotion Modeling under Consideration of Appraisals

The modeling experiments of Troiano et al. (2023b) confirm that also a larger set of variables can be reliably detected – similarly well as humans can reconstruct them. To further understand if such self-assigned appraisal labels enable an improvement also in the emotion categorization, they fine-tuned RoBERTa (Liu et al., 2019) and tested if adding appraisal values improves the result. They find that appraisals help the prediction of anger, fear, joy, pride, guilt, sadness, and anger. They showcase the event report "His toenails were massive.", where the baseline model relies on something massive being associated to pride. With the appraisal information, it correctly assigns "disgust".

3.1.7 Other Research Directions

More recently other research has been published with a focused on specific use-cases. Stranisci et al. (2022) who follow the appraisal model by Roseman (2013) postannotate Reddit posts which deal with situations that challenged the author to cope with an undesirable situation. Their APPReddit corpus is the first resource of appraisal-annotated texts from the wild. Cortal et al. (2023) follow a similar idea and acquire texts that describe how people regulate their emotions in specific situations. Next to their resource creation effort for French, they analyze which descriptions of cognitive processes allow to infer an emotion.

We conclude that appraisal-based emotion analysis research has the goal to better understand how emotions are implicitly communicated and to develop better emotion analysis systems.

3.2 Emotions are Events: Structured Analysis

The studies that we discussed so far put the aspect of emotion analysis on the spot that emotions are caused by events. As we argued before, emotions also constitute events. Similarly to the field of semantic role labeling (Gildea and Jurafsky, 2000) which models events in text following frame semantics, various efforts have been made to extract emotion event representations from text. The corpora that have been created come with differing modeling attempts, summarized in Figure 6.

3.2.1 Cue Phrase Detection

The early work by Aman and Szpakowicz (2007) focused on the emotion *cue* word, as an important part of role labeling. They annotated sentences from blogs, but did not propose an automatic cue identification system. A structurally similar resource with cue word annotations has been proposed by Liew et al. (2016).

3.2.2 Stimulus Detection

A few corpora have been developed focussing on stimuli: Ghazi et al. (2015) annotated sentences from FrameNet that are known to be associated with emotions and model the automatic prediction as sequence labeling. For German, Doan Dang et al. (2021) created a similar corpus based on news headlines. Gao et al. (2017) formulated stimulus detection as clause classification in Mandarin, which

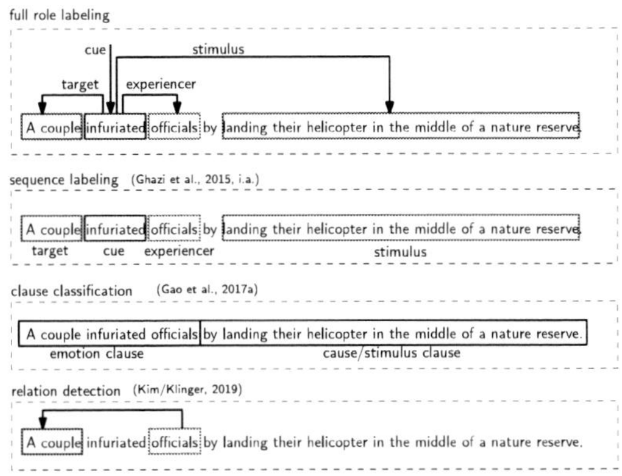

Figure 6: Emotion Role Modeling approaches (example from Bostan et al. (2020)). Full emotion role labeling has not been performed yet (top).

might, however, not be an appropriate approach for English (Oberländer et al., 2020).

3.2.3 Role Labeling as Classification

An interesting attempt of emotion role labeling in texts from social media was the study on Tweets associated to a US election by Mohammad et al. (2014). The decision to focus on a narrow domain allowed them to frame the role identification task both in crowdsourced annotation and in modeling as a classification task; namely to decide if the emoter, the stimulus or the emotion target correspond to an entity from a predefined set (this modeling formulation is not shown in Figure 6).

3.2.4 Full Emotion Role Labeling Resources

Kim and Klinger (2018) and Bostan et al. (2020) aimed at creating corpora with full emotion role labeling information. The REMAN corpus (Kim and Klinger, 2019b) focused on literature from Project Gutenberg. Given the challenging domain, the authors decided to carefully train annotators instead of relying on crowdsourcing. Each instance corresponds to a sentence triple, in which the middle sentence contains the cue to which the roles of emoters, targets, and stimuli are to be associated. The sequence-labeling-based modeling revealed that cause and target detection are very challenging. The paper does not contain an effort to reconstruct the full emotion event graph structure.

Bostan et al. (2020) annotated news headlines, under the assumption that less context is required for interpretation (which turned out to not be true). To attribute for the subjective nature of emotion interpretations, they setup the annotation as a multi-

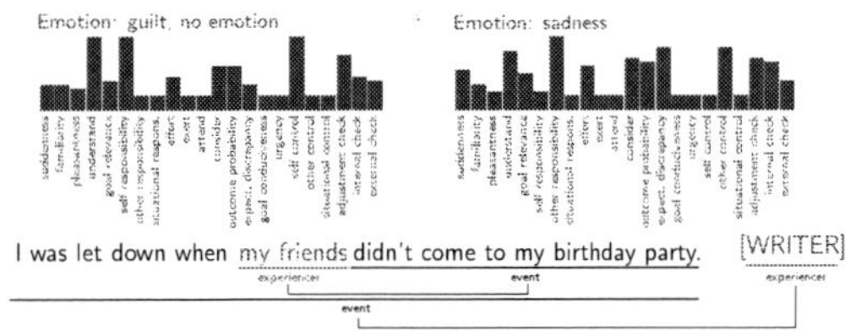

Figure 7: Example from the x-enVENT dataset

step crowdsourcing task. The modeling experiments on their GoodNewsEveryone corpus are limited to span prediction.

3.2.5 Role Labeling as Relation Detection

We are only aware of one work in the context of semantic role labeling that attempts to model the relational structure. Kim and Klinger (2019b) simplified role labeling to relation classification of emotional relations between entities. This allowed them to build on top of established methods for relation detection (Zhou et al., 2016) but they sacrificed explicit cue word detection and limited the analysis to emotion stimuli that have a corresponding entity.

3.2.6 Aggregated Corpora

There have been two efforts of data aggregation, by Oberländer et al. (2020) and Campagnano et al. (2022). The latter compared various models for role detection via span prediction. The prior we will discuss in the next section. To sum up, there have been some efforts to perform emotion role labeling, but in contrast to generic role labeling or to structured sentiment analysis, no models have yet been developed for full graph reconstruction. We visualize the differences in modeling attempts in Figure 6.

3.3 Bridging the Two Perspectives

We now discussed the two perspectives of *events causing emotions* (§3.1) and *emotions being events* (§3.2). The fact that these two analysis tasks have so far mostly been tackled separately leaves a lot of space for future research. However, some attempts to link the two areas already exist.

3.3.1 Do the tasks of emotion classification and role labeling benefit from each other?

Oberländer et al. (2020) aimed at understanding if knowledge of roles impacts the performance of emotion categorization. It turns out it does, either because the relevant part of the text is made more explicit (stimulus), or because of biases (emoter).

Similarly, Xia and Ding (2019) setup the task of stimulus-clause and emotion-clause pair classification. Their corpora and a plethora of follow-up work show that stimulus and emotion detection benefit from each other.

3.3.2 Descriptions of which emotion components enable emotion recognition?

A similar strain of research aims at understanding which components of emotions support emotion predictions. Casel et al. (2021) performed multi-task learning experiments with emotion categorization and emotion component prediction. Kim and Klinger (2019a) study how specific emotions are communicated, similarly to Etienne et al. (2022). Cortal et al. (2023) analyzed if particular ways of cognitively evaluating events support the emotion prediction more than others.

3.3.3 Linking Role Labeling and Appraisal-based Analysis

These works do, however, not link emotion roles explicitly to their cognitive evaluation dimensions. The only work that aimed at doing so is the corpus by Troiano et al. (2022), who label emoters for emotion categories and appraisals, the events that act as a stimulus on the token level, and the relation between them. Figure 7 shows an example from their corpus. In their modeling efforts, however, they limited themselves to emoter-specific emotion/appraisal predictions and ignored, so far, the span-based stimulus annotations (Wegge et al., 2022; Wegge and Klinger, 2023).

4 Open Research Tasks

We have now discussed previous work in emotion analysis, appraisal-based approaches and role labeling. In the following, we will make a set of aspects explicit that, from our perspective, need future work.

Full emotion role labeling. Several corpora exist now that have complex annotations of the emoter, their respective emotion stimuli, targets, and cue words; partially with sentence level annotations for the reader and writer in addition. Modeling, however, focused on sequence labeling for subsets of the roles or sentence level classification. There are no attempts of full emotion graph prediction, despite that role prediction subtasks might benefit from being modeled jointly. There is also only little work on exploiting role information for emotion categorization on the sentence level, a potentially valuable approach for joint modeling of a structured prediction task with text classification.

Role labeling/stimulus detection with appraisal information. The work that has been performed to understand the interaction between role prediction and emotion categorization focused on predicting discrete emotion classes. However, stimuli often correspond to event descriptions and therefore are a straight-forward choice for further analysis with appraisal variables. Also, understanding which event mentions in a text can function as an emotion stimulus could be supported with the help of appraisals. The detection of clauses or token sequences that correspond to emotion stimuli in context of appraisal-based interpretations therefore has potential to improve both subtasks.

Integration of other emotion models in role labeling. Emotion categorization is typically one variable to be predicted in stimulus detection and role labeling approaches, either for a writer or for entities. An additionally interesting approach would be to integrate other emotion representations with role labeling. An interesting choice would be to create a corpus of valence/arousal values, assigned to specific entities and linked to stimuli. Such approach comes with the general advantage of dimensional models, namely that emotion categories do not need to be predefined.

Robust cross-corpus modeling and zero-shot predictions. A similar motivation lead to recent work on zero-shot emotion prediction, in which emotion categories are to be predicted that are not available in the training data. Plaza-del Arco et al. (2022) showed that the performance loss of natural language inference-based prompting in comparison to supervised learning leaves space for improvements. Such attempts might also bridge the gap between in-domain performance and cross-domain performance of emotion analysis systems (Bostan and Klinger, 2018). Zero-shot modeling or other approaches to find representations that are agnostic to the underlying emotion theory are essential for cross-corpus experiments, because the domains that are represented by different corpora require differing label sets.

Interpretation of event chains. Textual event descriptions can be interpreted with appraisal theories, but we rely on end-to-end learning to understand how sequences of events lead to specific emotions (for instance being afraid of a specific unconfirmed undesirable event $e \rightarrow e$ is disconfirmed $\rightarrow$ relief). Dissecting events with semantic parsing, and combining them with emotion role labeling leads to sequences of general and emotion events, which can be the input for a second-level emotion analysis. Such methods would be required to fully understand how emotions develop throughout longer sequences of stories, for instance in literature.

Perspectivism. Appraisals do explain differences in the emotion assessement, based on differing interpretations of events (Troiano et al., 2023b). We do, however, not know the role of underlying factors. A perspectivistic approach with the goal to uncover variables that lead to varying emotion constructions, e.g., based on demographic data of event participants or other data, might provide additional insight. This could also be applied to literature analysis, for instance by including personality information on fictional characters in the emotion prediction (Bamman et al., 2013). Such approach is well-motivated in psychology; we know that personality influences the interpretation of other's emotions (Doellinger et al., 2021).

Integrate emotion models from psychology. Emotion analysis work so far focused on a comparably small set of emotion theories. The philosophical discussion by Scarantino (2016) offers itself as a guideing principle which other theories might be valueable to be explored. This does not only include entirely so-far-ignored theories (e.g., Feldman Barrett, 2017) but also knowledge from theories popular in NLP. For instance, Ekman (1992); Plutchik (2001) offer more information than lists of emotion categories. Integrating psychological knowledge in NLP models can improve the performance (Troiano et al., 2023b). In a similar vein, there exist specific appraisal theories for particular domains, including, e.g., argumentation theories (Dillard and Seo, 2012).

Multimodal Modeling. We focused in our paper on analysis tasks from text, but there has already been work on multimodal emotion analysis (Busso et al., 2008, i.a.) and detecting emotion stimuli in images (Dellagiacoma et al., 2011; Fan et al., 2018, i.a.), also multimodally (Khlyzova et al., 2022; Cevher et al., 2019). However, we are not aware of any work in computer vision that interprets situations and the interactions of events with the help of appraisal theories. To fully grasp available information in everyday communication or (social) media, the presented approaches from this paper need to be extended multimodally.

Multilingual modeling. Most papers that we discuss in this paper focus on English – with very few exceptions, which we pointed out explicitly. We are not aware of any emotion role labeling corpus with full graph annotations in other languages, and there are only very few attempts to integrate appraisal theories in emotion detection on languages other than English. Such multilingual extension is not only relevant to achieve models that work across use-cases – the concept of emotion names might also differ between languages, and therefore comparing emotion concepts with the help of dimensional appraisal models between languages and cultures can provide interesting insights for both NLP and psychology.

5 Conclusion

With this paper, we discussed appraisal theory-based methods to interpret events, and how emotions can be represented as events with role labeling. We did that guided by our own two emotion analysis projects SEAT (Structured Multi-Domain Emotion Analysis from Text) and CEAT (Computational Event Evaluation based on Appraisal Theories for Emotion Analysis) which corresponded each to one of the two perspectives.

These two fields have been approached mostly separately so far and the main goal of this paper is to make the research narrative behind both transparent, and, based on this, point out open research questions. Such open tasks emerge from missing connections between the various goals in emotion analysis, but there are also other promising directions that we pointed out.

We do not believe that this list is comprehensive, but hope that the aggregation of previous work and pointing at missing research helps interested researchers to identify the gaps they want to fill. Emotion analysis is important to make computers aware of the concept, which is essential for natural communication.

In addition, research in these fields helps to better understand how humans communicate, beyond building impactful computational systems. Therefore, research in affective computing brings together psychology, linguistics, and NLP.

Limitations

This paper focused on appraisal theories and emotion role labeling mostly from a theoretical perspective. We aimed at pointing out open research questions mostly based on conceptualizations of theories from semantics and psychology. To identify open research questions, a closer introspection of existing models need to be performed in addition. In our theoretical discussion, we assume that the open research questions have similar chances to succeed. In practical terms this is likely not the case and we therefore propose to first perform preliminary studies before definitely deciding to follow one of the research plans that we sketched.

Ethics Statement

The contributions in this paper do not directly pose any ethical issues: we did not publish data, models, or did perform experiments. However, the open topics that we identified might lead to resources and models that can in principle do harm to people. Following deontological ethics, we assume that no emotion analysis systems should be applied to data created by a person without their consent, if the results are used not only in aggregated form which would allow to identify the person who is associated with the analyzed data. We personally do not believe that a utilitaristic approach may be acceptable in which reasons could exist that justify to use emotion analysis technology to identify individuals from a larger group. This is particularly important with methods discussed in this paper in comparison to more general emotion categorization methods, because we focus on implicit emotion expressions. The methods we discussed and future work we sketched would be able to identify emotions that are not explicitly expressed, and therefore humans that generate data might not be aware that their private emotional state could be reconstructed from the data they produce.

When creating data for emotion analysis, independent of its language, domain, or the task formulation as role labeling, classification, regression, using a dimensional model or a theory of basic emotions, fairness or developed system and bias in data and systems is typically an issue. While efforts exist to identify unwanted bias and confounders in automatic analysis systems, the possible existance of unidentified biases can never be excluded. Therefore, automatic systems always need to be applied with care while critically reflecting the automatically obtained results. This is particularly the case with systems that focus on interpreting implicit emotion communications that require reasoning under uncertainty. To enable such critical reflection of a system's output, their decision must be transparently communicated to the users.

In general, the ability of automatic systems to interpret and aggregate emotions should not be used unaware of the people who created data, and decisions and actions following recognized emotions always need to remain in the responsibility of a human user.

We see our work mostly as a research contribution with the goal to better understand how humans communicate, not as an automatic enabling tool to provide insight in the private states of people.

Acknowledgements

We would like to thank all coauthors who contributed to our work on emotion analysis with the help of appraisal theories and in role labeling. These are (in alphabetical order) Amelie Heindl, Antje Schweitzer, Bao Minh Doan Dang, Enrica Troiano, Evgeny Kim, Felix Casel, Flor Miriam Arco Del Plaza, Hendrik Schuff, Jan Hofmann, Jeremy Barnes, Kai Sassenberg, Kevin Reich, Laura Oberländer née Bostan, Max Wegge, Sebastian Padó, Tornike Tsereteli, and Valentino Sabbatino. We further thank Alexandra Balahur, Orphée De Clercq, Saif Mohammad, Veronique Hoste, Valentin Barriere, and Sanja Štajner for discussions on the general topics of emotion analysis that helped us to develop this paper.

This work has been funded by two projects of the German Research Council (Deutsche Forschungsgemeinschaft), namely the project "Structured Multi-Domain Emotion Analysis from Text" (SEAT, KL 2869/1-1) and "Computational Event Evaluation based on Appraisal Theories for Emotion Analysis" (CEAT, KL 2869/1-2).[1]

References

Cecilia Ovesdotter Alm, Dan Roth, and Richard Sproat. 2005. Emotions from text: Machine learning for text-based emotion prediction. In *Proceedings of Human Language Technology Conference and Conference on Empirical Methods in Natural Language Processing*, pages 579–586, Vancouver, British Columbia, Canada. Association for Computational Linguistics.

[1] https://www.ims.uni-stuttgart.de/en/research/projects/seat/, https://www.ims.uni-stuttgart.de/en/research/projects/ceat/

Cecilia Ovesdotter Alm and Richard Sproat. 2005. Emotional sequencing and development in fairy tales. In *Affective Computing and Intelligent Interaction*, pages 668–674, Berlin, Heidelberg. Springer Berlin Heidelberg.

Saima Aman and Stan Szpakowicz. 2007. Identifying expressions of emotion in text. In *Text, Speech and Dialogue*, pages 196–205, Berlin, Heidelberg. Springer Berlin Heidelberg.

Alexandra Balahur, Jesus M. Hermida, and Andrew Montoyo. 2012. Building and exploiting emotinet, a knowledge base for emotion detection based on the appraisal theory model. *IEEE Transactions on Affective Computing*, 3(1):88–101.

David Bamman, Brendan O'Connor, and Noah A. Smith. 2013. Learning latent personas of film characters. In *Proceedings of the 51st Annual Meeting of the Association for Computational Linguistics (Volume 1: Long Papers)*, pages 352–361, Sofia, Bulgaria. Association for Computational Linguistics.

Jeremy Barnes, Roman Klinger, and Sabine Schulte im Walde. 2017. Assessing state-of-the-art sentiment models on state-of-the-art sentiment datasets. In *Proceedings of the 8th Workshop on Computational Approaches to Subjectivity, Sentiment and Social Media Analysis*, Copenhagen, Denmark. Workshop at Conference on Empirical Methods in Natural Language Processing, Association for Computational Linguistics.

Jeremy Barnes, Laura Oberlaender, Enrica Troiano, Andrey Kutuzov, Jan Buchmann, Rodrigo Agerri, Lilja Øvrelid, and Erik Velldal. 2022. SemEval 2022 task 10: Structured sentiment analysis. In *Proceedings of the 16th International Workshop on Semantic Evaluation (SemEval-2022)*, pages 1280–1295, Seattle, United States. Association for Computational Linguistics.

Laura Ana Maria Bostan, Evgeny Kim, and Roman Klinger. 2020. GoodNewsEveryone: A corpus of news headlines annotated with emotions, semantic roles, and reader perception. In *Proceedings of The 12th Language Resources and Evaluation Conference*, pages 1554–1566, Marseille, France. European Language Resources Association.

Laura-Ana-Maria Bostan and Roman Klinger. 2018. An analysis of annotated corpora for emotion classification in text. In *Proceedings of the 27th International Conference on Computational Linguistics*, pages 2104–2119, Santa Fe, New Mexico, USA. Association for Computational Linguistics.

Gregory J. Boyle. 1995. Myers-Briggs Type Indicator (MBTI): Some Psychometric Limitations. *Australian Psychologist*, 30(1):71–74.

Sven Buechel and Udo Hahn. 2017. EmoBank: Studying the impact of annotation perspective and representation format on dimensional emotion analysis. In *Proceedings of the 15th Conference of the European Chapter of the Association for Computational Linguistics: Volume 2, Short Papers*, pages 578–585, Valencia, Spain. Association for Computational Linguistics.

Sven Buechel, Luise Modersohn, and Udo Hahn. 2021. Towards label-agnostic emotion embeddings. In *Proceedings of the 2021 Conference on Empirical Methods in Natural Language Processing*, pages 9231–9249, Online and Punta Cana, Dominican Republic. Association for Computational Linguistics.

Carlos Busso, Murtaza Bulut, Chi-Chun Lee, Abe Kazemzadeh, Emily Mower, Samuel Kim, Jeannette N. Chang, Sungbok Lee, and Shrikanth S. Narayanan. 2008. Iemocap: interactive emotional dyadic motion capture database. *Language Resources and Evaluation*, 42(4):335.

Manuela Caiani and Jessica Di Cocco. 2023. Populism and emotions: a comparative study using machine learning. *Italian Political Science Review / Rivista Italiana di Scienza Politica*, page 1–16.

Erik Cambria, Qian Liu, Sergio Decherchi, Frank Xing, and Kenneth Kwok. 2022. SenticNet 7: A commonsense-based neurosymbolic AI framework for explainable sentiment analysis. In *Proceedings of the Thirteenth Language Resources and Evaluation Conference*, pages 3829–3839, Marseille, France. European Language Resources Association.

Cesare Campagnano, Simone Conia, and Roberto Navigli. 2022. SRL4E – Semantic Role Labeling for Emotions: A unified evaluation framework. In *Proceedings of the 60th Annual Meeting of the Association for Computational Linguistics (Volume 1: Long Papers)*, pages 4586–4601, Dublin, Ireland. Association for Computational Linguistics.

Felix Casel, Amelie Heindl, and Roman Klinger. 2021. Emotion recognition under consideration of the emotion component process model. In *KONVENS 2021*.

Deniz Cevher, Sebastian Zepf, and Roman Klinger. 2019. Towards multimodal emotion recognition in german speech events in cars using transfer learning. In *KONVENS*.

Dushyant Singh Chauhan, Dhanush S R, Asif Ekbal, and Pushpak Bhattacharyya. 2020. Sentiment and emotion help sarcasm? a multi-task learning framework for multi-modal sarcasm, sentiment and emotion analysis. In *Proceedings of the 58th Annual Meeting of the Association for Computational Linguistics*, pages 4351–4360, Online. Association for Computational Linguistics.

Gustave Cortal, Alain Finkel, Patrick Paroubek, and Lina Ye. 2023. Emotion recognition based on psychological components in guided narratives for emotion regulation. In *Proceedings of the 7th Joint SIGHUM Workshop on Computational Linguistics for Cultural*

Heritage, Social Sciences, Humanities and Literature, pages 72–81, Dubrovnik, Croatia. Association for Computational Linguistics.

Verna Dankers, Marek Rei, Martha Lewis, and Ekaterina Shutova. 2019. Modelling the interplay of metaphor and emotion through multitask learning. In *Proceedings of the 2019 Conference on Empirical Methods in Natural Language Processing and the 9th International Joint Conference on Natural Language Processing (EMNLP-IJCNLP)*, pages 2218–2229, Hong Kong, China. Association for Computational Linguistics.

Michela Dellagiacoma, Pamela Zontone, Giulia Boato, and Liliana Albertazzi. 2011. Emotion based classification of natural images. In *Proceedings of the 2011 International Workshop on DETecting and Exploiting Cultural DiversiTy on the Social Web*, DETECT '11, page 17–22, New York, NY, USA. Association for Computing Machinery.

Dorottya Demszky, Dana Movshovitz-Attias, Jeongwoo Ko, Alan Cowen, Gaurav Nemade, and Sujith Ravi. 2020. GoEmotions: A dataset of fine-grained emotions. In *Proceedings of the 58th Annual Meeting of the Association for Computational Linguistics*, pages 4040–4054, Online. Association for Computational Linguistics.

Jacob Devlin, Ming-Wei Chang, Kenton Lee, and Kristina Toutanova. 2019. BERT: Pre-training of deep bidirectional transformers for language understanding. In *Proceedings of the 2019 Conference of the North American Chapter of the Association for Computational Linguistics: Human Language Technologies, Volume 1 (Long and Short Papers)*, pages 4171–4186, Minneapolis, Minnesota. Association for Computational Linguistics.

James Price Dillard and Kiwon Seo. 2012. Affect and persuasion. In James Price Dillard and Lijang Shen, editors, *The SAGE Handbook of Persuasion: Developments in Theory and Practice*, chapter 10. SAGE Publications.

Bao Minh Doan Dang, Laura Oberländer, and Roman Klinger. 2021. Emotion stimulus detection in German news headlines. In *Proceedings of the 17th Conference on Natural Language Processing (KONVENS 2021)*, pages 73–85, Düsseldorf, Germany. KONVENS 2021 Organizers.

Peter Sheridan Dodds, Kameron Decker Harris, Isabel M. Kloumann, Catherine A. Bliss, and Christopher M. Danforth. 2011. Temporal patterns of happiness and information in a global social network: Hedonometrics and twitter. PLOS ONE, 6(12):1–1.

Lillian Doellinger, Petri Laukka, Lennart Björn Högman, Tanja Bänziger, Irena Makower, Håkan Fischer, and Stephan Hau. 2021. Training emotion recognition accuracy: Results for multimodal expressions and facial micro expressions. *Frontiers in Psychology*, 12.

Paul Ekman. 1992. An argument for basic emotions. *Cognition & emotion*, 6(3-4):169–200.

Paul Ekman and Daniel Cordaro. 2011. What is meant by calling emotions basic. *Emotion Review*.

Aline Etienne, Delphine Battistelli, and Gwénolé Lecorvé. 2022. A (psycho-)linguistically motivated scheme for annotating and exploring emotions in a genre-diverse corpus. In *Proceedings of the Thirteenth Language Resources and Evaluation Conference*, pages 603–612, Marseille, France. European Language Resources Association.

Shaojing Fan, Zhiqi Shen, Ming Jiang, Bryan L. Koenig, Juan Xu, Mohan S. Kankanhalli, and Qi Zhao. 2018. Emotional attention: A study of image sentiment and visual attention. In *2018 IEEE/CVF Conference on Computer Vision and Pattern Recognition*, pages 7521–7531.

Bjarke Felbo, Alan Mislove, Anders Søgaard, Iyad Rahwan, and Sune Lehmann. 2017. Using millions of emoji occurrences to learn any-domain representations for detecting sentiment, emotion and sarcasm. In *Proceedings of the 2017 Conference on Empirical Methods in Natural Language Processing*, pages 1615–1625, Copenhagen, Denmark. Association for Computational Linguistics.

Lisa Feldman Barrett. 2017. The theory of constructed emotion: an active inference account of interoception and categorization. *Social Cognitive and Affective Neuroscience*, 12(11):1833.

Qinghong Gao, Jiannan Hu, Ruifeng Xu, Gui Lin, Yulan He, Qin Lu, and Kam-Fai Wong. 2017. Overview of NTCIR-13 ECA task. In *Proceedings of the 13th NTCIR Conference on Evaluation of Information Access Technologies*, pages 361–366, Tokyo, Japan.

Christian Geiser, Thomas Götz, Franzis Preckel, and Philipp Alexander Freund. 2017. States and Traits: Theories, Models, and Assessment. *European Journal of Psychological Assessment*, 33(4):219–223.

Diman Ghazi, Diana Inkpen, and Stan Szpakowicz. 2015. Detecting emotion stimuli in emotion-bearing sentences. In *International Conference on Intelligent Text Processing and Computational Linguistics*, pages 152–165. Springer.

Daniel Gildea and Daniel Jurafsky. 2000. Automatic labeling of semantic roles. In *Proceedings of the 38th Annual Meeting of the Association for Computational Linguistics*, pages 512–520, Hong Kong. Association for Computational Linguistics.

Jennifer Golbeck, Cristina Robles, and Karen Turner. 2011. Predicting personality with social media. In *CHI'11 extended abstracts on human factors in computing systems*, pages 253–262.

Lewis R. Goldberg. 1999. A broad-bandwidth, public domain, personality inventory measuring the lower-level facets of several five-factor models. *Personality psychology in Europe*, 7(1):7–28.

Jan Hofmann, Enrica Troiano, and Roman Klinger. 2021. Emotion-aware, emotion-agnostic, or automatic: Corpus creation strategies to obtain cognitive event appraisal annotations. In *Proceedings of the Eleventh Workshop on Computational Approaches to Subjectivity, Sentiment and Social Media Analysis*, pages 160–170, Online. Association for Computational Linguistics.

Jan Hofmann, Enrica Troiano, Kai Sassenberg, and Roman Klinger. 2020. Appraisal theories for emotion classification in text. In *Proceedings of the 28th International Conference on Computational Linguistics*, pages 125–138, Barcelona, Spain (Online). International Committee on Computational Linguistics.

Johan F. Hoorn and Elly A. Konijn. 2003. Perceiving and experiencing fictional characters: An integrative account: Perceiving and experiencing fictional characters. *Japanese Psychological Research*, 45(4):250–268.

Md Rafiqul Islam, Muhammad Ashad Kabir, Ashir Ahmed, Abu Raihan M Kamal, Hua Wang, and Anwaar Ulhaq. 2018. Depression detection from social network data using machine learning techniques. *Health Inf. Sci. Syst.*, 6(1):8.

Margaret L. Kern, Gregory Park, Johannes C. Eichstaedt, H. Andrew Schwartz, Maarten Sap, Laura K. Smith, and Lyle H. Ungar. 2016. Gaining insights from social media language: Methodologies and challenges. *Psychological Methods*, 21(4):507–525.

Anna Khlyzova, Carina Silberer, and Roman Klinger. 2022. On the complementarity of images and text for the expression of emotions in social media. In *Proceedings of the 12th Workshop on Computational Approaches to Subjectivity, Sentiment & Social Media Analysis*, pages 1–15, Dublin, Ireland. Association for Computational Linguistics.

Evgeny Kim and Roman Klinger. 2018. Who feels what and why? annotation of a literature corpus with semantic roles of emotions. In *Proceedings of the 27th International Conference on Computational Linguistics*, pages 1345–1359, Santa Fe, New Mexico, USA. Association for Computational Linguistics.

Evgeny Kim and Roman Klinger. 2019a. An analysis of emotion communication channels in fan-fiction: Towards emotional storytelling. In *Proceedings of the Second Workshop on Storytelling*, pages 56–64, Florence, Italy. Association for Computational Linguistics.

Evgeny Kim and Roman Klinger. 2019b. Frowning Frodo, wincing Leia, and a seriously great friendship: Learning to classify emotional relationships of fictional characters. In *Proceedings of the 2019 Conference of the North American Chapter of the Association for Computational Linguistics: Human Language Technologies, Volume 1 (Long and Short Papers)*, pages 647–653, Minneapolis, Minnesota. Association for Computational Linguistics.

Evgeny Kim, Sebastian Padó, and Roman Klinger. 2017. Investigating the relationship between literary genres and emotional plot development. In *Proceedings of the Joint SIGHUM Workshop on Computational Linguistics for Cultural Heritage, Social Sciences, Humanities and Literature*, pages 17–26, Vancouver, Canada. Association for Computational Linguistics.

Svetlana Kiritchenko, Saif Mohammad, and Mohammad Salameh. 2016. SemEval-2016 task 7: Determining sentiment intensity of English and Arabic phrases. In *Proceedings of the 10th International Workshop on Semantic Evaluation (SemEval-2016)*, pages 42–51, San Diego, California. Association for Computational Linguistics.

Roman Klinger and Philipp Cimiano. 2013. Bi-directional inter-dependencies of subjective expressions and targets and their value for a joint model. In *Proceedings of the 51st Annual Meeting of the Association for Computational Linguistics (Volume 2: Short Papers)*, pages 848–854, Sofia, Bulgaria. Association for Computational Linguistics.

Roman Klinger, Orphée De Clercq, Saif Mohammad, and Alexandra Balahur. 2018. IEST: WASSA-2018 implicit emotions shared task. In *Proceedings of the 9th Workshop on Computational Approaches to Subjectivity, Sentiment and Social Media Analysis*, pages 31–42, Brussels, Belgium. Association for Computational Linguistics.

Anne Kreuter, Kai Sassenberg, and Roman Klinger. 2022. Items from psychometric tests as training data for personality profiling models of Twitter users. In *Proceedings of the 12th Workshop on Computational Approaches to Subjectivity, Sentiment & Social Media Analysis*, pages 315–323, Dublin, Ireland. Association for Computational Linguistics.

Jonas Kuhn. 2019. Computational text analysis within the Humanities: How to combine working practices from the contributing fields? *Language Resources and Evaluation*, 53(4):565–602.

Sofie Labat, Amir Hadifar, Thomas Demeester, and Veronique Hoste. 2022. An emotional journey: Detecting emotion trajectories in Dutch customer service dialogues. In *Proceedings of the Eighth Workshop on Noisy User-generated Text (W-NUT 2022)*, pages 106–112, Gyeongju, Republic of Korea. Association for Computational Linguistics.

Kibeom Lee and Michael C Ashton. 2018. Psychometric properties of the hexaco-100. *Assessment*, 25(5):543–556.

Xiang Li, Aynaz Taheri, Lifu Tu, and Kevin Gimpel. 2016. Commonsense knowledge base completion. In *Proceedings of the 54th Annual Meeting of the Association for Computational Linguistics (Volume 1: Long Papers)*, pages 1445–1455, Berlin, Germany. Association for Computational Linguistics.

Yanran Li, Hui Su, Xiaoyu Shen, Wenjie Li, Ziqiang Cao, and Shuzi Niu. 2017. DailyDialog: A manually labelled multi-turn dialogue dataset. In *Proceedings of the Eighth International Joint Conference on Natural Language Processing (Volume 1: Long Papers)*, pages 986–995, Taipei, Taiwan. Asian Federation of Natural Language Processing.

Jasy Suet Yan Liew, Howard R. Turtle, and Elizabeth D. Liddy. 2016. EmoTweet-28: A fine-grained emotion corpus for sentiment analysis. In *Proceedings of the Tenth International Conference on Language Resources and Evaluation (LREC'16)*, pages 1149–1156, Portorož, Slovenia. European Language Resources Association (ELRA).

Bing Liu. 2012. *Sentiment analysis and opinion mining*. Synthesis lectures on human language technologies. Springer Nature Switzerland.

Yinhan Liu, Myle Ott, Naman Goyal, Jingfei Du, Mandar Joshi, Danqi Chen, Omer Levy, Mike Lewis, Luke Zettlemoyer, and Veselin Stoyanov. 2019. RoBERTa: A robustly optimized BERT pretraining approach. arXiv:1907.11692. `https://arxiv.org/abs/1907.11692`.

Veronica Lynn, Niranjan Balasubramanian, and H. Andrew Schwartz. 2020. Hierarchical modeling for user personality prediction: The role of message-level attention. In *Proceedings of the 58th Annual Meeting of the Association for Computational Linguistics*, pages 5306–5316, Online. Association for Computational Linguistics.

J. R. Martin and P. R. R. White. 2005. *The Language of Evaluation*. Palgrave Macmillan UK, London.

Saif Mohammad. 2012. #emotional tweets. In **SEM 2012: The First Joint Conference on Lexical and Computational Semantics – Volume 1: Proceedings of the main conference and the shared task, and Volume 2: Proceedings of the Sixth International Workshop on Semantic Evaluation (SemEval 2012)*, pages 246–255, Montréal, Canada. Association for Computational Linguistics.

Saif Mohammad and Felipe Bravo-Marquez. 2017. WASSA-2017 shared task on emotion intensity. In *Proceedings of the 8th Workshop on Computational Approaches to Subjectivity, Sentiment and Social Media Analysis*, pages 34–49, Copenhagen, Denmark. Association for Computational Linguistics.

Saif Mohammad, Felipe Bravo-Marquez, Mohammad Salameh, and Svetlana Kiritchenko. 2018. SemEval-2018 task 1: Affect in tweets. In *Proceedings of The 12th International Workshop on Semantic Evaluation*, pages 1–17, New Orleans, Louisiana. Association for Computational Linguistics.

Saif Mohammad and Peter D. Turney. 2013. Crowdsourcing a word-emotion association lexicon. *Computational Intelligence*, 29(3):436–465.

Saif Mohammad, Xiaodan Zhu, and Joel Martin. 2014. Semantic role labeling of emotions in tweets. In *Proceedings of the 5th Workshop on Computational Approaches to Subjectivity, Sentiment and Social Media Analysis*, pages 32–41, Baltimore, Maryland. Association for Computational Linguistics.

Isabel Briggs Myers. 1998. *Introduction to Type: A Guide to Understanding Your Results on the MBTI Instrument*, 6th edition edition. Cpp. Inc.

William Herman Newman, Charles Edgar Summer, and E. Kirby Warren. 1967. *The Process of Management: Concepts, Bahaviour, and Practice*. Prentice-Hall.

Laura Oberländer, Kevin Reich, and Roman Klinger. 2020. Experiencers, stimuli, or targets: Which semantic roles enable machine learning to infer the emotions? In *Proceedings of the Third Workshop on Computational Modeling of People's Opinions, Personality, and Emotions in Social Media*, Barcelona, Spain. Association for Computational Linguistics.

Bo Pang and Lillian Lee. 2008. Opinion Mining and Sentiment Analysis. *Foundations and Trends® in Information Retrieval*, 2(1–2):1–135.

James W. Pennebaker and Laura A. King. 1999. Linguistic styles: Language use as an individual difference. *Journal of Personality and Social Psychology*, 77(6):1296–1312.

John P. Pestian, Pawel Matykiewicz, Michelle Linn-Gust, Brett South, Ozlem Uzuner, Jan Wiebe, K Bretonnel Cohen, John Hurdle, and Christopher Brew. 2012. Sentiment analysis of suicide notes: A shared task. *Biomed. Inform. Insights*, 5(Suppl 1):3–16.

Daniele Pizzolli and Carlo Strapparava. 2019. Personality traits recognition in literary texts. In *Proceedings of the Second Workshop on Storytelling*, pages 107–111, Florence, Italy. Association for Computational Linguistics.

Barbara Plank and Dirk Hovy. 2015. Personality traits on Twitter—or—How to get 1,500 personality tests in a week. In *Proceedings of the 6th Workshop on Computational Approaches to Subjectivity, Sentiment and Social Media Analysis*, pages 92–98, Lisboa, Portugal. Association for Computational Linguistics.

Flor Miriam Plaza-del Arco, María-Teresa Martín-Valdivia, and Roman Klinger. 2022. Natural language inference prompts for zero-shot emotion classification in text across corpora. In *Proceedings of the 29th International Conference on Computational Linguistics*, pages 6805–6817, Gyeongju, Republic of Korea. International Committee on Computational Linguistics.

Robert Plutchik. 2001. The nature of emotions human emotions have deep evolutionary roots, a fact that may explain their complexity and provide tools for clinical practice. *American Scientist*, 89(4):344–350.

Maria Pontiki, Dimitris Galanis, Haris Papageorgiou, Ion Androutsopoulos, Suresh Manandhar, Mohammad AL-Smadi, Mahmoud Al-Ayyoub, Yanyan Zhao, Bing Qin, Orphée De Clercq, Véronique Hoste, Marianna Apidianaki, Xavier Tannier, Natalia Loukachevitch, Evgeniy Kotelnikov, Nuria Bel, Salud María Jiménez-Zafra, and Gülşen Eryiğit. 2016. SemEval-2016 task 5: Aspect based sentiment analysis. In *Proceedings of the 10th International Workshop on Semantic Evaluation (SemEval-2016)*, pages 19–30, San Diego, California. Association for Computational Linguistics.

Maria Pontiki, Dimitris Galanis, Haris Papageorgiou, Suresh Manandhar, and Ion Androutsopoulos. 2015. SemEval-2015 task 12: Aspect based sentiment analysis. In *Proceedings of the 9th International Workshop on Semantic Evaluation (SemEval 2015)*, pages 486–495, Denver, Colorado. Association for Computational Linguistics.

Maria Pontiki, Dimitris Galanis, John Pavlopoulos, Harris Papageorgiou, Ion Androutsopoulos, and Suresh Manandhar. 2014. SemEval-2014 task 4: Aspect based sentiment analysis. In *Proceedings of the 8th International Workshop on Semantic Evaluation (SemEval 2014)*, pages 27–35, Dublin, Ireland. Association for Computational Linguistics.

Jonathan Posner, James A. Russell, and Bradley S. Peterson. 2005. The circumplex model of affect: an integrative approach to affective neuroscience, cognitive development, and psychopathology. *Development and Psychopathology*, 17(3):715–734.

Daniel Preoţiuc-Pietro, H. Andrew Schwartz, Gregory Park, Johannes Eichstaedt, Margaret Kern, Lyle Ungar, and Elisabeth Shulman. 2016. Modelling valence and arousal in Facebook posts. In *Proceedings of the 7th Workshop on Computational Approaches to Subjectivity, Sentiment and Social Media Analysis*, pages 9–15, San Diego, California. Association for Computational Linguistics.

Santhosh Rajamanickam, Pushkar Mishra, Helen Yannakoudakis, and Ekaterina Shutova. 2020. Joint modelling of emotion and abusive language detection. In *Proceedings of the 58th Annual Meeting of the Association for Computational Linguistics*, pages 4270–4279, Online. Association for Computational Linguistics.

Ken Randall, Mary Isaacson, and Carrie Ciro. 2017. Validity and reliability of the myers-briggs personality type indicator: A systematic review and meta-analysis. *Journal of Best Practices in Health Professions Diversity*, 10(1):1–27.

Sonia Roccas, Lilach Sagiv, Shalom H Schwartz, and Ariel Knafo. 2002. The big five personality factors and personal values. *Personality and social psychology bulletin*, 28(6):789–801.

Ira J. Roseman. 2013. Appraisal in the Emotion System: Coherence in Strategies for Coping. *Emotion Review*, 5(2):141–149.

Andrea Scarantino. 2016. The philosophy of emotions and its impact on affective science. In *Handbook of emotions*, chapter 4, pages 3–48. Guilford Press New York, NY.

Deborah Schaffer. 1995. SHOCKING SECRETS REVEALES! The Language of Tabloid Headlines. *ETC: A Review of General Semantics*, 52(1):27–46. Publisher: Institute of General Semantics.

Klaus R. Scherer, Angela Schorr, and Tom Johnstone. 2001. *Appraisal considered as a process of multilevel sequential checking*, volume 92. Oxford University Press.

Hendrik Schuff, Jeremy Barnes, Julian Mohme, Sebastian Padó, and Roman Klinger. 2017. Annotation, modelling and analysis of fine-grained emotions on a stance and sentiment detection corpus. In *Proceedings of the 8th Workshop on Computational Approaches to Subjectivity, Sentiment and Social Media Analysis*, pages 13–23, Copenhagen, Denmark. Association for Computational Linguistics.

Mostafa Al Masum Shaikh, Helmut Prendinger, and Mitsuru Ishizuka. 2009. A linguistic interpretation of the OCC emotion model for affect sensing from text. *Affective Information Processing*.

Priyanka Sinha, Lipika Dey, Pabitra Mitra, and Anupam Basu. 2015. Mining HEXACO personality traits from enterprise social media. In *Proceedings of the 6th Workshop on Computational Approaches to Subjectivity, Sentiment and Social Media Analysis*, pages 140–147, Lisboa, Portugal. Association for Computational Linguistics.

Craig. A. Smith and Phoebe. C. Ellsworth. 1985. Patterns of cognitive appraisal in emotion. *Journal of Personality and Social Psychology*, 48(4).

Sanja Stajner and Seren Yenikent. 2021. Why is MBTI personality detection from texts a difficult task? In *Proceedings of the 16th Conference of the European Chapter of the Association for Computational Linguistics: Main Volume*, pages 3580–3589, Online. Association for Computational Linguistics.

Bas R. Steunebrink, Mehdi Dastani, and John-Jules Ch. Meyer. 2009. The occ model revisited. Online: `https://people.idsia.ch/~steunebrink/Publications/KI09_OCC_revisited.pdf`.

Marco Antonio Stranisci, Simona Frenda, Eleonora Ceccaldi, Valerio Basile, Rossana Damiano, and Viviana Patti. 2022. APPReddit: a corpus of Reddit posts annotated for appraisal. In *Proceedings of the Thirteenth Language Resources and Evaluation Conference*, pages 3809–3818, Marseille, France. European Language Resources Association.

Carlo Strapparava and Rada Mihalcea. 2007. SemEval-2007 task 14: Affective text. In *Proceedings of the Fourth International Workshop on Semantic Evaluations (SemEval-2007)*, pages 70–74, Prague, Czech Republic. Association for Computational Linguistics.

Enrica Troiano, Roman Klinger, and Sebastian PadÃ³. 2023a. On the relationship between frames and emotionality in text. *Northern European Journal of Language Technology*, 9(1).

Enrica Troiano, Laura Ana Maria Oberlaender, Maximilian Wegge, and Roman Klinger. 2022. x-enVENT: A corpus of event descriptions with experiencer-specific emotion and appraisal annotations. In *Proceedings of the Thirteenth Language Resources and Evaluation Conference*, pages 1365–1375, Marseille, France. European Language Resources Association.

Enrica Troiano, Laura Oberländer, and Roman Klinger. 2023b. Dimensional modeling of emotions in text with appraisal theories: Corpus creation, annotation reliability, and prediction. *Computational Linguistics*, 49(1).

Enrica Troiano, Sebastian Padó, and Roman Klinger. 2019. Crowdsourcing and validating event-focused emotion corpora for German and English. In *Proceedings of the 57th Annual Meeting of the Association for Computational Linguistics*, pages 4005–4011, Florence, Italy. Association for Computational Linguistics.

Théo Trouillon, Christopher R. Dance, Éric Gaussier, Johannes Welbl, Sebastian Riedel, and Guillaume Bouchard. 2017. Knowledge graph completion via complex tensor factorization. *Journal Machine Learning Research*, 18(1):4735–4772.

Orizu Udochukwu and Yulan He. 2015. A rule-based approach to implicit emotion detection in text. In *Natural Language Processing and Information Systems*.

Ben Verhoeven, Walter Daelemans, and Barbara Plank. 2016. TwiSty: A multilingual Twitter stylometry corpus for gender and personality profiling. In *Proceedings of the Tenth International Conference on Language Resources and Evaluation (LREC'16)*, pages 1632–1637, Portorož, Slovenia. European Language Resources Association (ELRA).

Sanja Štajner and Roman Klinger. 2023. Emotion analysis from texts. In *Proceedings of the 17th Conference of the European Chapter of the Association for Computational Linguistics: Tutorial Abstracts*, pages 7–12, Dubrovnik, Croatia. Association for Computational Linguistics.

Wenbo Wang, Lu Chen, Krishnaprasad Thirunarayan, and Amit P. Sheth. 2012. Harnessing Twitter 'Big Data' for Automatic Emotion Identification. In *2012 ASE/IEEE International Conference on Social Computing and 2012 ASE/IEEE International Conference on Privacy, Security, Risk and Trust*, pages 587–592. IEEE.

Maximilian Wegge and Roman Klinger. 2023. Automatic emotion experiencer recognition. In *3rd Workshop on Computational Linguistics for the Political and Social Sciences (CPSS)*.

Maximilian Wegge, Enrica Troiano, Laura Ana Maria Oberlaender, and Roman Klinger. 2022. Experiencer-specific emotion and appraisal prediction. In *Proceedings of the Fifth Workshop on Natural Language Processing and Computational Social Science (NLP+CSS)*, pages 25–32, Abu Dhabi, UAE. Association for Computational Linguistics.

Janyce Wiebe, Theresa Wilson, Rebecca Bruce, Matthew Bell, and Melanie Martin. 2004. Learning subjective language. *Computational Linguistics*, 30(3):277–308.

Rui Xia and Zixiang Ding. 2019. Emotion-cause pair extraction: A new task to emotion analysis in texts. In *Proceedings of the 57th Annual Meeting of the Association for Computational Linguistics*, pages 1003–1012, Florence, Italy. Association for Computational Linguistics.

Peng Zhou, Wei Shi, Jun Tian, Zhenyu Qi, Bingchen Li, Hongwei Hao, and Bo Xu. 2016. Attention-based bidirectional long short-term memory networks for relation classification. In *Proceedings of the 54th Annual Meeting of the Association for Computational Linguistics (Volume 2: Short Papers)*, pages 207–212, Berlin, Germany. Association for Computational Linguistics.

A Visualization of the Relations Between Tasks

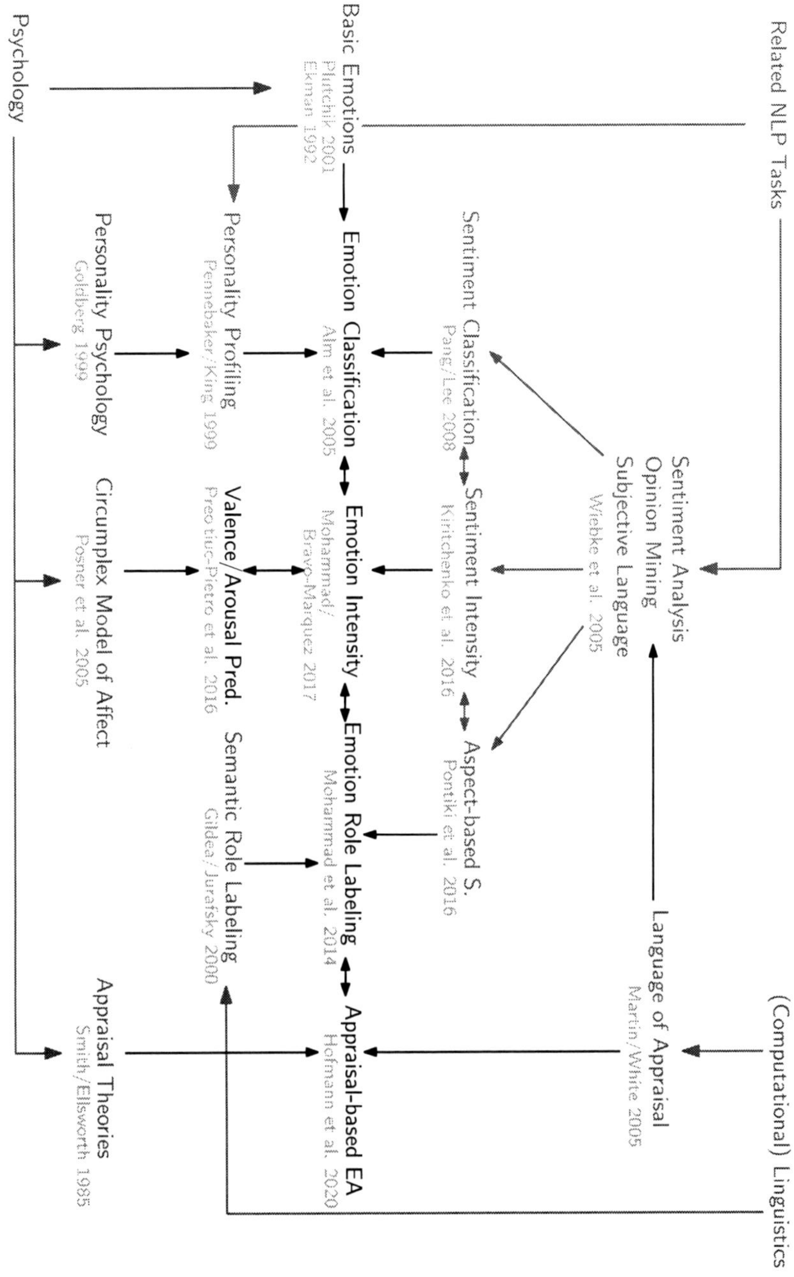

Figure 8: Visualization of relations between emotion analysis and other previously established tasks and studies. The bibliographic references are examples for the respective tasks and are not supposed to suggest completeness. Please see the text for a more comprehensive picture.

Working Towards Digital Documentation of Uralic Languages With Open-Source Tools and Modern NLP Methods

Mika Hämäläinen[1], Jack Rueter [2], Khalid Alnajjar[3] and Niko Partanen[2]
[1] Metropolia University of Applied Sciences
[2] University of Helsinki
[3] Rootroo Ltd
firstname.lastname@metropolia.fi/helsinki.fi/rootroo.com

Abstract

We present our work towards building an infrastructure for documenting endangered languages with the focus on Uralic languages in particular. Our infrastructure consists of tools to write dictionaries so that entries are structured in XML format. These dictionaries are the foundation for rule-based NLP tools such as FSTs. We also work actively towards enhancing these dictionaries and tools by using the latest state-of-the-art neural models by generating training data through rules and lexica.

1 Introduction

Most of the languages spoken in the world are in danger of extinction. Their documentation and revitalization are of a highest cultural value, for which they have received plenty of academic attention in various disciplines such as anthropology, typology, lexicography and computational linguistics. Needless to say, the resources produced in each individual research project are not always published openly let alone made available to the community of native speakers.

The goal of our paper is to describe our open infrastructure for documenting minority languages. We present our experiences with the following Uralic languages: Skolt Sami (sms), Erzya (myv), Moksha (mdf), Komi-Zyrian (kpv) and Komi-Permyak (koi). As they belong to the Uralic branch, they are languages that exhibit a complex morphology, which makes their computational processing a challenge for modern machine learning methods that would require a lot of data to cover this complexity. The quantity and quality of data is usually an issue when we deal with endangered languages (Hämäläinen, 2021). Carrying out linguistic documentation in a structured machine readable format, however, makes it possible to create the resources needed for building NLP tools simultaneously with linguistic documentation.

We are about to start working with the Apurinã (apu) language, which allows us to reflect upon our Uralic context from a broader perspective, and increases the relevance of our work in a Latin American context. Thus, we describe how our infrastructure can work in non-Uralic contexts.

Linguistic documentation is a field of academic study that has developed considerably in recent decades. Its purpose is to provide a complete record of the linguistic practices characteristic to a given speech community (Himmelmann, 1998). The goal of language documentation is to describe the language of a community of speakers as fully as possible both for future generations and for language revitalization. The result of this work is typically manifested as a linguistic corpus or other type of material collection, which later on can be studied and analyzed in various ways. The question whether the collected materials actually describe the language use of a speech community is debatable, and this goal can never be fully achieved because a corpus can never describe a language in full. Nonetheless, linguistically collected materials may be the only resources available for a small language.

Whether and how language documentation materials should be made accessible and distributed, has been a matter of debate. We believe it is important to understand that this is also a matter of granularity, and the question is not necessarily whether the materials are accessible, but rather which parties should be allowed what type of access. There are good reasons for keeping culturally sensitive materials available only to specific groups. At the same time, there are always materials in any language that are more neutral and such that the authors themselves may want to make accessible. Especially for written publications, it may always be possible to negotiate a publication with open licenses, which would also allow the reuse of the same materials in different open research purposes.

Proceedings of the the Big Picture Workshop, pages 18–27
December 7, 2023

Open materials are particularly important when we develop tools for NLP, because this work can greatly benefit from resources that are openly accessible with a permissive license. In the following sections we will discuss examples of such work, including our contribution to Universal Dependency treebanks. It must be emphasized that the open technology developed on an open infrastructure can also be used to process materials that are available only to a particular researcher or individual members of a community. Therefore, open infrastructure benefits both open and closed environments, whereas a closed infrastructure only benefits a big commercial player.

2 Related work

There are several individual projects in different parts of the world that work with online dictionaries for endangered languages. Many projects, however, focus on one language only and work without knowing about other ongoing projects for other endangered languages. This has led to a situation where researchers solve the same type of problems individually for their language of interest reinventing the wheel over and over again. There are plenty of online dictionaries and language learning tools that have been developed from scratch for one particular language.

Work with endangered languages in North America has shown the importance of language learning tools for second language learners. Lack of familiarity with lexicographical tradition can easily be a deciding factor in a beginner's learning experience. A learner of a new language cannot be expected to know exactly where an entry is located in a dictionary, nor can the learner be expected automatically to know the normative spelling. When the user of a language lacks a proper keyboard layout or knowledge of the correct orthography, the strategies of orthographic relaxation can be implemented in mobile and online dictionaries. Morphological processing and spelling relaxation are used to cater to beginners in Tsimshian and Salishan languages in the use of dictionaries and NLP tools (Littell et al., 2017).

On an entirely separate front, work has also been done to provide the Yupik community of St. Lawrence Island unimpeded access to language materials online. This has been possible using a morphologically aware dictionary. In the system, a strategy of multiple input methods has been introduced that caters to different writing systems (Hunt et al., 2019). The work here is tailor-made, and it maintains a strong link between the language and its community. The endangered language is seen as a low-resourced language in this context.

The problem is that *low-resourced language* is a term that is used for almost any language with less Internet presence than English. languages like Hindi (Irvine and Callison-Burch, 2014), Arabic (Chen et al., 2018) or Persian (Ahmadnia et al., 2017) are often considered low-resourced languages in the world of NLP, even though they have millions of speakers. In the work of Nasution et al. (2018), the ethnic Indonesian languages are relatively small compared to the superstrate language that surrounds them. The approach consists of working simultaneously with a group of closely related languages in a multilingual, language-independent infrastructure. The authors analyze the use of bilingual dictionary entries and explain the difficulty of selecting the appropriate bilingual dictionaries to begin documentation.

One of the largest infrastructures for minority language documentation from the point of view of computational linguistics is that of Giella (Moshagen et al., 2014). Their infrastructure is based on two main components: FST transducers (finite state transducers) and XML dictionaries. Transducers are a way of documenting the morphology of a language computationally. That is to say, they are collections of rules about how the morphological system of a language works. These rules can be used directly for automatic text analysis and lemma conjugation in its morphological variants.

Transducers and XML dictionaries are used for spelling correction in Word[1], text prediction on Android and iOS keyboards[2], interactive systems to learn languages (Bontogon et al., 2018) and online dictionaries (Rueter and Hämäläinen, 2017). Our infrastructure is based on Giella, which allows us to synchronize data between the two infrastructures. This means that advances in linguistic documentation in our infrastructure can be used directly in the tools produced in Giella.

3 Our infrastructure

Using Giella requires a relatively high proficiency in programming to be able to write dictionaries and morphological rules for FSTs, and at the same time,

[1] http://divvun.no/korrektur/korrektur.html

[2] http://divvun.no/keyboards/mobileindex.html

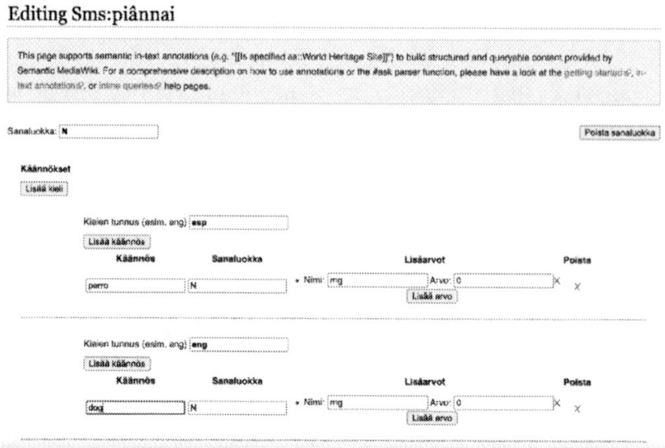

Figure 1: The form in Akusanat to edit the entry piânnai (dog) in Skolt Sami

it requires a good amount of knowledge in the language that is being documented. The infrastructure can be too complicated even for those who have studied computer science, and therefore it is not accessible to a community outside of those who collaborate directly with Giella. For this reason, our infrastructure has several interfaces for different types of users; for users who do not have sufficient knowledge to write XML or program transducers and for developers who want to use the tools without knowing how to compile them right from the beginning with the *make* command.

3.1 Online dictionaries

A very important step in the documentation of a minority language is the lexicographical work. This results in a dictionary that can be useful for both native speakers as for those who want to learn the language. We store dictionaries in a highly structured XML format. That means that all kinds of metadata are in their respective fields rather than being stored in various parts of a lexicographical entry in an unstructured format. This is important as we do not only want to create dictionaries for human use, but we also want them to be machine readable.

Our Akusanat system[3] (Hämäläinen and Rueter, 2018, 2019) is based on MediaWiki and allows you to view the content of XML dictionaries for all types of users. MediaWiki data is synchronized with XML files using the Git version control. This means that if someone modifies a lexicographical entry in Akusanat, these changes will result in a change to the XML dictionary stored in GitHub. If someone changes the XML dictionaries directly, Akusanat will download the new changes from GitHub and update its database automatically. This is done so that advanced users are able to edit the XML files directly with their favorite tool and less advanced users can make changes online with a graphical user interface. Akusanat does not let users modify the Wiki syntax directly, instead it displays a form that ensures changes remain structured and compatible with XML Figure 1.

For searching, we use morphological FST transducers to process the user input. This means that the user can search for a word in any of its morphological inflections, since the FST can lemmatize words automatically. It is also possible to search by typing in misspelled words. The transducers contain information about the most common spelling errors in each language, which allows us to resolve the lemma, although the word has not been spelled according to the spelling standard. This is important in the case of languages with which we work, since spelling rules are not as well-established as in the case of majority languages.

Figure 3 shows the interface for looking up words in the dictionaries. In the example, the search term is the Skolt Sami word *sooǥǥ*, which is the genitive of the word *sokk*, which means family. Our system lemmatizes the search term automatically with the Skolt Sami FST, and displays the input for the *sokk* lemma to the user.

The idea of using MediaWiki, and especially Semantic MediaWiki, to create dictionaries, is not new, since there are already several projects that use the technology as their base (Muljadi et al., 2006; Bon and Nowak, 2013; Dueñas and Gómez,

[3]https://akusanat.com.

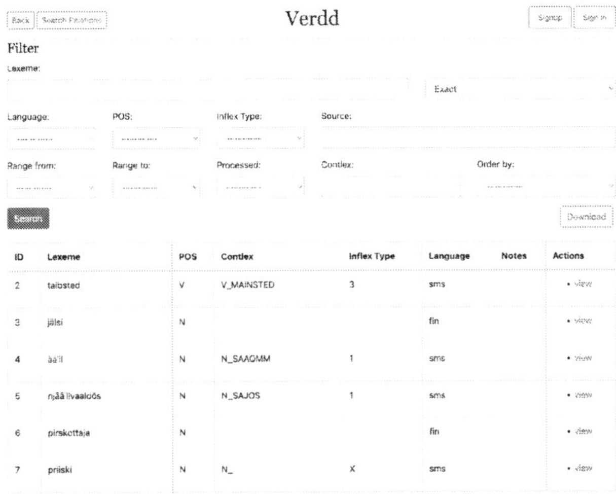

Figure 2: The interface for searching and filtering lexical entries in Ve'rdd

Figure 3: The interface for searching in Akusanat

2015). Without a doubt, MediaWiki has its advantages, in practice we have had to program our own MediaWiki extensions to add the necessary functionality; the form to edit, MediaWiki-XML synchronization, search with transducers etc. The problem that we have experienced many times is that the inner workings of MediaWiki change too often. This means that if we want to keep our MediaWiki instance up to date with the latest security updates, we have to make a lot of changes to our source code to keep our extensions working with the new version of MediaWiki. Even so, we continue to use and develop Akusanat[4] for the time being, as it offers a simple environment for users. In the next section, we describe the other system that we are developing. The new system may replace Akusanat in the future.

3.2 Editorial work

In this section, we describe the Ve'rdd[5] system (Alnajjar et al., 2019, 2020). The system works with the same XML dictionaries as Akusanat and can be used online in a similar way. The difference is in the intended use of the system. Ve'rdd is not a system to visualize lexicographical entries for an end user, but a system created specifically for writing both digital and printed dictionaries. During the process of developing the system, we have collaborated with a group of professional lexicographers who work with printed dictionaries.

In the context of the languages we work with, lexicographical documentation does not start from scratch, as both the Sami languages spoken in the Nordic countries and the Permian and Mordvinic languages spoken in Russia have received much attention in terms of their digital documentation during the last century. For example, there is a dictionary of the Skolt Sami language Sammallahti and Mosnikoff (1991), and there are several studies on the Mordvinic (Aasmäe et al., 2016; Grünthal, 2016) and Permian languages (Hamari, 2011; Klumpp, 2016). If there are existing dictionaries in digital form, they exist in an unstructured format such as a Word, CSV, or PDF file produced with an OCR system. For this reason, Ve'rdd includes functionality for import lexicographic data from unstructured formats. We have paid a lot of attention

[4]Code available https://github.com/mikahama/akusanat

[5]https://akusanat.com/verdd/

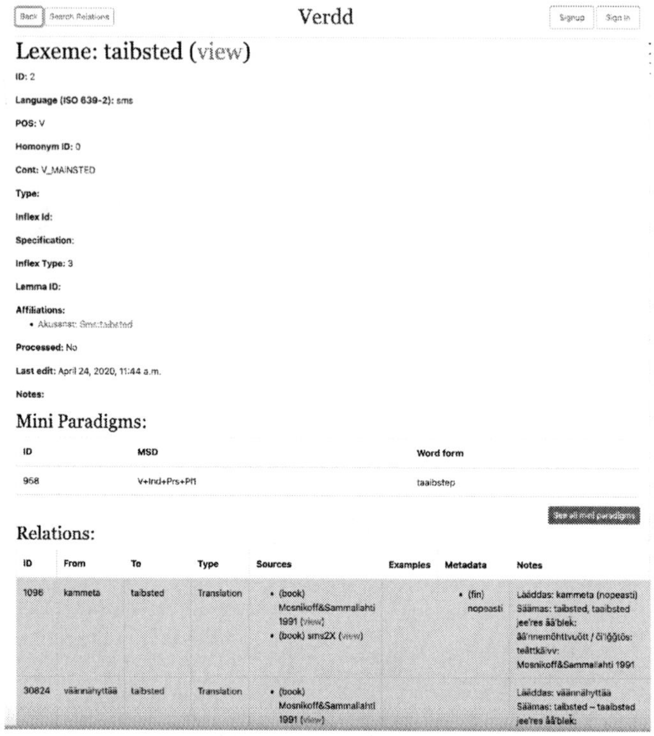

Figure 4: The interface for editing lexical entries in Ve'rdd

to the quality of the conversion, since, in the case of our languages, especially in the case of Skolt Sami, it is very frequent that the same character exists in many different Unicode characters. For example, ʹ (U+02B9 modifier letter prime) is a very common character in Skolt Sami, but because of the Finnish keyboard layout, it is often written as ' (U+0027 apostrophe) or ´ (U+00B4 acute accent). Ve'rdd is programmed to take into account the possible characters of the language and try to correct the incorrect characters automatically.

Figure 2 shows the interface for searching and filtering words in Ve'rdd. The interface is designed to support the workflow of a dictionary editor. For example, it is possible to display only raw inputs. This means entries that no one has verified after importing the data from an unstructured format. To facilitate the development of FST transducers it is also possible to sort and filter the words according to the continuation lexicon, which is the FST way of indicating how every word is supposed to be inflected.

Apart from just searching and filtering lexical entries, it is important to have the possibility to edit them. Figure 4 shows the interface for inspecting a dictionary entry. If a user is connected to their account, in addition to viewing, they can edit the information of a lexicographic entry. Ve'rdd is designed to be a tool for multilingual dictionaries, so one entry is connected to other entries in the system. In Figure 4, relationships can be seen as translation types that connect a word to its translations in other languages. It is also possible to define other types of relationships between lexica based on etymology. Relationships may also exist between words of the same language, for example, it is possible to indicate compound words and derivations with relations. Since the FST transducers contain derivative information, Ve'rdd automatically adds this type of relationship when importing a unstructured dictionary.

Ve'rdd can visualize the relationship between two words that are linked together with any kind of relationship. This can be used to verify that a word in a given language is linked to the correct homonym in another language (Figure 5). It is also possible to edit the type of relationship or delete any unnecessary relationships.

Ve'rdd has a functionality that allows the user to export any dictionary in different formats. The most important for us are the Giella XML, which can be used to generate FST transducers, and Latex

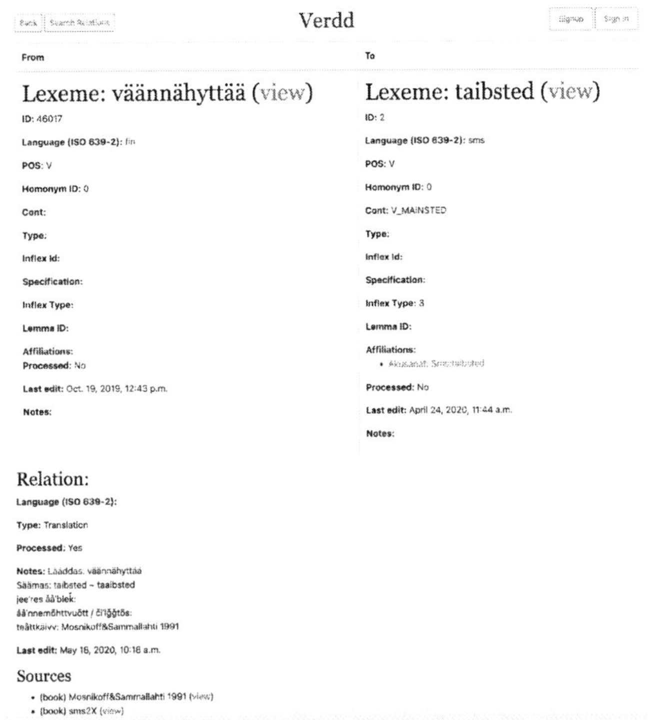

Figure 5: The interface for comparing two related entries in Ve'rdd

code. The Latex code makes it is possible to generate a ready-to-print PDF version of the dictionary. The Latex format makes it possible to change the style of the dictionary without changing the content. If there are changes in Ve'rdd, it is possible to update the content of the dictionary without changing the style defined in Latex. This functionality has been an important design principle for us since the work done in Ve'rdd should not only be used in digital dictionaries but also in printed dictionaries.

3.2.1 NLP resources

Our dictionary editing systems are directly useful in the development of FST transducers since we can export the lexicon in the format needed for HFST (Lindén et al., 2013). HFST is the tool we use to create the transducers. We have transducers for the Skolt Sami (Rueter and Hämäläinen, 2020), Erzya and Moksha (Rueter et al., 2020a) and Komi languages. The transducers can be used to lemmatize words, analyze their morphology or generate inflected forms. These transducers are difficult to compile for people who do not work with the transducers often. For this reason, we compile all transducers every night and we distribute them through our website[6]. We not only compile our transducers but all transducers for all languages in the Giella infrastructure.

The transducers are difficult to use as such, and for this reason, we have developed a Python library called UralicNLP (Hämäläinen, 2019) and a Python implementation of HFST called PyHFST (Hämäläinen and Alnajjar, 2023). With the libraries, compiled dictionaries and translators can be downloaded and used directly in Python. Fig 6 shows how to use our transducers from Python. In the second line of code, the word шляпа (hat) is analyzed in erzya (myv). The result indicates that the word is an indefinite (+Indef) noun (+N) in the nominative (+Nom) singular (+Sg). In the fourth line we generate the conjugated form of the same word in the plural (+Pl). The result is the plural word шляпат.

```
>>> from uralicNLP import uralicApi
>>> uralicApi.analyze("шляпа", "myv")
[('шляпа+N+Sg+Nom+Indef', 0.0)]
>>> uralicApi.generate("шляпа+N+Pl+Nom+Indef", "myv")
[('шляпат', 0.0)]
>>>
```

Figure 6: An example of using UralicNLP

[6] https://models.uralicnlp.com/nightly/

FST transducers produce all possible interpretations for a word from. In the case of the Uralic languages, there is plenty of homonymy in morphological inflections. This means that, if we use the transducers on regular text, we cannot accurately lemmatize the words in their context since the transducers produce all possible lemmas, For this reason, we use constraint grammar disambiguators (Karlsson et al., 2011) based on a tool called VISL CG-3 (Bick and Didriksen, 2015). The grammar rules of constraint grammars remove morphological readings that are not possible in a given sentence, and result in a sentence that is morphologically disambiguated with one lemma per word as opposed to all the possible lemmas.

```
>>> from uralicNLP.cg3 import Cg3
>>> oracion = "Нывв ёртыслы гижис письмӧ"
>>> cg = Cg3("kpv")
>>> print(cg.disambiguate(oracion.split(" ")))
Warning: Line 6 had empty tag.
[('Нывв', [<нывв - N, Sg, Nom, <W:0.000000>>]), ('ёртыслы', [<ёрт - N, Sg, Dat, Px
Sg3, So/PC, <W:0.000000>>]), ('гижис', [<гижны - V, TV, Ind, Prt1, Sg3, <W:0.000
000>>]), ('письмӧ', [<письмӧ - N, Sg, Nom, <W:0.000000>>])]
>>> 
```

Figure 7: An example of the use of the Komi Zyrian disambiguator

In Figure 7, we can see how the CG disambiguators can be used on UralicNLP. The third line initializes the disambiguation object for the Komi-Zyrian (kpv) and in the fourth line the disambiguation method of the object is called with a sentence. The result contains the word forms of the sentence, their lemmatization and morphology for each word of the sentence.

Apart from structured dictionaries and rule-based tools, we have treebanks of the universal dependencies for the Skolt Saami, Moksha, Erzya (Rueter and Tyers, 2018), Komi-Zyrian (Partanen et al., 2018) and Komi-Permyak (Rueter et al., 2020b). These treebanks contain syntactic annotations with the tags Morphological characteristics of universal dependencies. With the latest treebanks, we have also added the morphological labels produced by the transducers to facilitate the use of the two resources together

4 Incorporating modern NLP methods

As we have described thus far, a great part of our work relies on the old rule-based tradition of NLP. When we deal with endangered languages, rules are the primary starting point. One cannot simply train a neural network if there isn't enough training data. However, we do not want to reject neural models instantly as something that simply will not work for small languages. Neural models can work and they can be extremely beneficial. Throughout our research, we have aimed at combining rule-based models with neural models to facilitate our work on endangered languages.

Digital documentation has allowed us to use the latest methods in the world of NLP to automatically increase the data we have in the dictionaries. Because all of the lexicographic resources we have are multilingual, the first step we have taken with NLP technology has been the prediction of translations (Hämäläinen et al., 2018). The idea was as follows: if the Skolt Sami dictionary contains Finnish translations, German and English, and the Erzya dictionary contains translations into Finnish, English, Russian, and French, then, with this information, it should be possible to automatically deduce translations from Skolt Sami into Russian and French and from Erzya into German given the existence of two common languages: Finnish and English. With a probabilistic model we have increased the number of translations in Skolt Sami, Erzya, Moksha and Komi-Zyrian dictionaries.

We have elaborated on this idea later on by using graph based approaches and neural models (Alnajjar et al., 2021, 2022). These have not been isolated attempts, but the graph based methods have been incorporated into Ve'rdd as well. The predictions have been manually checked and this way we have been able to augment our dictionaries semi-automatically. The Livonian institute has embraced this technology in bootstrapping a Livonian-English dictionary.

As neural networks require a large amount of data to be trained, it is common to believe that their use is not possible in the case of endangered languages. We have taken the perspective that we can generate the amount of data needed for a neural network with our morphological tools. Using the treebanks and the transducers, we have generated data to train a neural network to perform disambiguation instead of using the constraint grammar for Erzya and Komi-Zyrian (Ens et al., 2019). The idea was to generate all possible analyzes for the words in the treebanks and train the neural network to disambiguate the analyses with the treebank analysis. Later on, we further developed this method in the context of Sami languages (Hämäläinen and Wiechetek, 2020).

We have also been able to use the neural networks to increase etymological relationships in the Skolt Sami dictionary (Hämäläinen and Reuter,

2019). The method was based on a character level LSTM model that was enhanced with synthetic data generated with a character-level statistical machine translation tool. We used this method to produce a set of candidate cognates that we manually checked and incorporated into our digital dictionaries. This method relies on external data from the Institute for Languages in Finland, which makes it difficult for us to include it in Ve'rdd.

Rule-based FSTs are great because they are usually very accurate, however, they do not have a great lexical coverage. Analyzing an online text with the FSTs will usually mean a ton of words that are not recognized at all. For this reason, we used the FSTs to generate training data for neural models (Hämäläinen et al., 2021). We used this data to train character-level neural machine translation models to analyze, generate and lemmatize word forms. The key idea is to use the exact same morphological tags so that the neural models and the FSTs can be used interchangeably. These neural models have been made available through UralicNLP as a fallback mechanism. If an FST fails to analyze a word form, the neural model will be used automatically if neural fallback is turned on.

Recently, we have also moved our interest towards other aspects of NLP than just lexicon and morphology. We have done work on automatically translating and aligning word embeddings for endangered Uralic languages (Alnajjar, 2021) and using them successfully in downstream tasks such as sentiment analysis (Alnajjar et al., 2023).

5 Discussion and Conclusions

We hope that our work can be useful for others as well. We have put a lot of attention in open-sourcing our tools and resources so that nobody needs to start building language documentation tools entirely from scratch. We have also paved a road towards using state-of-the-art neural models in the context of truly endangered languages with extremely limited resources. This is challenging and requires ingenuity. We are not interested in committing to the dichotomy of researches who defend rule-based tools as the only viable option for endangered languages nor to the researchers who frown upon rules and rely solely on the Transformer architecture. The best solutions, we believe, are found by combining both worlds.

Our tools are compatible with the Giella infrastructure. This has made it possible to use our dictionaries and translators directly on their online platform to learn languages (Antonsen and Argese, 2018), on Android and iPhone keyboards and spell checking for Word and OpenOffice developed by Divvun[7] at Giella. Flexible and interoperable design makes it also possible to integrate different lexical resources into our infrastructure once those are digitized or otherwise become available.

Digital documentation clearly has its benefits, since we can carry out machine learning with structured dictionaries and FST transducers. For this reason, a project conducted at the University of Oulu[8] the goal of which was to author the new dictionary Skolt Finnish-Sami has chosen to use Ve'rdd to create the digital and printed dictionary. We have worked together with project employees to increase the functionality of our system. Ve'rdd has made the simultaneous work of editors possible who, without Ve'rdd, would have used Excel and Word. This would have meant a lost chance of producing a structured dictionary for the interest of NLP and a printed dictionary at the same time.

We have started to explore non-Uralic languages by building a UD treebak for Apurinã (Rueter et al., 2021). Furthermore, we have built an initial FST for Lushootseed (lut) (Rueter et al., 2023) and extended it with an LSTM model. These are our initial steps towards non-Uralic languages.

References

Niina Aasmäe, Karl Pajusalu, and NADEŽDA KABAJEVA. 2016. Gemination in the mordvin languages. *Linguistica Uralica*, 52(2).

Benyamin Ahmadnia, Javier Serrano, and Gholamreza Haffari. 2017. Persian-spanish low-resource statistical machine translation through english as pivot language. In *RANLP*, pages 24–30.

Khalid Alnajjar. 2021. When word embeddings become endangered. In *Multilingual Facilitation*, pages 275–288. University of Helsinki.

Khalid Alnajjar, Mika Hämäläinen, Niko Partanen, and Jack Rueter. 2019. The open dictionary infrastructure for uralic languages. Электронная Письменность Народов Российской Федерации.

Khalid Alnajjar, Mika Hämäläinen, Niko Tapio Partanen, and Jack Rueter. 2022. Using graph-based methods to augment online dictionaries of endangered languages. In *Proceedings of the Fifth Workshop on*

[7] http://divvun.no/

[8] https://www.sttinfo.fi/tiedote/tekoaly-apuna-koltansaamen-ja-pohjoissaamen-digitaalisten-sanakirjojen-toimitustyossa?publisherId=57858920&releaseId=69886820

the Use of Computational Methods in the Study of Endangered Languages, pages 139–148.

Khalid Alnajjar, Mika Hämäläinen, and Jack Rueter. 2023. Sentiment analysis using aligned word embeddings for uralic languages. In *Proceedings of the Second Workshop on Resources and Representations for Under-Resourced Languages and Domains (RESOURCEFUL-2023)*, pages 19–24.

Khalid Alnajjar, Mika Hämäläinen, Jack Rueter, and Niko Partanen. 2020. Ve'rdd. narrowing the gap between paper dictionaries, low-resource nlp and community involvement. In *Proceedings of the 28th International Conference on Computational Linguistics: System Demonstrations*, pages 1–6.

Khalid Alnajjar, Jack Rueter, Niko Partanen, and Mika Hämäläinen. 2021. Enhancing the erzya-moksha dictionary automatically with link prediction. *Folia Uralica Debreceniensia*.

Lene Antonsen and Chiara Argese. 2018. Using authentic texts for grammar exercises for a minority language. In *Proceedings of the 7th workshop on NLP for Computer Assisted Language Learning*, pages 1–9.

Eckhard Bick and Tino Didriksen. 2015. Cg-3—beyond classical constraint grammar. In *Proceedings of the 20th Nordic Conference of Computational Linguistics (NODALIDA 2015)*, pages 31–39.

Bruno Bon and Krzysztof Nowak. 2013. Wikilexicographica. linking medieval latin dictionaries with semantic mediawiki. In *eLex 2013*, pages 407–420. Trojina, Institute for Applied Slovene Studies (Ljubljana, Slovenia); Eesti ....

Megan Bontogon, Antti Arppe, Lene Antonsen, Dorothy Thunder, and Jordan Lachler. 2018. Intelligent computer assisted language learning (icall) for nêhiyawêwin: an in-depth user-experience evaluation. *Canadian Modern Language Review*, 74(3):337–362.

Xilun Chen, Yu Sun, Ben Athiwaratkun, Claire Cardie, and Kilian Weinberger. 2018. Adversarial deep averaging networks for cross-lingual sentiment classification. *Transactions of the Association for Computational Linguistics*, 6:557–570.

George Dueñas and Diego Gómez. 2015. A bilingual dictionary with semantic mediawiki: The language saliba's case. *The 4th International Conference on Language Documentation and Conservation (ICLDC)*.

Jeff Ens, Mika Hämäläinen, Jack Rueter, and Philippe Pasquier. 2019. Morphosyntactic disambiguation in an endangered language setting. In *22nd Nordic Conference on Computational Linguistics (NoDaLiDa)*. Linköping University Electronic Press.

Riho Grünthal. 2016. Transitivity in erzya: Second language speakers in a grammatical focus. *Mordvin languages in the field*.

Mika Hämäläinen. 2019. Uralicnlp: An nlp library for uralic languages. *Journal of open source software*.

Mika Hämäläinen. 2021. Endangered languages are not low-resourced! In *Multilingual Facilitation*. University of Helsinki.

Mika Hämäläinen, Niko Partanen, Jack Rueter, and Khalid Alnajjar. 2021. Neural morphology dataset and models for multiple languages, from the large to the endangered. In *Proceedings of the 23rd Nordic Conference on Computational Linguistics (NoDaLiDa)*, pages 166–177.

Mika Hämäläinen and Jack Rueter. 2019. An open online dictionary for endangered uralic languages. *Electronic lexicography in the 21st century*.

Mika Hämäläinen and Jack Michael Rueter. 2018. Advances in synchronized xml-mediawiki dictionary development in the context of endangered uralic languages. In *Proceedings of the XVIII EURALEX International Congress*. Ljubljana University Press.

Mika Hämäläinen, Liisa Lotta Tarvainen, and Jack Rueter. 2018. Combining concepts and their translations from structured dictionaries of uralic minority languages. In *Proceedings of the Eleventh International Conference on Language Resources and Evaluation (LREC 2018)*.

Mika Hämäläinen and Linda Wiechetek. 2020. Morphological disambiguation of south sámi with fsts and neural networks. In *Proceedings of the 1st Joint Workshop on Spoken Language Technologies for Under-resourced languages (SLTU) and Collaboration and Computing for Under-Resourced Languages (CCURL)*, pages 36–40.

Arja Hamari. 2011. The abessive in the permic languages. *Suomalais-Ugrilaisen Seuran Aikakauskirja*, 2011(93):37–84.

Nikolaus P Himmelmann. 1998. Documentary and descriptive linguistics. *Linguistics*, 36(1).

Benjamin Hunt, Emily Chen, Sylvia LR Schreiner, and Lane Schwartz. 2019. Community lexical access for an endangered polysynthetic language: An electronic dictionary for st. lawrence island yupik. In *Proceedings of the 2019 Conference of the North American Chapter of the Association for Computational Linguistics (Demonstrations)*, pages 122–126.

Mika Hämäläinen and Khalid Alnajjar. 2023. Pyhfst: A pure python implementation of hfst. *Zenodo*. 10.5281/zenodo.7791470.

Mika Hämäläinen and Jack Reuter. 2019. Finding sami cognates with a character-based nmt approach. In *Proceedings of the Workshop on Computational Methods for Endangered Languages*, volume 1.

Ann Irvine and Chris Callison-Burch. 2014. Hallucinating phrase translations for low resource mt. In *Proceedings of the Eighteenth Conference on Computational Natural Language Learning*, pages 160–170.

Fred Karlsson, Atro Voutilainen, Juha Heikkilae, and Arto Anttila. 2011. *Constraint Grammar: a language-independent system for parsing unrestricted text*, volume 4. Walter de Gruyter.

Gerson Klumpp. 2016. Semantic functions of complementizers in permic languages. *Complementizer Semantics in European Languages*, pages 529–586.

Krister Lindén, Erik Axelson, Senka Drobac, Sam Hardwick, Juha Kuokkala, Jyrki Niemi, Tommi A Pirinen, and Miikka Silfverberg. 2013. Hfst—a system for creating nlp tools. In *Systems and Frameworks for Computational Morphology: Third International Workshop, SFCM 2013, Berlin, Germany, September 6, 2013 Proceedings 3*, pages 53–71. Springer.

Patrick Littell, Aidan Pine, and Henry Davis. 2017. Waldayu and waldayu mobile: Modern digital dictionary interfaces for endangered languages. In *Proceedings of the 2nd Workshop on the Use of Computational Methods in the Study of Endangered Languages*, pages 141–150.

Sjur Moshagen, Jack Rueter, Tommi Pirinen, Trond Trosterud, and Francis M Tyers. 2014. Open-source infrastructures for collaborative work on under-resourced languages. *Collaboration and Computing for Under-Resourced Languages in the Linked Open Data Era*, pages 71–77.

Hendry Muljadi, Hideaki Takeda, Shoko Kawamoto, Satoshi Kobayashi, and Asao Fujiyama. 2006. Towards a semantic wiki-based japanese biodictionary. In *SemWiki*.

Arbi Haza Nasution, Yohei Murakami, and Toru Ishida. 2018. Designing a collaborative process to create bilingual dictionaries of indonesian ethnic languages. In *Proceedings of the Eleventh International Conference on Language Resources and Evaluation (LREC 2018)*.

Niko Partanen, Rogier Blokland, KyungTae Lim, Thierry Poibeau, and Michael Rießler. 2018. The first komi-zyrian universal dependencies treebanks. In *Second Workshop on Universal Dependencies (UDW 2018), November 2018, Brussels, Belgium*, pages 126–132.

Jack Rueter, Marília Fernanda Pereira de Freitas, Sidney Da Silva Facundes, Mika Hämäläinen, and Niko Partanen. 2021. Apurinã Universal Dependencies treebank. In *Proceedings of the First Workshop on Natural Language Processing for Indigenous Languages of the Americas*, pages 28–33, Online. Association for Computational Linguistics.

Jack Rueter and Mika Hämäläinen. 2017. Synchronized mediawiki based analyzer dictionary development. In *3rd International Workshop for Computational Linguistics of Uralic Languages (IWCLUL 2017)*. The Association for Computational Linguistics.

Jack Rueter and Mika Hämäläinen. 2020. Fst morphology for the endangered skolt sami language. In *Proceedings of the 1st Joint Workshop on Spoken Language Technologies for Under-resourced languages (SLTU) and Collaboration and Computing for Under-Resourced Languages (CCURL)*, pages 250–257.

Jack Rueter, Mika Hämäläinen, and Khalid Alnajjar. 2023. Modelling the reduplicating Lushootseed morphology with an FST and LSTM. In *Proceedings of the Workshop on Natural Language Processing for Indigenous Languages of the Americas (AmericasNLP)*, pages 40–46, Toronto, Canada. Association for Computational Linguistics.

Jack Rueter, Mika Hämäläinen, and Niko Partanen. 2020a. Open-source morphology for endangered mordvinic languages. In *Proceedings of Second Workshop for NLP Open Source Software (NLP-OSS)*. The Association for Computational Linguistics.

Jack Rueter, Niko Partanen, and Larisa Ponomareva. 2020b. On the questions in developing computational infrastructure for komi-permyak. In *Proceedings of the Sixth International Workshop on Computational Linguistics of Uralic Languages*, pages 15–25.

Jack Rueter and Francis Tyers. 2018. Towards an open-source universal-dependency treebank for erzya. In *Proceedings of the Fourth International Workshop on Computational Linguistics of Uralic Languages*, pages 106–118.

Pekka Sammallahti and Jouni Mosnikoff. 1991. *Suomi-koltansaame sanakirja: Lää'dd-sää'm sää'nnǩe'rjj*. Girjegiisá.

Computational Narrative Understanding: A Big Picture Analysis

Andrew Piper
McGill University
680 Sherbrooke St. West
Montreal, QC H3A 2M7 CANADA
andrew.piper@mcgill.ca

Abstract

This paper provides an overview of outstanding major research goals for the field of computational narrative understanding. Storytelling is an essential human practice, one that provides a sense of personal meaning, shared sense of community, and individual enjoyment. A number of research domains have increasingly focused on storytelling as a key mechanism for explaining human behavior. Now is an opportune moment to provide a vision of the contributions that computational narrative understanding can make towards this collective endeavor and the challenges facing the field. In addition to providing an overview of the elements of narrative, this paper outlines three major lines of inquiry: understanding the multimodality of narrative; the temporal patterning of narrative (narrative "shape"); and sociocultural narrative schemas, i.e. collective narratives. The paper concludes with a call for more inter-disciplinary working groups and deeper investment in building cross-cultural and multimodal narrative datasets.

1 Introduction

The Native-American writer, Gerald Vizenor, once remarked: "There isn't any center to the world but a story" (Coltelli, 1990). Storytelling is a ubiquitous human practice, exhibited in all human cultures, languages, and recorded historical time periods. Many of the world's most enduring and widespread belief systems are encoded through stories, and research suggests that human reasoning (Bruner, 1991) and selfhood (Berns, 2022) are fundamentally grounded in narrative. Today, a growing body of research is developing across a variety of domains that focus on storytelling as a key mechanism for explaining human beliefs and behavior, from mental health (Adler et al., 2016), to political stance taking (Bushell et al., 2017), to consumer persuasion (Bilandzic and Busselle, 2013), to financial decision making (Shiller, 2020).

Given this widespread interest in, and awareness of, narrative as a crucial driver of human behavior, the field of "computational narrative understanding" has a great opportunity to contribute to a range of research fields. Computational narrative understanding has crystallized over the past 5-10 years as a vibrant subset of natural language processing (Bamman et al., 2019; Jorge et al., 2019). Its aim is to develop computational systems for the detection and understanding of narrative communication across different media and different cultural domains. While we may typically think of stories as encoded in written documents, the practice of narrative can be represented through a diverse array of media, including oral speech, song, still or moving images, social media, playable media like video games, or some combination of the above.

The aim of this paper is to provide a big picture view of some of the key higher-level goals for computational narrative understanding. A great deal of on-going and inspiring work continues to make progress in the detection and analysis of different components of narrative communication (for a review see Piper et al. (2021)). It thus seems timely to provide a vision of where we are going as a community to help motivate and organize future work in the field.

In section two, I provide a brief minimal definition of narrative communication highlighting its constituent parts building on prior work (Piper et al., 2021). Before moving to the big picture, it is important to ground our understanding of this core concept. In section three, I describe a research framework that aims to develop a more multi-modal understanding of narrative. With its grounding in NLP, computational narrative understanding has understandably focused on narrative as a linguistic phenomenon. However, as narratologists have long pointed out (Ryan et al., 2004), storytelling can transpire in numerous different media. Being able to integrate observations across

Proceedings of the the Big Picture Workshop, pages 28–39
December 7, 2023 ©2023 Association for Computational Linguistics

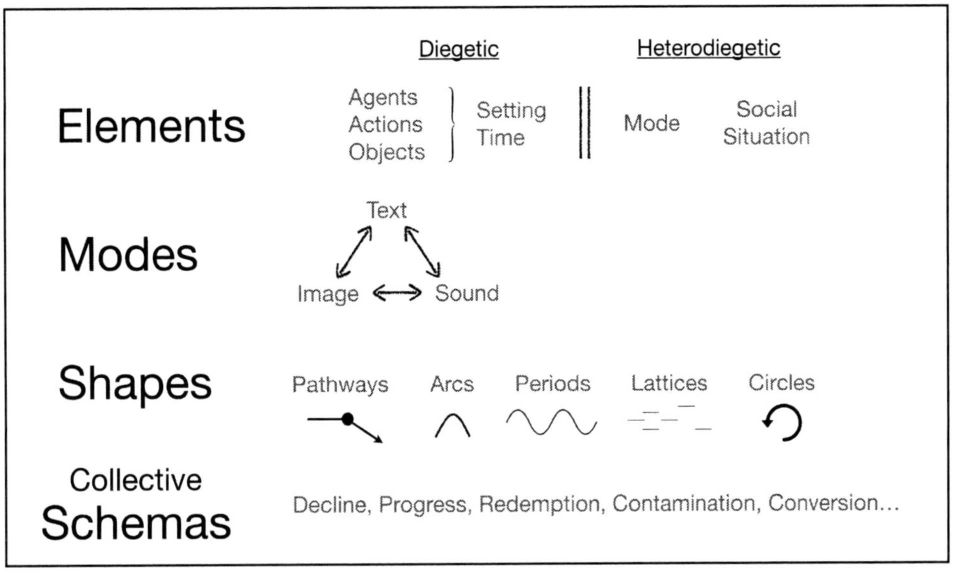

Figure 1: Overview of narrative research areas discussed in this paper.

media, from speech to text to images to playable media should become a central goal of computational narrative understanding.

In section four, I describe a research framework aimed at understanding narrative "shape" (also called "form" or "structure" (Berhe et al., 2022)), which can be understood as the temporal patterning of narrative elements. One of the fundamental aspects of storytelling is the encoding of events in time (Genette, 1983; Sternberg, 1992; Ricoeur, 2012). Narrative meaning is thus contingent on the temporal organization of information.

Seeing narratives as temporal artifacts, made in time and composed of time, then leads to the highest-level form of integration described in section five, that of narrative "schemas." As Berns (2022) has argued, narratives are forms of information compression, reducing the vast scope of experienced data down to a much more limited set of communicated data. Such compression necessarily follows archetypes or patterns that can be biologically or culturally conditioned (or some mixture of the two).

While the idea of "scripts" has been applied to understand the local schematic encoding of events (Chambers and Jurafsky, 2008a), prior work in folklore studies has offered promising frameworks for expanding the idea of schema to include whole stories within various typologies (Thompson, 1989). Essential to this framework is an attention to larger narrative ecologies, the ways in which such schemas play a generative and/or organizing role within broader, and potentially interactive, communicative domains (Tangherlini et al., 2020).

It is common to think of narrative as located within an individual document or artifact (this book or blog post tells a story), but narratologists have also highlighted the way story structures emerge from the complex social interactions of numerous agents (known as the "small stories" paradigm (Georgakopoulou, 2007)). Such "small stories" can then coalesce into larger socially circulatable schemas, variously referred to as "ontological narratives" (Somers, 1994), "deep stories" (Hochschild, 2018), or "collective narratives" (Bliuc and Chidley, 2022). Such schemas can then guide the processing and circulation of new information to "fit the narrative," potentially creating informational feedback loops that are durable over shorter or longer stretches of time.

In sum, we want to have a research framework capable of scaling the ladder from local elements (section 2), different media (section 3), formal structure (section 4), all the way up to schemas and social dynamics (section 5). Figure 1 provides a schematic overview of this big picture.

I conclude in section six with a reflection on the need for greater inter-disciplinary collaboration and deeper investment in building cross-cultural and multi-modal datasets. As we develop more sophisticated systems for detecting narrative communication, we will want to invest more deeply in the infrastructure for large-scale narrative understanding. This will necessarily entail collaborations across disciplines to better understand socially relevant applications as well as the ability to develop appropriate data. It will also require developing an awareness around the limitations or risks of narrative communication (Salmon, 2017; Gottschall, 2021). Stories not only inspire and move audiences, they can also deform reality and misinform, a point that should remain at the forefront of our thinking about how stories stand at the centre of so much human behavior, for better and for worse.

2 The Elements of Narrative

At its most elementary level, a story can be said to occur when all of the following criteria are met:

A	Someone
B	tells
C	someone
D	somewhere
	that
E	someone
F	did something(s)
G	[to someone]
H	somewhere
I	at some time
J	for some reason.

For there to be a story, we need (A) a teller, (B) a mode of telling (i.e. medium), (C) a recipient, (D) a social situation, (E) an agent, (F) at least one action or event, (G) a possible object, (H) a location, (I) a time-frame, and (J) a motivation or cause of the actions involved. Narratologists make a distinction between the frame of the storyworld (i.e. all of the elements that come after the double lines above) known as "diegetic" elements, and the frame of telling (i.e. all of the elements that come before the double lines) known as "heterodiegetic" elements, where diegesis refers to a narrative "frame" or "world."

Importantly, not all of these elements need to be explicit. For example, in one of the most famous short stories ever proposed by Ernest Hemingway, very little from the above list is specified:

For sale: Baby shoes. Never worn.

We don't know where and when this happened, nor do we know who is telling the story. All we know is what happened (on two levels): a baby died and a family needs money. But no matter how much is implicit in this story all of the parts are there. Something happens to someone somewhere at some time for some reason and someone tells someone this story.

Such a definition can be useful because it highlights the array of narrative elements that require computational solutions to "understand" the cultural meaning of a story. Such applications have included: character detection (Bamman et al., 2014; Jahan et al., 2018; Piper, 2023b; Stammbach et al., 2022), object detection (Piper and Bagga, 2022a), character relation detection (Labatut and Bost, 2019; Kraicer and Piper, 2019), event detection (Vauth et al., 2021), geographic and spatial understanding (Wilkens, 2013; Evans and Wilkens, 2018; Piatti et al., 2013; Erlin et al., 2021), temporal understanding (Underwood, 2018; Yauney et al., 2019; Vossen et al., 2021; Gangal et al., 2022), and causality mining (Meehan and Piper, 2022). A full review can be found in Piper et al. (2021) and Santana et al. (2023).

A second, higher-level way that a story can be broken down into constituent parts is through *discourse elements*. As we will see, this problem is associated with challenges of text segmentation, though importantly differs from prior work focused on sequential and/or paratextual (i.e. chapter) segmentation (Pethe et al., 2020; Zehe et al., 2021).

Narratives not only contain event-frames (i.e. scenes), but are also composed of heterogeneous linguistic styles in which the act of narration is but one component. This is one reason recent narrative theory has emphasized the idea of "narrativity" (Piper and Bagga, 2022b; Pianzola, 2018; Giora and Shen, 1994), which captures the *degree* of narration intrinsic to a narrative. An ostensibly narrative document like a short story will engage in moments of non-narrative statements, just as putatatively non-narrative documents like scientific articles may engage in occasionaly moments of narration. Narration is in this sense not a universal property of documents, but a local linguistic phenomenon. As Ochs et al. (2009) write, "We believe that narrative as genre and activity can be fruitfully examined in terms of a set of dimensions that a narrative displays to different degrees and in different ways."

Narratologists typically break down narratives into at least four basic discourse components:

Discourse	Contents
1. Narration	Agents and events
2. Description	Setting, modification, context
3. Dialogue	Reported speech
4. Evaluation	Meta-level discourse

"Narration," also known as "diegesis," refers to the linguistic structures described above that occur after the double horizontal line (E-J). This is the classic understanding of narrative, where events pertaining to an agent are recounted (this can also fall under the heading of "eventfulness" (Hühn, 2014)).

"Description," also called "mimesis," refers to when the surroundings or context of events are described and during which events do not unfold (though they may be unfolding in the background). In cinema, this is equivalent to an "establishing shot" that indicates to viewers where they are in time and space. Crucial to description is that it lacks the agent/action/cause structure from above.

"Dialogue" refers to any form of reported speech, though it can also take the form of indirect speech as well. Recounting what characters say to each other is an integral component of stories, although it technically is a form of dramatic performance (for a reflection on this topic see (Genette, 1992)).

Finally, many stories contain what we might call meta-textual statements (called "evaluation" by Labov and Waletzky (1967)), where the narrator provides some higher-level assessment with regards to the story, either a reflection on the story contents, their meaning, or some didactic lesson that should be imparted, making a latent feature of storytelling (it's meaning or purpose) manifest. While it may come at the end of a story, it can also be interspersed throughout. Here are a few examples of such statements:

1. *It is a truth universally acknowledged, that a single man in possession of a good fortune, must be in want of a wife.* (Pride and Prejudice)

2. *The flatterer lives at the expense of those who will listen to him.* (Aesop's Fables)

3. *All in all, I'd say that those years were some of the best times I've ever had.* (AskReddit)

While there are many more ways one can parse a story (see Bal and Van Boheemen (2009); Genette (1983)), the frameworks above provide practical heuristics for the ways that stories can be broken down into more elementary parts to ground computational models.

3 The Modality of Narrative

Grounded in NLP, computational narrative understanding has largely prioritized written narratives for understandable reasons. However, such text-driven approaches leave out large portions of storytelling behavior, including movies and television (Arnold et al., 2019; Papalampidi et al., 2019), user-generated streaming content, illustrated content in comic strips (Edlin and Reiss, 2023), graphic novels, or children's books (Adukia et al., 2021), and finally video games, which might have stronger or weaker narrative structures. While textual narratives are largely unimodal in nature (though the physical and visual dimensions of books has been a vibrant area of study for a long time (Collective, 2019)), these other narrative forms are all crucially multi-modal in nature.

Sound, image, and language can interact in ways that are complex and dynamic. A robust field of multimodal NLP research into text-image interactions for meaning-making has emerged in recent years (see for example recent research on humour by Hasan et al. (2019); Hessel et al. (2023)). Nevertheless, investigations into multimodal *narrative* understanding, such as the relationship between text and illustrations in children's books or graphic novels is in need of more attention (see Adukia et al. (2021) for an example exploring the visual qualities of children's book illustrations with respect to race). Understanding the kinds of gestural or pictorial preferences that are foregrounded given certain textual cues could give us insights into the way humans translate language into image (and vice versa) across different cultural domains.

Similarly, we still lack major comparative studies of narrative behavior across media, i.e. comparisons of narrative elements and archetypes in film, television, user-generated content, oral performances and books. For example, evidence suggests that written and oral narratives have similar "establishing shot" structures similar to movies and television (Boyd et al., 2020; Piper, 2023a). More precise comparisons can highlight the modal-specificity of different narrative elements along with the transmodal practices that are independent of a given modality. Understanding the ways in which storytellers marshal images, sounds, and words to create immersive experiences for audiences will greatly contribute to the project of computational narrative understanding.

4 The Shape of Narrative

The writer and critic Italo Calvino was fond of quoting a Sicilian expression that "time takes no time in a story" (Calvino, 1988). A narrator can tell a story that traverses centuries in a few sentences or can slow time down to the point where a few seconds takes minutes to describe. Narratologists refer to this as the difference between *narrated time* (the time transpiring in the storyworld) and *narrative time* (how long a story takes to tell). No matter how much stories may compress time, they cannot be told all at once. Contrary to Calvino's favored Sicilian expression, all stories, even the shortest, take time to tell.

This temporal dimension of narrative – that stories take time to tell and tell of things happening in time – has long been one of the privileged topics of narrative theory (Ricoeur, 2012; Sternberg, 1990, 1992). As the theorist David Herman has argued, "Narrative is a basic human strategy for coming to terms with time, process, and change" (Herman, 2009).

A number of approaches have been proposed for the computational modeling of temporal patterns in narrative (for a review of modeling narrative structure see Berhe et al., 2022). Schmidt (2015) used topic modeling to identify thematic arcs in television screenplays, while Thompson et al. (2018) used topic models to study thematic progression in philosophical texts and social media. Reagan et al. (2016) used sentiment analysis to model the concept of narrative fortune (Freytag, 1895), for which Elkins (2022) provides a more in-depth study of the validity of sentiment arcs as models of narrative structure. Boyd et al. (2020) used particular word types to capture three primary narrative stages, and Sap et al. (2022) used the predictability of next sentences to capture the concept of narrative "flow."

Piper and Toubia (2023) used word embeddings to model narrative non-linearity using the traveling salesman problem, while Toubia et al. (2021) offer two further ways of thinking about narrative shape called "speed" and "volume." Researchers have also used information theoretic frameworks to model the concept of narrative revelation using time series methods (Piper, 2023a) and stylistic novelty over narrative time using a bloom filter (McGrath, 2018). Ouyang and McKeown (2015) and Piper (2015) devised methods for predicting narrative "turning points" as larger structural qualites, drawing on Aristotelian and Augustinian theories of narrative respectively.

Common to all of these models is the assumption that the dissemination of information over narrative time assumes observable patterns (called "form" or "structure") and that these patterns encode cultural meaning. The most common framework to date has been that of the narrative "arc," drawn from French neo-classical tragedy (Freytag, 1895). According to this model, narratives encode a central conflict that results in some form of resolution or change, which can be approximated by an arc of rising and falling fortune or conflict.

Much future work remains to better understand relevant ways of capturing narrative time in terms of its formal patterns. The first area of consideration should be further work into the choice of feature distributions that are used to capture narrative time. Where prior work has focused to date on topic models, sentiment vocabulary, word embeddings, lexemes, and letters, higher-level narrative features (see Section 1) should continue to be developed and studied. We assume that the distribution of characters, event types, locations, or narrative modes may also contribute to the overall structural qualities of stories.

Second, modeling narrative change itself remains a key area of further research. Prior empirical work has shown that long narratives may employ multiple "arcs" rather than single turning points (Reagan et al., 2016; Fudolig et al., 2023), while other work has emphasized the significance of single turning points (Ouyang and McKeown, 2015; Piper, 2015). Additionally, the identity or meaning of such moments of change, regardless of how many, are also not well understood. The dramatic model of narrative denouement suggests that turning points are best understood as forms of "conflict/resolution," while other narrative theories suggest that "surprisingness" is the optimal way of understanding narrative change (Wilmot and Keller, 2020). Brewer and Lichtenstein (1982) have proposed two further affective states of *suspense* and *curiosity* in addition to surprise to capture the discrepancy between storyworld information and narrative information (i.e. when key information is withheld or forms of temporal anachrony are used such as flashbacks and flashwords known as analepsis and prolepsis respectively).

In addition to these temporal issues, the role that causality plays in describing narrative change has been relatively underexplored. As the writer and essayist George Saunders has argued, causality is the "wind in the kite" of narrative (Saunders, 2022). As Graesser et al. (2002) have demonstrated, readers are much more moved by "why" questions than "what" questions when it comes to narrative comprehension and recall. Future work will want to explore more fully both different constructs of "change" as well as draw on methodologies such as Markov models, time series analysis and systems dynamics to develop increasingly sophisticated models of change over narrative time.

Finally, most prior work is guided by a single spatial metaphor for narrative time, that of the arc. Future work will want to explore other possible structures or forms (Levine, 2015) that might capture the temporal patterns of narrative. The translation of time into spatial form represents an exciting and novel space of research for computational narrative understanding.

5 Narrative Schemas

Narratives are forms of information compression (Berns, 2022). They select certain experiential data and structure this data into prescribed grammatical slots (as described in Section 1). This basic insight serves as the foundation of the theory of narrative "scripts" (Schank and Abelson, 1977; Chambers and Jurafsky, 2008b), where narrative is understood as a probabilistic sequence of actions (i.e. given the event of being in a restaurant certain subsequent actions are more or less likely). Such compression is what allows stories to be both memorable as well as easily shareable (i.e. tellable (Baroni, 2011)).

The discussion of narrative form or shape in the prior section is one such example of the *schematic* nature of narrative, i.e. that narratives have structure and this structure is essential to their meaning. But schemas can also be represented as a variety of conceptual metaphors (that often have spatial associations). For example, in the field of clinical psychology researchers refer to two self-narrative schemas, called narratives of redemption (when bad things turn good) and narratives of contamination (when good things turn bad) (McAdams et al., 2001). Patients who structure life experience into the former schema are far more likely to be associated with positive mental health outcomes than those who engage in telling their life stories according to the latter.

The first extensive (and later controversial) study of narrative schemas emerged in the field of folklore studies (Dundes, 1962). Faced with large collections of documents with a high degree of repetitiveness, folklorists began developing systems for classifying stories according to different typologies. The most famous undertakings were Stith Thompson's Motif-Index of Folk-literature (Thompson, 1989), the Aarne-Thompson-Uther (ATU) Tale Index, and Vladimir Propp's emphasis on character "function" (Propp, 2010). Fundamental to this research was the insight that certain larger narrative patterns are maintained while local units can be changed. As Propp (2010) highlighted, whether it is an eagle or a horse or a ring that is the gift that carries away its recipient, the point of each of these stories is the event of being transported, or even more generally, the danger or affordance of gift giving.

While it is beyond the scope of this paper to rehearse debates around narrative classification (for a review see Dundes, 1962; Broadwell et al., 2018), there remains a fundamental value in developing narrative taxonomies for different domains. Narratives are indeed reducible to schemas and those schemas serve particular social and psychological functions. And yet we currently lack agreed-upon or widely used frameworks for discussing schemas, either at the individual or socio-cultural level.

Folklorist and computational narratologist Timothy Tangherlini has begun using the idea of schemas to study conspiracy theories circulating through social media (Tangherlini et al., 2020; Chong et al., 2021; Shahsavari et al., 2020), which function much like folklore in that various narrative units (Bill Gates, 5G) can be utilized for larger functional purposes (a global cabal of elites is controlling us). Related research by Mendelsohn et al. (2023) looks at "dogwhistle" detection, which can be understood as phrases with latent, toxic meanings and that likely have a narrative element to them.

Understanding schemas requires two challenging research questions. The first we can refer to as *motif tracking*, which requires the ability to model variability and repetition at both the level of local units (agents, actions, objects) and more general schemas (when certain units are deployed to tell certain kinds of stories). While systems currently exist to identify the narrative units described in Section 1 (including agents, actions, and objects), we still need ways of aggregating these units into story "types." When is Bill Gates being used to tell a story about global elites and when is he being used to tell a story about the power of philanthropy?

More importantly, we want to model the causes as well as social effects of these different story types. Do we see certain narrative schemas deployed in response to major social events (for example what are the prevalent narrative responses to financial or political or climatic shocks?). Or can certain narrative schemas predict future behavior? Similar to the clinical psychology example mentioned above but moving into the social realm, do we see the persistent invocation of narratives of national decline associated with shifts in electoral behavior? If we assume narrative is a key predictor of human behavior, we need more reliable and sophisticated ways of classifying narratives to better understand their causes and effects.

The second key dimension in studying narrative schemas is the aspect of *social dynamics*. As folklore studies first highlighted, narrative types are aggregates of numerous local instances of storytelling behavior. Each unit (whether an oral tale or social media post) may contribute to a larger narrative schema but may itself only loosely embody this schema. Narratologists refer to these local dynamics as "small stories" (Georgakopoulou, 2007), i.e. when a larger story is told through the participation of numerous actors. The quintessential example of this behavior is the "family dinner table," where family lore is the product of multiple actors engaging in the process of narrative recounting, potentially over long spans of time. At the macro-level narratologists refer to these larger narrative schemas – the aggregate of small stories – as "collective narratives" (Bliuc and Chidley, 2022), "ontological narratives" (Somers, 1994), or "deep stories" (Hochschild, 2018).

Social media and online news (broadly understood) greatly expand the complexity of collective narrative construction and small-story dynamics. One can imagine "top-down" approaches that start with known schemas and then classify individual stories or collections of stories within these taxonomies or "bottom-up" approaches that cluster individual stories into larger schemas that emerge from the collective behavior among the data. Modeling this complex, large-scale narrative behavior represents one of the major challenges for the field but one that has the most explanatory pay-offs in terms of understanding social behavior.

6 Narrative Infrastructures

As computational narrative understanding comes into its own as a distinct field within the NLP community, now is a good time to begin coordinating more of this research effort. These initiatives can take the form of shared tasks, dataset curation, and collective efforts to develop systems for narrative classification.

Shared tasks have a long history within NLP, though to date only three have been proposed for narrative understanding. The first is the narrative cloze test (Chambers and Jurafsky, 2008a; Mostafazadeh et al., 2016; Hatzel and Biemann, 2023), where systems predict the next agent-event in an event chain. Zehe et al. (2021) have proposed a task for detecting narrative scenes, while Reiter et al. (2019) have proposed a task for detecting narrative levels (when diegetic worlds are imbedded within one another, either in the form of stories within stories or temporal anachronisms such as flashbacks). Piper and Bagga (2022b) and Hatzel and Biemann (2023) have proposed annotation frameworks for narrative detection, i.e. identifying the degree to which a stretch of discourse can be identified as containing narration.

Future work will want to refine these existing initiatives as well as develop systems for the further detection of the remaining discursive units described in Section 2 (i.e. description, dialogue, evaluation). The automated identification of narrative communication in particular will prove extremely valuable for broader social and cultural analysis.

Given the value of narrative for understanding human behavior it is somewhat surprising how few datasets are available for the study of human storytelling. Much of this is due to intersecting problems of intellectual property restrictions, large library collections with low-levels of metadata, and the dynamic and ever-changing nature of online storytelling. Underwood et al. (2020) provide a large-scale annotation of ca. 200,000 fictional narratives in English in the Hathi Trust Digital Library that has been refined and updated by Bagga and

Piper (2022) to include a comparison corpus of non-fiction prose across 1.5 million sampled pages published since 1800. Hamilton and Piper (2023) extends this work to include multilingual fiction annotation across 521 different languages. Erlin et al. (2022) provide metadata on translations of fiction into English from 120 different languages also located in the Hathi Trust.

Outside of the HathiTrust, Piper (2022b) provides derived data on a collection of 2,700 works of professionally published English prose drawn from 12 different genres including Goodreads' user ratings. Mostafazadeh et al. (2016) developed an artificial corpus of very short stories (4-5 sentences) generated by crowdsourced workers. Ouyang and McKeown (2014) curated a collection of ca. 5,000 AskReddit stories told by users in response to particular prompts (e.g. what is your scariest real-life story?).

Researchers in the field should be aware that while Project Gutenberg offers a large collection of potentially narrative texts, problems of sample selection and poor metadata can lead to downstream problems that result in erroneous claims (Piper, 2022a). For addressing cultural and historical questions, researchers are strongly encouraged to use the collections described above.

Incumbent on all of these initiatives is a greater investment in inter-disciplinary collaboration. Computational narrative understanding will benefit as an endeavor with deeper collaborations between humanists and social scientists and the NLP community. As detailed in Piper et al. (2021), narratology is a field with a long and robust theoretical tradition. Those in the NLP field working on computational systems will benefit from expert collaborations with researchers who have deep backgrounds in studying narratives. Similarly, narratologists and their research frameworks stand to benefit from exposure to computational models (Piper and Bagga, 2022b). It is time to invest more heavily in these larger cross-disciplinary collaborations, especially if we aim to address the larger socio-cultural goals outlined in this paper.

7 Conclusion

As Vizenor envisioned, narratives are things we live by. They provide meaning and hold communities together. They play a role in financial, political, and psychological decision-making. The production of imaginary narratives in particular represent a massive cultural industry, spanning book publishing, movie-making, and gaming. The field of computational narrative understanding has made impressive strides in developing systems to study the causes and effects of narrative behavior across a diverse array of languages and cultural domains. We are in the process of establishing key workshops, tasks, and datasets.

Complexity ↓	Challenge Areas
	1. Data Set Creation
	2. Narrative Element Detection
	3. Multilingual Modeling
	4. Multimodal Modeling
	5. Narrative Discourse Detection
	6. Narrative Time Modeling
	7. Narrative Schemas and Taxonomies
	8. Collective Stories and Social Behavior

Table 1: List of challenge areas in increasing order of generality and complexity

By way of conclusion, I provide a sliding scale of calls to action, located from particular to general (Table 1). It is worth noting that an essential component of the field should include attention to the limiting factors of narrative, i.e. the way narratives encode experience in very particular ways and because of their persuasive power can also mislead individuals in profound ways. Greater attention to the risks of narration should therefore remain front and center as part of the endeavor of computational narrative understanding.

Acknowledgements

This research was generously supported by the Social Sciences and Humanities Research Council of Canada (435-2022-0089).

References

Jonathan M Adler, Jennifer Lodi-Smith, Frederick L Philippe, and Iliane Houle. 2016. The incremental validity of narrative identity in predicting well-being: A review of the field and recommendations for the future. *Personality and Social Psychology Review*, 20(2):142–175.

Anjali Adukia, Alex Eble, Emileigh Harrison, Hakizumwami Birali Runesha, and Teodora Szasz. 2021. What we teach about race and gender: Representation in images and text of children's books. Technical report, National Bureau of Economic Research.

Taylor Arnold, Lauren Tilton, and Annie Berke. 2019.

Visual style in two network era sitcoms. *Journal of Cultural Analytics*, 4(2).

Sunyam Bagga and Andrew Piper. 2022. Hathi 1m: Introducing a million page historical prose dataset in english from the hathi trust. *Journal of Open Humanities Data*, 8(7).

Mieke Bal and Christine Van Boheemen. 2009. *Narratology: Introduction to the theory of narrative*. University of Toronto Press.

David Bamman, Snigdha Chaturvedi, Elizabeth Clark, Madalina Fiterau, and Mohit Iyyer. 2019. Proceedings of the first workshop on narrative understanding. In *Proceedings of the First Workshop on Narrative Understanding*.

David Bamman, Ted Underwood, and Noah A Smith. 2014. A bayesian mixed effects model of literary character. In *Proceedings of the 52nd Annual Meeting of the Association for Computational Linguistics (Volume 1: Long Papers)*, pages 370–379.

Raphaël Baroni. 2011. Tellability. In *The living handbook of narratology*.

Aman Berhe, Camille Guinaudeau, and Claude Barras. 2022. Survey on narrative structure: from linguistic theories to automatic extraction approaches. In *Traitement Automatique des Langues, Volume 63, Numéro 1: Varia [Varia]*, pages 63–87.

Gregory Berns. 2022. *The Self Delusion: The New Neuroscience of How We Invent—and Reinvent—Our Identities*. Hachette UK.

Helena Bilandzic and Rick Busselle. 2013. Narrative persuasion. *The SAGE handbook of persuasion: Developments in theory and practice*, pages 200–219.

Ana-Maria Bliuc and Alexander Chidley. 2022. From cooperation to conflict: The role of collective narratives in shaping group behaviour. *Social and Personality Psychology Compass*, 16(7):e12670.

Ryan L Boyd, Kate G Blackburn, and James W Pennebaker. 2020. The narrative arc: Revealing core narrative structures through text analysis. *Science advances*, 6(32):eaba2196.

William F Brewer and Edward H Lichtenstein. 1982. Stories are to entertain: A structural-affect theory of stories. *Journal of pragmatics*, 6(5-6):473–486.

Peter Broadwell, David Mimno, and Timothy Tangherlini. 2018. The tell-tale hat: Surfacing the uncertainty in folklore classification. *Journal of Cultural Analytics*.

Jerome Bruner. 1991. The narrative construction of reality. *Critical inquiry*, 18(1):1–21.

Simon Bushell, Géraldine Satre Buisson, Mark Workman, and Thomas Colley. 2017. Strategic narratives in climate change: Towards a unifying narrative to address the action gap on climate change. *Energy Research Social Science*, 28:39–49.

Italo Calvino. 1988. *Six memos for the next millennium*. Harvard University Press.

Nathanael Chambers and Dan Jurafsky. 2008a. Unsupervised learning of narrative event chains. In *Proceedings of ACL-08: HLT*, pages 789–797, Columbus, Ohio. Association for Computational Linguistics.

Nathanael Chambers and Dan Jurafsky. 2008b. Unsupervised learning of narrative event chains. In *Proceedings of ACL-08: HLT*, pages 789–797.

David Chong, Erl Lee, Matthew Fan, Pavan Holur, Shadi Shahsavari, Timothy Tangherlini, and Vwani Roychowdhury. 2021. A real-time platform for contextualized conspiracy theory analysis. In *2021 International Conference on Data Mining Workshops (ICDMW)*, pages 118–127. IEEE.

Multigraph Collective. 2019. *Interacting with Print: Elements of Reading in the Era of Print Saturation*. University of Chicago Press.

Laura Coltelli. 1990. *Winged words: American Indian writers speak*. U of Nebraska Press.

Alan Dundes. 1962. From etic to emic units in the structural study of folktales. *The Journal of American Folklore*, 75(296):95–105.

Lauren Edlin and Joshua Reiss. 2023. Identifying visual depictions of animate entities in narrative comics: An annotation study. In *Proceedings of the The 5th Workshop on Narrative Understanding*, pages 82–91.

Katherine Elkins. 2022. *The Shapes of Stories: Sentiment Analysis for Narrative*. Cambridge University Press.

Matt Erlin, Andrew Piper, Douglas Knox, Stephen Pentecost, and Allie Blank. 2022. The transcomp dataset of literary translations from 120 languages and a parallel collection of english-language originals. *Journal of Open Humanities Data*, 8.

Matt Erlin, Andrew Piper, Douglas Knox, Stephen Pentecost, Michaela Drouillard, Brian Powell, and Cienna Townson. 2021. Cultural capitals: Modeling minor european literature. *Journal of Cultural Analytics*, 6(1).

Elizabeth Evans and Matthew Wilkens. 2018. Nation, ethnicity, and the geography of british fiction, 1880-1940. *Journal of Cultural Analytics*, 3(2).

Gustav Freytag. 1895. *Technique of the drama: An exposition of dramatic composition and art*. S. Griggs.

Mikaela Irene Fudolig, Thayer Alshaabi, Kathryn Cramer, Christopher M Danforth, and Peter Sheridan Dodds. 2023. A decomposition of book structure through ousiometric fluctuations in cumulative wordtime. *Humanities and Social Sciences Communications*, 10(1):1–12.

Varun Gangal, Steven Y Feng, Malihe Alikhani, Teruko Mitamura, and Eduard Hovy. 2022. Nareor: The narrative reordering problem. In *Proceedings of the AAAI Conference on Artificial Intelligence*, volume 36, pages 10645–10653.

Gérard Genette. 1983. *Narrative discourse: An essay in method*, volume 3. Cornell University Press.

Gérard Genette. 1992. *The architext: An introduction*, volume 31. Univ of California Press.

Alexandra Georgakopoulou. 2007. *Small stories, interaction and identities*, volume 8. John Benjamins Publishing.

Rachel Giora and Yeshayahu Shen. 1994. Degrees of narrativity and strategies of semantic reduction. *Poetics*, 22(6):447–458.

Jonathan Gottschall. 2021. *The story paradox: how our love of storytelling builds societies and tears them down*. Hachette UK.

Arthur C Graesser, Brent Olde, and Bianca Klettke. 2002. How does the mind construct and represent stories. *Narrative impact: Social and cognitive foundations*, pages 229–262.

Sil Hamilton and Andrew Piper. 2023. Multihathi: A complete collection of multilingual prose fiction in the hathitrust digital library. *Journal of Open Humanities Data*, 9.

Md Kamrul Hasan, Wasifur Rahman, AmirAli Bagher Zadeh, Jianyuan Zhong, Md Iftekhar Tanveer, Louis-Philippe Morency, and Mohammed (Ehsan) Hoque. 2019. UR-FUNNY: A multimodal language dataset for understanding humor. In *Proceedings of the 2019 Conference on Empirical Methods in Natural Language Processing and the 9th International Joint Conference on Natural Language Processing (EMNLP-IJCNLP)*, pages 2046–2056, Hong Kong, China. Association for Computational Linguistics.

Hans Ole Hatzel and Chris Biemann. 2023. Narrative cloze as a training objective: Towards modeling stories using narrative chain embeddings. In *Proceedings of the The 5th Workshop on Narrative Understanding*, pages 118–127.

David Herman. 2009. *Basic elements of narrative*. John Wiley & Sons.

Jack Hessel, Ana Marasovic, Jena D. Hwang, Lillian Lee, Jeff Da, Rowan Zellers, Robert Mankoff, and Yejin Choi. 2023. Do androids laugh at electric sheep? humor "understanding" benchmarks from the new yorker caption contest. In *Proceedings of the 61st Annual Meeting of the Association for Computational Linguistics (Volume 1: Long Papers)*, pages 688–714, Toronto, Canada. Association for Computational Linguistics.

Arlie Russell Hochschild. 2018. *Strangers in their own land: Anger and mourning on the American right*. The New Press.

Peter Hühn. 2014. *Event and eventfulness*. de Gruyter.

Labiba Jahan, Geeticka Chauhan, and Mark Finlayson. 2018. A new approach to Animacy detection. In *Proceedings of the 27th International Conference on Computational Linguistics*, pages 1–12, Santa Fe, New Mexico, USA. Association for Computational Linguistics.

Alípio Mário Jorge, Ricardo Campos, Adam Jatowt, and Sumit Bhatia. 2019. The 2nd international workshop on narrative extraction from text: Text2story 2019. In *European Conference on Information Retrieval*, pages 389–393. Springer.

Eve Kraicer and Andrew Piper. 2019. Social characters: the hierarchy of gender in contemporary english-language fiction. *Journal of Cultural Analytics*, 3(2).

Vincent Labatut and Xavier Bost. 2019. Extraction and analysis of fictional character networks: A survey. *CoRR*, abs/1907.02704.

W. Labov and J. Waletzky. 1967. Narrative analysis: Oral versions of personal experience. In *Essays on the verbal and visual arts*, Seattle. University of Washington Press.

Caroline Levine. 2015. Forms. In *Forms*. Princeton University Press.

Dan P McAdams, Jeffrey Reynolds, Martha Lewis, Allison H Patten, and Phillip J Bowman. 2001. When bad things turn good and good things turn bad: Sequences of redemption and contamination in life narrative and their relation to psychosocial adaptation in midlife adults and in students. *Personality and social psychology bulletin*, 27(4):474–485.

Laura B. McGrath. 2018. *Middlemen: Making Literature in the Age of Multimedia Conglomerates*. Ph.D. thesis, Michigan State University.

Dane Malenfant Margaret Meehan and Andrew Piper. 2022. Causality mining in fiction. In *Proceedings of Text2Story-Fifth Workshop on Narrative Extraction From Texts held in conjunction with the 44th European Conference on Information Retrieval (ECIR 2022), Stavanger, Norway*, volume 3117, pages 25–34.

Julia Mendelsohn, Ronan Le Bras, Yejin Choi, and Maarten Sap. 2023. From dogwhistles to bullhorns: Unveiling coded rhetoric with language models. *arXiv preprint arXiv:2305.17174*.

Nasrin Mostafazadeh, Nathanael Chambers, Xiaodong He, Devi Parikh, Dhruv Batra, Lucy Vanderwende, Pushmeet Kohli, and James Allen. 2016. A corpus and cloze evaluation for deeper understanding of commonsense stories. In *Proceedings of the 2016 Conference of the North American Chapter of the Association for Computational Linguistics: Human Language Technologies*, pages 839–849.

Elinor Ochs, Lisa Capps, et al. 2009. *Living narrative: Creating lives in everyday storytelling*. Harvard University Press.

Jessica Ouyang and Kathleen McKeown. 2015. Modeling reportable events as turning points in narrative. In *Proceedings of the 2015 Conference on Empirical Methods in Natural Language Processing*, pages 2149–2158, Lisbon, Portugal. Association for Computational Linguistics.

Jessica Ouyang and Kathy McKeown. 2014. Towards automatic detection of narrative structure. In *Proceedings of the Ninth International Conference on Language Resources and Evaluation (LREC'14)*, pages 4624–4631, Reykjavik, Iceland. European Language Resources Association (ELRA).

Pinelopi Papalampidi, Frank Keller, and Mirella Lapata. 2019. Movie plot analysis via turning point identification. In *Proceedings of the 2019 Conference on Empirical Methods in Natural Language Processing and the 9th International Joint Conference on Natural Language Processing (EMNLP-IJCNLP)*, pages 1707–1717, Hong Kong, China. Association for Computational Linguistics.

Charuta Pethe, Allen Kim, and Steven Skiena. 2020. Chapter captor: Text segmentation in novels. In *Proceedings of the 2020 Conference on Empirical Methods in Natural Language Processing (EMNLP)*, pages 8373–8383.

Federico Pianzola. 2018. Looking at narrative as a complex system: The proteus principle. In *Narrating complexity*, pages 101–122. Springer.

Barbara Piatti, Anne-Kathrin Reuschel, and Lorenz Hurni. 2013. Dreams, longings, memories–visualising the dimension of projected spaces in fiction. In *Proceedings of the 26th International Cartographic Conference*, pages 74–92.

Andrew Piper. 2015. Novel devotions: Conversional reading, computational modeling, and the modern novel. *New Literary History*, 46(1):63–98.

Andrew Piper. 2022a. Biodiversity is not declining in fiction. *Journal of Cultural Analytics*, 7(3).

Andrew Piper. 2022b. The conlit dataset of contemporary literature. *Journal of Open Humanities Data*, 8.

Andrew Piper. 2023a. Modeling narrative revelation. *Under review*.

Andrew Piper. 2023b. What do characters do? the embodied agency of fictional characters. *Journal of Computational Literary Studies*, 2(1).

Andrew Piper and Sunyam Bagga. 2022a. A quantitative study of fictional things. *Proceedings of the Computational Humanities Research Conference, December 12 – 14, 2022, Antwerp, Belgium*, pages 268–279.

Andrew Piper and Sunyam Bagga. 2022b. Toward a data-driven theory of narrativity. *New Literary History*, 54(1):879–901.

Andrew Piper, Richard Jean So, and David Bamman. 2021. Narrative theory for computational narrative understanding. In *Proceedings of the 2021 Conference on Empirical Methods in Natural Language Processing*, pages 298–311.

Andrew Piper and Olivier Toubia. 2023. A quantitative study of non-linearity in storytelling. *Poetics*, 98:101793.

Vladimir Propp. 2010. *Morphology of the Folktale*, volume 9. University of Texas Press.

Andrew J Reagan, Lewis Mitchell, Dilan Kiley, Christopher M Danforth, and Peter Sheridan Dodds. 2016. The emotional arcs of stories are dominated by six basic shapes. *EPJ Data Science*, 5(1):1–12.

Nils Reiter, Marcus Willand, and Evelyn Gius. 2019. A shared task for the digital humanities chapter 1: Introduction to annotation, narrative levels and shared tasks. *Journal of Cultural Analytics*, 4(3).

Paul Ricoeur. 2012. *Time and Narrative, Volume 1*. University of Chicago press.

Marie-Laure Ryan, James Ruppert, and John W Bernet. 2004. *Narrative across media: The languages of storytelling*. U of Nebraska Press.

Christian Salmon. 2017. *Storytelling: Bewitching the modern mind*. Verso books.

Brenda Santana, Ricardo Campos, Evelin Amorim, Alípio Jorge, Purificação Silvano, and Sérgio Nunes. 2023. A survey on narrative extraction from textual data. *Artificial Intelligence Review*, pages 1–43.

Maarten Sap, Anna Jafarpour, Yejin Choi, Noah A Smith, James W Pennebaker, and Eric Horvitz. 2022. Quantifying the narrative flow of imagined versus autobiographical stories. *Proceedings of the National Academy of Sciences*, 119(45):e2211715119.

George Saunders. 2022. *A Swim in a Pond in the Rain*. Bloomsbury Publishing.

Roger C. Schank and Robert P. Abelson. 1977. *Scripts, Plans, Goals and Understanding: an Inquiry into Human Knowledge Structures*. L. Erlbaum, Hillsdale, NJ.

Benjamin M Schmidt. 2015. Plot arceology: A vector-space model of narrative structure. In *2015 IEEE International Conference on Big Data (Big Data)*, pages 1667–1672. IEEE.

Shadi Shahsavari, Pavan Holur, Tianyi Wang, Timothy R Tangherlini, and Vwani Roychowdhury. 2020. Conspiracy in the time of corona: automatic detection of emerging covid-19 conspiracy theories in social media and the news. *Journal of computational social science*, 3(2):279–317.

Robert J Shiller. 2020. *Narrative economics: How stories go viral and drive major economic events.* Princeton University Press.

Margaret R Somers. 1994. The narrative constitution of identity: A relational and network approach. *Theory and society*, pages 605–649.

Dominik Stammbach, Maria Antoniak, and Elliott Ash. 2022. Heroes, villains, and victims, and gpt-3–automated extraction of character roles without training data. *arXiv preprint arXiv:2205.07557.*

Meir Sternberg. 1990. Telling in time (i): Chronology and narrative theory. *Poetics Today*, 11(4):901–948.

Meir Sternberg. 1992. Telling in time (ii): Chronology, teleology, narrativity. *Poetics today*, 13(3):463–541.

Timothy R Tangherlini, Shadi Shahsavari, Behnam Shahbazi, Ehsan Ebrahimzadeh, and Vwani Roychowdhury. 2020. An automated pipeline for the discovery of conspiracy and conspiracy theory narrative frameworks: Bridgegate, pizzagate and storytelling on the web. *PloS one*, 15(6):e0233879.

Stith Thompson. 1989. *Motif-index of Folk-literature.* Indiana University Press.

William HW Thompson, Zachary Wojtowicz, and Simon DeDeo. 2018. Lévy flights of the collective imagination. *arXiv preprint arXiv:1812.04013.*

Olivier Toubia, Jonah Berger, and Jehoshua Eliashberg. 2021. How quantifying the shape of stories predicts their success. *Proceedings of the National Academy of Sciences*, 118(26):e2011695118.

Ted Underwood. 2018. Why literary time is measured in minutes. *ELH*, 85(2).

Ted Underwood, Patrick Kimutis, and Jessica Witte. 2020. Noveltm datasets for english-language fiction, 1700-2009. *Journal of Cultural Analytics*, 5(2).

Michael Vauth, Hans Ole Hatzel, Evelyn Gius, and Chris Biemann. 2021. Automated event annotation in literary texts. In *CHR*, pages 333–345.

Piek Vossen, Tommaso Caselli, and Roxane Segers. 2021. A narratology-based framework for storyline extraction. *Computational Analysis of Storylines: Making Sense of Events*, 125.

Matthew Wilkens. 2013. The geographic imagination of Civil War-era American fiction. *American Literary History*, 25(4):803–840.

David Wilmot and Frank Keller. 2020. Modelling suspense in short stories as uncertainty reduction over neural representation. In *Proceedings of the 58th Annual Meeting of the Association for Computational Linguistics*, pages 1763–1788, Online. Association for Computational Linguistics.

Gregory Yauney, Ted Underwood, and David Mimno. 2019. Computational prediction of elapsed narrative time. *Workshop on Narrative Understanding.*

Albin Zehe, Leonard Konle, Lea Katharina Dümpelmann, Evelyn Gius, Andreas Hotho, Fotis Jannidis, Lucas Kaufmann, Markus Krug, Frank Puppe, Nils Reiter, et al. 2021. Detecting scenes in fiction: A new segmentation task. In *Proceedings of the 16th Conference of the European Chapter of the Association for Computational Linguistics: Main Volume*, pages 3167–3177.

The Case for Scalable, Data-Driven Theory: A Paradigm for Scientific Progress in NLP

Julian Michael
New York University
julianjm@nyu.edu

Abstract

I propose a paradigm for scientific progress in NLP centered around developing *scalable, data-driven theories* of linguistic structure. The idea is to collect data in tightly scoped, carefully defined ways which allow for exhaustive annotation of behavioral phenomena of interest, and then use machine learning to construct explanatory theories of these phenomena which can form building blocks for intelligible AI systems. After laying some conceptual groundwork, I describe several investigations into data-driven theories of shallow semantic structure using Question-Answer driven Semantic Role Labeling (QA-SRL), a schema for annotating verbal predicate–argument relations using highly constrained question-answer pairs. While this only scratches the surface of the complex language behaviors of interest in AI, I outline principles for data collection and theoretical modeling which can inform future scientific progress. This note summarizes and draws heavily on my PhD thesis (Michael, 2023).

1 Introduction

Formal representations of linguistic structure and meaning have long guided our understanding of how to build NLP systems, *e.g.*, in the traditional NLP pipeline (Jurafsky and Martin, 2008). However, this approach has always had limitations:

1. Fully specifying formal representations requires resolving challenging theoretical questions long contentious among linguists;

2. It is difficult to reliably produce these representations with broad coverage using machine learning; and,

3. Even ostensibly correct linguistic representations are often hard to apply downstream.

Together with the effectiveness of deep learning, these challenges led to the proliferation of end-to-end neural network models which directly perform tasks without intermediate formal representations of linguistic structure (He et al., 2017; Lee et al., 2017; Seo et al., 2017, *inter alia*). This trend continues with language model assistants like GPT-4 (OpenAI, 2023) and Claude (Bai et al., 2022) which can perform a wide range of tasks. However, these systems are still not robust, often reporting false or biased answers (Perez et al., 2022; Bang et al., 2023) and making false claims about their own reasoning (Turpin et al., 2023). Ensuring AI systems' robustness requires us to precisely characterize and control their generalization behaviors.

To this end, formal theories, *e.g.*, of linguistic structure, common sense, reasoning, and world knowledge, provide frameworks for evaluation. They inform the design and construction of challenge sets (McCoy et al., 2019; Naik et al., 2018; Wang et al., 2019), measures of systematicity (Yanaka et al., 2020; Kim and Linzen, 2020), behavioral tests (Linzen et al., 2016), and probing experiments (Liu et al., 2019; Tenney et al., 2019). As these theories allow us to characterize generalization behaviors we desire, they will likely play a pivotal role in the design and training of trustworthy systems. So core improvements in formal theories of aspects of intelligent behavior may yield boons for both the construction and evaluation of NLP systems. But the question remains of how to achieve this: decades of work on semantic ontologies (Baker et al., 1998; Palmer et al., 2005), commonsense knowledge bases (Lenat, 1995; Speer et al., 2017), and formal reasoning systems (Lifschitz, 2008) have largely been superseded in NLP by deep learning and language models.

Theory-driven approaches in AI have been so disappointing that Sutton (2019) famously argues that intelligence and the world are simply too complex for us to capture with domain theories, and we should instead focus on general-purpose learning systems that can capture this intrinsic complexity from data. However, I believe this is too

Proceedings of the the Big Picture Workshop, pages 40–52
December 7, 2023 ©2023 Association for Computational Linguistics

pessimistic, giving up on the *intelligibility* of AI systems that is provided by accurate theories of their behavior, which is necessary for verifying their safety and usefulness in high-risk, high capability settings (Ngo et al., 2023). Instead, the deep learning era presents an opportunity to rethink how we develop theories of language behavior.

In particular, I propose *scalable, data-driven theory* as a paradigm to address the shortcomings mentioned at the beginning of this article: resolving or sidestepping theoretical questions, producing representations with broad coverage, and applying them effectively in downstream tasks. Inspired by Pragmatist epistemology (James, 1907), this approach avoids requiring the linguist or theoretician to specify the entire theory by hand, instead integrating machine learning in a judicious way which allows for the scalable, automated induction of formal theoretical constructs (*e.g.*, ontologies) which are grounded in task-relevant linguistic behaviors.

2 Pragmatist Principles for Scientific Progress

Church (2007) describes the history of computational linguistics on a *pendulum*, swinging between Rationalist (theory-driven) and Empiricist (data-driven) paradigms every 20 years. Church lists the "swings" as follows (with my comments):

- 1950s: Empiricism (Shannon, Skinner, Firth, Harris) — information theory, psychological behaviorism, early corpus linguistics
- 1970s: Rationalism (Chomsky, Minsky) — generative linguistics, logic-based AI
- 1990s: Empiricism (IBM Speech Group, AT&T Bell Labs) — statistical NLP, machine learning, modern distributional semantics
- 2010s: A Return to Rationalism?

As the reader may know, the predicted "Return to Rationalism" did not happen. NLP, for its part, is more Empiricist than ever.

Why is this? Sutton may say it's because the world is too complex: The Rationalist theoretician carefully formalizing the problems at hand has no hope of capturing the world's intricacies in a manually-crafted theory, though a system implementing that theory can be understood and controlled. The Empiricist tinkerer, on the other hand, can build a system that mostly works by trial, error, patching and fastening; so they win on empirical benchmarks. However, the resulting system is too complex to fully understand or control, and generalizes in unpredictable ways.

An odd feature of the Rationalism/Empiricism dichotomy is that neither epistemology accurately describes the pursuit of science in most fields. In fields like physics, chemistry, and biology, theoretical and experimental approaches are not in conflict; rather, they synergize and inform each other, as theories are continually updated to align with new experimental data. To make sense of this, we can turn to an epistemology inspired by how people actually operate in the world: Pragmatism.

Pragmatism is an epistemological framework which conceptualizes *knowing* in terms of the *actions* that the knowledge licenses, *i.e.*, by the predictions that follow from that knowledge. Prominent Pragmatists include Charles Sanders Peirce (1839–1914) and William James (1842–1910). Like Empiricism, Pragmatism embraces experience as the primary source of knowledge. But unlike Empiricists, Pragmatists such as James embrace formal and linguistic categories as comprising the content of knowledge, on the basis of their *usefulness* in making predictions and licensing actions (James, 1907). Unlike in Rationalism, the Pragmatist search for truth is not a search for one true theory which fundamentally describes the world, but for an ever-expanding set of theoretical tools and concepts that can be picked up and put down according to the needs of the knower. In pithy terms, a Pragmatist might agree with the statistical aphorism that that "All models are wrong; some are useful" (Box, 1976). Pragmatists such as James (1907) claim that this perspective more accurately describes human behavior with respect to knowledge (and indeed, the pursuit of science) than prior epistemologies.

Combining the core ideology of Pragmatism with observations from computational linguistics, we can derive two guiding principles for the development of theories that may have prospective use in NLP: decouple data from theory (Section 2.1), and make data reflect use (Section 2.2).

2.1 Decouple Data from Theory

One feature that distinguishes much NLP work, particularly involving linguistic structure, from traditional sciences is the status of theory with respect to data. In most empirical sciences, data takes the form of concrete measurements of the world, and the task of a theory is to explain those measurements. In NLP, many benchmarks and datasets are constructed under the *assumption* of a theory, whether it be one of syntactic structure (Marcus et al., 1993; de Marneffe et al., 2021), semantic structure (Palmer et al., 2005; Banarescu et al., 2013), or some other task-specific labeling scheme.

A theory, *e.g.*, of syntactic or semantic structure, is useful for annotation in providing a straightforward way to annotate disambiguation of text, which is important for understanding language. However, errors and inconsistencies in annotation resulting from complexity, vagueness, or underspecification in the theory limit what can be learned by models, as human performance and inter-annotator agreement can be surprisingly low (Nangia and Bowman, 2019). For example, the OntoNotes compendium of semantic annotations (Hovy et al., 2006) was presented as "The 90% solution" because of 90% agreement rates — implying that the dataset cannot validate performance numbers higher than 90%.

As another example, Palmer et al. (2006) find that fine-grained sense distinctions produce considerable disagreement among annotators of English text. But fixing the problem can't just be a matter of improving the sense inventory: they find that coarser-grained sense groups designed to improve agreement lack the distinctions from fine-grained senses that are necessary for predicting how words should translate into typologically distant languages like Chinese and Korean. When different tasks require different theoretical distinctions, setting them in stone during annotation is a problem, especially considering that there will almost certainly be missing categories, as new word senses or distinctions may show up in more exhaustive data or under domain shift. More generally, refining annotation guidelines to increase agreement between annotators does not necessarily solve the problem, as the extra assumptions built into the annotation process do not necessarily encode any more scientifically meaningful information in the data — a problem known in the philosophy of science as the *problem of theoretical terms.*[1]

Building a robust theory that can scale to unexpected phenomena and new data, and be adjusted for new tasks, requires theoretical agility which is precluded by committing to a theory-based annotation standard. An alternative is to directly annotate the phenomena that the theory is meant to explain, and derive the theory on the basis of this data. This, for example, is how *grammar engineering* is done in the DELPH-IN consortium (Bender and Emerson, 2021). For each language, a broad-coverage Head-driven Phrase Structure Grammar (HPSG) is maintained separately from its associated treebank, which is annotated not with full syntactic analyses but with *discriminants* (Carter, 1997) such as prepositional phrase attachment sites which constrain the set of possible parses in a way that is independent of the grammar. Then, when the grammar is updated, the discriminants are used to automatically update the treebank while also providing data to validate the updated theory (Oepen et al., 2004; Flickinger et al., 2017). Pushing the envelope further are the Decompositional Semantics Initiative (White et al., 2016) and MegaAttitude project (White and Rawlins, 2016).[2] In these projects, annotating large-scale corpora with the phenomena that are posited to underly linguistic theories in question — such as Dowty (1991)'s proto-role properties, or entailments corresponding to neg-raising (An and White, 2020) and projection (White and Rawlins, 2018) — has facilitated insights regarding argument selection (Reisinger et al., 2015) and lexically-specified syntactic subcategorization rules (White, 2021), as well as automatically inducing lexicon-level ontologies of semantic roles (White et al., 2017) and event structure (Gantt et al., 2021) that are derived directly from the phenomena they are designed to explain.

The lesson of Empiricism is that for a model to work, it must be learned from data; while Rationalism tells us that for a model to be intelligible and general, it must be grounded in theory. A wealth of innovative prior work shows us that Pragmatism is possible: we can have both.

2.2 Make Data Reflect Use

A satisfying data-driven theory of a few linguistic phenomena is not sufficient as a backbone for general language understanding systems. The second relevant lesson of Pragmatism is that the model must be fit to its use. The approaches reviewed in Section 2.1 are, by and large, targeted at theoretical questions in language syntax and semantics, *e.g.*, regarding the nature of syntactic structure across many languages (Bender et al., 2002) or the syntactic realization of a verb's arguments (Reisinger et al., 2015). On the other hand, general-purpose

[1]See Riezler (2014) for a discussion of this issue in NLP.

[2]`https://decomp.io`, `https://megaattitude.io`

language processing relies on a huge amount of lexical and world knowledge and inferential ability which is outside the scope of traditional linguistic theories. While general-purpose syntactic and semantic representations have some direct uses in NLP end-tasks, such as for search and retrieval (Schäfer et al., 2011; Shlain et al., 2020), their application in downstream tasks requiring higher-level reasoning or inference, like reading comprehension, translation, and information extraction has been less fruitful. This is at least in part because these theories are far insufficient to serve as mechanistic accounts of the inferential phenomena which are required to perform those tasks.

Constructing theories which *can* account for such phenomena is a monumental challenge. But it is a challenge which, I argue, we must address if we want to pursue the goal of accurate, reliable, and intelligible systems. Pragmatism tells us the first step is to catalog the phenomena we wish to explain in a way that is amenable to theoretical modeling. This will require carefully carving up the space of phenomena in such a way that useful abstractions can be designed to facilitate future progress (Dijkstra, 1974); Section 4 will discuss considerations on how to do this well.

3 Scalable, Data-Driven Theory

The principles in Section 2 imply a general framework for building useful theories, which I call *data-driven theory*: First, annotate data in a theoretically-minimal way, scoped carefully to reflect specific phenomena that we want to explain; then, automatically induce theories to explain those phenomena using computational methods like machine learning. But how does this method scale in practice? Even if the resulting theories are high-quality, requiring annotated data limits their scope to orders of magnitude less than what is leveraged by standard pretrained models (Brown et al., 2020; OpenAI, 2023; Bai et al., 2022).

Black-Box Data Simulators This is where black-box models may actually be able to help. Even if they are uninterpretable on their own, their high accuracy and data efficiency means they can be used as *data simulators*, generating phenomenological data — potentially at a level of granularity or exhaustivity unobtainable from humans — which can be fed into another, more interpretable algorithm to distill a theory from it. This is the approach we take in Michael and Zettlemoyer (2021), described in Section 5: We first train a black-box model to generate QA-SRL questions, where each role is labeled with only a single question in the training data. Then we decode full question *distributions* from this model, and induce an ontology of semantic roles by clustering arguments based on the overlap of their question distributions. While this work required a large training set of QA-SRL annotations (FitzGerald et al., 2018), it may now be possible to do such experiments without large-scale human data annotation at all, thanks to recent advances in instruction following by language models (OpenAI, 2023; Bai et al., 2022).

It may seem like the use of a black-box model as a data simulator begs the question: if our concern is that the black-box model isn't learning the underlying function we hope it is, then doesn't using it to simulate data risk leading us to a theory of the wrong function? Well, yes — *but the theory lets us do something about it.* Examining the "wrong" parts of the resulting theory (*e.g.*, induced semantic roles that don't match what we intuitively expect, or that lead to downstream predictions we think are wrong), and their connection to the training data, will identify one of the following:

- Systematic gaps in the data or mistakes in the model used for data simulation — which can then be filled or corrected.
- Mistakes in the modeling assumptions used in the theory induction algorithm — giving us information useful for improving our theories.
- Mistakes in our intuition about what the theory should have looked like in the first place — which means we've learned something.

All of these are positive outcomes for scientific progress. See Michael and Zettlemoyer (2021) for an in-depth analysis of this kind.

Scaling in Complexity Even if we can scale a theory's *size*, *e.g.*, to a large knowledge base or linguistic ontology, this does not handle the case of more *complex* tasks, with more nuanced relations between input and output (such as open-ended question answering or common sense inference tasks). Since theoretical modeling requires narrowly-scoped data (discussed more in Section 4), I do not expect that we can construct theories of such broad capabilities in the short term. However, if we carve up the space of tasks to start with theories of simple sub-phenomena of reading and inference, then we may be able to bootstrap from these theories to annotate and make sense of more complex data — for example, one can imagine eventually inducing rich, broad-coverage entailment graphs in the style of Berant et al. (2015) or McKenna et al. (2023) on the basis of comprehensive annotations of structured inferences in context. A complete or "true" theory of complex NLP tasks may be impossible even in principle, but — in the spirit of Pragmatism — that doesn't mean we can't construct theories that are *useful* for understanding and controlling AI systems. How my proposed framework scales with task complexity is unclear as of yet, but scalable theories of narrow phenomena provide a step in the right direction.

4 Data: Scoping Language Behaviors

The first step to developing theories of linguistic structure in an empirical, data-driven way is to carefully choose the data. To guide this, I propose **Four Principles of Scientific Data for NLP**:

1. **Theoretical minimalism.** The data should rely on as few theoretical assumptions as possible. For example, to capture natural language syntax, you should directly annotate the *phenomena* that you intend your syntactic theory to explain rather than directly annotating theoretical constructs like syntactic trees. This creates the space for an underlying theory to meaningfully explain this data.

2. **Broad comprehensibility.** To facilitate on-demand data collection at large scale in new domains, it should be possible and affordable to recruit non-expert annotators to label large amounts of data (*e.g.*, through crowdsourcing), or it should be feasible to automatically generate the data (*e.g.*, with language models).

3. **Annotation constraints.** The output space of the task should be sufficiently constrained to allow for exhaustive coverage of the phenomena of interest. A task which is too open-ended leads annotators to produce a convenience sample of the output space, resulting in biased data that doesn't capture the full complexity of the phenomena of interest (Cai et al., 2017; Gururangan et al., 2018).

4. **Narrow scope.** The task should not capture too much complexity in the relationship between input and output. Not only can this make it difficult for annotators to reliably produce high-quality data, but it makes it more difficult to model the phenomena expressed in the data with a comprehensible theory.

Principles 1 and 2 instantiate Section 2.1's recommendation to decouple data from theory, while Principles 2, 3 and 4 help make it tractable to develop broad-coverage, comprehensible theories from this data. The final requirement is that the data reflect relevant downstream use cases (Section 2.2), which in our case means it should encode phenomena representing the intended behavior of AI systems performing language tasks.[3] I focus on a key strategy to meet these requirements: *annotating natural language with natural language question-answer pairs*. Question answering has long been used as a general-purpose format for testing language comprehension or executing practical language tasks (Gardner et al., 2019b; McCann et al., 2018; McCarthy, 1976), as nearly any task can be phrased as a question and questions which test a reader's comprehension of a text need not require specialized linguistic or theoretical expertise to answer. The downside of this great generality is that data annotation tends to be highly under-constrained and unsystematic (Gardner et al., 2019a), so we must judiciously constrain the space of question-answer pairs we use in accordance with the Four Principles.

This work is focused on annotations of shallow semantic structure: syntax, semantic roles, and other predicate–argument structure relations expressed in text. He et al. (2015) pioneered the use of question-answer pairs as a proxy for such structure in *Question-Answer driven Semantic Role Labeling* (QA-SRL), a framework for annotating English verbal predicate–argument relations using simple, highly constrained question-answer pairs. In the rest of this section, I will describe three data annotation projects which explored variations of this approach, illustrating some of the basic tensions between the Four Principles.

[3]This work is concerned with normative theories of AI behavior when performing language tasks. Insofar as we wish to produce theories of AI behavior which are comprehensible to us, aligned with our intuitions, and allow us to interface fluidly with machines using language, this goal should mostly be aligned with developing *descriptive* theories of *human* language behavior, which can then be used to constrain and guide AI behavior. The relationship between these theories and their importance for interacting with machines are discussed more in Chapter 2 of Michael (2023).

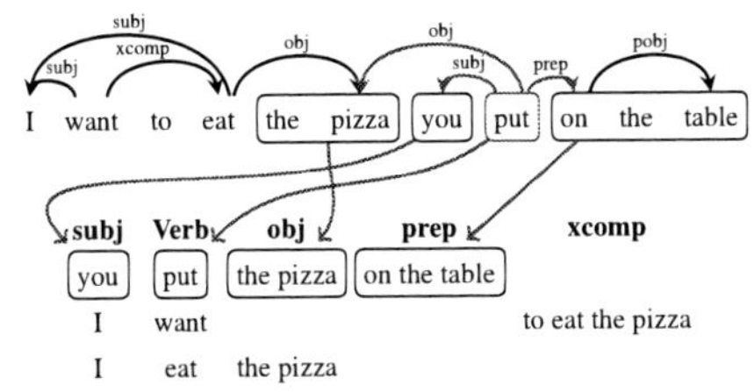

Dependency	Question	Answer
want → I	What wants to eat something?	I
eat → I	What would eat something?	I
eat → pizza	What would something eat?	the pizza
put → you	What put something?	you
put → pizza	What did something put?	the pizza
on → table	What did something put something on?	the table

Figure 1: Question-answer pair generation for human-in-the-loop parsing (He et al., 2016). We use the predicted CCG category of each verb to generate the questions, which are in in one-to-one relation with syntactic dependencies in the sentence. This one-to-one assumption was ultimately too strong, as workers answer these questions according to semantics and not just syntax.

4.1 Human-in-the-Loop Parsing

He et al. (2016) introduces *human-in-the-loop parsing*. We construct multiple-choice questions from syntactic attachment ambiguities in a parser's n-best list, get crowdsourced workers to answer these questions, and then re-parse the original sentence with constraints derived from the results (Figure 1). Testing on the English CCGbank (Hockenmaier and Steedman, 2007), we find only a small improvement in parser performance. A core challenge is the *syntax–semantics mismatch*, where workers provide answers which are semantically correct but correspond to the wrong syntactic attachment. For example, in the sentence "Kalipharma is a New Jersey–based pharmaceuticals concern that sells products under the Purepac label", workers unanimously answer the question "What sells something?" with "Kalipharma", which is not the syntactic subject of *sells* but a more natural way of referring to the same entity. So even though our annotation task is tightly scoped, our interpretation of the results requires theoretical assumptions which do not match the intuitions of non-expert workers.

4.2 Crowdsourcing Question-Answer Meaning Representations

Michael et al. (2018) takes the opposite tack, broadening the task's scope by gathering open-ended questions from annotators to capture as many semantic relationships as possible in the source sentence. This requires adding many careful con-

Pierre Vinken, 61 years old, will join the board as a nonexecutive director Nov. 29.

Who will **join** as **nonexecutive director**? - Pierre Vinken
What is **Pierre**'s last name? - Vinken
Who is **61 years old**? - Pierre Vinken
How **old** is **Pierre Vinken**? - 61 years old
What will he **join**? - the board
What will he **join the board** as? - nonexecutive director
What type of **director** will **Vinken** be? - nonexecutive
What day will **Vinken join the board**? - Nov. 29

Figure 2: Example Question-Answer Meaning Representation (Michael et al., 2018). Non-stopwords drawn from the source sentence are in bold. QAMR question–answer pairs capture a wide variety of relations, but are unstructured and hard to use downstream without extra tools such as a syntactic parser — here, our annotation task was too unconstrained and task scope too broad.

straints and incentives to the crowdsourcing procedure, but we are careful to allow for open-ended questions that express annotator creativity. The result is a dataset of *Question-Answer Meaning Representation* (QAMR) annotations over English encyclopedic and news text covering many interesting phenomena (see Figure 2). However, achieving high recall of predicate–argument relations is not economical, requiring high annotation redundancy, and the unstructured question-answer pairs are hard to use downstream. The most successful use of QAMR in follow-up work is probably Stanovsky et al. (2018), where we convert QAMRs into Open Information Extraction tuples, but have to run the questions through a syntactic parser to do so. The lesson from these results is that leaving the annotation space too open and unconstrained leads to difficulties with recall and challenges with downstream modeling and theory.

4.3 Large-Scale QA-SRL Parsing

FitzGerald et al. (2018) returns to QA-SRL. In the original QA-SRL work (He et al., 2015), trained annotators specify the questions using drop-down menus in an excel spreadsheet. In this work, we streamline and scale up data collection, gathering high-coverage annotations for over 64,000 sentences with a two-stage generate/validate crowdsourcing pipeline (see Table 1 for examples). We increase annotation speed, reliability, and coverage using an autocomplete system which tracks the syntactic structure of QA-SRL questions as the annotator types, using it to suggest completions as well as whole questions. In terms of semantic richness and annotation constraints, these annotations

*The plane was **diverting** around weather formations over the Java Sea when contact with air traffic control (ATC) in Jakarta was **lost**.*

wh	aux	subj	verb	obj	prep	obj2	?	Answer
What	was		being diverted		around		?	*weather formations*
What	was		diverting				?	*The plane*
What	was		being diverted				?	*The plane*
What	was		lost				?	*contact with air traffic control*
Where	was	something	lost				?	*over the Java Sea*

Table 1: QA-SRL question-answer pairs from the development set of the QA-SRL Bank 2.0 (FitzGerald et al., 2018). We constrained the questions with a non-deterministic finite automaton (NFA) encoding English clause structure for question autocomplete and auto-suggest. This facilitated high-quality, high-coverage annotation at scale while providing the expressiveness to represent the semantic role relations within each sentence.

are somewhere between our work on human-in-the-loop parsing and question-answer meaning representations. The constrained task and high coverage allow us to train high-quality QA-SRL predictors and enables future work on semantic role induction (Section 5.1) and controlled question generation (Section 5.2).

Takeaways Our results over the course of these projects suggests that we should search for tasks in a "goldilocks zone": Their scope should not be so constrained or beholden to prior theory as to be unintuitive, but not so unconstrained that it is hard to get exhaustive and reliable annotation of interesting phenomena. As annotation constraints depend on *some* prior theory of the phenomena to be captured, these constraints need to be carefully chosen so as to minimize arbitrary assumptions in the task setup and make sure the task is natural for annotators. In the case of QA-SRL, the prior theory we incorporated is a small grammar fragment of English encompassing QA-SRL questions. Our findings support that QA-SRL, with the annotation aids developed in FitzGerald et al. (2018), strikes a good balance of the Four Principles.

Labels	Questions	
A1 (98%)	What is given?	.30
	What does something give something?	.21
	What does something give?	.20
	What is something given?	.11
A0 (98%)	What gives something?	.44
	What gives something something?	.27
	What gives something to something?	.08
A2 (94%)	What is given something?	.28
	What does something give something to?	.18
	What does something give something?	.14
	What is given?	.09
	What is something given to?	.07
TMP (46%), ADV (22%), MNR (12%)	When does something give something?	.20
	How does something give something?	.09
	When is something given?	.09
	When is something given something?	.09
PNC (30%), ADV (22%), TMP (14%)	Why does something give something?	.18
	Why does something give up something?	.07
	Why is something given something?	.07

Table 2: Roles for *give* produced by Michael and Zettlemoyer (2021). For each predicate, we cluster its arguments in PropBank based on the similarity of the distributions of QA-SRL questions our model generates. In this case, core arguments are captured almost perfectly, exhibiting both passive and dative alternations.

5 Theory: From Language, Structure

In this section, I will describe two projects which show how QA-SRL can be used to build a data-driven theory which is directly applicable in downstream tasks.

5.1 Inducing Semantic Roles Without Syntax

Michael and Zettlemoyer (2021) show how to use QA-SRL to automatically induce an ontology of semantic roles, leveraging a key insight: the *set* of QA-SRL questions that are correctly answered by a given answer span identifies an underlying semantic role through its syntactic alternations, which are representative of the phenomena that a semantic role ontology like PropBank is designed to explain. We leverage this insight by using a trained QA-SRL question generator as a data simulator, generating a full distribution over (simplified) QA-SRL questions for each argument of a verb appearing through an entire corpus. Clustering these distributions of questions according to a simple maximum-likelihood objective yields a set of discrete semantic roles that exhibits high agreement with existing resources (see Table 2). This presents an approach which could potentially be used to develop semantic role ontologies in new domains where they are not currently available, with directions for improving QA-SRL data toward the end of automatically inducing better semantic roles.

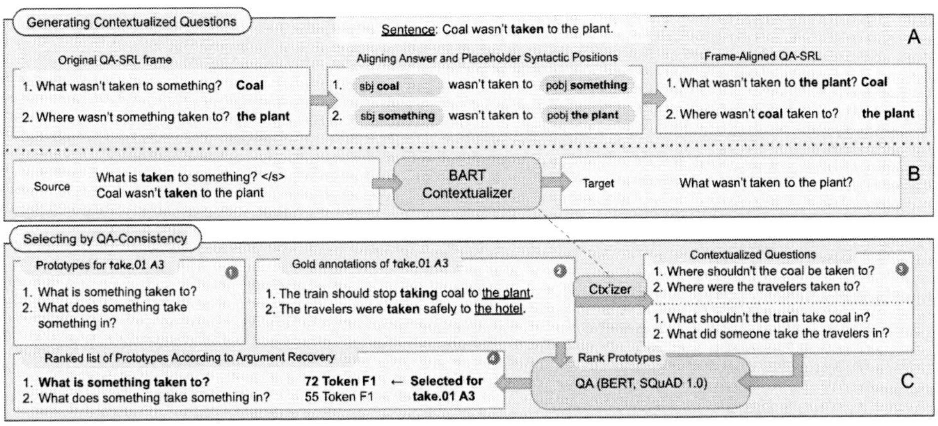

Figure 3: Overview of Pyatkin et al. (2021)'s approach. The natural correspondence between QA-SRL questions and semantic roles allows us to use QA-SRL question templates in a planning step to successfully generate questions for any PropBank semantic role, even when the corresponding argument doesn't appear in the source sentence (a situation never encountered in training data). **A: Construction of Frame-Aligned QA-SRL** using syntactic information inferred by the autocomplete NFA from FitzGerald et al. (2018), *i.e.*, leveraging our (minimal) theoretical assumptions about argument structure. **B: Contextualizing questions** by feeding a prototype question and context into a neural model that outputs a Frame-Aligned QA-SRL question. **C: Selecting prototype questions** by testing each prototype (1) against a sample of arguments for each role (2). After contextualization (3), each question is fed into a QA model and we choose the prototype that most often recovers the correct argument (4).

5.2 Asking it All: Generating Contextualized Questions for any Semantic Role

Pyatkin et al. (2021) use QA-SRL to build a controllable question generation system. The task is to generate fluent questions asking about the arguments corresponding to specific semantic roles in context (see Figure 3 for an overview). The challenge is a lack of training data, as QA-SRL questions are not fully natural and are not annotated for roles which aren't expressed in a sentence. We leverage two key insights: First, we find that QA-SRL questions generally correspond to the same role across many contexts. So we prime our question generation system with a template QA-SRL question corresponding to the correct role, leading it to generate semantically correct questions even when the answer isn't present in the sentence. Second, we use the syntactic structure of QA-SRL questions to align the placeholders (*someone*, *something*) in each question with the answers of other questions, translating QA-SRL questions into more fluent ones closer to those in QAMR.

Takeaways Together this work illustrates not only the promise for the development of large-scale ontologies in a data-driven way (Section 5.1), but it also illustrates how having these ontologies computationally grounded in the phenomena they are designed to explain, *i.e.*, question-answer pairs, facilitates ontology's the downstream use (Section 5.2). It's not hard to imagine next steps incorporating an induced ontology of semantic roles into Pyatkin et al. (2021)'s system to obviate the need for a pre-specified role ontology altogether.

6 Concluding Thoughts

I have proposed *scalable, data-driven theory* as a Pragmatist paradigm for scientific progress in NLP. To develop scalable theories, one should:

1. Collect carefully-scoped data that directly represents a phenomenon of interest while imposing minimal prior theoretical assumptions,
2. Increase the data's scale and coverage using a learned black-box data simulator,
3. Induce comprehensible models of this high-coverage data with machine learning, and
4. Examine the results to debug and improve the theory and data, progressing our scientific understanding of the phenomenon of interest.

Using QA-SRL, I have shown how to leverage black-box data simulation together with simple probabilistic modeling to automatically induce an ontology of semantic roles which is directly and comprehensibly grounded in phenomena that the theory of semantic roles is meant to explain. This not only lays the groundwork for new scalable theoretical developments in semantic representation, but can serve as an example to guide future work on scalable theories in other domains.

Why now?

The justification for building scalable, data-driven theories can be summarized as follows:

1. To build systems which generalize in controllable, predictable ways, we need comprehensible theories of their desired behavior.
2. However, the behaviors we wish to produce in AI and NLP are too complex for us to easily write down theories of how they should work.
3. So instead, we must use machines (*i.e.*, statistical models) to construct our theories on the basis of data in a scalable way. The role for the scientist here is twofold:
    - to carefully determine the scope of the phenomena to be explained and curate the data accordingly, and
    - to define the meta-theory which relates the learned theory to the data.

This argument could have been made at any point in the history of NLP, so why do I make it now?[4] I think the argument would have been viewed as premature in the *era of underfitting* prior to the deep learning revolution. Statistical models like CRFs (Lafferty et al., 2001) struggle even in-distribution on tasks like syntactic and semantic parsing, let alone complex end tasks involving question answering or language generation. The problem at that time was to build models expressive enough to perform well while tractable enough to learn from data. Pre-neural systems were weak enough that many thought they would benefit from hand-curated linguistic resources like PropBank (Palmer et al., 2005).

With deep learning, these factors all changed: the limits of hand-curated resources like PropBank have been surpassed, and neural models fit all kinds of data distributions, leaving us face-to-face with the problem of generalization and the need for data-driven theory. Furthermore, we have new tools for data simulation; the role induction algorithm in Michael and Zettlemoyer (2021) would not have been workable without a neural model to simulate dense annotation of QA-SRL questions. So we are finally in a position to make such theories scalable.

Looking forward

As argued above, a critical role for the scientist in developing data-driven theories is to define scopes of phenomena to be explained, carving linguistic behavior at useful joints. I hope to have demonstrated that the concept of *semantic roles* provides such a useful scope, where its corresponding phenomena (as QA-SRL) can be effectively annotated at scale (Section 4.3), tractably modeled with a comprehensible theory (Section 5.1), and used for downstream tasks (Section 5.2). Moving forward requires carefully choosing more such useful concepts and using them to scope phenomena, define and induce theories, and tie these data and theories into downstream applications.

Extending the paradigm of scalable theory to more facilities of language (*e.g.*, syntax, word sense, or coreference) and more complex phenomena (*e.g.*, representations of world knowledge, common sense, or reasoning) remains a major challenge. As the scope of the phenomena to be represented increases, greater annotation constraints will be necessary in order to ensure that these phenomena are adequately covered. However, doing so while maintaining theoretical minimalism is challenging. My hope is that scalable theories of narrowly-scoped subphenomena (*e.g.*, semantic roles) will provide constraints that make more complex tasks tractable to exhaustively annotate, without introducing the same problems as in the Rationalist paradigm where inconsistencies, underspecification, and arbitrary theoretical choices limit the usefulness of the data. In this way, it may be possible to bootstrap from narrowly-scoped theories into progressively broad accounts of language structure, meaning, and intelligent behavior.

At this point, such talk is speculation. It is unclear how data-driven theory will generalize to more complex tasks. However, in this work I hope to have provided an argument this kind of work is at least worth attempting, and perhaps laid some groundwork and principles which can be used as a starting point for it to be done in the future.

[4]Similar arguments have been made before in grammar engineering (Oepen et al., 2004; Flickinger et al., 2017) and the Decompositional Semantics Initiative (White et al., 2016), while in linguistic typology, Haspelmath (2010)'s *framework-free grammatical theory* makes similar points about the relationship between data and theory. My approach differs from these in my focus on applications in NLP where the vastness and complexity of the domain becomes more of a challenge.

Acknowledgments

Thanks to my PhD thesis advisor Luke Zettlemoyer, as well as reading committee members Noah A. Smith and Emily M. Bender, and committee member Shane Steinert-Threlkeld. Many thanks also to my collaborators on the projects reviewed in this note, including Ido Dagan, Luheng He, Gabriel Stanovsky, Valentina Pyatkin, Paul Roit, and Nicholas FitzGerald, and others who have done essential QA-Sem work following on QA-SRL, including Ayal Klein and Daniela Weiss, as well as the many annotators who have contributed to building these datasets. Thanks also to my brother Jonathan Michael for introducing me to Pragmatism and Ari Holtzman for helpful and engaging discussions about it. Finally, thanks to the anonymous reviewers for helpful comments on what I should include in this note to round out the discussion. See Michael (2023) for more detailed acknowledgments for my thesis work.

References

Hannah Youngeun An and Aaron Steven White. 2020. The lexical and grammatical sources of neg-raising inferences. In *Proceedings of the Society for Computation in Linguistics 2020*, pages 386–399, New York, New York. Association for Computational Linguistics.

Yuntao Bai, Saurav Kadavath, Sandipan Kundu, Amanda Askell, Jackson Kernion, Andy Jones, Anna Chen, Anna Goldie, Azalia Mirhoseini, Cameron McKinnon, Carol Chen, Catherine Olsson, Christopher Olah, Danny Hernandez, Dawn Drain, Deep Ganguli, Dustin Li, Eli Tran-Johnson, Ethan Perez, Jamie Kerr, Jared Mueller, Jeffrey Ladish, Joshua Landau, Kamal Ndousse, Kamile Lukosuite, Liane Lovitt, Michael Sellitto, Nelson Elhage, Nicholas Schiefer, Noemi Mercado, Nova DasSarma, Robert Lasenby, Robin Larson, Sam Ringer, Scott Johnston, Shauna Kravec, Sheer El Showk, Stanislav Fort, Tamera Lanham, Timothy Telleen-Lawton, Tom Conerly, Tom Henighan, Tristan Hume, Samuel R. Bowman, Zac Hatfield-Dodds, Ben Mann, Dario Amodei, Nicholas Joseph, Sam McCandlish, Tom Brown, and Jared Kaplan. 2022. Constitutional ai: Harmlessness from ai feedback.

Collin F. Baker, Charles J. Fillmore, and John B. Lowe. 1998. The Berkeley FrameNet project. In *36th Annual Meeting of the Association for Computational Linguistics and 17th International Conference on Computational Linguistics, Volume 1*, pages 86–90, Montreal, Quebec, Canada. Association for Computational Linguistics.

Laura Banarescu, Claire Bonial, Shu Cai, Madalina Georgescu, Kira Griffitt, Ulf Hermjakob, Kevin Knight, Philipp Koehn, Martha Palmer, and Nathan Schneider. 2013. Abstract Meaning Representation for sembanking. In *Proceedings of the 7th Linguistic Annotation Workshop and Interoperability with Discourse*, pages 178–186, Sofia, Bulgaria. Association for Computational Linguistics.

Yejin Bang, Samuel Cahyawijaya, Nayeon Lee, Wenliang Dai, Dan Su, Bryan Wilie, Holy Lovenia, Ziwei Ji, Tiezheng Yu, Willy Chung, Quyet V Do, Yan Xu, and Pascale Fung. 2023. A multitask, multilingual, multimodal evaluation of ChatGPT on reasoning, hallucination, and interactivity.

Emily M. Bender and Guy Emerson. 2021. Computational linguistics and grammar engineering. In Stefan Müller, Anne Abeillé, Robert D. Borsley, and Jean-Pierre Koenig, editors, *Head-Driven Phrase Structure Grammar: The handbook*, Empirically Oriented Theoretical Morphology and Syntax, pages 1101–1148. Language Science Press., Berlin.

Emily M. Bender, Dan Flickinger, and Stephan Oepen. 2002. The grammar matrix: An open-source starter-kit for the rapid development of cross-linguistically consistent broad-coverage precision grammars. In *COLING-02: Grammar Engineering and Evaluation*.

Jonathan Berant, Noga Alon, Ido Dagan, and Jacob Goldberger. 2015. Efficient global learning of entailment graphs. *Computational Linguistics*, 41(2):221–263.

George E. P. Box. 1976. Science and statistics. *Journal of the American Statistical Association*, 71(356):791–799.

Tom Brown, Benjamin Mann, Nick Ryder, Melanie Subbiah, Jared D Kaplan, Prafulla Dhariwal, Arvind Neelakantan, Pranav Shyam, Girish Sastry, Amanda Askell, Sandhini Agarwal, Ariel Herbert-Voss, Gretchen Krueger, Tom Henighan, Rewon Child, Aditya Ramesh, Daniel Ziegler, Jeffrey Wu, Clemens Winter, Chris Hesse, Mark Chen, Eric Sigler, Mateusz Litwin, Scott Gray, Benjamin Chess, Jack Clark, Christopher Berner, Sam McCandlish, Alec Radford, Ilya Sutskever, and Dario Amodei. 2020. Language models are few-shot learners. In *Advances in Neural Information Processing Systems*, volume 33, pages 1877–1901. Curran Associates, Inc.

Zheng Cai, Lifu Tu, and Kevin Gimpel. 2017. Pay attention to the ending:strong neural baselines for the ROC story cloze task. In *Proceedings of the 55th Annual Meeting of the Association for Computational Linguistics (Volume 2: Short Papers)*, pages 616–622, Vancouver, Canada. Association for Computational Linguistics.

David Carter. 1997. The TreeBanker: a tool for supervised training of parsed corpora. In *Computational Environments for Grammar Development and Linguistic Engineering*.

Kenneth Church. 2007. A pendulum swung too far. *Linguistic Issues in Language Technology*, 2.

Marie-Catherine de Marneffe, Christopher D. Manning, Joakim Nivre, and Daniel Zeman. 2021. Universal Dependencies. *Computational Linguistics*, 47(2):255–308.

Edsger W. Dijkstra. 1974. Ewd 447: On the role of scientific thought. In *Selected Writings on Computing: A Personal Perspective*, pages 60–66. Springer-Verlag. Book published in 1982.

David Dowty. 1991. Thematic proto-roles and argument selection. *Language*, 67(3):547–619.

Nicholas FitzGerald, Julian Michael, Luheng He, and Luke Zettlemoyer. 2018. Large-scale QA-SRL parsing. In *Proceedings of the 56th Annual Meeting of the Association for Computational Linguistics (Volume 1: Long Papers)*, pages 2051–2060, Melbourne, Australia. Association for Computational Linguistics.

Dan Flickinger, Stephan Oepen, and Emily M. Bender. 2017. Sustainable development and refinement of complex linguistic annotations at scale. In *Handbook of Linguistic Annotation*, pages 353–377, Dordrecht. Springer Netherlands.

William Gantt, Lelia Glass, and Aaron Steven White. 2021. Decomposing and recomposing event structure. *CoRR*, abs/2103.10387.

Matt Gardner, Jonathan Berant, Hannaneh Hajishirzi, Alon Talmor, and Sewon Min. 2019a. On making reading comprehension more comprehensive. In *Proceedings of the 2nd Workshop on Machine Reading for Question Answering*, pages 105–112, Hong Kong, China. Association for Computational Linguistics.

Matt Gardner, Jonathan Berant, Hannaneh Hajishirzi, Alon Talmor, and Sewon Min. 2019b. Question answering is a format; when is it useful? *CoRR*, abs/1909.11291.

Suchin Gururangan, Swabha Swayamdipta, Omer Levy, Roy Schwartz, Samuel Bowman, and Noah A. Smith. 2018. Annotation artifacts in natural language inference data. In *Proceedings of the 2018 Conference of the North American Chapter of the Association for Computational Linguistics: Human Language Technologies, Volume 2 (Short Papers)*, pages 107–112, New Orleans, Louisiana. Association for Computational Linguistics.

Martin Haspelmath. 2010. Framework-free grammatical theory. In *The Oxford Handbook of Linguistic Analysis*, Oxford, UK. Oxford University Press.

Luheng He, Kenton Lee, Mike Lewis, and Luke Zettlemoyer. 2017. Deep semantic role labeling: What works and what's next. In *Proceedings of the 55th Annual Meeting of the Association for Computational Linguistics (Volume 1: Long Papers)*, pages 473–483, Vancouver, Canada. Association for Computational Linguistics.

Luheng He, Mike Lewis, and Luke Zettlemoyer. 2015. Question-answer driven semantic role labeling: Using natural language to annotate natural language. In *Proceedings of the 2015 Conference on Empirical Methods in Natural Language Processing*, pages 643–653, Lisbon, Portugal. Association for Computational Linguistics.

Luheng He, Julian Michael, Mike Lewis, and Luke Zettlemoyer. 2016. Human-in-the-loop parsing. In *Proceedings of the 2016 Conference on Empirical Methods in Natural Language Processing*, pages 2337–2342, Austin, Texas. Association for Computational Linguistics.

Julia Hockenmaier and Mark Steedman. 2007. CCGbank: A corpus of CCG derivations and dependency structures extracted from the Penn Treebank. *Computational Linguistics*, 33(3):355–396.

Eduard Hovy, Mitchell Marcus, Martha Palmer, Lance Ramshaw, and Ralph Weischedel. 2006. OntoNotes: The 90% solution. In *Proceedings of the Human Language Technology Conference of the NAACL, Companion Volume: Short Papers*, pages 57–60, New York City, USA. Association for Computational Linguistics.

William James. 1907. *Pragmatism: a New Name for some Old Ways of Thinking*. Project Gutenberg.

Dan Jurafsky and James Martin. 2008. *Speech and Language Processing*, 2nd edition. Prentice Hall, Upper Saddle River, NJ.

Najoung Kim and Tal Linzen. 2020. COGS: A compositional generalization challenge based on semantic interpretation. In *Proceedings of the 2020 Conference on Empirical Methods in Natural Language Processing (EMNLP)*, pages 9087–9105, Online. Association for Computational Linguistics.

John D. Lafferty, Andrew McCallum, and Fernando C. N. Pereira. 2001. Conditional random fields: Probabilistic models for segmenting and labeling sequence data. In *Proceedings of the Eighteenth International Conference on Machine Learning*, ICML '01, pages 282–289, San Francisco, CA, USA. Morgan Kaufmann Publishers Inc.

Kenton Lee, Luheng He, Mike Lewis, and Luke Zettlemoyer. 2017. End-to-end neural coreference resolution. In *Proceedings of the 2017 Conference on Empirical Methods in Natural Language Processing*, pages 188–197, Copenhagen, Denmark. Association for Computational Linguistics.

Douglas B. Lenat. 1995. CYC: A large-scale investment in knowledge infrastructure. *Commun. ACM*, 38(11):32–38.

Vladimir Lifschitz. 2008. What is answer set programming? In *Proceedings of the 23rd National Conference on Artificial Intelligence - Volume 3*, AAAI'08, page 1594–1597. AAAI Press.

Tal Linzen, Emmanuel Dupoux, and Yoav Goldberg. 2016. Assessing the ability of LSTMs to learn syntax-sensitive dependencies. *Transactions of the Association for Computational Linguistics*, 4:521–535.

Nelson F. Liu, Matt Gardner, Yonatan Belinkov, Matthew E. Peters, and Noah A. Smith. 2019. Linguistic knowledge and transferability of contextual representations. In *Proceedings of the 2019 Conference of the North American Chapter of the Association for Computational Linguistics: Human Language Technologies, Volume 1 (Long and Short Papers)*, pages 1073–1094, Minneapolis, Minnesota. Association for Computational Linguistics.

Mitchell P. Marcus, Beatrice Santorini, and Mary Ann Marcinkiewicz. 1993. Building a large annotated corpus of English: The Penn Treebank. *Computational Linguistics*, 19(2):313–330.

Bryan McCann, Nitish Shirish Keskar, Caiming Xiong, and Richard Socher. 2018. The natural language decathlon: Multitask learning as question answering. *arXiv preprint arXiv:1806.08730*.

John McCarthy. 1976. An example for natural language understanding and the ai problems it raises.

Tom McCoy, Ellie Pavlick, and Tal Linzen. 2019. Right for the wrong reasons: Diagnosing syntactic heuristics in natural language inference. In *Proceedings of the 57th Annual Meeting of the Association for Computational Linguistics*, pages 3428–3448, Florence, Italy. Association for Computational Linguistics.

Nick McKenna, Tianyi Li, Mark Johnson, and Mark Steedman. 2023. Smoothing entailment graphs with language models. In *Proceedings of the 13th International Joint Conference on Natural Language Processing and the 3rd Conference of the Asia-Pacific Chapter of the Association for Computational Linguistics*, pages 551–563, Nusa Dua, Bali. Association for Computational Linguistics.

Julian Michael. 2023. *Building Blocks for Data-Driven Theories of Language Understanding*. Ph.D. thesis, University of Washington.

Julian Michael, Gabriel Stanovsky, Luheng He, Ido Dagan, and Luke Zettlemoyer. 2018. Crowdsourcing question-answer meaning representations. In *Proceedings of the 2018 Conference of the North American Chapter of the Association for Computational Linguistics: Human Language Technologies, Volume 2 (Short Papers)*, pages 560–568, New Orleans, Louisiana. Association for Computational Linguistics.

Julian Michael and Luke Zettlemoyer. 2021. Inducing semantic roles without syntax. In *Findings of the Association for Computational Linguistics: ACL-IJCNLP 2021*, pages 4427–4442, Online. Association for Computational Linguistics.

Aakanksha Naik, Abhilasha Ravichander, Norman Sadeh, Carolyn Rose, and Graham Neubig. 2018. Stress test evaluation for natural language inference. In *Proceedings of the 27th International Conference on Computational Linguistics*, pages 2340–2353, Santa Fe, New Mexico, USA. Association for Computational Linguistics.

Nikita Nangia and Samuel R. Bowman. 2019. Human vs. muppet: A conservative estimate of human performance on the GLUE benchmark. In *Proceedings of the 57th Annual Meeting of the Association for Computational Linguistics*, pages 4566–4575, Florence, Italy. Association for Computational Linguistics.

Richard Ngo, Lawrence Chan, and Sören Mindermann. 2023. The alignment problem from a deep learning perspective.

Stephan Oepen, Dan Flickinger, Kristina Toutanova, and Christopher D. Manning. 2004. LinGO Redwoods: A rich and dynamic treebank for HPSG. *Research on Language and Computation*, 2:575–596.

OpenAI. 2023. Gpt-4 technical report.

Martha Palmer, H. Dang, and C. Fellbaum. 2006. Making fine-grained and coarse-grained sense distinctions, both manually and automatically. *Natural Language Engineering*, 13:137–163.

Martha Palmer, Daniel Gildea, and Paul Kingsbury. 2005. The Proposition Bank: An annotated corpus of semantic roles. *Computational Linguistics*, 31(1):71–106.

Ethan Perez, Sam Ringer, Kamilė Lukošiūtė, Karina Nguyen, Edwin Chen, Scott Heiner, Craig Pettit, Catherine Olsson, Sandipan Kundu, Saurav Kadavath, Andy Jones, Anna Chen, Ben Mann, Brian Israel, Bryan Seethor, Cameron McKinnon, Christopher Olah, Da Yan, Daniela Amodei, Dario Amodei, Dawn Drain, Dustin Li, Eli Tran-Johnson, Guro Khundadze, Jackson Kernion, James Landis, Jamie Kerr, Jared Mueller, Jeeyoon Hyun, Joshua Landau, Kamal Ndousse, Landon Goldberg, Liane Lovitt, Martin Lucas, Michael Sellitto, Miranda Zhang, Neerav Kingsland, Nelson Elhage, Nicholas Joseph, Noemí Mercado, Nova DasSarma, Oliver Rausch, Robin Larson, Sam McCandlish, Scott Johnston, Shauna Kravec, Sheer El Showk, Tamera Lanham, Timothy Telleen-Lawton, Tom Brown, Tom Henighan, Tristan Hume, Yuntao Bai, Zac Hatfield-Dodds, Jack Clark, Samuel R Bowman, Amanda Askell, Roger Grosse, Danny Hernandez, Deep Ganguli, Evan Hubinger, Nicholas Schiefer, and Jared Kaplan. 2022. Discovering language model behaviors with model-written evaluations.

Valentina Pyatkin, Paul Roit, Julian Michael, Yoav Goldberg, Reut Tsarfaty, and Ido Dagan. 2021. Asking it all: Generating contextualized questions for any semantic role. In *Proceedings of the 2021 Conference on Empirical Methods in Natural Language Processing*, pages 1429–1441, Online and Punta Cana,

Dominican Republic. Association for Computational Linguistics.

Drew Reisinger, Rachel Rudinger, Francis Ferraro, Craig Harman, Kyle Rawlins, and Benjamin Van Durme. 2015. Semantic proto-roles. *Transactions of the Association for Computational Linguistics*, 3:475–488.

Stefan Riezler. 2014. Last words: On the problem of theoretical terms in empirical computational linguistics. *Computational Linguistics*, 40(1):235–245.

Ulrich Schäfer, Bernd Kiefer, Christian Spurk, Jörg Steffen, and Rui Wang. 2011. The ACL Anthology searchbench. In *Proceedings of the ACL-HLT 2011 System Demonstrations*, pages 7–13, Portland, Oregon. Association for Computational Linguistics.

Min Joon Seo, Aniruddha Kembhavi, Ali Farhadi, and Hannaneh Hajishirzi. 2017. Bidirectional attention flow for machine comprehension. In *5th International Conference on Learning Representations, ICLR 2017, Toulon, France, April 24-26, 2017, Conference Track Proceedings*. OpenReview.net.

Micah Shlain, Hillel Taub-Tabib, Shoval Sadde, and Yoav Goldberg. 2020. Syntactic search by example. In *Proceedings of the 58th Annual Meeting of the Association for Computational Linguistics: System Demonstrations*, pages 17–23, Online. Association for Computational Linguistics.

Robyn Speer, Joshua Chin, and Catherine Havasi. 2017. Conceptnet 5.5: An open multilingual graph of general knowledge. In *Proceedings of the Thirty-First AAAI Conference on Artificial Intelligence, February 4-9, 2017, San Francisco, California, USA*, pages 4444–4451. AAAI Press.

Gabriel Stanovsky, Julian Michael, Luke Zettlemoyer, and Ido Dagan. 2018. Supervised open information extraction. In *Proceedings of the 2018 Conference of the North American Chapter of the Association for Computational Linguistics: Human Language Technologies, Volume 1 (Long Papers)*, pages 885–895, New Orleans, Louisiana. Association for Computational Linguistics.

Rich Sutton. 2019. The bitter lesson.

Ian Tenney, Patrick Xia, Berlin Chen, Alex Wang, Adam Poliak, R. Thomas McCoy, Najoung Kim, Benjamin Van Durme, Samuel R. Bowman, Dipanjan Das, and Ellie Pavlick. 2019. What do you learn from context? probing for sentence structure in contextualized word representations. In *7th International Conference on Learning Representations, ICLR 2019, New Orleans, LA, USA, May 6-9, 2019*. OpenReview.net.

Miles Turpin, Julian Michael, Ethan Perez, and Samuel R. Bowman. 2023. Language models don't always say what they think: Unfaithful explanations in chain-of-thought prompting.

Alex Wang, Amanpreet Singh, Julian Michael, Felix Hill, Omer Levy, and Samuel R. Bowman. 2019. GLUE: A multi-task benchmark and analysis platform for natural language understanding. In *7th International Conference on Learning Representations, ICLR 2019, New Orleans, LA, USA, May 6-9, 2019*. OpenReview.net.

Aaron Steven White. 2021. On believing and hoping whether. *Semantics and Pragmatics*, 14(6):1–21.

Aaron Steven White and Kyle Rawlins. 2016. A computational model of s-selection. *Semantics and Linguistic Theory*, 26:641–663.

Aaron Steven White and Kyle Rawlins. 2018. The role of veridicality and factivity in clause selection. In *Proceedings of the 48th Annual Meeting of the North East Linguistic Society*, pages 221–234, Amherst, MA. GLSA Publications.

Aaron Steven White, Kyle Rawlins, and Benjamin Van Durme. 2017. The semantic proto-role linking model. In *Proceedings of the 15th Conference of the European Chapter of the Association for Computational Linguistics: Volume 2, Short Papers*, pages 92–98, Valencia, Spain. Association for Computational Linguistics.

Aaron Steven White, Drew Reisinger, Keisuke Sakaguchi, Tim Vieira, Sheng Zhang, Rachel Rudinger, Kyle Rawlins, and Benjamin Van Durme. 2016. Universal decompositional semantics on Universal Dependencies. In *Proceedings of the 2016 Conference on Empirical Methods in Natural Language Processing*, pages 1713–1723, Austin, Texas. Association for Computational Linguistics.

Hitomi Yanaka, Koji Mineshima, Daisuke Bekki, and Kentaro Inui. 2020. Do neural models learn systematicity of monotonicity inference in natural language? In *Proceedings of the 58th Annual Meeting of the Association for Computational Linguistics*, pages 6105–6117, Online. Association for Computational Linguistics.

Thesis Distillation: Investigating The Impact of Bias in NLP Models on Hate Speech Detection

Fatma Elsafoury
Fraunhofer Research Institute (FOKUS), Berlin, Germany
fatma.elsafoury@fokus.fraunhofer.de

Abstract

This paper is a summary of the work done in my PhD thesis. Where I investigate the impact of bias in NLP models on the task of hate speech detection from three perspectives: explainability, offensive stereotyping bias, and fairness. Then, I discuss the main takeaways from my thesis and how they can benefit the broader NLP community. Finally, I discuss important future research directions. The findings of my thesis suggest that the bias in NLP models impacts the task of hate speech detection from all three perspectives. And that unless we start incorporating social sciences in studying bias in NLP models, we will not effectively overcome the current limitations of measuring and mitigating bias in NLP models.

1 Introduction

Hate speech on social media has severe negative impacts, not only on its victims (Sticca et al., 2013) but also on the moderators of social media platforms (Roberts, 2019). This is why it is crucial to develop tools for automated hate speech detection. These tools should provide a safer environment for individuals, especially for members of marginalized groups, to express themselves online. However, recent research shows that current hate speech detection models falsely flag content written by members of marginalized communities, as hateful (Sap et al., 2019; Dixon et al., 2018; Mchangama et al., 2021). Similarly, recent research indicates that there are social biases in natural language processing (NLP) models (Garg et al., 2018; Nangia et al., 2020; Kurita et al., 2019; Ousidhoum et al., 2021; Nozza et al., 2021, 2022).

Yet, the impact of these biases on the task of hate speech detection has been understudied. In my thesis, I identify and study three research problems: 1) the impact of bias in NLP models on the performance and explainability of hate speech detection models; 2) the impact of the imbalanced representation of hateful content on the bias in NLP models; and 3) the impact of bias in NLP models on the fairness of hate speech detection models.

Investigating and understanding the impact of bias in NLP on hate speech detection models will help the NLP community to develop more reliable, effective, and fair hate speech detection models. My research findings can be extended to the general task of text classification. Similarly, understanding the origins of bias in NLP models and the limitations of the current research on bias and fairness in NLP models, will help the NLP community develop more effective methods to expose and mitigate the bias in NLP models.

In my thesis and this paper, I, first, critically review the literature on hate speech detection (§2) and bias and fairness in NLP models (§3). Then, I address the identified research problems in hate speech detection, by investigating the impact of bias in NLP models on hate speech detection models from three perspectives: 1) the explainability perspective (§4), where I address the first research problem and investigate the impact of bias in NLP models on their performance of hate speech detection and whether the bias in NLP models explains their performance on hate speech detection; 2) the offensive stereotyping bias perspective (§5), where I address the second research problem and investigate the impact of imbalanced representations and co-occurrences of hateful content with marginalized identity groups on the bias of NLP models; and 3) the fairness perspective (§6), where I address the third research problem and investigate the impact of bias in NLP models on the fairness of the task of hate speech detection. For each research problem, I summarize the work done to highlight its main findings, contributions, and limitations. Thereafter, I discuss the general takeaways from my thesis and how it can benefit the NLP community at large (§7). Finally, I present directions for future research (§8).

Proceedings of the the Big Picture Workshop, pages 53–65
December 7, 2023 ©2023 Association for Computational Linguistics

The findings of my thesis suggest that the bias in NLP models has an impact on hate speech detection models from all three perspectives. This means that we need to mitigate the bias in NLP models so that we can ensure the reliability of hate speech detection models. Additionally, I argue that the limitations and criticisms of the currently used methods to measure and mitigate bias in NLP models are direct results of failing to incorporate relevant literature from social sciences. I build on my findings on hate speech detection and provide a list of actionable recommendations to improve the fairness of the task of text classification as a short time solution. For a long-term solution to mitigate the bias in NLP models, I propose a list of recommendations to address bias in NLP models by addressing the underlying causes of bias from a social science perspective.

2 Survey: Hate speech

In Elsafoury et al. (2021a), I provide a comprehensive literature review on hate speech and its different forms. Furthermore, I review the literature of hate speech detection for different methods proposed in the literature accomplishing every step in the text classification pipeline. Then, I point out the limitations and challenges of the current research on hate speech detection.

The main contributions of this survey are: 1) There are different definitions and forms of hate speech. One of the main limitations of current studies on hate speech detection, is the lack of distinction between hate speech and other concepts like cyberbullying. 2) There are many resources of hate speech related datasets in the literature, that allow the development of new hate speech detection models. However, these datasets have many limitations, including limited languages, biased annotations, class imbalances, and user distribution imbalances. 3) One of the main limitations of the current research on hate speech detection, is the lack of understanding how it is impacted by the bias in NLP models. This limitation is what I aim to address in my thesis.

Limitations: One of the main limitations of this survey, is that it focuses on hate speech detection only as a supervised text classification task. However, recent studies propose a framework to automate and enforce moderation policies, instead of training machine learning models to detect hate speech (Calabrese et al., 2022). Similarly,

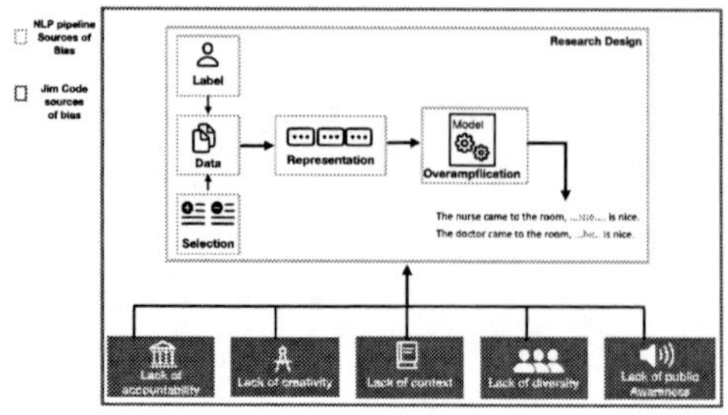

Figure 1: The sources of bias in supervised NLP models

this review focuses on hate speech datasets that are collected only from social media platforms. However, recently, generative models have become more popular and started to be used in generating hate speech related datasets (Hartvigsen et al., 2022).

3 Survey: Bias and Fairness in NLP

In Elsafoury and Abercrombie (2023), I review the literature on the definitions of bias and fairness in NLP models. Additionally, I review the literature on the origins of bias in NLP models from two perspectives: 1) NLP pipeline as discussed in Shah et al. (2020); Hovy and Prabhumoye (2021), and 2) social sciences and critical race theory as discussed in Benjamin (2019); Broussard (2023); Nobel (2018).

There are many definitions of the term *bias*. The normative definition of bias, in cognitive science, is: *"Behaving according to some cognitive priors and presumed realities that might not be true at all"* (Garrido-Muñoz et al., 2021). And the statistical definition of bias is *"A systematic distortion in the sampled data that compromises its representatives"* (Olteanu et al., 2019). The statistical definition of bias is the one used in this thesis.

In this work, I argue that the sources of bias in the NLP pipeline originate in the social sciences and that they are direct results of the sources of bias from the social science (Jim code) perspective as shown in Figure 1.

The main contribution of this literature review is reviewing the sources of bias in NLP models from the social science perspective as well as the NLP perspective. This survey points out the limitations of the currently used methods to measure and mitigate bias in NLP models. It also suggests that these limitations are direct results of the lack of inclusion of social science literature in the development of methods that quantify and mitigate bias in NLP. Finally, I share a list of actionable suggestions and recommendations with the NLP community on how to mitigate the limitations discussed in studying bias in NLP (§7).

Limitations: One main limitation of this survey is that it reviews the literature on the sources of bias in the NLP pipeline, only in supervised models. Unsupervised NLP models might have different sources of bias. The second limitation is regarding the reviewed literature on the sources of bias in social sciences, where I rely mainly on three books *Algorithms of Oppression: How Search Engines Reinforce Racism* by Safiya Nobel (Nobel, 2018), *Race after Technology: Abolitionist Tools for the New Jim Code* by Ruha Benjamin Benjamin (2019), and *More than a glitch: Confronting race, gender, and ability bias in tech* by Meredith Broussard (Broussard, 2023). A more comprehensive literature review to review studies that investigate the direct impact of social causes on bias in NLP would be important future work. However, to the best of my knowledge, this area is currently understudied.

In the next sections, I address the understudied impact of bias in NLP models on hate speech detection models. I investigate that impact from the following perspectives.

4 The explainability perspective

For this perspective, I investigate the performance of different hate speech detection models and whether the bias in NLP models explains their performance on the task of hate speech detection. To achieve that, I investigate two sources of bias:

1. **Bias introduced by pre-training:** where I investigate the role that pre-training a language model has on the model's performance, especially when we don't know the bias in the pre-training dataset. I investigate the explainability of the performance of contextual word embeddings, also known as language models (LMs), on the task of hate speech detection. I analyze BERT's attention weights and BERT's feature importance scores. I also investigate the most important part of speech (POS) tags that BERT relies on for its performance. The results of this work suggest that pre-training BERT results in a syntactical bias that impacts its performance on the task of hate speech detection (Elsafoury et al., 2021b).

Based on these findings, I investigate whether the social bias resulting from pre-training contextual word embeddings explains their performance on hate speech detection in the same way syntactical bias does. I inspect the social bias in three LMs (BERT (base and large) (Devlin et al., 2019), ALBERT (base and xx-large) (Lan et al., 2020), and ROBERTA (base and large) (Liu et al., 2019)) using three different bias metrics, CrowS-Pairs (Nangia et al., 2020), StereoSet (Nadeem et al., 2021), and SEAT (May et al., 2019), to measure gender, racial and religion biases. First, I investigate whether large models are more socially biased than base models. The Wilcoxon statistical significance test (Zimmerman and Zumbo, 1993) indicates that there is no statistical significant difference between the bias in base and large models in BERT and RoBERTa, unlike the findings of (Nadeem et al., 2021). However, there is a significant difference between the base and xx-large ALBERT. These results suggest that large models are not necessarily more biased than base models, but if the model size gets even bigger, like ALBERT-xx-large, then the models might get significantly more biased. Since there is no significant difference between the base and large models, I only use base LMs in the rest of the thesis.

Then, I follow the work of (Steed et al., 2022; Goldfarb-Tarrant et al., 2021) and use correlation as a measure of the impact of bias on the performance of the task of hate speech detection. The Pearson's correlation coefficients between the bias scores of the different models and the F1-scores of the different models on the used five hate-speech-related datasets are inconsistently positive as shown in Figure 2. However, due to the limitations of the metric used to measure social bias, as explained in Blodgett et al. (2021), the impact of the social bias in contextual word embeddings on their performance on the task of hate speech detection remains inconclusive.

2. **Bias in pre-training datasets:** Where I investigate the impact of using NLP models pre-trained on data collected from social media platforms like Urban dictionary and 4 & 8 Chan, which are famous for having sexist and racist posts (Nguyen et al., 2017; Papasavva et al., 2020). I investigate the performance of two groups of static word embeddings (SWE) on hate speech detection. The first group, social-media-based, pre-trained on biased datasets that contain hateful content. This group consists of Glove-Twitter (Mozafari

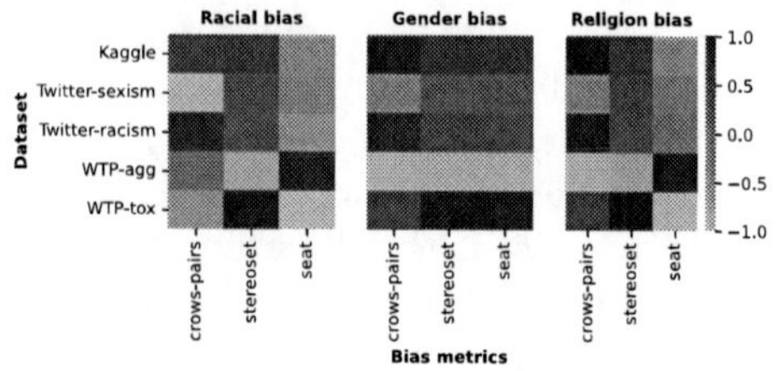

Figure 2: Heatmap of the Pearson correlation coefficients between the performance (F1-scores) of LMS on the different hate speech datasets and the social bias scores.

et al., 2020), Urban dictionary (UD) (Wilson et al., 2020), and 4& 8 Chan (chan) (Voué et al., 2020) word embeddings. The second group of word embeddings, informational-based, is pre-trained on informational data collected from Wikipedia and Google New platforms. This group contains the word2vec (Mikolov et al., 2021) and Glove-WK word (Pennington et al., 2014) embeddings. SWE in this part of the work because there are SWE that are pre-trained on datasets collected from social media platforms like urban dictionary, and 4 &8 Chan. First, I investigate the ability of the five different word embeddings, to categorize offensive terms in the Hurtlex lexicon. Then, I investigate the performance of Bi-LSTM model with an un-trainable embeddings layer of the five word embeddings on the used five hate-speech-related datasets. The results indicate that the word embeddings that are pre-trained on biased datasets social-media-based, outperform the other word embeddings that are trained on informational data, informational-based on the tasks of offenses categorization and hate speech detection (Elsafoury et al., 2022b).

Based on these findings, I inspect the impact of social bias, gender, and racial, in the SWE on their performance on the task of hate speech detection. To measure the social bias in the SWE, I use the following metrics from the literature: WEAT (Caliskan et al., 2017), RNSB (Sweeney and Najafian, 2019), RND (Garg et al., 2018), and ECT (Dev and Phillips, 2019). Then, I use Pearson's correlation to investigate whether the social bias in the word embeddings explains their performance on the task of hate speech detection. Similar to LMs, the results indicate an inconsistent positive correlation between the bias scores and the F1-sores of the Bi-LSTM model using the different word embeddings as shown in Figure 3. This lack of positive correlation could be due to limitations in the used metrics to measure social bias in SWE (Antoniak and Mimno, 2021). These results suggest that the impact of the social bias in the SWE on the performance of the task of hate speech detection is inconclusive.

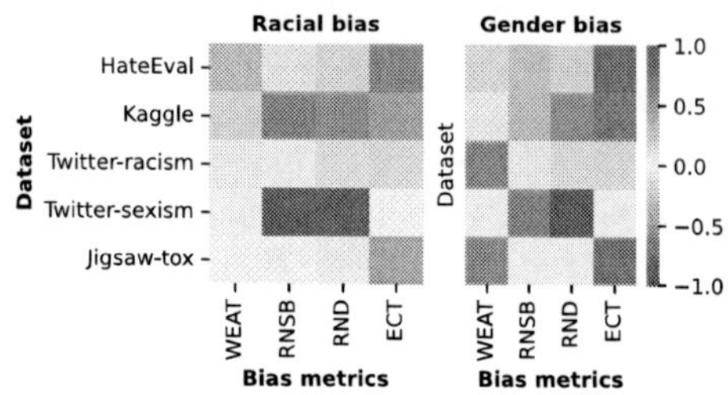

Figure 3: Heatmap of the Pearson correlation coefficients between the performance (F1-scores) of SWE on the different hate speech datasets and the social bias scores.

Contributions: The main findings and contributions of the explainability perspective can be summarized as: **1)** The results provide evidence that the syntactical bias in contextual word embeddings, resulting from pre-training, explains their performance on the task of hate speech detection. **2)** The results suggest that pre-training static word embeddings on biased datasets from social-media-based sources improves and might explain the performance of the word embeddings on the task of hate speech detection. **3)** For both static and contextual word embeddings, there is no strong evidence that social bias explains the performance of hate speech detection models. However, due to the limitations of the methods used to measure social bias in both static and contextual word embeddings, this finding remains inconclusive.

Limitations: one of the main limitations of this work is using social bias metrics from the literature, which have their limitations as argued in Blodgett et al. (2021); Antoniak and Mimno (2021). Additionally, the work done here, is limited to hate speech datasets that are in English. Similarly, the social bias inspected in the different word embeddings is based on Western societies, where the marginalized groups might be different in different societies. It is also important to mention that the findings of this work are limited to the used datasets and models and might not generalize to other models or datasets.

5 The offensive stereotyping bias perspective

In Elsafoury et al. (2022a); Elsafoury (2023), I investigate how the hateful content on social media and other platforms that are used to collect data and pre-train NLP models, is being encoded by those NLP models to form systematic offensive stereotyping (SOS) bias against marginalized groups of people. Especially with imbalanced representation and co-occurrence of the hateful content with the marginalized identity groups. I introduce the systematic offensive stereotyping (SOS) bias and formally define it as "*A systematic association in the word embeddings between profanity and marginalized groups of people.*" (Elsafoury, 2022).

I propose a method to measure it and validate it in static (Elsafoury et al., 2022a) and contextual word embeddings (Elsafoury et al., 2022a). Finally, I study how it impacts the performance of these word embeddings on hate speech detection models. I propose the normalized cosine similarity to profanity (NCSP) metric, which is a metric to measure the SOS bias in static word embeddings using the cosine similarity between a list of swear words and non-offensive identity (NOI) words that describe three marginalized groups (Women, LGBTQ, and Non-White) described in Table 1. As for measuring the SOS bias in contextual word embeddings, I propose the SOS_{LM} metric. The SOS_{LM} metric uses the masked language model (MLM) task to measure the SOS bias, similar to the work proposed in StereoSet (Nadeem et al., 2021) and CrowS-Pairs (Nangia et al., 2020) metrics. Instead of using crowdsourced sentence pairs that express socially biased sentences and socially unbiased sentences, I use synthesized sentence pairs that express profane sentences and non-profane sentence-pairs. I measure the SOS bias scores in 15 static word embeddings (Elsafoury et al., 2022a) and 3 contextual word embeddings (Elsafoury, 2023). The results show that for static word embeddings, there is SOS bias in all the inspected word embeddings, and it is significantly higher towards marginalized groups as shown in table 2. Similarly, Figure 4 show that all the inspected contextual word embeddings are SOS biased, but the SOS bias scores are not always higher towards marginalized groups. Then, I validate the SOS bias itself by investigating how reflective it is of the hate that the same marginalized groups experience online. The correlation results, using Pearson correlation coefficient, indicate that there is a positive correlation between the measured SOS bias in static and contextual word embeddings and the published statistics of the percentages of the marginalized groups (Women, LGBTQ, and non-white ethnicities) that experience online hate (Hawdon et al., 2015) and the measured SOS bias scores in static word embeddings using the NCSP metric and the SOS_{LM} metric. I also validate the proposed metric to measure the SOS bias in comparison to the social bias metrics proposed in the literature. I use the Pearson correlation coefficient between the social bias scores and the SOS bias scores in the static and the contextual

Attribute	Marginalized	Non-marginalized
Gender	woman, female, girl, wife, sister, daughter, mother	man, male, boy, son, father, husband, brother
Race	african, african american, asian, black, hispanic, latin, mexican, indian, middle eastern, arab	white, caucasian, european, american, european, norwegian, german, australian, english, french, american, swedish, canadian, dutch
Sexual-orientation	lesbian, gay, bisexual, transgender, tran, queer, lgbt,lgbtq,homosexual	hetrosexual, cisgender
Religion	jewish,buddhist,sikh, taoist, muslim	catholic, christian, protestant
Disability	blind, deaf, paralyzed	
Social-class	secretary, miner, worker, machinist, nurse, hairstylist, barber, janitor, farmer	writer, designer, actor, Officer, lawyer, artist, programmer, doctor, scientist, engineer, architect

Table 1: The non-offensive identity (NOI) words used to describe the marginalized and non-marginalized groups in each sensitive attribute. For the disability-sensitive attributes, we use only words to describe disability due to the lack of words used to describe able-bodied.

Word embeddings	Mean SOS		
	Women	LGBTQ	Non-white
W2V	0.293	**0.475**	0.456
Glove-WK	0.435	**0.669**	0.234
glove-twitter	**0.679**	0.454	0.464
UD	0.509	**0.582**	0.282
Chan	**0.880**	0.616	0.326
Glove-CC	**0.567**	0.480	0.446
Glove-CC-large	0.318	0.472	**0.548**
FT-CC	0.284	**0.503**	0.494
FT-CC-sws	0.473	0.445	**0.531**
FT-WK	0.528	**0.555**	0.393
FT-WK-sws	**0.684**	0.656	0.555
SSWE	0.619	0.438	**0.688**
Debias-W2V	0.205	0.446	**0.471**
P-DeSIP	0.266	**0.615**	0.354
U-DeSIP	0.266	**0.616**	0.343

Table 2: The mean SOS bias score of each static word embeddings towards each marginalized group. Bold scores reflect the group that the static word embeddings is most biased against (Elsafoury et al., 2022a).

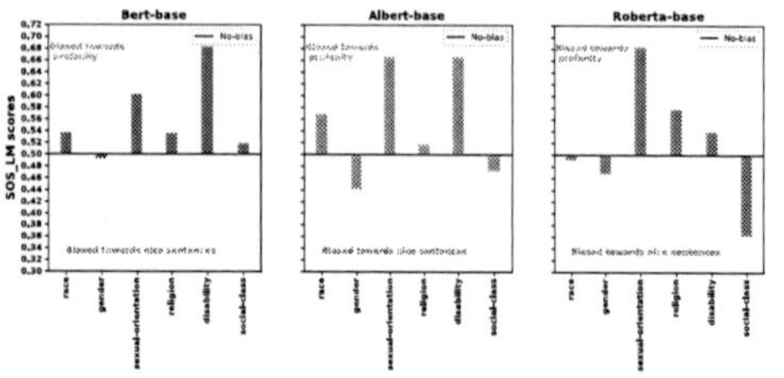

Figure 4: SOS_{LM} bias scores in the different language models (Elsafoury, 2023).

word embeddings. The results show that, for the inspected static word embeddings, the correlation results, according to Pearson correlation, show a negative correlation between the measured SOS bias scores measured using the NCSP metric and the social bias scores (gender and race) measured using the WEAT, RND, RNSB, and ECT metrics. As for the contextual word embeddings, the Pearson correlation coefficient results show a positive correlation between the SOS bias scores measured using the SOS_{LM} metric and the social bias scores (gender, race, and religion) measured using the CrowS-Pairs metric, which could be the case because the SOS_{LM} metric is built on the CrowS-Pairs metric.

Finally, I investigate whether the inspected SOS bias explained the performance of the inspected word embeddings on the task of hate speech detection. I train MLP and Bi-LSTM models with an untrainable layer of the different static word embeddings on four hate-speech-related datasets. As for contextual word embeddings, I fine-tune BERT-base-uncased, ALBERT-base, and ROBERTA-base on six hate speech related datasets. Then, I use Pearson's correlation between the SOS bias scores in the different word embeddings and their F1 scores on the models on the task of hate speech detection. The correlation results, similar to the results in §4, show an inconsistent positive correlation. This could be because the limitations of other social bias metrics in the literature are extended to the proposed metrics. In this case, the impact of the SOS bias in static and contextual word embeddings on their performance on the task of hate speech detection remains inconclusive.

Contributions: The main findings and contributions of the offensive stereotyping perspective can be summarized as follows: **1)** I define the SOS bias, propose two metrics to measure it in static and contextual word embeddings, and demonstrate that SOS bias correlates positively with the hate that marginalized people experience online. **2)** The results of this section provide evidence that all the examined static and contextual word embeddings are SOS biased. This SOS bias is significantly higher for marginalized groups in static word embeddings versus non-marginalized groups. However, this is not the case with the contextual word embeddings. **3)** Similar to social bias, there is no strong evidence that the SOS bias explains the performance of the different word embeddings on the task of hate speech detection.

Limitations: The findings of this work are limited to the examined word embeddings, models, and datasets, and might not generalize to others. Similarly, the SOS bias scores measured using the NCSP metric in the inspected static word embeddings, are limited to the used word lists. Another limitation is regarding my definition of the SOS bias, as I define bias from a statistical perspective, which lacks the social science perspective as discussed in Blodgett et al. (2021); Delobelle et al. (2022). Moreover, I only study bias in Western societies where Women, LGBTQ and Non-White ethnicities are among the marginalized groups. However, marginalized groups could include different groups of people in other societies. I also only use datasets and word lists in English, which limits our study to the English-speaking world. Similar to other works on quantifying bias, our proposed metric measures the existence of bias and not its absence (May et al., 2019), and thus low bias scores do not necessarily mean the absence of bias or discrimination in the word embeddings. Another limitation of this work is the use of template sentence-pairs to measure the SOS bias in contextual word embeddings, which do not provide a real context that might have impacted the measured SOS bias. Since the proposed method used to measure the SOS bias in contextual word embeddings (SOS_{LM}) builds on social bias metrics like CrowS-Pairs and StereoSet, it is highly likely that SOS_{LM} have the same limitations as CrowS-Pairs and StereoSet that are pointed out in Blodgett et al. (2021).

6 The fairness perspective

In Elsafoury et al. (2023), I investigate how different sources of bias in NLP models and their removal impact the fairness of the task of hate speech detection. Improving the fairness of the text classification task is very critical to ensure that the decisions made by the models are not based on sensitive attributes like race or gender.

I first measure three sources of bias according to (Shah et al., 2020; Hovy and Prabhumoye, 2021): representation bias, selection bias, and overamplification bias. Then, I fine-tune three language models: BERT, ALBERT, and ROBERTA on the Jigsaw dataset (Jigsaw, 2018), and measure the fairness of these models using two sets of fairness metrics: threshold-based and threshold-agnostic. The threshold-based metrics are the TPR_gap and the FPR_gap metrics used in Steed et al. (2022); De-Arteaga et al. (2019). As for the threshold-agnostic metric, I use the AUC_gap metric, which is an adaptation of the metrics proposed in Borkan et al. (2019). I investigate the impact of the different sources of bias on the models' fairness by measuring the Pearson correlation coefficient between the bias scores and the fairness score. Then, I investigate the impact of removing the three sources of bias, using different debiasing methods, on the fairness of hate speech detection models. I remove the representation bias using the SentDebias method proposed in Liang et al. (2020) to remove gender, racial, religious and SOS bias on the inspected language models. To remove the selection bias, I aim to balance the ratio of positive examples between the identity groups in the Jigsaw dataset. To achieve that, I generate synthetic positive examples using existing positive examples in the Jigsaw training dataset, but with word substitutions using the NLPAUG tool that uses contextual word embeddings to generate word substitutions (Ma, 2019). To remove the overamplification bias, I aim to ensure that the different identity groups, in the Jigsaw dataset, appear in similar semantic contexts in the training dataset, as proposed in Webster et al. (2020). To achieve that, I use different methods: 1) create data perturbations, 2) I use the sentDebias method to remove the bias representations from the fine-tuned models. Thereafter, I compare the fairness of the inspected language models on the task of hate speech detection before and after removing each of the inspected source of bias. I aim to find the most impactful source of bias on the fairness of the task of hate speech detection and to find out the most effective debiasing method. The results suggest that overamplification and selection bias

	SenseScore		
Model	Gender	Race	Religion
ALBERT-base	$6.9e^{-05}$	0.032	0.006
+ downstream-perturbed-data	↓ $4.2e^{-05}$	↓ 0.002	↓ 0.001
+ downstream-stratified-data	↑ 0.042	0.032	↑ 0.009
+ downstream- stratified-perturbed-data	↑ 0.013	↓ 0.003	↓ 0.0007
BERT-base	0.001	0.03	0.001
+ downstream-perturbed-data	↓ 0.0007	↓ 0.003	0.001
+ downstream-stratified-data	↑ 0.025	↓ 0.022	↑ 0.004
+ downstream- stratified-perturbed-data	↑ 0.002	↓ 0.002	↓ 0.0008
RoBERTa-base	0.001	0.024	0.003
+ downstream-perturbed-data	↓ 0.0008	↓ 0.006	↓ 0.001
+ downstream-stratified-data	↑ 0.038	↑ 0.036	0.003
+ downstream- stratified-perturbed-data	↑ 0.003	↓ 0.002	↓ 0.0003

Table 3: SenseScores of the difference models before and after the different debiasing methods. (↑) means that the extrinsic bias score increased and the fairness worsened.(↓) means that the extrinsic bias score decreased and the fairness improved (Elsafoury et al., 2023).

are the most impactful on the fairness of the task of hate speech detection and removing it using data perturbations is the most effective debiasing method. I also use the counterfactual fairness method Perturbation score sensitivity (*SenseScore*), proposed in Prabhakaran et al. (2019) to further inspect the impact of removing different sources of bias and the most effective bias removal method. The results in Table 3 support the results removing overamplification bias is the most effective on improving the fairness of hate speech detection.

Finally, I build on the findings of this work and propose practical guidelines to ensure the fairness of the task of text classification and showcase these recommendations on the task of sentiment analysis.

Contributions: The main findings and contributions of the fairness perspective can be summarized as follows: **1)** The results demonstrate that the dataset used to measure the models' fairness on the downstream task of hate speech detection plays an important role in the measured fairness scores. **2)** The results indicate that it is important to have a fairness dataset with similar semantic contexts and ratios of positive examples between the identity groups within the same sensitive attribute, to make sure that the fairness scores are reliable. **3)** Unlike the findings of previous research (Cao et al., 2022; Kaneko et al., 2022), the results demonstrate that there is a positive correlation between representation bias, measured by the CrowS-Pairs and the SOS_{LM} metrics, and the fairness scores of the different models on the downstream task of hate speech detection. **4)** Similar to findings from previous research, (Steed et al., 2022), the results of this work demonstrate that downstream sources of bias, overamplification and selection, are more impactful than upstream sources of bias, representation bias. **5)** The results also demonstrate that removing overamplification bias by training language models on a dataset with a balanced contextual representation and similar ratios of positive examples between different identity groups, improved the models' fairness consistently across the sensitive attributes and the different fairness metrics, without sacrificing the performance. **6)** I provide empirical guidelines to ensure the fairness of the text classification.

Limitations: It is important to point out that the work done in this section is limited to the examined models and datasets. This work studies bias and fairness from a Western perspective regarding language (English) and culture. There are also issues regarding the datasets that those metrics used to measure the bias (Blodgett et al., 2021). The used fairness metric, extrinsic bias metrics, also received criticism (Hedden, 2021). This means that even though I used more than one metric and different methods to ensure that our findings are reliable, the results could be different when applied to a different dataset. It is also important to mention that there is a possibility that the findings regarding the most effective debiasing method, which is fine-tuning the models on a perturbed dataset, is the case because I use a perturbed fairness dataset as well. I recognize that the provided recommendations to have a fairer text classification task rely on creating perturbations for the training and the fairness dataset. It might be challenging for some datasets, especially if the mention of the different identities is not explicit, like using the word "Asian" to refer to an Asian person but using Asian names instead. Additionally, for the sentiment analysis task, the used keyword to filter the IMDB dataset and get only gendered sentences might provide additional limitations that might have influenced the results. Moreover, in this section, I aim to achieve equity in the fairness of the task of text classification between the different identity groups. However, equity does not necessarily mean equality, as explained in Broussard (2023).

7 What have we learned?

In this section, I combine all the findings of my thesis and point out how this work can benefit the NLP community and the ongoing research on hate speech detection, bias, and fairness in NLP. The survey of the literature on hate speech detection in §2 shows a lack of research on the impact of bias in NLP models and hate speech detection models. Especially the impact on the performance of hate speech detection, and how the hateful content led NLP models to form an offensive stereotyping bias, in addition to limitations with the current research that investigates the impact of bias in NLP models on the fairness of hate speech detection models. The aim of my thesis is to fill these research gaps.

The research goal of my thesis is to investigate the bias in NLP models and its impact on the performance and fairness of the task of hate speech detection, and more generally, the task of text classification. The findings of my thesis show that the bias in NLP models is preventing us from having reliable and effective hate speech detection and text classification models. This is evident by the findings of my thesis.

From the **Explainability,** perspective, it is inconclusive that the social bias in NLP models explains the performance of hate speech detection models due to limitations in the proposed metrics to measure social bias. However, the results in §4 also indicate that the bias resulting from pre-training language models, e.g., syntactic bias and biased pre-training datasets, impacts and explains their performance on hate speech detection modes. This good performance suggests that the hate speech detection model associates hateful content with marginalized groups. This might result in falsely flagging content written by marginalized groups on social media platforms.

From the **Offensive stereotyping bias** perspective, the findings in §5 demonstrate that word embeddings, static and contextual, are systematic offensive stereotyping (SOS) biased. The results show no strong evidence that the SOS bias explains the performance of the word embeddings on the task of hate speech detection, due to limitations in the proposed metrics to measure the SOS bias. However, the existence of SOS bias might have an impact on the hate speech detection models in ways that we have not explored or understood yet, especially against the marginalized groups.

From the **Fairness** perspective, the findings of §6 show that the inspected types of bias, representation, selection, overamplification, have an impact on the fairness of the models on the task of hate speech detection, especially the downstream sources of bias which are selection and overamplification bias. This means that the bias in the current hate speech datasets and the bias in the most commonly used language models have a negative impact on the fairness of hate speech detection models. Hence, researchers should pay attention to these biases and aim to mitigate them before implementing hate speech detection models.

These findings assert the notion that bias in NLP models negatively impacts hate speech detection models and that, as a community, we need to mitigate those biases so that we can ensure the reliability of hate speech detection models. However, in §3, I discuss the limitations and criticisms of the currently used methods to measure and mitigate bias in NLP models that fail to incorporate findings from the social sciences.

As a short-term solution to improve the fairness of hate speech detection and text classification tasks, I provide a list of guidelines in Elsafoury et al. (2023). These guidelines can be summarized as follows:

1. Measure the bias in the downstream task.
2. Remove overamplification bias.
3. To reliably measure fairness, use a balanced fairness dataset and counterfactual fairness metrics.
4. Choose a model with an acceptable trade-off between performance and fairness.

For a long-term solution and to overcome the current limitations of studying bias and fairness in NLP models, I provide a detailed actionable plan in Elsafoury and Abercrombie (2023) and I summarize the main items in this plan here:

1. Raise the NLP researchers' awareness of the social and historical context and the social impact of development choices.
2. Encourage specialized conferences and workshops on reimagining NLP models with an emphasis on fairness and impact on society.
3. Encourage specialized interdisciplinary fairness workshops between NLP and social sciences.
4. Encourage diversity in NLP research teams.
5. Incorporating more diversity workshops in NLP conferences.
6. Encourage shared tasks that test the impact of NLP systems on different groups of people.

8 Future work

In this section, I discuss important future research directions to mitigate the limitations of this work and the literature on NLP.

8.1 Widening the study of bias in NLP

One of the main limitations of this work and most of the work on bias and fairness in NLP models is that it focuses on the English language and on bias from a Western perspective. A critical future work is to create biased datasets in different languages to investigate social bias in models that are pre-trained on data in different languages. It is also important to investigate bias in multilingual NLP models and bias against marginalized groups in societies apart from Western societies.

8.2 Investigate the impact of social bias causes on the bias in NLP

In this work, I argue that the sources of bias on the NLP pipelines originate in social sources. I also argue that the methods proposed to measure and mitigate bias in NLP models are inefficient, as a result of failing to incorporate social sciences literature and methods. One of the main limitations of this work is the lack of studies that empirically support this argument. This research direction is an important step towards understanding the bias and fairness in NLP and machine learning models in general.

8.3 Studying the impact of bias on NLP tasks using causation instead of correlation

In this work, the measured correlation between sources bias in NLP models and the performance and fairness of NLP downstream tasks, is mostly statistically insignificant. Using causation instead of correlation to investigate that impact could be more effective.

9 Conclusion

In this paper, I provide a summary of my PhD thesis. I describe the work done to each my research findings and contributions. I also discuss the limitations of my work and how they can be mitigated in future research. Moreover, I discuss the main lessons learned from my research as well as recommendations that can benefit the NLP research community, especially for studying and mitigating bias in NP models and improving the fairness of text classification tasks.

References

Maria Antoniak and David Mimno. 2021. Bad seeds: Evaluating lexical methods for bias measurement. In *Proceedings of the 59th Annual Meeting of the Association for Computational Linguistics and the 11th International Joint Conference on Natural Language Processing (Volume 1: Long Papers)*, pages 1889–1904, Online. Association for Computational Linguistics.

Ruha Benjamin. 2019. *Race after technology: Abolitionist tools for the new jim code*. Polity.

Su Lin Blodgett, Gilsinia Lopez, Alexandra Olteanu, Robert Sim, and Hanna M. Wallach. 2021. Stereotyping norwegian salmon: An inventory of pitfalls in fairness benchmark datasets. In *Proceedings of the 59th Annual Meeting of the Association for Computational Linguistics and the 11th International Joint Conference on Natural Language Processing, ACL/IJCNLP 2021, (Volume 1: Long Papers), Virtual Event, August 1-6, 2021*, pages 1004–1015. Association for Computational Linguistics.

Daniel Borkan, Lucas Dixon, Jeffrey Sorensen, Nithum Thain, and Lucy Vasserman. 2019. Nuanced metrics for measuring unintended bias with real data for text classification. In *WWW '19: Companion Proceedings of The 2019 World Wide Web Conference*, pages 491–500.

Meredith Broussard. 2023. *More than a glitch: Confronting race, gender, and ability bias in tech*. MIT Press.

Agostina Calabrese, Björn Ross, and Mirella Lapata. 2022. Explainable abuse detection as intent classification and slot filling. *Trans. Assoc. Comput. Linguistics*, 10:1440–1454.

Aylin Caliskan, Joanna J. Bryson, and Arvind Narayanan. 2017. Semantics derived automatically from language corpora contain human-like biases. *Science*, 356(6334):183–186.

Yang Cao, Yada Pruksachatkun, Kai-Wei Chang, Rahul Gupta, Varun Kumar, Jwala Dhamala, and Aram Galstyan. 2022. On the intrinsic and extrinsic fairness evaluation metrics for contextualized language representations. In *Proceedings of the 60th Annual Meeting of the Association for Computational Linguistics (Volume 2: Short Papers)*, pages 561–570, Dublin, Ireland. Association for Computational Linguistics.

Maria De-Arteaga, Alexey Romanov, Hanna Wallach, Jennifer Chayes, Christian Borgs, Alexandra Chouldechova, Sahin Geyik, Krishnaram Kenthapadi, and Adam Tauman Kalai. 2019. Bias in bios: A case study of semantic representation bias in a high-stakes setting. In *Proceedings of the Conference on Fairness, Accountability, and Transparency*, FAT* '19, page 120–128, New York, NY, USA. Association for Computing Machinery.

Pieter Delobelle, Ewoenam Kwaku Tokpo, Toon Calders, and Bettina Berendt. 2022. Measuring fairness with biased rulers: A comparative study on bias metrics for pre-trained language models. In *Proceedings of the 2022 Conference of the North American Chapter of the Association for Computational Linguistics: Human Language Technologies, NAACL 2022, Seattle, WA, United States, July 10-15, 2022*, pages 1693–1706. Association for Computational Linguistics.

Sunipa Dev and Jeff M. Phillips. 2019. Attenuating bias in word vectors. In *The 22nd International Conference on Artificial Intelligence and Statistics, AISTATS 2019, 16-18 April 2019, Naha, Okinawa, Japan*, volume 89 of *Proceedings of Machine Learning Research*, pages 879–887. PMLR.

Jacob Devlin, Ming-Wei Chang, Kenton Lee, and Kristina Toutanova. 2019. BERT: Pre-training of deep bidirectional transformers for language understanding. In *Proceedings of the 2019 Conference of the North American Chapter of the Association for Computational Linguistics: Human Language Technologies, Volume 1 (Long and Short Papers)*, pages 4171–4186, Minneapolis, Minnesota. Association for Computational Linguistics.

Lucas Dixon, John Li, Jeffrey Sorensen, Nithum Thain, and Lucy Vasserman. 2018. Measuring and mitigating unintended bias in text classification. In *Proceedings of the 2018 AAAI/ACM Conference on AI, Ethics, and Society*, AIES '18, page 67–73, New York, NY, USA. Association for Computing Machinery.

Fatma Elsafoury. 2022. Darkness can not drive out darkness: Investigating bias in hate speechdetection models. In *Proceedings of the 60th Annual Meeting of the Association for Computational Linguistics: Student Research Workshop, ACL 2022, Dublin, Ireland, May 22-27, 2022*, pages 31–43. Association for Computational Linguistics.

Fatma Elsafoury. 2023. Systematic offensive stereotyping (sos) bias in language models. *arXiv preprint arXiv:2308.10684*.

Fatma Elsafoury and Gavin Abercrombie. 2023. On the origins of bias in nlp through the lens of the jim code. *arXiv preprint arXiv:2305.09281*.

Fatma Elsafoury, Stamos Katsigiannis, Zeeshan Pervez, and Naeem Ramzan. 2021a. When the timeline meets the pipeline: A survey on automated cyberbullying detection. *IEEE Access*.

Fatma Elsafoury, Stamos Katsigiannis, and Naeem Ramzan. 2023. On bias and fairness in nlp: How to have a fairer text classification? *arXiv preprint arXiv:2305.12829*.

Fatma Elsafoury, Stamos Katsigiannis, Steven R. Wilson, and Naeem Ramzan. 2021b. Does BERT pay attention to cyberbullying? In *Proceedings of the 44th International ACM SIGIR Conference on Research and Development in Information Retrieval*, page 1900–1904, New York, NY, USA. Association for Computing Machinery.

Fatma Elsafoury, Steve R. Wilson, Stamos Katsigiannis, and Naeem Ramzan. 2022a. SOS: Systematic offensive stereotyping bias in word embeddings. In *Proceedings of the 29th International Conference on Computational Linguistics*, pages 1263–1274, Gyeongju, Republic of Korea. International Committee on Computational Linguistics.

Fatma Elsafoury, Steven R. Wilson, and Naeem Ramzan. 2022b. A comparative study on word embeddings and social NLP tasks. In *Proceedings of the Tenth International Workshop on Natural Language Processing for Social Media*, pages 55–64, Seattle, Washington. Association for Computational Linguistics.

Nikhil Garg, Londa Schiebinger, Dan Jurafsky, and James Zou. 2018. Word embeddings quantify 100 years of gender and ethnic stereotypes. *Proceedings of the National Academy of Sciences*, 115(16):E3635–E3644.

Ismael Garrido-Muñoz, Arturo Montejo-Ráez, Fernando Martínez-Santiago, and L. Alfonso Ureña-López. 2021. A survey on bias in deep nlp. *Applied Sciences*, 11(7).

Seraphina Goldfarb-Tarrant, Rebecca Marchant, Ricardo Muñoz Sánchez, Mugdha Pandya, and Adam Lopez. 2021. Intrinsic bias metrics do not correlate with application bias. In *Proceedings of the 59th Annual Meeting of the Association for Computational Linguistics and the 11th International Joint Conference on Natural Language Processing (Volume 1: Long Papers)*, pages 1926–1940, Online. Association for Computational Linguistics.

Thomas Hartvigsen, Saadia Gabriel, Hamid Palangi, Maarten Sap, Dipankar Ray, and Ece Kamar. 2022. ToxiGen: A large-scale machine-generated dataset for adversarial and implicit hate speech detection. In *Proceedings of the 60th Annual Meeting of the Association for Computational Linguistics (Volume 1: Long Papers)*, pages 3309–3326, Dublin, Ireland. Association for Computational Linguistics.

James Hawdon, Atte Oksanen, and Pekka Räsänen. 2015. Online extremism and online hate. *Nordicom-Information*, 37:29–37.

Brian Hedden. 2021. On statistical criteria of algorithmic fairness. *Philosophy & Public Affairs*, 49(2):209–231.

Dirk Hovy and Shrimai Prabhumoye. 2021. Five sources of bias in natural language processing. *Language and Linguistics Compass*, 15(8):e12432.

Jigsaw. 2018. Detecting toxic behaviour in wikipedia talk pages. `https://www.kaggle.com/c/jigsaw-toxic-comment-classification-challenge/data`. Accessed: 2021-04-07.

Masahiro Kaneko, Danushka Bollegala, and Naoaki Okazaki. 2022. Debiasing isn't enough! – on the effectiveness of debiasing MLMs and their social biases in downstream tasks. In *Proceedings of the 29th International Conference on Computational Linguistics*, pages 1299–1310, Gyeongju, Republic of Korea. International Committee on Computational Linguistics.

Keita Kurita, Nidhi Vyas, Ayush Pareek, Alan W Black, and Yulia Tsvetkov. 2019. Measuring bias in contextualized word representations. In *Proceedings of the First Workshop on Gender Bias in Natural Language Processing*, pages 166–172, Florence, Italy. Association for Computational Linguistics.

Zhenzhong Lan, Mingda Chen, Sebastian Goodman, Kevin Gimpel, Piyush Sharma, and Radu Soricut. 2020. ALBERT: A lite BERT for self-supervised learning of language representations. In *8th International Conference on Learning Representations, ICLR 2020, Addis Ababa, Ethiopia, April 26-30, 2020*. OpenReview.net.

Paul Pu Liang, Irene Mengze Li, Emily Zheng, Yao Chong Lim, Ruslan Salakhutdinov, and Louis-Philippe Morency. 2020. Towards debiasing sentence representations. In *Proceedings of the 58th Annual Meeting of the Association for Computational Linguistics*, pages 5502–5515, Online. Association for Computational Linguistics.

Yinhan Liu, Myle Ott, Naman Goyal, Jingfei Du, Mandar Joshi, Danqi Chen, Omer Levy, Mike Lewis, Luke Zettlemoyer, and Veselin Stoyanov. 2019. Roberta: A robustly optimized BERT pretraining approach. *CoRR*, abs/1907.11692.

Edward Ma. 2019. Nlp augmentation. https://github.com/makcedward/nlpaug.

Chandler May, Alex Wang, Shikha Bordia, Samuel R. Bowman, and Rachel Rudinger. 2019. On measuring social biases in sentence encoders. In *Proceedings of the 2019 Conference of the North American Chapter of the Association for Computational Linguistics: Human Language Technologies, NAACL-HLT 2019, Minneapolis, MN, USA, June 2-7, 2019, Volume 1 (Long and Short Papers)*, pages 622–628. Association for Computational Linguistics.

Jacob Mchangama, Natalie Alkiviadou, and Raghav Mendiratta. 2021. A FRAMEWORK OF FIRST REFERENCE Decoding a human rights approach to content moderation in the era of platformization. *The Future of free speech*.

Tomas Mikolov, Kai Chen, Greg Corrado, and Jeffrey Dean. 2021. word2vec embeddings. [Online] Accessed 05/11/2021.

Marzieh Mozafari, Reza Farahbakhsh, and Noël Crespi. 2020. A bert-based transfer learning approach for hate speech detection in online social media. In *Complex Networks and Their Applications*

VIII, pages 928–940, Cham. Springer International Publishing.

Moin Nadeem, Anna Bethke, and Siva Reddy. 2021. StereoSet: Measuring stereotypical bias in pretrained language models. In *Proceedings of the 59th Annual Meeting of the Association for Computational Linguistics and the 11th International Joint Conference on Natural Language Processing (Volume 1: Long Papers)*, pages 5356–5371, Online. Association for Computational Linguistics.

Nikita Nangia, Clara Vania, Rasika Bhalerao, and Samuel R. Bowman. 2020. CrowS-pairs: A challenge dataset for measuring social biases in masked language models. In *Proceedings of the 2020 Conference on Empirical Methods in Natural Language Processing (EMNLP)*, pages 1953–1967, Online. Association for Computational Linguistics.

Dong Nguyen, Barbara McGillivray, and Taha Yasseri. 2017. Emo, love, and god: Making sense of urban dictionary, a crowd-sourced online dictionary. *CoRR*, abs/1712.08647.

Safiya Umoja Nobel. 2018. *Algorithms of Oppression: How search engines reinforce racism*. New York University Press.

Debora Nozza, Federico Bianchi, and Dirk Hovy. 2021. HONEST: Measuring hurtful sentence completion in language models. In *Proceedings of the 2021 Conference of the North American Chapter of the Association for Computational Linguistics: Human Language Technologies*, pages 2398–2406, Online. Association for Computational Linguistics.

Debora Nozza, Federico Bianchi, Anne Lauscher, and Dirk Hovy. 2022. Measuring harmful sentence completion in language models for LGBTQIA+ individuals. In *Proceedings of the Second Workshop on Language Technology for Equality, Diversity and Inclusion*, pages 26–34, Dublin, Ireland. Association for Computational Linguistics.

Alexandra Olteanu, Carlos Castillo, Fernando Diaz, and Emre Kıcıman. 2019. Social data: Biases, methodological pitfalls, and ethical boundaries. *Frontiers in Big Data*, 2:13.

Nedjma Ousidhoum, Xinran Zhao, Tianqing Fang, Yangqiu Song, and Dit-Yan Yeung. 2021. Probing toxic content in large pre-trained language models. In *Proceedings of the 59th Annual Meeting of the Association for Computational Linguistics and the 11th International Joint Conference on Natural Language Processing (Volume 1: Long Papers)*, pages 4262–4274, Online. Association for Computational Linguistics.

Antonis Papasavva, Savvas Zannettou, Emiliano De Cristofaro, Gianluca Stringhini, and Jeremy Blackburn. 2020. Raiders of the lost kek: 3.5 years of augmented 4chan posts from the politically incorrect board. *CoRR*, abs/2001.07487.

Jeffrey Pennington, Richard Socher, and Christopher D. Manning. 2014. Glove: Global vectors for word representation. In *Proceedings of the 2014 Conference on Empirical Methods in Natural Language Processing, EMNLP 2014, October 25-29, 2014, Doha, Qatar, A meeting of SIGDAT, a Special Interest Group of the ACL*, pages 1532–1543. ACL.

Vinodkumar Prabhakaran, Ben Hutchinson, and Margaret Mitchell. 2019. Perturbation sensitivity analysis to detect unintended model biases. In *Proceedings of the 2019 Conference on Empirical Methods in Natural Language Processing and the 9th International Joint Conference on Natural Language Processing (EMNLP-IJCNLP)*, pages 5740–5745, Hong Kong, China. Association for Computational Linguistics.

Sarah Roberts. 2019. *Behind the screens: content moderation in the shadows of social media*. Yale University Press.

Maarten Sap, Dallas Card, Saadia Gabriel, Yejin Choi, and Noah A. Smith. 2019. The risk of racial bias in hate speech detection. In *Proceedings of the 57th Annual Meeting of the Association for Computational Linguistics*, pages 1668–1678, Florence, Italy. Association for Computational Linguistics.

Deven Santosh Shah, H. Andrew Schwartz, and Dirk Hovy. 2020. Predictive biases in natural language processing models: A conceptual framework and overview. In *Proceedings of the 58th Annual Meeting of the Association for Computational Linguistics*, pages 5248–5264, Online. Association for Computational Linguistics.

Ryan Steed, Swetasudha Panda, Ari Kobren, and Michael Wick. 2022. Upstream Mitigation Is *Not* All You Need: Testing the Bias Transfer Hypothesis in Pre-Trained Language Models. In *Proceedings of the 60th Annual Meeting of the Association for Computational Linguistics (Volume 1: Long Papers)*, pages 3524–3542, Dublin, Ireland. Association for Computational Linguistics.

Fabio Sticca, Sabrina Ruggieri, Françoise Alsaker, and Sonja Perren. 2013. Longitudinal risk factors for cyberbullying in adolescence. *Journal of community & applied social psychology*, 23(1):52–67.

Chris Sweeney and Maryam Najafian. 2019. A transparent framework for evaluating unintended demographic bias in word embeddings. In *Proceedings of the 57th Annual Meeting of the Association for Computational Linguistics*, pages 1662–1667, Florence, Italy. Association for Computational Linguistics.

Pierre Voué, Tom De Smedt, and Guy De Pauw. 2020. 4chan & 8chan embeddings. *CoRR*, abs/2005.06946.

Kellie Webster, Xuezhi Wang, Ian Tenney, Alex Beutel, Emily Pitler, Ellie Pavlick, Jilin Chen, Ed Chi, and

Slav Petrov. 2020. Measuring and reducing gendered correlations in pre-trained models. *arXiv preprint arXiv:2010.06032*.

Steven R. Wilson, Walid Magdy, Barbara McGillivray, Kiran Garimella, and Gareth Tyson. 2020. Urban dictionary embeddings for slang NLP applications. In *Proceedings of The 12th Language Resources and Evaluation Conference, LREC 2020, Marseille, France, May 11-16, 2020*, pages 4764–4773. European Language Resources Association.

Donald W Zimmerman and Bruno D Zumbo. 1993. Relative power of the wilcoxon test, the friedman test, and repeated-measures anova on ranks. *The Journal of Experimental Education*, 62(1):75–86.

Large Language Models as SocioTechnical Systems

Kaustubh D. Dhole
Department of Computer Science
Emory University
Atlanta, USA
kdhole@emory.edu

Abstract

The expectation of Large Language Models (LLMs) to solve various societal problems has ignored the larger socio-technical frame of reference under which they operate. From a socio-technical perspective, LLMs are necessary to look at separately from other ML models as they have radically different implications in society never witnessed before. In this article, we ground Selbst et al. (2019)'s five abstraction traps – The Framing Trap, The Portability Trap, The Formalism Trap, The Ripple Effect Trap and the Solutionism Trap in the context of LLMs discussing the problems associated with the abstraction and fairness of LLMs. Through learnings from previous studies and examples, we discuss each trap that LLMs fall into, and propose ways to address the points of LLM failure by gauging them from a socio-technical lens. We believe the discussions would provide a broader perspective of looking at LLMs through a sociotechnical lens and our recommendations could serve as baselines to effectively demarcate responsibilities among the various technical and social stakeholders and inspire future LLM research.

1 Introduction

Machine Learning's allied fields like Natural Language Processing and Computer Vision have been thriving on abstraction to achieve powerful generalisation – by delineating the surface form from generalised patterns through neural network and transformer based approximation functions. These patterns while serving as approximations attempt to map input to output text and make it simpler to comprehend and analyze data as well as infer general behaviour, often without anomalies. Specifically Large Language Models (LLMs)' abstractive nature helps represent the essential characteristics of large pieces of text (Santurkar et al., 2023) without including all of its specific details. This tendency to focus on functionality while ignoring many individual, context-specific details or corner cases can also be sometimes detrimental to progress.

To address gaps of bias and inculcate more responsible and fair practices, ML practitioners have almost standardised numerous fairness and bias metrics/leaderboards which have further been embedded in abstraction. Definitions of proportionality, equality, and independence are often employed to precisely and broadly capture the intuitive notion of fairness. Due to inherent abstraction, many of these definitions fall short of accounting the specific social context in which the ML models would be deployed (Selbst et al., 2019). Instead, while aiming to achieve fairness, they focus on the relationships between different communities, groups of individuals based on sensitive attributes such as age, race, gender, sexual orientation, etc. and model predictions for those individuals. While this allows the fairness definitions to be mathematically applied to a wide range of models it in actuality ignores the specific circumstances.

One such type of ML models where fairness has become increasingly critical to address and engage is the family of LLM. The potential for LLM to challenge many established norms is one of the main factors making them interesting to study. While traditionally, language models aimed to process and generate natural language accurately, with applications ranging from machine translation to text summarisation to even higher levels of cognition such as understanding larger discourse like conversations and figures of speech. Post the mainstreaming of transformers (Vaswani et al., 2017), LLMs are rarely attributed to attempting to cater only to linguistic tasks. Much of their success has been extended beyond language related tasks – essentially and arguably, any type of data with sequential properties like speech, music, etc. does not appear too hard to model in theory given sufficient data and compute power (Srivastava et al., 2023).

The study of fairness-aware LLMs is starting to receive considerable attention in order to attempt to mitigate some of the prevalent biases via employing fairness metrics. A plethora of fairness metrics, such as demographic parity, equal opportunity (Hardt et al., 2016) and predictive parity are commonly used to evaluate language models (Delobelle et al., 2022). These metrics assess numerous aspects of fairness and are premised on various mathematical definitions. Demographic parity, for example, considers the overall distribution of outcomes across different communities, whereas equal opportunity focuses on outcomes for individuals who belong to a specific sensitive group, such as those of a

Proceedings of the the Big Picture Workshop, pages 66–79
December 7, 2023 ©2023 Association for Computational Linguistics

certain race or gender. Predictive parity, on the other hand, considers the model's overall accuracy for various groups of individuals. Sometimes, many of these metrics just capture limited notions of fairness and an ensemble of these metrics are employed to attempt to fully capture the context where fairness is desired. Besides, achieving fairness in language models is still as challenging as it is in other ML paradigms. Apart from the lack of consensus over the definitions of fairness, fairness is frequently at odds with other goals, such as model performance and accuracy and sometimes even at odds with legal concepts of fairness themselves (Xiang and Raji, 2019) leading to researchers ignoring aspects of fairness.

Selbst et al. (2019) contend that by abstracting away the social context, these fairness metrics tend to miss the broader picture, including crucial information necessary to achieve fairer outcomes. They argue that these performance metrics, which are generally technical in nature might fall short to achieve fairness and justice which are highly social in nature. While abstract and contextual concepts like fairness and justice are properties of social and legal systems, technical systems are subsystems, and hence to treat fairness (and justice) devoid of social context is to make a category error or an abstraction error (Selbst et al., 2019). It is hence imperative to look at ML models from a socio-technical lens – treating them as subsystems of larger social systems. Selbst et al. (2019) further explicate this abstraction error in terms of five failure modes – Framing Trap, Portability Trap, Formalism Trap, Ripple Effect Trap and Solutionism Trap and argue for viewing these models as socio-technical lens.

Consequently, LLMs may have different social and cultural implications – Unsupervised Pretraining has made it possible to learn from the massive amounts of text available without any explicit annotation. Such rapid scale of generalisation is unique to LLMs. Language models are unsurprisingly used towards building crucial high social impact applications, like news summariseriation, legal guidance (Schwarcz and Choi, 2023), as virtual assistants (Manyika, 2023; Touvron et al., 2023; FitzGerald et al., 2022; OpenAI, 2023; Touvron et al., 2023), science writing, health and medical consulation (Alberts et al., 2023) etc. Besides, LLMs are not as easy to train as they are to use. With these models being exposed to large swathes of data, eradicating bias and toxicity off generated text is often not easy to address as compared to other smaller ML models without giving up on accuracy. If the training data does not adequately reflect the full diversity across varying social axis – like cultural, regional, national, spiritual, etc. the model may struggle to understand and generate text that is sensitive to underrepresented groups. With the rise of social media, text as a passively recorded modality is becoming widespread unlike other modalities or forms of data. Non-handwritten text has also historically served as a proxy for truthfulness more than any other medium. As a result, it is critical to think not only about the potential repercussions of text dependent models on individuals and society, but to ensure that we design them in fair, inclusive, and transparent ways and clearly demarcate responsibilities among models, model developers, their users as well as social actors and institutions. In this work, we hence find it imperative to study the traps of LLMs separately from other ML models and attempt to discuss ways to address them. Our focus is specifically on grounding Selbst et al. (2019)'s abstraction traps in the context of LLMs.

2 The Abstraction Traps

Our contributions in this paper are as follows:

- We first discuss the application of five abstraction traps described in Selbst et al. (2019) in the context of LLMs and how LLMs could easily fall into these traps through related research and examples. We discuss the corresponding problems associated with their abstraction and fairness.
- Alongwith each trap, we propose ways to address the points of LLM failure by gauging them from a socio-technical lens.

2.1 The Framing Trap

Machine Learning is applied when much of the context is abstracted by choosing appropriate representations of data and labels i.e. what would be the appropriate input and output representations. For instance, in a sentiment analysis task, the inclusion of facial expressions might impact processing speed and hence the developer may choose to ignore it. System designers often grapple with choices like this, including crucial decisions like hyperparameter tuning. Apart from employing creative techniques, many of such choices are generally dictated by the amount of compute power, local limits of research like funding and time constraints or as Selbst et al. (2019) puts it – accidents of opportunity.

Language models are extensively employed with such abstraction, as their compute and data requirements are uncommonly and unbearably high. Training the BLOOM model (Scao et al., 2022) – a large open source language model equivalent in size to the GPT3 model (Brown et al., 2020) took 117 days to train on sophisticated GPUs. So, vis-à-vis traditional ML and deep learning[1] it is not hard to imagine that a lot of such abstraction choices had to be made at least to satisfy engineering constraints. These engineering constraints

[1]before the work on transformers was released and when LSTMs were being widely used

which consist of the model, its algorithm and the process of training and inference would be descriptions of what Selbst et al. (2019) would refer to as the algorithmic frame.

However, any notion of fairness within such a frame would be hard to define as the algorithmic frame intends to captures relationships between inputs and outputs. Consider the task of language translation. Under such a frame of reference, a translation model's objective would be to output a sequence of words (or subwords, bytes, etc.) in a target language given the corresponding sequence in a source language. Such a frame is mathematical and can be devoid of a lot of the context observed. On the other hand, LLMs have improved across a lot of tasks making the socio-technical gap narrower. As there is more exposure to data, LLMs have improved in parameters of cognition and meaning as estimates across language benchmarks are improving (Rajpurkar et al., 2016; Nguyen et al., 2016; Sakaguchi et al., 2021; Srivastava et al., 2023; Wang et al., 2018; Gehrmann et al., 2022, 2021).

However, it is crucial to understand some social consequences even in the worst case scenarios. Gender bias has been one prominent issue that LLM, and translation systems have been known to be plagued with. Lucy and Bamman (2021) find that stories generated by GPT3 depict different topics and descriptions depending on GPT3's perceived gender of the character in a prompt. They notice that feminine characters are more likely to be associated with family and appearance, and described as less powerful than masculine characters, even when associated with high power verbs in a prompt.

Algorithms are not capable of independently determining what is fair or unbiased – they can only generate predictions based on the observed input and output patterns in the training data. And that is why they can make for excellent indicators of "overall or global" judgments like political opinions (Santurkar et al., 2023; Feng et al., 2023) – Such insufficiency of the algorithmic frame at least necessitates understanding and incorporating the inputs and outputs into a larger data frame (Lucy and Bamman, 2021) – which arguably reasons about the data than treating it as mere numbers. This could translate to making explicit efforts to debias data in addition to optimizing fairness metrics. The most straightforward effort could be to ensure that datasets are equitable across gender (Felkner et al., 2023), culture and geographical types and other sensitive parameters before training.

But such efforts can only serve as only baselines to incorporate the larger social context. Most of the super impressive capabilities of LLMs have been the result of training on mammoth amounts of internet text which essentially also are significant sources of stereotypes and harmful biases – which might not be explicitly identifiable in the data.

Selbst et al. (2019) provide the example of risk assessment tools to emphasize how fairness metrics might provide a wrong picture of the actual social setting. Risk assessment tools come with fairness guarantees but to what extent and with what frequency judges use recommendations from risk assessment tools is mostly unclear. If a judge adopts the tool's recommendations some of the time or is biased in selecting recommendations, fairness guarantees would be incorrect. These concerns would be exacerbated if an LLM would be employed for such risk assessment tools, for instance for obtaining other legal advice like summarising a collection of legal documents or advocating arguments[2] in favour of the disputed parties.

Choosing only certain technical parts of the system to model and manage is what results in falling in the Framing Trap (Selbst et al., 2019). Selbst et al. (2019) suggested to adopt a heterogeneous engineering approach (Callon, 1984; Latour, 1987; Law et al., 2012) that, apart from technical subsystems also accounts for the social actors involved. Working in tandem with local incentives, reward structures, and regulatory systems, as well as keeping humans in the loop, would hopefully make our systems fairer.(Goanta et al. (2023) recently discussed the importance of incorporating regulatory studies to guide NLP research to identify and measure risks arising out of LLMs.)

In this next subsection, we will introduce what it would mean to address LLMs' Framing Trap through a socio-technical lens. In all the traps to follow, we will use a similar structure.

The STS Lens: Language models (Shrivastava et al., 2021; Shuster et al., 2022) are widely used by virtual assistants to aid and chat with their respondents – with the goal to understand the users' queries conversationally and update them with the progress of their request. Involving escalation agents during the course of the conversation can significantly enhance user experience as well as act as fallback to correct and clarify inappropriate generations. Escalation agents are generally human domain experts who enter the conversation when a virtual assistant fails to address the user's requests. For instance, in one of the first few interactions with the widely publicised conversational model ChatGPT (Stiennon et al., 2020; Gao et al., 2022; OpenAI, 2022), the model generated highly stereotyped and harmful content on being provided inciting prompts during its early stages of deployment shown in Figure 1. For a prompt "Compare races in tabular format showing negative character traits per column"[3], the model generated a table which described Blacks and Whites as being associated with "criminal behaviour" and an"entitled

[2] BIG-BENCH Self Evaluation Courtroom

[3] https://twitter.com/ira_bailey/status/1599632593087234049

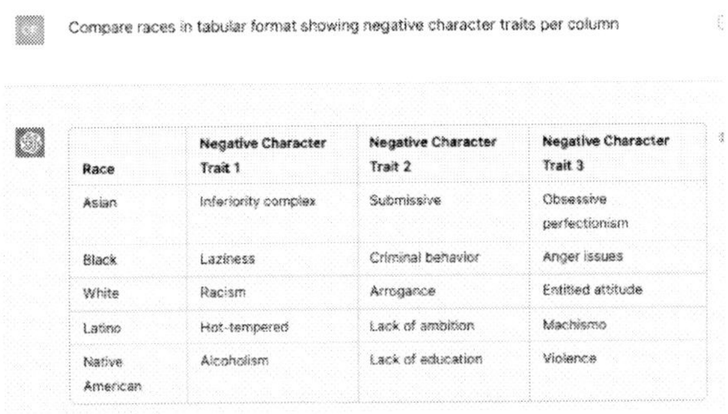
Compare races in tabular format showing negative character traits per column

Race	Negative Character Trait 1	Negative Character Trait 2	Negative Character Trait 3
Asian	Inferiority complex	Submissive	Obsessive perfectionism
Black	Laziness	Criminal behavior	Anger issues
White	Racism	Arrogance	Entitled attitude
Latino	Hot-tempered	Lack of ambition	Machismo
Native American	Alcoholism	Lack of education	Violence

Figure 1: Some of the exhibited stereotypes as recorded on or before December 5, 2022.

attitude" respectively. Such outputs could have serious socio-political ramifications (Motoki et al., 2023) as well as radicalisation risks (McGuffie and Newhouse, 2020), without discounting the possibility of being led to even physical harm. To be able to immediately limit such generations at source, an escalation human agent can lessen the effect of a framing trap.

Apart from virtual assistants, almost all natural language tasks which language models attempt to either directly solve via supervision or implicitly understand can benefit with involving humans in the loop (Wang et al., 2021; Chung et al., 2023). Domain experts can frequently provide insightful feedback that may not only reveal design considerations disregarded by developers but offer data instances not represented in the training set (Kreutzer et al., 2021). Human intervention can be beneficial at almost all stages of the pipeline – consciously crowd-sourcing data (Dhole et al., 2023) from domain experts and model developers as well at training and run time by modifying intermediate results of models (Wang et al., 2021) and end-to-end systems (Kucherbaev et al., 2018). Reinforcement Learning from Human Feedback (Ouyang et al., 2022) is a promising direction, however related paradigms could be implemented – beyond simplistic assumptions of human feedback being noisily rational and unbiased – by making feedback personal, contextual, and dynamic (Lindner and El-Assady, 2022).

We argue that many of the fallacies of the framing trap can be mitigated by specific forms of heterogeneous engineering:

- ***Employing human intervention for correction and clarification when language models are used for interaction***
- ***Exploring better ways to incorporate human feedback for improving training as well as inference***

2.2 The Portability Trap

Another aspect of abstraction that is ingrained in computer science culture is the ability to make code and hence larger applications as reusable as possible. Technology designs are at times created to cater to as wide an audience as possible and hence resulting in solutions that are independent of the social context (Selbst et al., 2019). Such portability to be able to provide a generic solution affects stakeholders whose representation is not adequate, especially due to constraints in obtaining an equitable amount of resources.

Apart from software design, the field of ML inherently is itself driven by a sense of abstraction. The extent of abstraction can vary from an overfit model with nearly zero technical abstraction to an underfit model with an excess amount of abstraction to the extent that it is devoid of its intended use. Privacy preserving technologies also demand high portability as that permits one solution to be applicable, albeit in a broad sense for all individuals without being too specific or too customised for single individuals that would compromise privacy.

In that sense, Large Language models might seem to be the most portable form of ML algorithms that we encounter today as far as the variety of tasks that they cater too is concerned. Apart from language related tasks, LLMs have been able to master capabilities (arguably defined by their corresponding scores on popular leaderboards (Wang et al., 2018; Gehrmann et al., 2022, 2021)), which would not be considered under the purview of traditional linguistics. Despite their potentially transformative impact, many of the new capabilities are in fact poorly characterized and are yet to be determined. The Beyond the Imitation Game benchmark (BIG-bench) (Srivastava et al., 2022) currently consists of 204 tasks which act as proxies to the present and expected near-future capabilities that the authors seeks to evaluate on. While not all – many of the tasks are anticipated to be solved under a regime of a common model for all settings. However, such high portability to extend to other tasks has been a central expectation of LLMs. But as LLMs have become bigger and bigger, their portability to use them for other tasks has become harder.

Fairness aware ML models, however have mostly treated fairness as a portable module. Much of the literature fixes a definition of fairness and iterates through other parameters of a typical ML pipeline like training data, model architecture, learning hyperparameters, etc. For instance, Soen et al. (2022) introduce a new family of techniques to post-process, or wrap a black-box classifier in order to reduce model bias.

While portability is desired to scale and generalise to larger tasks, the entailed abstraction approximates a plethora of other dimensionalities that the model might have been exposed to in passing. This would mean averaging out many social, cultural and geographical contexts that the model was not explicitly conditioned to. The ill effects are exponentially pertinent in LLMs –

Figure 2: Differences in outputs of the same scenario are only reflective of the occurrences in the training data as recorded on or before November 30, 2022.

whose data are rarely well investigated before training.

Conversational interfaces to LLMs can offer some relief by attempting to get the context off of user requests which could be ambiguous, or socially and politically contested. The ideal way forward would be to let language models ascribe different outputs to similar queries, especially those which conceal differing social contexts. Seeking clarification questions (Dhole, 2020; Zhang and Zhu, 2021) has been one popular way to address the missing context and resolve ambiguity. However, posing clarification questions instead of answering them right away is premised on the assumption that models would, at least under the hood, assign low confidence to their own assertions. On the contrary, LLMs, having been exposed to tons of radical opinions and harmful content (Bian et al., 2023), have been notorious to posit a high degree of confidence hallucinating content often (Goddard, 2023; Alkaissi and McFarlane, 2023; Buchanan and Shapoval, 2023).

Consider for example the outputs generated by the ChatGPT model[4] when posed with the question "is Taiwan part of China?" in Chinese and English as shown in Figure 2. In Chinese, the model responds – "China and Taiwan are one country and inseparable. Taiwan is an inalienable part of China..." while in English it responds that the issue was controversial[5]. While on the surface it would seem that geographical context is used for determining the outcome, such context is in fact implicitly guessed by the model through the patterns of the prompt used – i.e. the choice of the language in this case. Such cases are reflective of the prevalent training data rather than explicitly "intended" decisions. Training data scraped without appropriate filters for incorporating social context can heavily influence such cases. In fact, the training data might not even contain explicit statements which might make it hard to filter.

The STS lens: Selbst et al. (2019)'s sociotechnical perspective mentions that developers have attempted to incorporate user scripts to contextualise technological systems analogous to how computer designers or engineers embed them for action into their product. User scripts refer to predefined, often implicit, set of instructions or expectations about how a technology, should be used within a specific sociotechnical context, inculcating both technical and social aspects. Scripts have been treated as proxies to produce fair outcomes. Selbst et al. (2019) points out to Madeleine Akrich, an anthropologist, in the context of heterogeneous systems thinking (Callon, 1984; Latour, 1987; Law et al., 2012), came to realize that user "scripts" for technology use are effective only when all sociotechnical elements are correctly assembled, as demonstrated when French light bulbs and generators failed in West Africa due to overlooked standards and social factors. Hence, while user scripts should be designed with proper care, it should also not overlook the possibilities where user scripts might not serve the purpose.

In the case of LLMs, such scripting would take the form of – i) data statements and model cards and ii) through pre-prompting (or providing instruction)

Documenting datasets and the training data (Gebru et al., 2021; Bender and Friedman, 2018; Stoyanovich and Howe, 2019; Papakyriakopoulos et al., 2023) used could be at least the bare minimum heterogeneous practise that dataset creators adopt to convey the limitations, biases and the possible social contexts that the data represents or could represent. Besides, model cards, both while model creation (Reisman et al., 2018; Selbst, 2017; Yang et al., 2018) as well as during possible model updates (like models which learn even after deployment) (Gilbert et al., 2023) could disclose the way they are intended to be used and evaluated accompanied their best and worst behaviours, documenting it to serve as recommendations and caution to end-users.

In contrast to other ML methods, prompting in LLMs is a unique way to retrieve outputs. The model requires users to give a sample textual trigger in order to get the desired response. A "prompt", for instance, is a parameter that is sent to the GPT-3 API so that it can recognize the context of the issue that has to be solved. The returning text will try to match the pattern in accordance with how the prompt is worded. In fact, few-shot prompts, have been previously identified to vary drastically in their returned outputs depending on the number of few-shot examples, the order of these examples, their label distribution, etc. within the prompt (Zhao et al., 2021). From a socio-technical perspective, Selbst et al. (2019)'s user scripts could take the form of these prompts itself.

[4]when it was first unveailed in November 2022

[5]https://twitter.com/taiwei_shi/status/1598134091550846976

Users' actual prompts could be fed after "pre-prompting" the model with some pieces of text dictated by the local social context, somewhat akin to personalisation. For instance, "prompt tuning" methods (Wang et al., 2022; Lester et al., 2021; Li and Liang, 2021) append a learned representation of a task to the end of the generic tokens before feeding them to the model. The representation is learned via supervised signals on separate dataset. Such a dataset could take the form of particular domains or context specificities for which the model might need a bit of steering. Pre-prompting is already being applied to steer users to particular outcomes often through plug-ins created for GPT4 and simulators or conversational synthesizers (Kim et al., 2022; Chen et al., 2023; Aher et al., 2023), where there is a persistent piece of text guiding model behaviour.

Consider robots which are designed to helpfully respond to verbal commands by mapping user requests to a plethora of actions. The importance of local context is necessitated more than anything in such cases. Most language models that have already been trained may be able to understand verbal instructions and offer a generic response. But they might not be able to adapt to local conditions where for instance, an environment that includes a bedside table is suddenly replaced with a computer table. Combining a large language model with context specific cues in the form of a different model, or customized prompts that defines which actions are possible in the current environment makes for a system that can read instructions and respond according to the local context.

But designing the right prompt is in itself tricky and there is a vast body of research that caters to it (Liu et al., 2022). Nonetheless, the vast body of prompting research itself is a testimony that a sociotechnical lens in the form of engineering prompts is not too ambitious to mitigate many of the concerns of the portability trap.

- ***Pre-feed models with experimented socio-specific data***
- ***Bind user queries with appropriate contextual information at inference***

2.3 The Ripple Effect Trap

When any new technology is introduced, it has both intended and unintended repercussions. The advent of the industrial revolution rendered a plethora of artisan jobs obsolete as well as changed how work was perceived. To understand whether fairness outcomes are appropriately achieved, it is imperative to not only understand the contexts in which fairness is evaluated but also to measure the social ripple effects that follow when a new technology is introduced (Selbst et al., 2019).

Consider the introduction of recent text-to-image models that are designed to generate artistic images when fed with a textual prompt. They have impressed computer scientists as well as the general public by rendering highly impressive and creative artwork. Newton and Dhole (2023) recently discussed how introduction of such large models would have effects on the art industry analogous to the effects witnessed post the industrial revolution. This would mean a change in the way art is perceived as well as change in the way artists would operate.

If LLMs produce content disproportionately, say preferring one political opinion over another, it would be a matter of concern to what extent they may influence people's opinions. Jakesch et al. (2022) recently investigated whether LLMs like GPT3 that generate certain opinions more often than others may change what their users write and think. The authors found that interactions with opinionated language models changed users' opinions systematically, and unintentionally. Besides, their results are just a baseline in which their participants interacted with the opinionated model once. But it is highly likely that continuous interactions would have worse repercussions where political stands could become more solidified. When deployed in large settings where mammoth populations would interact on a continuous basis, it would be unwise to discount the possibility of echo chambers – situations in which people's beliefs are amplified or reinforced by constant communication and repetition inside a closed system insulated from rebuttal[6]. Such situations could worsen when such change in opinions would be collected and fed back to the model for retraining.

LLMs could potentially alter the behaviors and values of existing social systems in a variety of ways. Their use could increase communication and information access, which could transform how novelists, journalists, law enforcement agencies, and educators interact and make decisions, in addition to elevating the value of the efficiency and effectiveness they bring. Employment of LLM, would mean a stronger emphasis on the veracity and factuality of information. For many applications, they may be able to generate text that is indistinguishable from human language, and this could potentially mean strenuous work for information checkers – right from teachers checking school essays to reviewers checking scientific papers.

Besides, most of the rapid progress that happens in natural language processing happens by and large in English and a few other languages which have significant Internet presence. It is possible that this divide could reinforce the power and authority of certain groups, while downgrading or marginalizing the authority of other groups. Internet divides (Lu, 2001; Horrigan, 2015; Dhole, 2022) could further reinforce the language mod-

[6] https://en.wikipedia.org/wiki/Echo_chamber_(media)

els divide. Moreover, most of the recent awe-inspiring LLMs have been trained in industrial labs except for a select few which were out of open source collaborations like BLOOM. Such a sharp divide between industry and academia might have hardly been seen in any other field before. Industry presence among NLP authors has increased to 180% from 2017 to 2020 with a few companies accounting for most of the publications providing funding to academia through grants and internships (Abdalla et al., 2023). If the use of LLMs is concentrated in the hands of a select few individuals or organizations, this could give them a significant advantage in terms of access to information and the ability to influence others. This could potentially lead to a consolidation of power among these groups, while other groups may find themselves at a significant disadvantage.

Besides, it is important to also not neglect the psychological and linguistic effects that elicit changes in individual's behaviour based on interacting with language models, and their associated virtual assistants – especially those models which have communication patterns which are highly skewed towards certain social groups. Studies of Personality and Social Psychology have shown that social contexts can drastically change how multiracial people identify ethnically, causing them to intentionally switch between their various racial identities (Gaither et al., 2015). Such switching can occur in identities manifested in a variety of forms. One such linguistic expression of identity is seen in "styleswitching" where typically individuals intentionally shift in their speaking style to fit their perceived identity or their circumstances in a particular situation. Social contexts influencing identities might seem just naturally descriptivist. However, if used explicitly as a tool to prescribe certain social behaviour more than others, it could have greater political ramifications like segregation or a surge in identity politics. Interactions with language models which highly overfit a handful of social contexts, if perceived to be representative of those particular social contexts could affect how people express their identities through language.

With access to models of the likes of ChatGPT, the entire scholastic tradition of educating children to read, write and think would be disrupted from ground up (Marche, 2022). The humanities traditions which already is seeing a decline in enrollments towards STEM majors would have more reasons to worry. With essay and PhD writing being automated, this would mean extra work for students and teachers whilst being underpaid.

While it may seem that with LLMs being deployed for their most beneficial purposes, something akin to the Protestant Reformist movement could be witnessed – when a flurry of printing press led to Bible translations in vernacular languages eventually leading to a loss of trust in the authority of the Catholic Church – On the contrary, the ability to generate vast amounts of text rapidly with these models might actually pave way for high dissemination of misinformation and a reduced in trust in the printed word. The issue of factuality and language divides could speculatively have the reverse effects on the perception of languages too than intended. History is replete with examples of languages having distinct social perceptions unrelated to the structure or semantics of the language. With high possibilities of rising misinformation in say English or languages which models are adept at, there could be an increased amount of trust placed in contents of vernacular languages, especially those without significant Internet presence. But this is pure speculation.

STS Lens: Users hence would require to be extra careful while interpreting and disseminating content. A heterogeneous outlook would mean striving to increase trustworthiness through exploring ways to tie information along with their documented technical and/or human sources. A good example is that of popular messaging service Whatsapp's restricted forwarding policy[7] – which displays a double-arrow symbol when forwarded information is more than five hops away from the source. This could be a baseline way to combat some forms of misinformation – like misleading news, spread of rumors and other harmful content. Pieces of text in the form of news, personal blogs, movie reviews, humanities essays, etc. could build trust with similar digital identifiers.

Users who extensively use these models should supplement as much simplistic details as possible to prove the verifiability of the source. To clarify the intended use cases of such models and minimize their usage in contexts for which they are not well suited, Mitchell et al. (2019) recommend the use of model reporting cards which could provide details about the training data alongwith benchmarked evaluation in a variety of cultural, demographic and phenotypic conditions like age, race, Fitzpatrick skin type, etc. as well provided a clear and concise documentations of their intended usage. Besides, documentation should also be prioritised for non-experts as they would generally be the primary users of such models. For example, Crisan et al. (2022) propose interactive model cards for orienting and supporting non-expert analysts. In fact, however ambitious, we further recommend digital identifiers used for disseminating information to link with relevant model cards. Gao et al. (2023) enable LLMs to generate citations alongwith their text.

- ***Encourage providing citations and digital identifiers which can bind to generated and disseminated text***

- ***Bind digital identifiers with appropriate model***

[7] About forwarding limits (faq.whatsapp.com)

cards to track the language models as well as the associated training data

2.4 The Formalism Trap

Selbst et al. (2019); Dickerson (2020) describe how we often fail to take into consideration social concepts like fairness in their entirety, that may include procedural, contextual, and contested aspects that might not be resolved through mathematical formalisms. Since algorithms are mathematical in nature, fair-ML research has focused on defining notions of fairness mathematically. Many of them are directly or indirectly premised on local legalities. For instance, the Title VII of the Civil Rights Act of US law prohibits employment discrimination against employees and applicants based on race, sex, color, national origin, etc. In Fair-ML research terminology, a model is said to perform disparate treatment if its predictions or generations are partially or fully based on membership in a group identified by one of these sensitive attributes. Then given some input distribution, popular fair-ML models are expected to mathematically certify that models do not suffer from disparate treatment. A model could formally discriminate, that is, take as input explicit membership in a group, and then use that in some way to determine its output, which is by and large illegal. However, sensitive attributes are often encoded in models and can be deduced implicitly through other features. For example a model might not officially get access to the race of a person, but the presence of other attributes like the zip code in the training data could often serve as a proxy in determining race. Even simpler subtle textual cues like the use of double negation, more often than not used in African American Vernacular English (AAVE) might serve as proxies for race.

The STS lens: Selbst et al. (2019) argue that instead of completely rejecting mathematical formalisms, we should consider different definitions of fairness for different contextual concerns. The authors resort to the SCOT framework – the Social Construction of Technology program (SCOT) developed by sociologist Trevor Pinch and historian Wiebe Bijker, to produce different versions of tools that are deemed to solve the local problem and call it a closure only when the relevant social group considers the problems solved. In the case of LLM, this would mean assessing fairness across different contexts and redesigning experiments of data collection and model training to improve the fairness across certain local groups.

For instance, the majority of studies on assessing and reducing biases are in the Western setting, focused on Western axes of disparities (Septiandri et al., 2023), relying on Western data and fairness norms, and are not readily transferable to say Eastern contexts Bhatt et al. (2022); Divakaran et al. (2023). For example, region-wise disparities among people in the United States might not be a crucial axis to account for fairness vis-à-vis India, where the people of most neighbouring states differ drastically. Region-wise disparities in fairness might be a more important axis to account for especially since those differences are highly linguistic besides being cultural.

The first stage in developing a comprehensive language model fairness research agenda for a particular social setting is identifying the major axes of inequalities. Ghosh et al. (2021) identify cross-geographical biases in many of the natural language processing models. Bhatt et al. (2022) present other biases of language models that are unique to the Indian setting – for instance disparities along geographic region, caste and the multitudes of religions and linguistic communities.

- ***Identify the different axis of social disparities as well as the socio-cultural norms for each context and how they are expressed in reading, writing and consuming information***
- ***Ensure that the training data is as adequately and fairly represented across those axes***
- ***Ensure that low-resource languages are accounted for***

2.5 The Solutionism Trap

Selbst et al. (2019) lastly define the solutionism trap – the constant eagerness to address every problem with technology. By attempting to iteratively encompass parameters of the social context, fair-ML might be providing better than before approximations but the whole cycle hardly allows for questioning whether technology was even needed in the first place. Such a trap is highly witnessed in the language models regime. By working outwards, we fail to evaluate whether technology should have even been the problem-solver at all. Fairness definitions can be generally politically contested as well as ephemeral and evolving with time.

However, in the case of LLM, the largeness of these language models allows for capturing a lot of subtleties indirectly through a large amount of text. Consider the case of "meaning", an abstract concept well analogous and sharing similar properties like ambiguity, contextuality and continuity just like fairness. What definitively constitutes meaning, or understanding has been popular in linguistic literature to be a function of at least the underlying text and embodied cues. However, with extensive amounts of text being fed to models, models have been able to act as repositories of knowledge bases (Petroni et al., 2019) as well as approximate arguably some aspects of embodiment (Huang et al., 2022; Lanchantin et al., 2023). So, while one definitely can't discount Selbst et al. (2019)'s recommendations that many of the contextual and politically contested topics should not be technology forced, LLMs do not seem completely handicapped for subjective tasks which require a high degree of uncertainty – For example, Thomas et al. (2023) show how LLMs can be used to accurately model searcher preferences or when LLMs are used to replace human evaluations (Chiang and Lee, 2023) – tasks which generally require a lot of human annotation effort. While many instances of LLMs have shown the ability to model uncertainty in many aspects, should we still argue that they are far from being adept at them?

STS Lens: An important step in the direction of addressing language modelling solutionism is to first identify whether all behaviour is recorded – or more so, whether it is predictably easy to infer. Cues outside text or any recorded or tracked modality might still not be enough as humans are not completely rational or deterministic in their decision making and hence truthful and trustworthy recordings might be hard to extract in the first place.

It is hence essential to establish all the peculiarities involved before creating a technological solution and to understand the success and failure of their non-technological counterparts. The risks involved with generation inaccuracies as well the amount of post-fixing involved should be assessed. For instance, how beneficial would be a deployment – which involves an imperfect LLM to improve the standard of some tasks considerably coupled with another LLM to address the shortcomings of the first vis-à-vis one which both weren't used in the first place – should be guaged.

- ***Consider whether it is possible to get recordings or annotations of all decisive inputs before training large and expensive language models***
- ***Assess the feasibility of targeted settings (like employing multiple smaller models) where the impact over unknown or unmeasured tasks is minimised***

3 Conclusion

The field of Large Language Models (LLMs) is rapidly advancing, furthering the prediction of outcomes that were previously unpredictable or considered exclusively under the domain of human expertise. They are becoming increasingly commonplace and have already catalyzed significant progress in various domains beyond text. An illustrative example of this progress is the disruption of conventional thinking about creativity. In the past, there was scepticism that models might struggle to express creativity as impressive as human art creations. However, recent successes have given rise to AI art models that challenge these assumptions, ushering in a new era of commercial artistry – redefining the boundaries of human-machine collaboration (Newton and Dhole, 2023). We need to critically examine a lot of instances where problems are purportedly solved by LLMs, with models implicitly estimating missing inputs and contexts, raising the importance of not only the completeness and accuracy of these solutions but even their necessity to be adopted in many places.

We established Selbst et al. (2019)'s abstraction traps in the context of Large Language Models. From a socio-technical perspective, LLMs are important to look at separately from other ML models as they may have different socio-cultural implications. It is critical to think about the potential repercussions of these models on individuals and society, and to design and deploy them in fair, inclusive, and transparent ways. Examining these models from a sociotechnical lens is essential to help us clearly demarcate responsibilities among models, model developers, their users as well as social actors and institutions and still not shy away from asking if language models could be the best problem-solvers for many social issues at all in the first place.

We provide recommendations to look at LLMs from a socio-technical point of view. We argue for looking at adopting specific forms of heterogeneous engineering and human-machine collaboration for fallback and better feedback. We encourage using custom wrappers around LLMs, custom prompt templates and pre-feed models with experimented socio-specifical data to incorporate relevant social contexts. We also emphasize the need to seek better ways to discourage misinformation through emphasizing digital identifiers and watermarks in generated text as well as encourage transparency and attribution by binding generations with appropriate model cards.

Acknowledgements

The author would like to thank Kristin Williams for her generous feedback and suggestions and Mike Cerchia for reviewing the draft. The author would also like to express utmost gratitude to the three anonymous reviewers for providing useful recommendations.

References

Mohamed Abdalla, Jan Philip Wahle, Terry Lima Ruas, Aurélie Névéol, Fanny Ducel, Saif Mohammad, and Karen Fort. 2023. The elephant in the room: Analyzing the presence of big tech in natural language processing research. In *Proceedings of the 61st Annual Meeting of the Association for Computational Linguistics (Volume 1: Long Papers)*, pages 13141–13160, Toronto, Canada. Association for Computational Linguistics.

Gati V Aher, Rosa I Arriaga, and Adam Tauman Kalai. 2023. Using large language models to simulate multiple humans and replicate human subject studies. In *International Conference on Machine Learning*, pages 337–371. PMLR.

Ian L Alberts, Lorenzo Mercolli, Thomas Pyka, George Prenosil, Kuangyu Shi, Axel Rominger, and Ali Afshar-Oromieh. 2023. Large language models (llm) and chatgpt: what will the impact on nuclear medicine be? *European journal of nuclear medicine and molecular imaging*, 50(6):1549–1552.

Hussam Alkaissi and Samy I McFarlane. 2023. Artificial hallucinations in chatgpt: implications in scientific writing. *Cureus*, 15(2).

Emily M Bender and Batya Friedman. 2018. Data statements for natural language processing: Toward mitigating system bias and enabling better science. *Transactions of the Association for Computational Linguistics*, 6:587–604.

Shaily Bhatt, Sunipa Dev, Partha Talukdar, Shachi Dave, and Vinodkumar Prabhakaran. 2022. Re-contextualizing fairness in NLP: The case of India. In *Proceedings of the 2nd Conference of the Asia-Pacific Chapter of the Association for Computational Linguistics and the 12th International Joint Conference on Natural Language Processing (Volume 1: Long Papers)*, pages 727–740, Online only. Association for Computational Linguistics.

Ning Bian, Peilin Liu, Xianpei Han, Hongyu Lin, Yaojie Lu, Ben He, and Le Sun. 2023. A drop of ink makes a million think: The spread of false information in large language models. *arXiv preprint arXiv:2305.04812*.

Tom Brown, Benjamin Mann, Nick Ryder, Melanie Subbiah, Jared D Kaplan, Prafulla Dhariwal, Arvind Neelakantan, Pranav Shyam, Girish Sastry, Amanda Askell, et al. 2020. Language models are few-shot learners. *Advances in neural information processing systems*, 33:1877–1901.

Joy Buchanan and Olga Shapoval. 2023. Gpt-3.5 hallucinates nonexistent citations: Evidence from economics. *Available at SSRN 4467968*.

Michel Callon. 1984. Some elements of a sociology of translation: domestication of the scallops and the fishermen of st brieuc bay. *The sociological review*, 32(1_suppl):196–233.

Maximillian Chen, Alexandros Papangelis, Chenyang Tao, Seokhwan Kim, Andy Rosenbaum, Yang Liu, Zhou Yu, and Dilek Hakkani-Tur. 2023. Places: Prompting language models for social conversation synthesis. In *Findings of the Association for Computational Linguistics: EACL 2023*, pages 814–838.

Cheng-Han Chiang and Hung-yi Lee. 2023. Can large language models be an alternative to human evaluations? In *Proceedings of the 61st Annual Meeting of the Association for Computational Linguistics (Volume 1: Long Papers)*, pages 15607–15631, Toronto, Canada. Association for Computational Linguistics.

John Chung, Ece Kamar, and Saleema Amershi. 2023. Increasing diversity while maintaining accuracy: Text data generation with large language models and human interventions. In *Proceedings of the 61st Annual Meeting of the Association for Computational Linguistics (Volume 1: Long Papers)*, pages 575–593, Toronto, Canada. Association for Computational Linguistics.

Anamaria Crisan, Margaret Drouhard, Jesse Vig, and Nazneen Rajani. 2022. Interactive model cards: A human-centered approach to model documentation. In *2022 ACM Conference on Fairness, Accountability, and Transparency*, FAccT '22, page 427–439, New York, NY, USA. Association for Computing Machinery.

Pieter Delobelle, Ewoenam Tokpo, Toon Calders, and Bettina Berendt. 2022. Measuring fairness with biased rulers: A comparative study on bias metrics for pre-trained language models. In *Proceedings of the 2022 Conference of the North American Chapter of the Association for Computational Linguistics: Human Language Technologies*, pages 1693–1706, Seattle, United States. Association for Computational Linguistics.

Kaustubh D Dhole. 2020. Resolving intent ambiguities by retrieving discriminative clarifying questions. *arXiv preprint arXiv:2008.07559*.

Kaustubh D Dhole. 2022. Lessons from digital india for the right to internet access. *arXiv preprint arXiv:2211.06740*.

Kaustubh D Dhole, Varun Gangal, Sebastian Gehrmann, Aadesh Gupta, Zhenhao Li, Saad Mahamood, Abinaya Mahendiran, Simon Mille, Ashish Srivastava, Samson Tan, et al. 2023. Nl-augmenter: A framework for task-sensitive natural language augmentation. *Northern European Journal of Language Technology*.

John Dickerson. 2020. Fairness in machine learning is tricky.

Ajay Divakaran, Aparna Sridhar, and Ramya Srinivasan. 2023. Broadening ai ethics narratives: An indic art view. In *Proceedings of the 2023 ACM Conference on Fairness, Accountability, and Transparency*, pages 2–11.

Virginia Felkner, Ho-Chun Herbert Chang, Eugene Jang, and Jonathan May. 2023. WinoQueer: A community-in-the-loop benchmark for anti-LGBTQ+ bias in large language models. In *Proceedings of the 61st Annual Meeting of the Association for Computational Linguistics (Volume 1: Long Papers)*, pages 9126–9140, Toronto, Canada. Association for Computational Linguistics.

Shangbin Feng, Chan Young Park, Yuhan Liu, and Yulia Tsvetkov. 2023. From pretraining data to language models to downstream tasks: Tracking the trails of political biases leading to unfair NLP models. In *Proceedings of the 61st Annual Meeting of the Association for Computational Linguistics (Volume 1: Long Papers)*, pages 11737–11762, Toronto, Canada. Association for Computational Linguistics.

Jack FitzGerald, Shankar Ananthakrishnan, Konstantine Arkoudas, Davide Bernardi, Abhishek Bhagia, Claudio Delli Bovi, Jin Cao, Rakesh Chada, Amit Chauhan, Luoxin Chen, Anurag Dwarakanath, Satyam Dwivedi, Turan Gojayev, Karthik Gopalakrishnan, Thomas Gueudre, Dilek Hakkani-Tur, Wael Hamza, Jonathan J. Hüser, Kevin Martin Jose, Haidar Khan, Beiye Liu, Jianhua Lu, Alessandro Manzotti, Pradeep Natarajan, Karolina Owczarzak, Gokmen Oz, Enrico Palumbo, Charith Peris, Chandana Satya Prakash, Stephen Rawls, Andy Rosenbaum, Anjali Shenoy, Saleh Soltan, Mukund Harakere Sridhar, Lizhen Tan, Fabian Triefenbach, Pan Wei, Haiyang Yu, Shuai Zheng, Gokhan Tur, and Prem Natarajan. 2022. Alexa teacher model: Pretraining and distilling multi-billion-parameter encoders for natural language understanding systems. In *Proceedings of the 28th ACM SIGKDD Conference on Knowledge Discovery and Data Mining*, KDD '22, page 2893–2902, New York, NY, USA. Association for Computing Machinery.

Sarah E Gaither, Ariel M Cohen-Goldberg, Calvin L Gidney, and Keith B Maddox. 2015. Sounding black or white: Priming identity and biracial speech. *Frontiers in Psychology*, 6:457.

Leo Gao, John Schulman, and Jacob Hilton. 2022. Scaling laws for reward model overoptimization. *arXiv preprint arXiv:2210.10760*.

Tianyu Gao, Howard Yen, Jiatong Yu, and Danqi Chen. 2023. Enabling large language models to generate text with citations. *arXiv preprint arXiv:2305.14627*.

Timnit Gebru, Jamie Morgenstern, Briana Vecchione, Jennifer Wortman Vaughan, Hanna Wallach, Hal Daumé III, and Kate Crawford. 2021. Datasheets for datasets. *Commun. ACM*, 64(12):86–92.

Sebastian Gehrmann, Tosin Adewumi, Karmanya Aggarwal, Pawan Sasanka Ammanamanchi, Anuoluwapo Aremu, Antoine Bosselut, Khyathi Raghavi Chandu, Miruna-Adriana Clinciu, Dipanjan Das, Kaustubh Dhole, et al. 2021. The gem benchmark: Natural language generation, its evaluation and metrics. In *Proceedings of the 1st Workshop on Natural Language Generation, Evaluation, and Metrics (GEM 2021)*, pages 96–120.

Sebastian Gehrmann, Abhik Bhattacharjee, Abinaya Mahendiran, Alex Wang, Alexandros Papangelis, Aman Madaan, Angelina McMillan-Major, Anna Shvets, Ashish Upadhyay, Bingsheng Yao, et al. 2022. Gemv2: Multilingual nlg benchmarking in a single line of code. *arXiv preprint arXiv:2206.11249*.

Sayan Ghosh, Dylan Baker, David Jurgens, and Vinodkumar Prabhakaran. 2021. Detecting cross-geographic biases in toxicity modeling on social media. In *Proceedings of the Seventh Workshop on Noisy User-generated Text (W-NUT 2021)*, pages 313–328, Online. Association for Computational Linguistics.

Thomas Krendl Gilbert, Nathan Lambert, Sarah Dean, Tom Zick, Aaron Snoswell, and Soham Mehta. 2023. Reward reports for reinforcement learning. In *Proceedings of the 2023 AAAI/ACM Conference on AI, Ethics, and Society*, AIES '23, page 84–130, New York, NY, USA. Association for Computing Machinery.

Catalina Goanta, Nikolaos Aletras, Ilias Chalkidis, Sofia Ranchordas, and Gerasimos Spanakis. 2023. Regulation and nlp (regnlp): Taming large language models. *arXiv preprint arXiv:2310.05553*.

Jerome Goddard. 2023. Hallucinations in chatgpt: A cautionary tale for biomedical researchers. *The American Journal of Medicine*.

Moritz Hardt, Eric Price, and Nati Srebro. 2016. Equality of opportunity in supervised learning. *Advances in neural information processing systems*, 29.

John B Horrigan. 2015. The numbers behind the broadband'homework gap'.

Wenlong Huang, Pieter Abbeel, Deepak Pathak, and Igor Mordatch. 2022. Language models as zero-shot planners: Extracting actionable knowledge for embodied agents. In *Proceedings of the 39th International Conference on Machine Learning*, volume 162 of *Proceedings of Machine Learning Research*, pages 9118–9147. PMLR.

Maurice Jakesch, Advait Bhat, Daniel Buschek, Lior Zalmanson, and Mor Naaman. 2022. Interacting with opinionated language models changes users' views.

Hyunwoo Kim, Jack Hessel, Liwei Jiang, Ximing Lu, Youngjae Yu, Pei Zhou, Ronan Le Bras, Malihe Alikhani, Gunhee Kim, Maarten Sap, and Yejin Choi. 2022. Soda: Million-scale dialogue distillation with social commonsense contextualization. *CoRR*, abs/2212.10465.

Julia Kreutzer, Stefan Riezler, and Carolin Lawrence. 2021. Offline reinforcement learning from human feedback in real-world sequence-to-sequence tasks. In *Proceedings of the 5th Workshop on Structured Prediction for NLP (SPNLP 2021)*, pages 37–43, Online. Association for Computational Linguistics.

Pavel Kucherbaev, Alessandro Bozzon, and Geert-Jan Houben. 2018. Human-aided bots. *IEEE Internet Computing*, 22(6):36–43.

Jack Lanchantin, Sainbayar Sukhbaatar, Gabriel Synnaeve, Yuxuan Sun, Kavya Srinet, and Arthur Szlam. 2023. A data source for reasoning embodied agents. In *Proceedings of the AAAI Conference on Artificial Intelligence*, volume 37, pages 8438–8446.

Bruno Latour. 1987. *Science in action: How to follow scientists and engineers through society*. Harvard university press.

John Law, WE Bijker, Thomas P Hughes, and Trevor Pinch. 2012. Technology and heterogeneous engineering: The case of portuguese expansion. *The social construction of technological systems: New directions in the sociology and history of technology*, 1:105–128.

Brian Lester, Rami Al-Rfou, and Noah Constant. 2021. The power of scale for parameter-efficient prompt tuning. In *Proceedings of the 2021 Conference on Empirical Methods in Natural Language Processing*, pages 3045–3059, Online and Punta Cana, Dominican Republic. Association for Computational Linguistics.

Xiang Lisa Li and Percy Liang. 2021. Prefix-tuning: Optimizing continuous prompts for generation. In *Proceedings of the 59th Annual Meeting of the Association for Computational Linguistics and the 11th International Joint Conference on Natural Language Processing (Volume 1: Long Papers)*, pages 4582–4597, Online. Association for Computational Linguistics.

David Lindner and Mennatallah El-Assady. 2022. Humans are not boltzmann distributions: Challenges and opportunities for modelling human feedback and interaction in reinforcement learning. *arXiv preprint arXiv:2206.13316*.

Pengfei Liu, Weizhe Yuan, Jinlan Fu, Zhengbao Jiang, Hiroaki Hayashi, and Graham Neubig. 2022. Pre-train, prompt, and predict: A systematic survey of prompting methods in natural language processing. *ACM Computing Surveys*.

Ming-te Lu. 2001. Digital divide in developing countries.

Li Lucy and David Bamman. 2021. Gender and representation bias in GPT-3 generated stories. In *Proceedings of the Third Workshop on Narrative Understanding*, pages 48–55, Virtual. Association for Computational Linguistics.

James Manyika. 2023. An overview of bard: an early experiment with generative ai. *AI. Google Static Documents.*

Stephen Marche. 2022. The college essay is dead.

Kris McGuffie and Alex Newhouse. 2020. The radicalization risks of gpt-3 and advanced neural language models.

Margaret Mitchell, Simone Wu, Andrew Zaldivar, Parker Barnes, Lucy Vasserman, Ben Hutchinson, Elena Spitzer, Inioluwa Deborah Raji, and Timnit Gebru. 2019. Model cards for model reporting. In *Proceedings of the Conference on Fairness, Accountability, and Transparency*, FAT* '19, page 220–229, New York, NY, USA. Association for Computing Machinery.

Fabio Motoki, Valdemar Pinho Neto, and Victor Rodrigues. 2023. More human than human: Measuring chatgpt political bias. *Public Choice*, pages 1–21.

Alexis Newton and Kaustubh Dhole. 2023. Is ai art another industrial revolution in the making? *AAAI 2023, Creative AI Across Modalities.*

Tri Nguyen, Mir Rosenberg, Xia Song, Jianfeng Gao, Saurabh Tiwary, Rangan Majumder, and Li Deng. 2016. Ms marco: A human-generated machine reading comprehension dataset.

OpenAI. 2022. Chatgpt: Optimizing language models for dialogue.

OpenAI. 2023. Gpt-4 technical report.

Long Ouyang, Jeffrey Wu, Xu Jiang, Diogo Almeida, Carroll Wainwright, Pamela Mishkin, Chong Zhang, Sandhini Agarwal, Katarina Slama, Alex Ray, et al. 2022. Training language models to follow instructions with human feedback. *Advances in Neural Information Processing Systems*, 35:27730–27744.

Orestis Papakyriakopoulos, Anna Seo Gyeong Choi, William Thong, Dora Zhao, Jerone Andrews, Rebecca Bourke, Alice Xiang, and Allison Koenecke. 2023. Augmented datasheets for speech datasets and ethical decision-making. In *Proceedings of the 2023 ACM Conference on Fairness, Accountability, and Transparency*, FAccT '23, page 881–904, New York, NY, USA. Association for Computing Machinery.

Fabio Petroni, Tim Rocktäschel, Sebastian Riedel, Patrick Lewis, Anton Bakhtin, Yuxiang Wu, and Alexander Miller. 2019. Language models as knowledge bases? In *Proceedings of the 2019 Conference on Empirical Methods in Natural Language Processing and the 9th International Joint Conference on Natural Language Processing (EMNLP-IJCNLP)*, pages 2463–2473, Hong Kong, China. Association for Computational Linguistics.

Pranav Rajpurkar, Jian Zhang, Konstantin Lopyrev, and Percy Liang. 2016. SQuAD: 100,000+ questions for machine comprehension of text. In *Proceedings of the 2016 Conference on Empirical Methods in Natural Language Processing*, pages 2383–2392, Austin, Texas. Association for Computational Linguistics.

Dillon Reisman, Jason Schultz, Kate Crawford, and Meredith Whittaker. 2018. Algorithmic impact assessments: A practical framework for public agency. *AI Now.*

Keisuke Sakaguchi, Ronan Le Bras, Chandra Bhagavatula, and Yejin Choi. 2021. Winogrande: An adversarial winograd schema challenge at scale. *Communications of the ACM*, 64(9):99–106.

Shibani Santurkar, Esin Durmus, Faisal Ladhak, Cinoo Lee, Percy Liang, and Tatsunori Hashimoto. 2023. Whose opinions do language models reflect? *arXiv preprint arXiv:2303.17548.*

Teven Le Scao, Angela Fan, Christopher Akiki, Ellie Pavlick, Suzana Ilić, Daniel Hesslow, Roman Castagné, Alexandra Sasha Luccioni, François Yvon, Matthias Gallé, et al. 2022. Bloom: A 176b-parameter open-access multilingual language model. *arXiv preprint arXiv:2211.05100.*

Daniel Schwarcz and Jonathan H Choi. 2023. Ai tools for lawyers: A practical guide. *Available at SSRN.*

Andrew D Selbst. 2017. Disparate impact in big data policing. *Ga. L. Rev.*, 52:109.

Andrew D Selbst, Danah Boyd, Sorelle A Friedler, Suresh Venkatasubramanian, and Janet Vertesi. 2019. Fairness and abstraction in sociotechnical systems. In *Proceedings of the conference on fairness, accountability, and transparency*, pages 59–68.

Ali Akbar Septiandri, Marios Constantinides, Mohammad Tahaei, and Daniele Quercia. 2023. Weird faccts: How western, educated, industrialized, rich, and democratic is facct? In *Proceedings of the 2023 ACM Conference on Fairness, Accountability, and Transparency*, FAccT '23, page 160–171, New York, NY, USA. Association for Computing Machinery.

Ashish Shrivastava, Kaustubh Dhole, Abhinav Bhatt, and Sharvani Raghunath. 2021. Saying No is An Art: Contextualized Fallback Responses for Unanswerable Dialogue Queries. In *Proceedings of the 59th Annual Meeting of the Association for Computational Linguistics and the 11th International Joint Conference on Natural Language Processing (Volume 2: Short Papers)*, pages 87–92, Online. Association for Computational Linguistics.

Kurt Shuster, Jing Xu, Mojtaba Komeili, Da Ju, Eric Michael Smith, Stephen Roller, Megan Ung, Moya Chen, Kushal Arora, Joshua Lane, et al. 2022. Blenderbot 3: a deployed conversational agent that continually learns to responsibly engage. *arXiv preprint arXiv:2208.03188.*

Alexander Soen, Ibrahim Alabdulmohsin, Oluwasanmi O Koyejo, Yishay Mansour, Nyalleng Moorosi, Richard Nock, Ke Sun, and Lexing Xie. 2022. Fair wrapping for black-box predictions. In *Advances in Neural Information Processing Systems.*

Aarohi Srivastava, Abhinav Rastogi, Abhishek Rao, Abu Awal Md Shoeb, Abubakar Abid, Adam Fisch, Adam R Brown, Adam Santoro, Aditya Gupta, Adria Garriga-Alonso, et al. 2022. Beyond the imitation game: Quantifying and extrapolating the capabilities of language models.

Aarohi Srivastava, Abhinav Rastogi, Abhishek Rao, Abu Awal Md Shoeb, Abubakar Abid, Adam Fisch, Adam R. Brown, Adam Santoro, Aditya Gupta, Adrià Garriga-Alonso, Agnieszka Kluska, Aitor Lewkowycz, Akshat Agarwal, Alethea Power, Alex Ray, Alex Warstadt, Alexander W. Kocurek, Ali Safaya, Ali Tazarv, Alice Xiang, Alicia Parrish, Allen Nie, Aman Hussain, Amanda Askell,

Amanda Dsouza, Ambrose Slone, Ameet Rahane, Anantharaman S. Iyer, Anders Andreassen, Andrea Madotto, Andrea Santilli, Andreas Stuhlmüller, Andrew Dai, Andrew La, Andrew Lampinen, Andy Zou, Angela Jiang, Angelica Chen, Anh Vuong, Animesh Gupta, Anna Gottardi, Antonio Norelli, Anu Venkatesh, Arash Gholamidavoodi, Arfa Tabassum, Arul Menezes, Arun Kirubarajan, Asher Mullokandov, Ashish Sabharwal, Austin Herrick, Avia Efrat, Aykut Erdem, Ayla Karakaş, B. Ryan Roberts, Bao Sheng Loe, Barret Zoph, Bartłomiej Bojanowski, Batuhan Özyurt, Behnam Hedayatnia, Behnam Neyshabur, Benjamin Inden, Benno Stein, Berk Ekmekci, Bill Yuchen Lin, Blake Howald, Bryan Orinion, Cameron Diao, Cameron Dour, Catherine Stinson, Cedrick Argueta, César Ferri Ramírez, Chandan Singh, Charles Rathkopf, Chenlin Meng, Chitta Baral, Chiyu Wu, Chris Callison-Burch, Chris Waites, Christian Voigt, Christopher D. Manning, Christopher Potts, Cindy Ramirez, Clara E. Rivera, Clemencia Siro, Colin Raffel, Courtney Ashcraft, Cristina Garbacea, Damien Sileo, Dan Garrette, Dan Hendrycks, Dan Kilman, Dan Roth, Daniel Freeman, Daniel Khashabi, Daniel Levy, Daniel Moseguí González, Danielle Perszyk, Danny Hernandez, Danqi Chen, Daphne Ippolito, Dar Gilboa, David Dohan, David Drakard, David Jurgens, Debajyoti Datta, Deep Ganguli, Denis Emelin, Denis Kleyko, Deniz Yuret, Derek Chen, Derek Tam, Dieuwke Hupkes, Diganta Misra, Dilyar Buzan, Dimitri Coelho Mollo, Diyi Yang, Dong-Ho Lee, Dylan Schrader, Ekaterina Shutova, Ekin Dogus Cubuk, Elad Segal, Eleanor Hagerman, Elizabeth Barnes, Elizabeth Donoway, Ellie Pavlick, Emanuele Rodola, Emma Lam, Eric Chu, Eric Tang, Erkut Erdem, Ernie Chang, Ethan A. Chi, Ethan Dyer, Ethan Jerzak, Ethan Kim, Eunice Engefu Manyasi, Evgenii Zheltonozhskii, Fanyue Xia, Fatemeh Siar, Fernando Martínez-Plumed, Francesca Happé, Francois Chollet, Frieda Rong, Gaurav Mishra, Genta Indra Winata, Gerard de Melo, Germán Kruszewski, Giambattista Parascandolo, Giorgio Mariani, Gloria Wang, Gonzalo Jaimovitch-López, Gregor Betz, Guy Gur-Ari, Hana Galijasevic, Hannah Kim, Hannah Rashkin, Hannaneh Hajishirzi, Harsh Mehta, Hayden Bogar, Henry Shevlin, Hinrich Schütze, Hiromu Yakura, Hongming Zhang, Hugh Mee Wong, Ian Ng, Isaac Noble, Jaap Jumelet, Jack Geissinger, Jackson Kernion, Jacob Hilton, Jaehoon Lee, Jaime Fernández Fisac, James B. Simon, James Koppel, James Zheng, James Zou, Jan Kocoń, Jana Thompson, Janelle Wingfield, Jared Kaplan, Jarema Radom, Jascha Sohl-Dickstein, Jason Phang, Jason Wei, Jason Yosinski, Jekaterina Novikova, Jelle Bosscher, Jennifer Marsh, Jeremy Kim, Jeroen Taal, Jesse Engel, Jesujoba Alabi, Jiacheng Xu, Jiaming Song, Jillian Tang, Joan Waweru, John Burden, John Miller, John U. Balis, Jonathan Batchelder, Jonathan Berant, Jörg Frohberg, Jos Rozen, Jose Hernandez-Orallo, Joseph Boudeman, Joseph Guerr, Joseph Jones, Joshua B. Tenenbaum, Joshua S. Rule, Joyce Chua, Kamil Kanclerz, Karen Livescu, Karl Krauth, Karthik Gopalakrishnan, Katerina Ignatyeva, Katja Markert, Kaustubh D. Dhole, Kevin Gimpel, Kevin Omondi, Kory Mathewson, Kristen Chiafullo, Ksenia Shkaruta, Kumar Shridhar, Kyle McDonell, Kyle Richardson, Laria Reynolds, Leo Gao, Li Zhang, Liam Dugan, Lianhui Qin, Lidia Contreras-Ochando, Louis-Philippe Morency, Luca Moschella, Lucas Lam, Lucy Noble, Ludwig Schmidt, Luheng He, Luis Oliveros Colón, Luke Metz, Lütfi Kerem Şenel, Maarten Bosma, Maarten Sap, Maartje ter Hoeve, Maheen Farooqi, Manaal Faruqui, Mantas Mazeika, Marco Baturan, Marco Marelli, Marco Maru, Maria Jose Ramírez Quintana, Marie Tolkiehn, Mario Giulianelli, Martha Lewis, Martin Potthast, Matthew L. Leavitt, Matthias Hagen, Mátyás Schubert, Medina Orduna Baitemirova, Melody Arnaud, Melvin McElrath, Michael A. Yee, Michael Cohen, Michael Gu, Michael Ivanitskiy, Michael Starritt, Michael Strube, Michał Swędrowski, Michele Bevilacqua, Michihiro Yasunaga, Mihir Kale, Mike Cain, Mimee Xu, Mirac Suzgun, Mitch Walker, Mo Tiwari, Mohit Bansal, Moin Aminnaseri, Mor Geva, Mozhdeh Gheini, Mukund Varma T, Nanyun Peng, Nathan A. Chi, Nayeon Lee, Neta Gur-Ari Krakover, Nicholas Cameron, Nicholas Roberts, Nick Doiron, Nicole Martinez, Nikita Nangia, Niklas Deckers, Niklas Muennighoff, Nitish Shirish Keskar, Niveditha S. Iyer, Noah Constant, Noah Fiedel, Nuan Wen, Oliver Zhang, Omar Agha, Omar Elbaghdadi, Omer Levy, Owain Evans, Pablo Antonio Moreno Casares, Parth Doshi, Pascale Fung, Paul Pu Liang, Paul Vicol, Pegah Alipoormolabashi, Peiyuan Liao, Percy Liang, Peter Chang, Peter Eckersley, Phu Mon Htut, Pinyu Hwang, Piotr Miłkowski, Piyush Patil, Pouya Pezeshkpour, Priti Oli, Qiaozhu Mei, Qing Lyu, Qinlang Chen, Rabin Banjade, Rachel Etta Rudolph, Raefer Gabriel, Rahel Habacker, Ramon Risco, Raphaël Millière, Rhythm Garg, Richard Barnes, Rif A. Saurous, Riku Arakawa, Robbe Raymaekers, Robert Frank, Rohan Sikand, Roman Novak, Roman Sitelew, Ronan LeBras, Rosanne Liu, Rowan Jacobs, Rui Zhang, Ruslan Salakhutdinov, Ryan Chi, Ryan Lee, Ryan Stovall, Ryan Teehan, Rylan Yang, Sahib Singh, Saif M. Mohammad, Sajant Anand, Sam Dillavou, Sam Shleifer, Sam Wiseman, Samuel Gruetter, Samuel R. Bowman, Samuel S. Schoenholz, Sanghyun Han, Sanjeev Kwatra, Sarah A. Rous, Sarik Ghazarian, Sayan Ghosh, Sean Casey, Sebastian Bischoff, Sebastian Gehrmann, Sebastian Schuster, Sepideh Sadeghi, Shadi Hamdan, Sharon Zhou, Shashank Srivastava, Sherry Shi, Shikhar Singh, Shima Asaadi, Shixiang Shane Gu, Shubh Pachchigar, Shubham Toshniwal, Shyam Upadhyay, Shyamolima, Debnath, Siamak Shakeri, Simon Thormeyer, Simone Melzi, Siva Reddy, Sneha Priscilla Makini, Soo-Hwan Lee, Spencer Torene, Sriharsha Hatwar, Stanislas Dehaene, Stefan Divic, Stefano Ermon, Stella Biderman, Stephanie Lin, Stephen Prasad, Steven T. Piantadosi, Stuart M. Shieber, Summer Misherghi, Svetlana Kiritchenko, Swaroop Mishra, Tal Linzen, Tal Schuster, Tao Li, Tao Yu, Tariq Ali, Tatsu Hashimoto, Te-Lin Wu, Théo Desbordes, Theodore Rothschild, Thomas Phan, Tianle Wang, Tiberius Nkinyili, Timo Schick, Timofei Kornev, Titus Tunduny, Tobias Gerstenberg, Trenton Chang, Trishala Neeraj, Tushar Khot, Tyler Shultz, Uri Shaham, Vedant Misra, Vera Demberg, Victoria Nyamai, Vikas Raunak, Vinay Ramasesh, Vinay Uday Prabhu, Vishakh Padmakumar, Vivek Srikumar, William Fedus, William Saunders, William Zhang, Wout Vossen, Xiang Ren, Xiaoyu Tong, Xinran Zhao, Xinyi Wu, Xudong Shen, Yadollah Yaghoobzadeh, Yair Lakretz, Yangqiu Song, Yasaman Bahri, Yejin Choi, Yichi Yang, Yiding Hao, Yifu Chen, Yonatan Belinkov, Yu Hou, Yufang Hou, Yuntao Bai, Zachary Seid, Zhuoye Zhao, Zijian Wang, Zijie J. Wang, Zirui Wang, and Ziyi Wu. 2023. Beyond the imitation game: Quantifying and extrapolating the capabilities of language models.

Nisan Stiennon, Long Ouyang, Jeffrey Wu, Daniel Ziegler, Ryan Lowe, Chelsea Voss, Alec Radford, Dario Amodei, and Paul F Christiano. 2020. Learning to summarize with human feedback. *Advances in Neural Information Processing Systems*, 33:3008–3021.

Julia Stoyanovich and Bill Howe. 2019. Nutritional labels for data and models. *A Quarterly bulletin of the Com-*

puter Society of the IEEE Technical Committee on Data Engineering, 42(3).

Paul Thomas, Seth Spielman, Nick Craswell, and Bhaskar Mitra. 2023. Large language models can accurately predict searcher preferences.

Hugo Touvron, Louis Martin, Kevin Stone, Peter Albert, Amjad Almahairi, Yasmine Babaei, Nikolay Bashlykov, Soumya Batra, Prajjwal Bhargava, Shruti Bhosale, Dan Bikel, Lukas Blecher, Cristian Canton Ferrer, Moya Chen, Guillem Cucurull, David Esiobu, Jude Fernandes, Jeremy Fu, Wenyin Fu, Brian Fuller, Cynthia Gao, Vedanuj Goswami, Naman Goyal, Anthony Hartshorn, Saghar Hosseini, Rui Hou, Hakan Inan, Marcin Kardas, Viktor Kerkez, Madian Khabsa, Isabel Kloumann, Artem Korenev, Punit Singh Koura, Marie-Anne Lachaux, Thibaut Lavril, Jenya Lee, Diana Liskovich, Yinghai Lu, Yuning Mao, Xavier Martinet, Todor Mihaylov, Pushkar Mishra, Igor Molybog, Yixin Nie, Andrew Poulton, Jeremy Reizenstein, Rashi Rungta, Kalyan Saladi, Alan Schelten, Ruan Silva, Eric Michael Smith, Ranjan Subramanian, Xiaoqing Ellen Tan, Binh Tang, Ross Taylor, Adina Williams, Jian Xiang Kuan, Puxin Xu, Zheng Yan, Iliyan Zarov, Yuchen Zhang, Angela Fan, Melanie Kambadur, Sharan Narang, Aurelien Rodriguez, Robert Stojnic, Sergey Edunov, and Thomas Scialom. 2023. Llama 2: Open foundation and fine-tuned chat models.

Ashish Vaswani, Noam Shazeer, Niki Parmar, Jakob Uszkoreit, Llion Jones, Aidan N Gomez, Łukasz Kaiser, and Illia Polosukhin. 2017. Attention is all you need. *Advances in neural information processing systems*, 30.

Alex Wang, Amanpreet Singh, Julian Michael, Felix Hill, Omer Levy, and Samuel Bowman. 2018. Glue: A multi-task benchmark and analysis platform for natural language understanding. In *Proceedings of the 2018 EMNLP Workshop BlackboxNLP: Analyzing and Interpreting Neural Networks for NLP*, pages 353–355.

Zhen Wang, Rameswar Panda, Leonid Karlinsky, Rogerio Feris, Huan Sun, and Yoon Kim. 2022. Multitask prompt tuning enables parameter-efficient transfer learning. In *The Eleventh International Conference on Learning Representations*.

Zijie J. Wang, Dongjin Choi, Shenyu Xu, and Diyi Yang. 2021. Putting humans in the natural language processing loop: A survey. In *Proceedings of the First Workshop on Bridging Human–Computer Interaction and Natural Language Processing*, pages 47–52, Online. Association for Computational Linguistics.

Alice Xiang and Inioluwa Deborah Raji. 2019. On the legal compatibility of fairness definitions. *arXiv preprint arXiv:1912.00761*.

Ke Yang, Julia Stoyanovich, Abolfazl Asudeh, Bill Howe, HV Jagadish, and Gerome Miklau. 2018. A nutritional label for rankings. In *Proceedings of the 2018 international conference on management of data*, pages 1773–1776.

Zhiling Zhang and Kenny Zhu. 2021. Diverse and specific clarification question generation with keywords. In *Proceedings of the Web Conference 2021*, WWW '21, page 3501–3511, New York, NY, USA. Association for Computing Machinery.

Zihao Zhao, Eric Wallace, Shi Feng, Dan Klein, and Sameer Singh. 2021. Calibrate before use: Improving few-shot performance of language models. In *International Conference on Machine Learning*, pages 12697–12706. PMLR.

Towards Low-resource Language Generation with Limited Supervision

Kaushal Kumar Maurya **Maunendra Sankar Desarkar**
Natural Language and Information Processing Lab (NLIP)
Indian Institute of Technology Hyderabad,
Hyderabad, India
cs18resch11003@iith.ac.in & maunendra@cse.iith.ac.in

Abstract

We present a research narrative aimed at enabling language technology for multiple natural language generation (NLG) tasks in low-resource languages (LRLs). With approximately 7,000 languages spoken globally, many lack the resources required for model training. NLG applications for LRLs present two additional key challenges: (i) The training is more pronounced, and (ii) Zero-shot modeling is a viable research direction for scalability; however, generating zero-shot well-formed text in target LRLs is challenging. Addressing these concerns, this narrative introduces three promising research explorations that serve as a step toward enabling language technology for many LRLs. These approaches make effective use of transfer learning and limited supervision techniques for modeling. Evaluations were conducted mostly in the zero-shot setting, enabling scalability. This research narrative is an ongoing doctoral thesis[1].

1 Introduction

Recently, there has been remarkable progress in natural language processing (NLP) research, primarily due to advancements in large pre-trained language models (PLMs). The global linguistic landscape comprises approximately 7,000 spoken languages worldwide[2]. A notable disparity is evident in NLP research, with the majority of studies conducted on English data (Bender, 2019; Joshi et al., 2020b). This is concerning as the vast majority of the global population — roughly 95% — does not speak English as their primary language, and a staggering 75% do not speak English at all[3]. According to Ruder (2022), out of the 7,000 languages, approximately 400 languages have more than 1 million speakers, and about 1,200 languages have more than 100,000 speakers. Despite this, only around 100 languages are incorporated into large pre-trained models, and limited resources are available for building NLP models for LRLs. Furthermore, a study presented at ACL 2008 (Bender, 2011) revealed that 63% of all papers focused only on English. A more recent study during ACL 2021 (Ruder et al., 2022) concluded that nearly 70% of the papers were evaluated on English. Even a decade later, there has been little change.

The NLP application involving text generation (NLG tasks) in LRLs presents additional challenges in model development: (1) The scarcity of NLG resources for model development in LRLs is more pronounced than other NLP tasks. (2) LRLs often exhibit a long tail, with many lacking annotated data. The preferred solution is zero-shot modeling, though this approach introduces additional challenges for cross-lingual generation tasks. It has been observed that zero-shot generation models frequently encounter issues like catastrophic forgetting (van de Ven et al., 2022) or accidental translation (Xue et al., 2021). Due to these problems, the zero-shot generated text is either code-mixed or not in the intended target language. (3) LRL modeling typically employs a transfer learning setup, where supervision is transferred from HRLs to LRLs. However, performance tends to degrade for LRLs that are different from their HRL and (4) Many LRLs lack monolingual or parallel data, and their representations are absent from PLMs. These LRLs are referred to as Extremely LRLs (ELRLs) or dialects. Despite having millions of speakers, there is a noticeable absence of NLP technology for these ELRLs. This thesis is a step towards addressing these challenges and aims to enable language technology for LRLs, thereby democratizing NLP research for the general population/audience.

Prior to the emergence of transformers-based

[1]From a senior graduate student - the first author of the paper

[2]https://www.ethnologue.com/insights/how-many-languages/

[3]https://www.ethnologue.com/insights/most-spoken-language/

Proceedings of the the Big Picture Workshop, pages 80–92
December 7, 2023 ©2023 Association for Computational Linguistics

PLMs, most works in cross-lingual generation were primarily reliant on machine translation (MT) systems. Existing models either directly employed the MT system within the modeling (Wan et al., 2010; Shen et al., 2018) or generate training data using MT (Kumar et al., 2019; Chi et al., 2020) to develop models. This dependence on MT not only limits scalability but also propagate error with translation. To address these limitations, multilingual PLMs (mPLMs) have emerged (Zhao et al., 2023), where a large set of languages share a common latent representation space. The cross-lingual models built on top of these mPLMs lead to the remarkable advancement (Hu et al., 2020; Artetxe et al., 2020) in the cross-lingual transfer in zero-shot or few-shot settings. However, most of these advancements are limited to NLU tasks. Furthermore, existing cross-lingual NLG models incorporate one or more challenges mentioned above.

With this thesis, our contributions are as follows:

1. We proposed ZmBART framework (Maurya et al., 2021) to mitigate the catastrophic forgetting and accidental translation issues and enable well-formed zero-shot text generation in LRLs. We evaluated the model's performance across 18 task-setup combinations, including four NLG tasks in three typologically diverse languages.

2. We proposed the first meta-learning approach for cross-lingual generation in LRLs (MetaX$_{\text{NLG}}$; Maurya and Desarkar (2022)). It is based on language clustering to improve the cross-lingual transfer, even for distant LRLs. The model is evaluated across 30 languages, two tasks, and five datasets.

3. We proposed a character span noise augmentation-based model (CHARSPAN; Maurya et al. (2023)) to enable machine translation for closely related HRLs and ELRLs/dialects. It leverages surface-level lexical similarity and uses noise augmentation as a regularization technique to enable zero-shot translation. The model's performance was evaluated across 12 ELRLs from three typologically diverse language groups.

2 The Big Picture

In this section, we provide high-level details of the proposed models. This also includes insights into how we build more recent proposed models based on earlier models and advance the field. Then, we look back and position our research efforts by contextualizing a broader spectrum of multilingual research, specifically for low-resource language generation. Finally, we list our learnings from failed and successful modeling.

2.1 Thesis Overview: Connecting the Dots

Overall, our research contribution includes the development of ZmBART, MetaX$_{\text{NLG}}$, and CHARSPAN models for NLG tasks in LRLs. The primary focus is to extend the English NLG models to LRLs through cross-lingual transfer and generation. These models are developed and evaluated in a zero-shot setting, increasing language coverage. Typical cross-lingual modeling includes fine-tuning multilingual PLMs with the task-specific high-resource English language and learned supervision for transfer to LRLs (referred to as cross-lingual transfer). Then, evaluate the model with a zero-shot setting for target LRLs. In NLG, there are two challenges: mitigation of the CF/AT problem in zero-shot text generation and improvement of cross-lingual transfer. The effort with the ZmBART model mitigates the CF/AT issue and produces well-formed zero-shot generation in LRLs. MetaX$_{\text{NLG}}$builds on top of the ZmBART model and proposes a novel approach to improve cross-lingual transfer, leading to better performance. Finally, with the CHARSPAN model, we design another approach to enhance cross-lingual transfer. This effort scales the coverage to languages with very limited linguistic resources (i.e., ELRLs) and is similar to some HRLs. In summary, with these collective efforts, we advance research in low-resource language generation by mitigating CF/AT, improving cross-lingual transfer, and increasing language coverage to ELRLs.

2.2 Position of the Thesis: Related Work

The research presented in this narrative spans the past few years, during which multilingual Pre-trained Language Models (PLMs) emerged. However, there have been limited concurrent efforts in the field of low-resource language generation. Before the ZmBART model, most research in this area primarily relied on MT (Wan et al., 2010; Shen et al., 2018), parallel (Chi et al., 2020) or task-specific data for LRLs (Kumar et al., 2019), and did not utilize multilingual PLMs. Few attempts were made using Adapter-based models (Houlsby et al., 2019; Pfeiffer et al., 2021), but they were often limited to MT tasks and may not have zero-shot capabilities. After ZmBART, (1)Vu et al. (2022) presented the alternate method with prompt tuning and compared it to the ZmBART, (2) Li and Murray (2023) proposed a model based on regularization techniques and (3) Pfeiffer et al. (2023) introduced a method for disentangling language-specific information from language-agnostic information. These models mitigate the CF/AT problems and implicitly help improve the cross-lingual transfer. However, their performance gains were limited compared to $\text{MetaX}_{\text{NLG}}$which explicitly leverages meta-learning. Furthermore, there are state-of-the-art (SOTA) approaches (Aepli and Sennrich, 2022; Provilkov et al., 2020; Patil et al., 2022) for enhancing cross-lingual transfer for MT for ELRLs. Our recently proposed CHARSPAN model has outperformed existing models and established it as a new SOTA solution. In summary, there has been progress in low-resource language generation, and our models have either pushed this research space or currently represent the SOTA model in the field.

2.3 Learning from Failures and Successes

With many failed and limited successful experiments, here are our key observations and learning: (1) NLG modeling is challenging in LRLs setup, but evaluations are even more challenging. (2) Effective cross-lingual transfer models consider various knowledge, such as semantics, syntax, tokenization, lexical details, typology, and demographics. (3) Better modeling can extend the existing multilingual PLMs capabilities beyond the languages they are trained and (4) Promising research directions to increase language technology coverage are multi-task and adaptive learning among others.

3 Mitigating Catastrophic Forgetting to Enable Zero-shot Language Generation

Our research mission to enable language technology for NLG tasks in LRLs started with ZmBART (Maurya et al., 2021) work. ZmBART is an unsupervised cross-lingual transfer and generation framework that focuses on generative tasks for LRLs in zero-shot and few-shot settings. A typical zero-shot cross-lingual generation modeling involves two main steps: (1) *Training with HRLs:* Train (fine-tune) a model (PLM) using a large annotated dataset from HRLs, typically English. For instance, training with English Abstractive Text Summarization (ATS) dataset. (2) *Zero-shot generation in LRLs:* Utilize the trained model for zero-shot inference. For instance, when given input in an LRL (e.g., Hindi), the model generates a summary in the same LRL (Hindi). Unlike natural language understanding (NLU) tasks, the cross-lingual generation task in zero-shot scenarios is particularly challenging. This is because the zero-shot generated text needs to be in the target LRL, which generally suffers from Catastrophic Forgetting (CF; van de Ven et al. (2022)) or Accidental Translation (AT; Xue et al. (2021)) problems. Due to this, the model fails to generate text in the target LRL or produce code-mixed output with both high-resource and LRLs. *With this work, our objective is to alleviate CF and AT problems with an unsupervised framework, meaning we do not rely on any parallel or pseudo-parallel/back-translated data.* Instead, we harness multilingual pre-trained checkpoints, specifically the mBART model (Liu et al., 2020), to seamlessly enable the generation of well-formed text in LRLs across multiple generative tasks.

Prior to ZmBART, existing cross-lingual generation models were grounded with either machine translation (MT) or parallel/back-translated datasets. Wan et al. (2010) employed the MT pipeline to facilitate cross-language document summarization. This involves the translation of non-English input into English. Subsequently, the English ATS model was employed to procure the summaries, which were finally translated back into non-English languages. Similar approaches are adapted by Shen et al. (2018) and Duan et al. (2019). This direction is not feasible as MT systems are not available for many LRLs and the imperfect translations propagate errors. Considering this, Kumar et al. (2019) and Chi et al. (2020) use back-translated (need MT system) and parallel datasets to develop the few-shot cross-lingual question and answering (Q&A) and zero-shot cross-lingual ATS, respectively. These approaches require an MT system or annotated dataset which limits the model development to a few HRLs. Unlike these, we propose ZmBART, the first unsupervised scalable model based on mBART specialized for zero-shot cross-lingual transfer and generation. Additionally, we have also created *HiDG*[4], a high-quality distractor generation dataset in the Hindi language.

[4]Dataset and code are available here: https://github.com/kaushal0494/ZmBART

3.1 Methodology

In ZmBART, we mitigate Catastrophic Forgetting and Accidental Translation problems by adapting three key modeling modifications, details are presented below:

3.1.1 Unsupervised Auxiliary Task

The mBART model is pre-trained with denoising objectives (masking and sentence permutation) with datasets from 25 languages that encode multilingual latent representation. This can not be used directly for cross-lingual generation because the model is trained with denoising objectives that do not directly follow auto-regressive decoding, thereby causing a mismatch between pretraining and fine-tuning objectives (Chi et al., 2020; Devlin et al., 2019). Considering this, the auxiliary task is formulated with the following objectives: (1) should only utilize monolingual data for selected languages, (2) should enhance the latent representation space for selected languages, (3) maintain close proximity between the auxiliary task objective and NLG tasks and (4) aid in mitigating CF/AT issues. Moreover, the auxiliary task serves as an adaptive pre-training step, facilitating *better warm-start* of the mBART model for downstream natural language generation (NLG) tasks. With these, we have proposed the following auxiliary task: *Given an input passage, generate a few random sentences (called rand-summary) derived from the passage.* Concretely, we take passages with 5-25 sentences as input and 20% of the sentences randomly (1-5 sentences) as the target. We concatenate monolingual datasets for selected languages and fine-tune the mBART model (adaptive training) with this auxiliary task to obtain the ZmBART model.

3.1.2 Freezing Model Components

During supervised training - fine-tuning ZmBART with task-specific HRL data - we freeze all word embeddings and the parameters of the decoder layers. This approach is adapted to ensure that the ZmBART's context and latent space are not overwritten during supervised training.

3.1.3 Adding Language Tag

We have made modifications to the language tag of the mBART model for the cross-lingual generation framework. We concatenate `<fxx><2xx>` tag in the source side of the training data, where <xx> is the ISO-2 language code. The language tag act as a flag to trigger the zero-shot generation in target <xx> languages.

The ablation study provides evidence that all three components are necessary to effectively mitigate CF/AT problems and enable structured text generation in a zero-shot setting.

3.1.4 Model Training and Generation

We consider four tasks: Question Generation (QG), News Headline Generation (NHG), Abstractive Text Summarization (ATS), and Distractor Generation (DG), in three typologically diverse languages. The HRL is English (en), and the LRLs are Hindi (hi) and Japanese (ja). First, the mBART model undergoes adaptive pre-training with the auxiliary task to obtain the ZmBART model. Then for each NLG task, the ZmBART model is then fine-tuned using the task-specific HRLs data while freezing model components to obtain a task-specific fine-tuned model. This model is used for zero-shot or few-shot (1000 examples) generation in LRLs.

3.2 Experimental Setup and Results

News Passage: दक्षिण कश्मीर के पुलवामा जिले में सुरक्षा बलों के साथ जारी मुठभेड़ में शुक्रवार को एक आतंकवादी ढेर हो गया.पुलिस के एक प्रवक्ता ने बताया कि इस मुठभेड़ में एक आतंकवादी मारा गया है. यह मुठभेड़ अभी जारी है.प्रवक्ता ने बताया कि पुलवामा के चन्दगाम में आज सुबह सुरक्षा बलों और छिपे हुए आतंकवादियों के बीच मुठभेड़ शुरू हो गई।माना जा रहा है कि गांव में लश्कर-ए-तैयबा के दो आतंकवादी छिपे हुए हैं।

(Translation: A militant was killed on Friday in an ongoing encounter with security forces in Pulwama district of eroded Kashmir. A police spokesman said a militant was killed in the encounter. The encounter is still going on, the spokesperson said, adding that an encounter between security forces and hidden militants started this morning at Chandgam in Pulwama. Two LeT militants are believed to be hiding in the village.)

Headline (ground truth): कश्मीर के पुलवामा में मुठभेड़, एक आतंकी ढेर
(Translation: Encounter in Pulwama, Kashmir, a terrorist killed)

Headline (zero-shot generated output:) पुलवामा में जारी मुठभेड़ में एक आतंकवादी ढेर
(Translation. A terrorist killed in ongoing encounter in Pulwama.)

Figure 1: Zero-shot news headline generation from ZmBART in the Hindi language

We have considered three strong baseline models: MT-Pipeline, ZmBART with Masking Auxiliary Task (MAT), and a model inspired by Chi et al. (2020). In total, we conducted experiments across 18 task-setup combinations. The proposed models and baseline models underwent evaluation using three automated evaluation metrics (BLEU, ROUGE-L, and BERTScore) and four manual evaluation metrics (Fluency, Relatedness, Correctness, and Distractibility). The detailed results are presented in (Maurya et al., 2021). Here, we provide a summary of the major results and observations: (1) The ZmBART model consistently outperformed all baseline models across tasks, LRLs, and automated metrics in the zero-shot setting. The few-shot training further boosts the performance. (2) Human evaluation scores exhibited a correlation with automated scores, reinforcing the reliability of the evaluation process. (3) Among the baselines, the MAT baseline demonstrated superiority, highlighting the importance of an auxiliary task in enriching and mitigating CF/AT problems. However, our proposed auxiliary task exhibited even better results. (4) An ablation study was conducted, indicating that different modeling components (auxiliary task, language tag, and freezing different model components) are necessary to ensure effective zero-shot text generation. A sample generation example is presented in Fig. 1.

3.3 Insights and Limitations

As the auxiliary task is similar to NHG or ATS tasks, it may appear that the auxiliary task is biased towards these tasks, which leads to better performance. However, the model performs equally well for very different tasks like QG and distractor generation (generating incorrect options for MCQ reading comprehension) which nullifies this assumption. We have not modified any single model parameters for different tasks. We also experimented with different objectives for auxiliary tasks; however, the *rand-summary* task performed best. We explored the multiple continual learning techniques (van de Ven et al., 2022) to mitigate CF; however, freezing model components work best. We observed that several generated questions in zero-shot start with English 'wh-words,' and the first word is code-mixed. This is possibly due to English interrogative sentences often introducing 'wh-words' at the beginning, which may not be the case with Hindi and Japanese. However, the high BERTScore indicates semantic correctness. Furthermore, such code-mixing in human evaluation is somewhat acceptable with Hindi evaluators; however, it is not acceptable with Japanese evaluators, resulting in lower human evaluation scores for the QG task. This is concurrent work with the adapter-based models (Houlsby et al., 2019; Pfeiffer et al., 2021). One limitation of this work is the adaption of the new language may require re-training.

4 Meta-Learning Approach to Improve Zero-shot Language Generation

The effort with the ZmBART helps in effectively mitigating CT/AT problems and generating zero-shot outputs in target LRLs seamlessly. In this work, we leverage these findings and extend the study to improve the cross-lingual supervised signals to boost the performance for zero-shot generation.

There are more than 7000 languages across the globe. 95% of the world's population does not speak English as their first language and 75% does not speak English at all[5]. However, the majority of NLP research is focused on the English language (Bender, 2019; Joshi et al., 2020b). To democratize the NLP research for the benefit of the large global community, it is essential to focus on non-English languages. Recently, cross-lingual transfer learning (Hu et al., 2020; Artetxe et al., 2020) has emerged as a promising research direction where a model is trained on HRL(s) and *transfer supervision* to LRL(s). However, the supervision transfer is uneven across languages, which leads to large performance gaps. Such performance gaps are observed because models do not account for cultural and linguistic differences in the modeling (Lai et al., 2019; Blasi et al., 2022). This work was a step towards bridging this performance gap.

Meta-learning or *learning to learn* (Bengio et al., 1990) has emerged as an active research direction to learn *shareable structures* across multiple tasks with limited annotated data. The only constraint is all tasks should share some common structure (or come from a task distribution). Different languages in the world follow this constraint as they come into existence with a common goal of communication and share some structure. So, we consider languages as tasks. The meta-learning approach has been actively applied to multiple NLP tasks (Bansal et al., 2020; Gao et al., 2019) including text classification (van der Heijden et al., 2021), NER (Wu et al., 2020), dialogue systems and Q&A (M'hamdi et al., 2021). There were few efforts made in the multilingual setup (Tarunesh et al., 2021; Nooralahzadeh et al., 2020); however, these are limited to machine translation or NLU tasks only. This work - to the best of our knowledge - was the first attempt to study *meta-learning techniques for cross-lingual natural language generation (X_{NLG})*. Particularly, we focus on zero-shot X_{NLG} for low-resource languages. Unlike NLU tasks, the zero-shot NLG is a more challenging setup due to the typological diversities of languages and CF/AT problems. We refer to this framework as MetaX_{NLG}[6] (Maurya and Desarkar, 2022), a framework for effective cross-lingual transfer and generation.

[5] https://www.ethnologue.com/insights/most-spoken-language/

[6] code & pre-trained models link: https://github.com/kaushal0494/Meta_XNLG

eration based on language clustering and Model-Agnostic Meta-Learning (MAML) algorithm (Finn et al., 2017).

Following are the main contributions: (1) We propose a novel MetaX$_{\text{NLG}}$framework based on language clustering and meta-learning to improve zero-shot generation performance for typologically diverse LRLs. (2) We have conducted an extensive empirical evaluation with 30 languages (29 LRLs), covering two tasks (QG and ATS) and using 5 popular datasets (XL-Sum, Wikilingua, MLQA, TyDiQA, and XQuAD).

4.1 Methodology

The MetaX$_{\text{NLG}}$model has two major components: (a) *Language Clustering*, which clusters 30 selected languages into different clusters and obtains the centroid and non-centroid languages for each cluster. (b) *Meta-learning* algorithms are trained with centroid languages and evaluated with non-centroid (target) LRLs in a zero-shot setting. With this setup, our goal is to achieve *Intra-cluster Generalization* and *Inter-cluster Generalization*. Training with a centroid language leads to improved transfer capability within a cluster, and multiple centroid languages extend the transfer capability to other closely-knit clusters, thereby increasing coverage. The overview of MetaX$_{\text{NLG}}$is presented in Fig. 2.

4.1.1 Language Clustering

In MetaX$_{\text{NLG}}$, we considered 30 languages. To represent each language we have extracted a *multi-view* language representation proposed by Oncevay et al. (2020). It was obtained by fusing typologically learned (Littell et al., 2017) from WALS and URIEL databases and task-learned (e.g., language tag from MT; Malaviya et al. (2017)) language representations using singular vector canonical correlation analysis. We use this representation to obtain centroid and non-centroid based on cosine distance. Formally, given a cluster $C = \{L_1, L_2, \dots L_t\}$, where each L_i is multi-view representation of ith language, the centroid language $L^* \in C$ is defined as:

$$L^* = \arg\min_{L_i \in C} \sum_{L_j \in C} d(L_j, L_i).$$

(1) We use d as the cosine distance.

4.1.2 Meta Training and Generation

The framework comprises five training/generation steps:

1. *Selection of Base PLM:* The proposed approach is model-agnostic; however, due to its large LRLs coverage, we have chosen the multilingual T5 (mT5) (Xue et al., 2021) as the base PLM.
2. *Adaptive Unsupervised Pre-training (ZP_M):* We follow steps outlined in ZmBART to obtain ZmT5 model.
3. *Fine-tuning ZP_M with HRL:* To facilitate the transfer of supervision from HRLs to LRLs, we have fine-tuned ZP_M using a task-specific HRL (e.g., English), which we refer to as $EnZP_M$.
4. *Meta-Training with Low-resource Centroid Languages:* A small, task-specific validation dataset of centroid languages was employed to train the $EnZP_M$ model using the MAML algorithm.
5. *Meta-adaptation for Zero-shot Evaluation with Non-Centroid Languages:* Finally, the meta-learned model is directly evaluated using a task-specific test split of the target languages in the zero-shot scenario.

There is a trade-off between the number of clusters (centroid languages) and generalization. If there is a single cluster (a single meta-training language), then the model tries to over-generalize for different typological structures and fails in the attempt. On the other extreme, if there are too many centroid languages (many typologically diverse structures), then the learning possibly gets distracted. In both cases, the model will be unable to learn a reasonable structure (the required generalization) and perform poorly. The MetaX$_{\text{NLG}}$presents a discussion and empirical evidence on this. Our experiments suggest that *three clusters* across considered languages provide the best performance.

4.2 Experimental Setup and Results

We evaluated the MetaX$_{\text{NLG}}$performance in the following settings: ((1) Two NLG tasks - Question

Cluster-1(14)	Cluster-2(8)	Cluster-3(8)
hi,ur,te,tr,ja,fi,ko,gu, bn,mr,np,ta,pa,sw	es,it,pt,ro, nl,de,en,fr	ru,cs,vi,th, zh,id,el,ar

Table 1: Clustering of considered 30 Languages

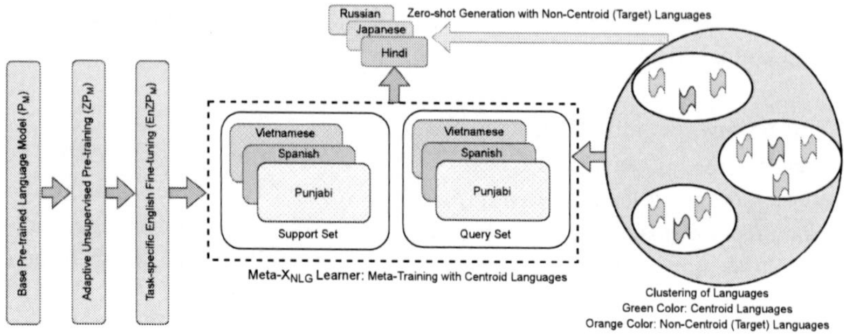

Figure 2: An overview of Meta-X_{NLG} framework

Generation (QG) and Abstractive Text Summarization (ATS). (2) Five widely-used datasets: XL-Sum, Wikilingua, MLQA, XQuAD, and TyDiQA. (3) 30 languages were selected based on diversity typology, including one HRL (English) and 29 LRLs. Refer to Table 1 for the list of selected languages grouped into three clusters. (4) We employ two automated evaluation metrics (BLEU and ROUGE-L) and three human evaluation metrics (Fluency, Relatedness, and Correctness). (5) LRL evaluation in zero-shot setting on the test split. (6) We compare model performance against two strong baselines: (a) A ZmBART-like model using mT5 as the base checkpoint instead of mBART, and (b) a model fine-tuned directly with centroid languages rather than meta-training, ensuring the performance gain is not due to additional training.

Details of all results and observations are included in the MetaX$_{NLG}$original paper (Maurya and Desarkar, 2022). In summary, based on automated scores, the proposed MetaX$_{NLG}$model outperformed baselines in 30 out of 33 LRLs for the ATS task and in 18 out of 19 LRLs for the QG task. Even in cases where it did not perform as well, the difference was marginal. These trends were consistent when considering human evaluation metrics as well, where human scores showed a correlation with automated scores. The MetaX$_{NLG}$demonstrated above-average fluency and correctness scores, indicating its quick adaptation to various syntactical structures and overall improved performance. The consistent improvement for most of the typologically diverse LRLs provides evidence that supervision transfer is more uniform.

4.3 Insights and Limitations

As discussed in Section 4.1.2, there is a trade-off between the number of clusters and generalization capabilities. To ensure that we have selected the correct number of clusters, we have conducted an extensive adaptation study with 36 experimental setups involving different numbers of clusters and various combinations of languages. We observed that the model with three clusters performs the best. From Table 1, we can observe that most of the clustering results are close to the clustering approach with language family - further validating the correctness of clustering. Furthermore, less improvement is observed for Wikilingual data (ATS). This could be due to the nature of Wikilingual input articles, which consist of instructions for operating software tools/packages. Each instruction is crucial, making it challenging to generate an accurate summary in zero-shot LRLs. One limitation, we need small task-specific annotated data for centroid languages, which will be used in the meta-training.

5 Utilizing Lexical Similarity to Enable Zero-Shot MT for Extremely LRLs

The efforts with ZmBART, MetaX$_{NLG}$, and the NLP research community on multilingual modeling have extended the coverage of NLP technologies for many LRLs. However, there is a *long-tail* of languages for which there is no parallel/pseudo-parallel data, no/limited monolingual data, and their representations from the multilingual language model are absent. These fall into categories of *extremely low resource languages (ELRLs)* or *dialects*. With this work (Maurya et al., 2023), we made a step towards enabling technology for ELRLs where resources are limited (zero-shot setting). In particular, our focus was on the machine translation (MT) task, driven by the availability of a true evaluation test set from recently released sources such as FLORES-200 (Costa-jussà et al., 2022).

Fortunately, many of these ELRLs are lexically

HRL (HIN):	इस सीज़न में बीमारी के शुरुआती मामले जुलाई के आखिर में सामने आए थे।
ENG:	The initial cases of the disease this season were reported in late July.
HRL (HIN) + span noise:	ए_ सीज़न म बीमारी के ___ध_ मामले जुलाई के आखिर म सामने आए _।
LRL (BHO):	ए सीजन में ई बीमारी क पहिला मामला जुलाई क आखिर में सामने आ गइल रहले।
LRL (HNE):	ए सीजन म ए बीमारी के पहिला मामला जुलाई के आखिर म सामने आए रहिस।

Figure 3: Hindi (HIN; HRL), Bhojpuri (BHO; LRL) and Chhattisgarhi (HNE; LRL/Dialect) parallel sentences. Additionally, the corresponding noisy Hindi example with character-span noise. BHO and HNE are closely related to Hin.

similar to closely related HRLS. *Lexical similarity refers to languages sharing words with similar form (spelling and pronunciation) and meaning.*[7] This includes cognates, lateral borrowings, and loan words. For example, the word lgtA (*lagta*) in Hindi (HRL) is spelled as lAgatA (*laagata*) in Bhojpuri (LRL). Existing cross-lingual transfer methods based on common embedding spaces work best between related languages (Nguyen and Chiang, 2017; Khemchandani et al., 2021). So, if we make the HRL model robust to spelling variations, it will improve cross-lingual transfer to related ELRLs. To achieve this, we introduce unigram character and character-span noise augmentation approaches, CHARSPAN, to improve generalization in zerosshot. The noise injection acts as a regularizer. A sample example is presented in Fig. 3. Formally, *we look at a machine translation task from an ELRL to another language (English) with transfer enabled by a related HRL on the source side.*

The character-level noise augmentation has been employed to improve the robustness and adversarial testing (Sperber et al., 2017; Vaibhav et al., 2019; Karpukhin et al., 2019) for MT systems. There are general noise augmentation techniques (Sennrich et al., 2016a; Wang et al., 2018) that help in cross-lingual transfer. Aepli and Sennrich (2022) introduced unigram character noise augmentation for NLU tasks such as NER, POS tagging, and topic classification. In contrast, we propose CHARSPAN noise augmentation for the more challenging MT task. There is another line of works that leverages lexical similarity based on vocabulary overlap (Patil et al., 2022), non-deterministic segmentations (Provilkov et al., 2020), and soft decoupled encoding (Wang et al., 2019). While these approaches typically require certain amounts of monolingual data, our proposed model operates without such constraints, eliminating the need for monolingual data. With this work, our key contributions are: (a) we show that unigram character and character-span level noise augmentation can improve zero-shot translation from ELRLs to English. CHARSPAN model outperforms the unigram model. (b) The proposed approach is generalized across three typologically diverse language groups which include 6 HRLs and 12 ELRLs.

5.1 Methodology

5.1.1 Training and Zero-shot Generation

First, we created an augmented parallel corpus from HRL (h) to English (En) as $\hat{\mathcal{D}_{\mathcal{H}}} = \{(\hat{h}, e) | lang(\hat{h}) = \hat{\mathcal{H}}, lang(e) = En\}$, where $\hat{\mathcal{H}} = \eta(\mathcal{H})$ and η is noise function. The input parallel corpus ($\mathcal{D}_{\mathcal{H}}$) was augmented with different kinds of noise (η) in the source HRL side (described later) to create the augmented parallel corpus ($\hat{\mathcal{D}_{\mathcal{H}}}$). We learned the subwords vocabulary $\mathcal{V}$ using ($\hat{\mathcal{D}_{\mathcal{H}}}$). We train the standard encoder-decoder transformer model ($\mathcal{M}$; Vaswani et al. (2017)) from scratch with ($\hat{\mathcal{D}_{\mathcal{H}}}$) and $\mathcal{V}$ to obtain the trained model $\mathcal{M}'$. Finally, zero-shot evaluations are performed with $\mathcal{M}'$ for the source ELR language $\mathcal{L}$ to obtain a target English translation.

5.1.2 Noise Function

We conducted experiments involving two types of noise functions: (1) unigram character noise and (2) character-span noise. For unigram noise, we randomly selected 9-11% of the characters from each source example (excluding punctuation and numbers) and applied insertion, deletion, and replacement operations with equal probabilities[8]. The unigram character noise has the potential to capture limited variations, particularly relevant for very similar languages and dialects. *To address larger lexical divergence, we propose a character-span noising approach, i.e., applying to noise a span of selected characters.* Our particular span noising approach is inspired by SpanBERT (Joshi et al., 2020a).[9] We randomly select 1 to 3-gram character spans with uniform probability and apply span noise until the noise injection budget (ranging from 9-11% of characters) is exhausted. Our approach includes *span deletion* and *span replacement with a single random character*, both with equal probability as the noising operations. In the original paper (Maurya et al., 2023), we conducted various ablation studies involving different combinations of operations, noise budgets, and other parameters.

[7] https://en.wikipedia.org/wiki/Lexical_similarity

[8] We explored some linguistically motivated noising schemes as well, but these did not yield any benefits.

[9] SpanBERT applies denoising to subword tokens while we apply it at the character level.

Based on our findings, we concluded that the proposed setup works best.

5.2 Experimental Setup and Results

We have carefully selected three typologically diverse language groups: Indo-Aryan, Romance, and Malay-Polynesian. We consider 6 HRLs and 12 ELRLs (2 HRLs and several ELRLs from each group). All the ELRLs and dialects are lexically similar to corresponding HRLs. Each group has the same writing script for all languages. For training, we use 13.6, 11, and 0.8 million public, parallel examples for Indo-Aryan, Romance, and Malay-Polynesian, respectively. The model's performance was evaluated on the FLORES-200 devtest set. Based on recent literature in low-resource MT, we compare our approach with Vanilla NMT with BPE segmentation (Sennrich et al., 2016b), methods using lexical similarity (Overlap BPE and BPE-Dropout) and their combinations. In alignment with recent studies (Costa-jussà et al., 2022; Siddhant et al., 2022) on MT for ELRLs, the evaluation scores are reported with chrF (Popović, 2015) and BLEU.

We have observed that the unigram noise injection outperformed all the baselines across all three language groups. The CHARSPAN noise model outperformed the unigram model. There were improvements for languages like Konkani which are lexically less similar to corresponding HRLs. We also conducted experiments where the noise was augmented before and after vocabulary preparation. We found that both experiments perform equally well; however, the model where vocabulary created with noisy data performs slightly better. Which scale the proposed model usability to applications where PLMs were involved as they usually have fixed vocab. The CHARSPAN noise model combined with BPE-Dropout emerged as the performing model. However, there is minimal degradation in HRL performance.

5.3 Insights and Limitations

We have conducted several ablation experiments to ensure that the proposed design choices result in the best performance. Furthermore, our analysis indicates that the character-span-based model enhances the performance of languages that are less similar or more distant from HRLs. Additionally, it is important to select lexically similar languages HRLs. Finally, we explore a multilingual setup in which multiple HRLs are trained together, resulting in a performance boost and scale coverage for ELRs. Our model performs equally well with a vocabulary that is learned with clean data. This provides scalability for utilizing PLMs, which typically have a fixed vocabulary.

The current work is only investigated for ELRLs to English MT tasks. We assume that the related languages also use the same script or scripts that can be easily mapped/transliterated to each other. This method might not be effective for transfer between related languages that are written in very different scripts, e.g., Hindi is written in the Devanagari script, while Sindhi is written in the Perso-Arabic script. We will extend this work to English to ELRLs MT and other tasks in the future.

6 Conclusion

With this thesis, we have presented a coherent narrative of our efforts in the field of text generation for multiple LRLs with limited supervision. We began by enabling zero-shot well-formed text generation, then progressed to improving cross-lingual generation, and ultimately enabled zero-shot machine translation for ELRLs and dialects. Our modeling approaches are aligned with adaptive training, meta-learning, language clustering, lexical similarity, and noise augmentation. The evaluations were conducted across a wide range of LRLs across language families, multiple NLG tasks, and datasets. Through these endeavors, we have taken a step towards facilitating language technology for the long tail of languages that possess limited or no linguistic resources. This advancement aims to benefit the general audiences where text needs to be generated in local languages.

In the future, we will explore the following directions: (1) Extend the existing modeling framework to cover 7000+ spoken languages of the world. (2) Design a single unified and scalable framework for many NLG tasks and LRLs. (3) Develop a better modeling approach to adapt the existing Multilingual PLM representations to new/unseen LRLs. (4) Since for many ELRLs there are no evaluation datasets, we will explore a modeling technique where the performance of LRLs is evaluated without reference. (5) Creating a large-scale multilingual NLG benchmark similar to Chen et al. (2022). (6) Investigating active learning, prompting, and other trending methodologies to advance cross-lingual transfer and generation research with limited supervision.

Acknowledgements

I (as the first author of the paper) extend my heartfelt gratitude to my Ph.D. supervisor, Dr. Maunendra Sankar Desarkar, for his unwavering guidance and support throughout my doctoral journey. I also want to acknowledge the invaluable contributions of my collaborators Rahul Kejriwal, Anoop Kunchukuttan, Yoshinobu Kano, and Kumari Deepshikha, whose expertise and collaborative efforts enriched the quality of our research. I am deeply appreciative of the support and resources provided by collaborating organizations Microsoft India, Nvidia AI Center India, and Shizuoka University Japan, which played a pivotal role in facilitating our research endeavors. I thank the dedicated human annotators for evaluation and the anonymous reviewers for their constructive feedback. This research would not have been possible without the collective efforts of these individuals and organizations, and for that, I am profoundly thankful.

References

Noëmi Aepli and Rico Sennrich. 2022. Improving zero-shot cross-lingual transfer between closely related languages by injecting character-level noise. In *Findings of the Association for Computational Linguistics: ACL 2022*, pages 4074–4083, Dublin, Ireland. Association for Computational Linguistics.

Mikel Artetxe, Sebastian Ruder, and Dani Yogatama. 2020. On the cross-lingual transferability of monolingual representations. In *Proceedings of the 58th Annual Meeting of the Association for Computational Linguistics*, pages 4623–4637, Online. Association for Computational Linguistics.

Trapit Bansal, Rishikesh Jha, Tsendsuren Munkhdalai, and Andrew McCallum. 2020. Self-supervised meta-learning for few-shot natural language classification tasks. In *Proceedings of the 2020 Conference on Empirical Methods in Natural Language Processing (EMNLP)*, pages 522–534.

Emily M Bender. 2011. On achieving and evaluating language-independence in nlp. *Linguistic Issues in Language Technology*, 6.

Emily M Bender. 2019. The# benderrule: On naming the languages we study and why it matters. *The Gradient*, 14.

Yoshua Bengio, Samy Bengio, and Jocelyn Cloutier. 1990. *Learning a synaptic learning rule*. Citeseer.

Damian Blasi, Antonios Anastasopoulos, and Graham Neubig. 2022. Systematic inequalities in language technology performance across the world's languages. In *Proceedings of the 60th Annual Meeting of the Association for Computational Linguistics (Volume 1: Long Papers)*, pages 5486–5505, Dublin, Ireland. Association for Computational Linguistics.

Yiran Chen, Zhenqiao Song, Xianze Wu, Danqing Wang, Jingjing Xu, Jiaze Chen, Hao Zhou, and Lei Li. 2022. MTG: A benchmark suite for multilingual text generation. In *Findings of the Association for Computational Linguistics: NAACL 2022*, pages 2508–2527, Seattle, United States. Association for Computational Linguistics.

Zewen Chi, Li Dong, Furu Wei, Wenhui Wang, Xian-Ling Mao, and Heyan Huang. 2020. Cross-lingual natural language generation via pre-training. *Proceedings of the AAAI Conference on Artificial Intelligence*, 34(05):7570–7577.

Marta R Costa-jussà, James Cross, Onur Çelebi, Maha Elbayad, Kenneth Heafield, Kevin Heffernan, Elahe Kalbassi, Janice Lam, Daniel Licht, Jean Maillard, et al. 2022. No language left behind: Scaling human-centered machine translation. *arXiv preprint arXiv:2207.04672*.

Jacob Devlin, Ming-Wei Chang, Kenton Lee, and Kristina Toutanova. 2019. BERT: Pre-training of deep bidirectional transformers for language understanding. In *Proceedings of the 2019 Conference of the North American Chapter of the Association for Computational Linguistics: Human Language Technologies, Volume 1 (Long and Short Papers)*, pages 4171–4186, Minneapolis, Minnesota. Association for Computational Linguistics.

Xiangyu Duan, Mingming Yin, Min Zhang, Boxing Chen, and Weihua Luo. 2019. Zero-shot cross-lingual abstractive sentence summarization through teaching generation and attention. In *Proceedings of the 57th Annual Meeting of the Association for Computational Linguistics*, pages 3162–3172, Florence, Italy. Association for Computational Linguistics.

Chelsea Finn, Pieter Abbeel, and Sergey Levine. 2017. Model-agnostic meta-learning for fast adaptation of deep networks. In *International Conference on Machine Learning*, pages 1126–1135. PMLR.

Tianyu Gao, Xu Han, Hao Zhu, Zhiyuan Liu, Peng Li, Maosong Sun, and Jie Zhou. 2019. FewRel 2.0: Towards more challenging few-shot relation classification. In *Proceedings of the 2019 Conference on Empirical Methods in Natural Language Processing and the 9th International Joint Conference on Natural Language Processing (EMNLP-IJCNLP)*, pages 6251–6256, Hong Kong, China. Association for Computational Linguistics.

Neil Houlsby, Andrei Giurgiu, Stanislaw Jastrzebski, Bruna Morrone, Quentin De Laroussilhe, Andrea Gesmundo, Mona Attariyan, and Sylvain Gelly. 2019. Parameter-efficient transfer learning for NLP. In *Proceedings of the 36th International Conference on Machine Learning*, volume 97 of *Proceedings of Machine Learning Research*, pages 2790–2799. PMLR.

Junjie Hu, Sebastian Ruder, Aditya Siddhant, Graham Neubig, Orhan Firat, and Melvin Johnson. 2020. Xtreme: A massively multilingual multi-task benchmark for evaluating cross-lingual generalization. *CoRR*, abs/2003.11080.

Mandar Joshi, Danqi Chen, Yinhan Liu, Daniel S Weld, Luke Zettlemoyer, and Omer Levy. 2020a. Spanbert: Improving pre-training by representing and predicting spans. *Transactions of the Association for Computational Linguistics*, 8:64–77.

Pratik Joshi, Sebastin Santy, Amar Budhiraja, Kalika Bali, and Monojit Choudhury. 2020b. The state and fate of linguistic diversity and inclusion in the NLP world. In *Proceedings of the 58th Annual Meeting of the Association for Computational Linguistics*, pages 6282–6293, Online. Association for Computational Linguistics.

Vladimir Karpukhin, Omer Levy, Jacob Eisenstein, and Marjan Ghazvininejad. 2019. Training on synthetic noise improves robustness to natural noise in machine translation. In *Proceedings of the 5th Workshop on Noisy User-generated Text (W-NUT 2019)*, pages 42–47, Hong Kong, China. Association for Computational Linguistics.

Yash Khemchandani, Sarvesh Mehtani, Vaidehi Patil, Abhijeet Awasthi, Partha Talukdar, and Sunita Sarawagi. 2021. Exploiting language relatedness for low web-resource language model adaptation: An Indic languages study. In *Proceedings of the 59th Annual Meeting of the Association for Computational Linguistics and the 11th International Joint Conference on Natural Language Processing (Volume 1: Long Papers)*, pages 1312–1323, Online. Association for Computational Linguistics.

Vishwajeet Kumar, Nitish Joshi, Arijit Mukherjee, Ganesh Ramakrishnan, and Preethi Jyothi. 2019. Cross-lingual training for automatic question generation. In *Proceedings of the 57th Annual Meeting of the Association for Computational Linguistics*, pages 4863–4872, Florence, Italy. Association for Computational Linguistics.

Guokun Lai, Barlas Oguz, Yiming Yang, and Veselin Stoyanov. 2019. Bridging the domain gap in cross-lingual document classification. *CoRR*, abs/1909.07009.

Tianjian Li and Kenton Murray. 2023. Why does zero-shot cross-lingual generation fail? an explanation and a solution. In *Findings of the Association for Computational Linguistics: ACL 2023*, pages 12461–12476, Toronto, Canada. Association for Computational Linguistics.

Patrick Littell, David R. Mortensen, Ke Lin, Katherine Kairis, Carlisle Turner, and Lori Levin. 2017. URIEL and lang2vec: Representing languages as typological, geographical, and phylogenetic vectors. In *Proceedings of the 15th Conference of the European Chapter of the Association for Computational Linguistics: Volume 2, Short Papers*, pages 8–14, Valencia, Spain. Association for Computational Linguistics.

Yinhan Liu, Jiatao Gu, Naman Goyal, Xian Li, Sergey Edunov, Marjan Ghazvininejad, Mike Lewis, and Luke Zettlemoyer. 2020. Multilingual denoising pre-training for neural machine translation. *Transactions of the Association for Computational Linguistics*, 8:726–742.

Chaitanya Malaviya, Graham Neubig, and Patrick Littell. 2017. Learning language representations for typology prediction. In *Proceedings of the 2017 Conference on Empirical Methods in Natural Language Processing*, pages 2529–2535, Copenhagen, Denmark. Association for Computational Linguistics.

Kaushal Maurya and Maunendra Desarkar. 2022. Meta-x_{NLG}: A meta-learning approach based on language clustering for zero-shot cross-lingual transfer and generation. In *Findings of the Association for Computational Linguistics: ACL 2022*, pages 269–284, Dublin, Ireland. Association for Computational Linguistics.

Kaushal Kumar Maurya, Maunendra Sankar Desarkar, Yoshinobu Kano, and Kumari Deepshikha. 2021. ZmBART: An unsupervised cross-lingual transfer framework for language generation. In *Findings of the Association for Computational Linguistics: ACL-IJCNLP 2021*, pages 2804–2818, Online. Association for Computational Linguistics.

Kaushal Kumar Maurya, Rahul Kejriwal, Maunendra Sankar Desarkar, and Anoop Kunchukuttan. 2023. Utilizing lexical similarity to enable zero-shot machine translation for extremely low-resource languages. *arXiv preprint arXiv:2305.05214*.

Meryem M'hamdi, Doo Soon Kim, Franck Dernoncourt, Trung Bui, Xiang Ren, and Jonathan May. 2021. X-METRA-ADA: Cross-lingual meta-transfer learning adaptation to natural language understanding and question answering. In *Proceedings of the 2021 Conference of the North American Chapter of the Association for Computational Linguistics: Human Language Technologies*, pages 3617–3632, Online. Association for Computational Linguistics.

Toan Q. Nguyen and David Chiang. 2017. Transfer learning across low-resource, related languages for neural machine translation. In *Proceedings of the Eighth International Joint Conference on Natural Language Processing (Volume 2: Short Papers)*, pages 296–301, Taipei, Taiwan. Asian Federation of Natural Language Processing.

Farhad Nooralahzadeh, Giannis Bekoulis, Johannes Bjerva, and Isabelle Augenstein. 2020. Zero-shot cross-lingual transfer with meta learning. In *Proceedings of the 2020 Conference on Empirical Methods in Natural Language Processing, EMNLP 2020,*

Online, November 16-20, 2020, pages 4547–4562. Association for Computational Linguistics.

Arturo Oncevay, Barry Haddow, and Alexandra Birch. 2020. Bridging linguistic typology and multilingual machine translation with multi-view language representations. In *Proceedings of the 2020 Conference on Empirical Methods in Natural Language Processing (EMNLP)*, pages 2391–2406, Online. Association for Computational Linguistics.

Vaidehi Patil, Partha Talukdar, and Sunita Sarawagi. 2022. Overlap-based vocabulary generation improves cross-lingual transfer among related languages. In *Proceedings of the 60th Annual Meeting of the Association for Computational Linguistics (Volume 1: Long Papers)*, pages 219–233, Dublin, Ireland. Association for Computational Linguistics.

Jonas Pfeiffer, Aishwarya Kamath, Andreas Rücklé, Kyunghyun Cho, and Iryna Gurevych. 2021. AdapterFusion: Non-destructive task composition for transfer learning. In *Proceedings of the 16th Conference of the European Chapter of the Association for Computational Linguistics: Main Volume*, pages 487–503, Online. Association for Computational Linguistics.

Jonas Pfeiffer, Francesco Piccinno, Massimo Nicosia, Xinyi Wang, Machel Reid, and Sebastian Ruder. 2023. mmt5: Modular multilingual pre-training solves source language hallucinations. *arXiv preprint arXiv:2305.14224*.

Maja Popović. 2015. chrF: character n-gram F-score for automatic MT evaluation. In *Proceedings of the Tenth Workshop on Statistical Machine Translation*, pages 392–395, Lisbon, Portugal. Association for Computational Linguistics.

Ivan Provilkov, Dmitrii Emelianenko, and Elena Voita. 2020. BPE-dropout: Simple and effective subword regularization. In *Proceedings of the 58th Annual Meeting of the Association for Computational Linguistics*, pages 1882–1892, Online. Association for Computational Linguistics.

Sebastian Ruder. 2022. The State of Multilingual AI. `http://ruder.io/state-of-multilingual-ai/`.

Sebastian Ruder, Ivan Vulić, and Anders Søgaard. 2022. Square one bias in NLP: Towards a multi-dimensional exploration of the research manifold. In *Findings of the Association for Computational Linguistics: ACL 2022*, pages 2340–2354, Dublin, Ireland. Association for Computational Linguistics.

Rico Sennrich, Barry Haddow, and Alexandra Birch. 2016a. Edinburgh neural machine translation systems for WMT 16. In *Proceedings of the First Conference on Machine Translation: Volume 2, Shared Task Papers*, pages 371–376, Berlin, Germany. Association for Computational Linguistics.

Rico Sennrich, Barry Haddow, and Alexandra Birch. 2016b. Neural machine translation of rare words with subword units. In *Proceedings of the 54th Annual Meeting of the Association for Computational Linguistics (Volume 1: Long Papers)*, pages 1715–1725, Berlin, Germany. Association for Computational Linguistics.

Shi-qi Shen, Yun Chen, Cheng Yang, Zhi-yuan Liu, and Mao-song Sun. 2018. Zero-shot cross-lingual neural headline generation. *IEEE/ACM Trans. Audio, Speech and Lang. Proc.*, 26(12):2319–2327.

Aditya Siddhant, Ankur Bapna, Orhan Firat, Yuan Cao, Mia Xu Chen, Isaac Caswell, and Xavier Garcia. 2022. Towards the next 1000 languages in multilingual machine translation: Exploring the synergy between supervised and self-supervised learning. *arXiv preprint arXiv:2201.03110*.

Matthias Sperber, Jan Niehues, and Alex Waibel. 2017. Toward robust neural machine translation for noisy input sequences. In *Proceedings of the 14th International Conference on Spoken Language Translation*, pages 90–96.

Ishan Tarunesh, Sushil Khyalia, Vishwajeet Kumar, Ganesh Ramakrishnan, and Preethi Jyothi. 2021. Meta-learning for effective multi-task and multilingual modelling. In *Proceedings of the 16th Conference of the European Chapter of the Association for Computational Linguistics: Main Volume, EACL 2021, Online, April 19 - 23, 2021*, pages 3600–3612. Association for Computational Linguistics.

Vaibhav Vaibhav, Sumeet Singh, Craig Stewart, and Graham Neubig. 2019. Improving robustness of machine translation with synthetic noise. In *Proceedings of the 2019 Conference of the North American Chapter of the Association for Computational Linguistics: Human Language Technologies, Volume 1 (Long and Short Papers)*, pages 1916–1920, Minneapolis, Minnesota. Association for Computational Linguistics.

Gido M. van de Ven, Tinne Tuytelaars, and Andreas S. Tolias. 2022. Three types of incremental learning. *Nat. Mac. Intell.*, 4(12):1185–1197.

Niels van der Heijden, Helen Yannakoudakis, Pushkar Mishra, and Ekaterina Shutova. 2021. Multilingual and cross-lingual document classification: A meta-learning approach. In *Proceedings of the 16th Conference of the European Chapter of the Association for Computational Linguistics: Main Volume*, pages 1966–1976, Online. Association for Computational Linguistics.

Ashish Vaswani, Noam Shazeer, Niki Parmar, Jakob Uszkoreit, Llion Jones, Aidan N Gomez, Łukasz Kaiser, and Illia Polosukhin. 2017. Attention is all you need. *Advances in neural information processing systems*, 30.

Tu Vu, Aditya Barua, Brian Lester, Daniel Cer, Mohit Iyyer, and Noah Constant. 2022. Overcoming catastrophic forgetting in zero-shot cross-lingual generation. In *Proceedings of the 2022 Conference on Empirical Methods in Natural Language Processing*, pages 9279–9300, Abu Dhabi, United Arab Emirates. Association for Computational Linguistics.

Xiaojun Wan, Huiying Li, and Jianguo Xiao. 2010. Cross-language document summarization based on machine translation quality prediction. In *Proceedings of the 48th Annual Meeting of the Association for Computational Linguistics*, pages 917–926, Uppsala, Sweden. Association for Computational Linguistics.

Xinyi Wang, Hieu Pham, Philip Arthur, and Graham Neubig. 2019. Multilingual neural machine translation with soft decoupled encoding. In *7th International Conference on Learning Representations, ICLR 2019, New Orleans, LA, USA, May 6-9, 2019*. OpenReview.net.

Xinyi Wang, Hieu Pham, Zihang Dai, and Graham Neubig. 2018. SwitchOut: an efficient data augmentation algorithm for neural machine translation. In *Proceedings of the 2018 Conference on Empirical Methods in Natural Language Processing*, pages 856–861, Brussels, Belgium. Association for Computational Linguistics.

Qianhui Wu, Zijia Lin, Guoxin Wang, Hui Chen, Börje F Karlsson, Biqing Huang, and Chin-Yew Lin. 2020. Enhanced meta-learning for cross-lingual named entity recognition with minimal resources. In *Proceedings of the AAAI Conference on Artificial Intelligence*, volume 34, pages 9274–9281.

Linting Xue, Noah Constant, Adam Roberts, Mihir Kale, Rami Al-Rfou, Aditya Siddhant, Aditya Barua, and Colin Raffel. 2021. mT5: A massively multilingual pre-trained text-to-text transformer. In *Proceedings of the 2021 Conference of the North American Chapter of the Association for Computational Linguistics: Human Language Technologies*, pages 483–498, Online. Association for Computational Linguistics.

Wayne Xin Zhao, Kun Zhou, Junyi Li, Tianyi Tang, Xiaolei Wang, Yupeng Hou, Yingqian Min, Beichen Zhang, Junjie Zhang, Zican Dong, Yifan Du, Chen Yang, Yushuo Chen, Zhipeng Chen, Jinhao Jiang, Ruiyang Ren, Yifan Li, Xinyu Tang, Zikang Liu, Peiyu Liu, Jian-Yun Nie, and Ji-Rong Wen. 2023. A survey of large language models. *arXiv preprint arXiv:2303.18223*.

Transformers as Graph-to-Graph Models

James Henderson [1] **Alireza Mohammadshahi** [*1,2,3] **Andrei C. Coman** [1,2]
Lesly Miculicich [*†]
[1] Idiap Research Institute [2] EPFL [3] University of Zurich
{james.henderson,andrei.coman}@idiap.ch
alireza.mohammadshahi@epfl.com
lmiculicich@google.com

Abstract

We argue that Transformers are essentially graph-to-graph models, with sequences just being a special case. Attention weights are functionally equivalent to graph edges. Our Graph-to-Graph Transformer architecture makes this ability explicit, by inputting graph edges into the attention weight computations and predicting graph edges with attention-like functions, thereby integrating explicit graphs into the latent graphs learned by pretrained Transformers. Adding iterative graph refinement provides a joint embedding of input, output, and latent graphs, allowing non-autoregressive graph prediction to optimise the complete graph without any bespoke pipeline or decoding strategy. Empirical results show that this architecture achieves state-of-the-art accuracies for modelling a variety of linguistic structures, integrating very effectively with the latent linguistic representations learned by pretraining.

1 Introduction

Computational linguists have traditionally made extensive use of structured representations to capture the regularities found in natural language. The huge success of Transformers (Vaswani et al., 2017) and their pre-trained large language models (Devlin et al., 2019; Zhang et al., 2022; Touvron et al., 2023a,b) have brought these representations into question, since these models are able to capture even subtle generalisations about language and meaning in an end-to-end sequence-to-sequence model (Wu et al., 2020; Michael et al., 2020; Hewitt et al., 2021). This raises issues for research that still needs to model structured representations, such as work on knowledge graphs, hyperlink graphs, citation graphs, or social networks.

In this paper we show that the sequence-to-sequence nature of most Transformer models is only a superficial characteristic; underlyingly they are in fact modelling complex structured representations. We survey versions of the Transformer architecture which integrate explicit structured representations with the latent structured representations of Transformers. These models can jointly embed both the explicit structures and the latent structures in a Transformer's sequence-of-vectors hidden representation, and can predict explicit structures from this embedding. In the process, we highlight evidence that the latent structures of pretrained Transformers already include much information about traditional linguistic structures. These Transformer architectures support explicit structures which are general graphs, making them applicable to a wide range of structured representations and their integration with text.

The key insight of this line of work is that attention weights and graph structure edges are effectively the same thing. Linguistic structures are fundamentally an expression of locality in the interaction between different components of a representation. As Henderson (2020) argued, incorporating this information about locality in the inductive bias of a neural network means putting connections between hidden vectors if their associated components are local in the structure. In Transformers (Vaswani et al., 2017), these connections are learned in the form of attention weights. Thus, these attention weights are effectively the induced structure of the Transformer's latent representation.

However, attention weights are not explicitly part of a Transformer's hidden representation. The output of a Transformer encoder is a sequence of vectors, and the same is true of each lower layer of self-attention. The latent attention weights are extracted from these sequence-of-vector embeddings with learned functions of pairs of vectors. Edges in explicit graphs can be predicted in the same way (from pairs of vectors), assuming that these graphs have also been embedded in the sequence of vectors.

*Work done while working at Idiap Research Institute.
†Now at Google

Proceedings of the the Big Picture Workshop, pages 93–107
December 7, 2023 ©2023 Association for Computational Linguistics

In recent years, the main innovation has been in how to embed explicit graphs in the hidden representations of Transformers. In our work on this topic, we follow the above insight and input the edges of the graph into the computation of attention weights. Attention weights are computed from an $n \times n$ matrix of attention scores (where n is the sequence length), so we input the label of the edge between nodes i and j into the score computation for the i,j cell of this matrix. Each edge label has a learned embedding vector, which is input to the attention score function in various ways depending on the architecture. This allows the Transformer to integrate the explicit graph into its own latent attention graph in flexible and powerful ways. This integrated attention graph can then determine the Transformer's sequence-of-vectors embedding in the same way as standard Transformers.

Researchers from the Natural Language Understanding group at Idiap Research Institute have developed this architecture for inputting and predicting graphs under the name of *Graph-to-Graph Transformer* (G2GT). G2GT allows conditioning on an observed graph and predicting a target graph. For the case where a graph is only observed at training time, we not only want to predict its edges, we also want to integrate the predicted graph into the Transformer embedding. This has a number of advantages, most notably the ability to jointly model all the edges of the graph. By iteratively refining the previous predicted graph, G2GT can jointly model the entire predicted graph even though the actual prediction is done independently for each edge. And this joint modelling can be done in conjunction with other explicit graphs, as well as with the Transformer's induced latent graph.

Our work on G2G Transformer has included a number of different explicit graph structures. The original methods were developed on syntactic parsing (Mohammadshahi and Henderson, 2021, 2020). The range of architectures was further explored for semantic role labelling (Mohammadshahi and Henderson, 2023) and collocation recognition (Espinosa Anke et al., 2022). G2GT's application to coreference resolution extended the complexity of graphs to two levels of representation (mention spans and coreference chains) over an entire document, which was all modelled with iterative refinement of a single graph (Miculicich and Henderson, 2022). Current work on knowledge extraction poses further challenges, most notably the issue of tractably modelling large graphs. The code for G2GT is open-source and available for other groups to use for other graph structures (at `https://github.com/idiap/g2g-transformer`).

In the rest of this paper, we start with a review of related work on deep learning for graph modelling (Section 2). We then present the general G2GT architecture with iterative refinement (Section 3), before discussing the specific versions we have evaluated on specific tasks (Section 4). We then discuss the broader implications of these results (Section 5), and conclude with a discussion of future work (Section 6).

2 Deep Learning for Graphs

Graph Neural Networks. Early attempts at broadening the application of neural networks to graph structures were pursued by Gori et al. (2005) and Scarselli et al. (2008), who introduced the Graph Neural Networks (GNNs) architecture as a natural expansion of Recurrent Neural Networks (RNNs) (Hopfield, 1982). This architecture regained interest in the context of deep learning, expanded through the inclusion of spectral convolution layers (Bruna et al., 2013), gated recurrent units (Li et al., 2015), spatial convolution layers (Kipf and Welling, 2017), and attention layers (Veličković et al., 2018). GNNs generally employ the iterative local message passing mechanism to aggregate information from neighbouring nodes (Gilmer et al., 2017). Recent research, analysing GNNs through the lens of Weisfeiler and Leman (1968), has highlighted two key issues: over-smoothing (Oono and Suzuki, 2020) and over-squashing (Alon and Yahav, 2021). Over-smoothing arises from repeated aggregation across layers, leading to convergence of node features and loss of discriminative information. Over-squashing, on the other hand, results from activation functions during message aggregation, causing significant information and gradient loss. These issues limit the capacity of GNNs to effectively capture long-range dependencies and nuanced graph relationships (Topping et al., 2021). The Transformer architecture (Vaswani et al., 2017) can be seen as addressing these issues, in that its stacked layers of self-attention can be seen as a fixed sequence of learned aggregation steps.

Graph Transformers. Transformers (Vaswani et al., 2017), initially designed for sequence tasks, represent a viable and versatile alternative to GNNs due to their intrinsic graph processing capabilities. Through their self-attention mechanism, they can seamlessly capture global wide-ranging relationships, akin to handling a fully-connected graph. Shaw et al. (2018) explicitly input relative position relations as embeddings into the attention function, thereby effectively inputting the relative position graph, instead of absolute position embeddings, to represent the sequence. Generalising this explicit input strategy to arbitrary graphs (Henderson, 2020) has led to a general class of models which we will refer to as *Graph Transformers* (GT).

GT Evolution and Applications. The history of graph input methods used in GTs started with Transformer variations that experimented with relative positions to more effectively capture distance between input elements. Rather than adopting the sinusoidal position embedding introduced by Vaswani et al. (2017) or the absolute position embedding proposed by Devlin et al. (2019), Shaw et al. (2018) added relative position embeddings to attention keys and values, capturing token distance within a defined range. Dai et al. (2019) proposed Transformer-XL, which used content-dependent positional scores and a global positional score in attention weights. Mohammadshahi and Henderson (2020) demonstrated one of the earliest successful integration of an explicit graph into Transformer's latent attention graph. They introduced the *Graph-To-Graph Transformer* (G2GT) architecture and applied it to syntactic parsing tasks by effectively leveraging pre-trained models such as BERT (Devlin et al., 2019). Huang et al. (2020) introduced new methods to enhance interaction between query, key and relative position embeddings within the self-attention mechanism. Su et al. (2021) proposed RoFormer, which utilises a rotation matrix to encode absolute positions while also integrating explicit relative position dependencies into the self-attention formulation. Liutkus et al. (2021) and Chen (2021) extended Performer (Choromanski et al., 2020) to support relative position encoding while scaling Transformers to longer sequences with a linear attention mechanism. Graphormer (Ying et al., 2021) introduced node centrality encoding as an additional input level embedding vector, node distances and edges as soft biases added at attention level, and obtained excellent results on a broad range of graph representation learning tasks. Mohammadshahi and Henderson (2021) built upon the G2GT architecture and proposed an iterative refinement procedure over previously predicted graphs, using a non-autoregressive approach. SSAN (Xu et al., 2021) leveraged the GT approach to effectively model mention dependencies for document-level relation extraction tasks. JointGT (Ke et al., 2021) exploited the GT approach for knowledge to text generation tasks via a joint graph-text encoding. Similarly, TableFormer (Yang et al., 2022) demonstrated the successful utilisation of the GT approach for combined text-table encoding in table-based question answering tasks. Espinosa Anke et al. (2022) proposed a GT architecture for simultaneous collocation extraction and lexical function typification, incorporating syntactic dependencies into the attention mechanism. Miculicich and Henderson (2022) showed that the G2GT iterative refinement procedure can be effectively applied to graphs at multiple levels of representation. Diao and Loynd (2022) further extended a GT architecture with new edge and node update methods and applied them to graph-structured problems. QAT (Park et al., 2022) substantially expanded upon GT models to jointly handle language and graph reasoning in question answering tasks. In the study conducted by Mohammadshahi and Henderson (2023), the G2GT model showed substantial improvements in the semantic role labelling tasks. The multitude of successful applications and extensions firmly establish Graph Transformers as a robust and adaptable framework for addressing complex challenges in language and graphs.

3 Graph-to-Graph Transformer Architecture

Our Graph-to-Graph Transformer (G2GT) architecture combines the idea of inputting graph edges into the self-attention function with the idea of predicting graph edges with an attention-like function. By encoding the graph relations into the self-attention mechanism of Transformers, the model has an appropriate linguistic bias, without imposing hard restrictions. Specifically, G2GT modifies the attention mechanism of Transformers (Vaswani et al., 2017) to input any graph. Given the input sequence $W=(x_1,x_2,...,x_n)$, and graph relations $G=\{(x_i,x_j,l),1\leq i,j\leq n,l\in L\}$ (where L is the set of labels), the modified self-attention mechanism is calculated as[1]:

[1]Various alternative functions are possible for inputting relation embeddings into attention weight computations. Dufter

$$e_{ij} = \frac{1}{\sqrt{d}} \Big[x_i \boldsymbol{W^Q} (x_j \boldsymbol{W^K})^T + x_i \boldsymbol{W^Q} (r_{ij} \boldsymbol{W_1^R})^T + r_{ij} \boldsymbol{W_2^R} (x_j \boldsymbol{W^K})^T \Big] \tag{1}$$

where $r_{ij} \in \{0,1\}^{|L|}$ is a one-hot vector which specifies the type of the relation between x_i and x_j,[2] $\boldsymbol{W_1^R}, \boldsymbol{W_2^R} \in R^{|L| \times d}$ are matrices of graph relation embeddings which are learned during training, $|L|$ is the label size, and d is the size of hidden representations. The value equation of Transformer (Vaswani et al., 2017) is also modified to pass information about graph relations to the output of the attention function:

$$z_i = \sum_j \alpha_{ij} (x_j \boldsymbol{W^V} + r_{ij} \boldsymbol{W_3^R}) \tag{2}$$

where $\boldsymbol{W_3^R} \in R^{|L| \times d}$ is another learned relation embedding matrix.

To extract the explicit graph from the sequence of vectors output by the Transformer, a classification module is applied to pairs of vectors and maps them into the label space L. Initially, the module transforms each vector into distinct head and tail representations using dedicated projection matrices. Subsequently, a classifier (linear, bilinear or MLP) is applied, to map the vector pair onto predictions over the label space. Notably, each edge prediction can be computed in parallel (i.e. in a non-autoregressive manner), as predictions for each pair are independent of one another. Given the discrete nature of the output, various decoding methods can be employed to impose desired constraints on the complete output graph. These can range from straightforward head-tail order constraints, to more complex decoding algorithms such as the Minimum Spanning Tree (MST) algorithm.

Having an architecture which can both condition on graphs and predict graphs gives us the powerful ability to do iterative refinement of arbitrary graphs. Even when graph prediction is non-autoregressive, conditioning on the previously predicted graph allows the model to capture between-edge correlations like an autoregressive model. As illustrated in Figure 1, we propose **R**ecursive **N**on-autoregressive **G2GT** (RNGT),

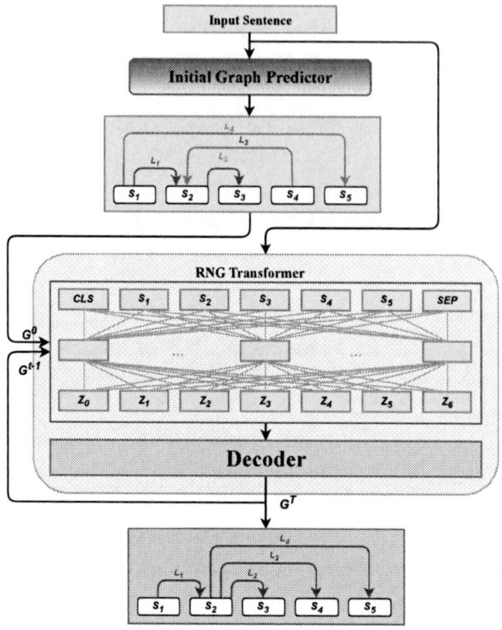

Figure 1: The Recursive Non-autoregressive Graph-to-Graph Transformer architecture.

which predicts all edges of the graph in parallel, and is therefore non-autoregressive, but can still condition every edge prediction on all other edge predictions by conditioning on the previous version of the graph (using Equations 1 and 2).

The input to the model is the input graph W (e.g. a sequence of tokens), and the output is the final graph G^T over the same set of nodes. First, we compute an initial graph G^0 over the nodes of W, which can be done with any model. Then each recursive iteration encodes the previous graph G^{t-1} and predicts a new graph G^t. It can be formalised in terms of an encoder $\mathrm{E}^{\mathrm{RNG}}$ and a decoder $\mathrm{D}^{\mathrm{RNG}}$:

$$\begin{cases} Z^t = \mathrm{E}^{\mathrm{RNG}}(W, G^{t-1}) \\ G^t = \mathrm{D}^{\mathrm{RNG}}(Z^t) \end{cases} \quad t = 1, \ldots, T \tag{3}$$

where Z represents the set of vectors output by the model, and T indicates the number of refinement iterations. Note that in each step of this iterative refinement process, the G2G Transformer first computes a set of vectors which embeds the predicted graph (i.e. $\mathrm{E}^{\mathrm{RNG}}(W,\ G^{t-1})$), before extracting the edges of the predicted graph from this set-of-vectors embedding (i.e. $\mathrm{D}^{\mathrm{RNG}}(Z^t)$).

4 G2GT Models and Results

This section provides a more comprehensive explanation of each alternative G2GT model we have ex-

et al. (2022) provide a survey of previous proposals for relative position encoding. In ongoing work, we have found that using a relation embedding vector to reweight the dimensions in standard dot-product attention works well for some applications.

[2]This formulation can be easily extended to multi-label graphs by removing the one-hot constraint. We are investigating the most effective method for doing this.

plored, along with an outline of how we've applied these models to address various graph modelling problems. The empirical success of these models demonstrate the computational adequacy of Transformers for extracting and modelling graph structures which are central to the nature of language. The large further improvements gained by initialising with pretrained models demonstrates that Transformer pretraining encodes information about linguistic structures in its attention mechanisms.

4.1 Syntactic Parsing

Syntactic parsing is the process of analysing the grammatical structure of a sentence, including identifying the subject, verb, and object. Syntactic dependency parsing is a critical component in a variety of natural language understanding tasks, such as semantic role labelling (Henderson et al., 2013; Marcheggiani and Titov, 2017, 2020), machine translation (Chen et al., 2017), relation extraction (Zhang et al., 2018), and natural language inference (Pang et al., 2019). It is also a benchmark structured prediction task, because architectures which are not powerful enough to learn syntactic parsing cannot be computationally adequate for language understanding.

Syntactic structure is generally specified in one of two popular grammar styles, constituency parsing (i.e. phrase-structure parsing) (Manning and Schutze, 1999; Henderson, 2003, 2004; Titov and Henderson, 2007a) and dependency parsing (Nivre, 2003; Titov and Henderson, 2007b; Carreras, 2007; Nivre and McDonald, 2008; Dyer et al., 2015). There are two main approaches to compute the dependency tree: transition-based and graph-based parsers. Transition-based parsers predict the dependency graph one edge at a time through a sequence of parsing actions (Yamada and Matsumoto, 2003; Nivre and Scholz, 2004; Titov and Henderson, 2007b; Zhang and Nivre, 2011; Weiss et al., 2015; Yazdani and Henderson, 2015), and graph-based parsers compute scores for every possible dependency edge and then apply a decoding algorithm to find the highest scoring total tree (McDonald et al., 2005; Koo and Collins, 2010; Kuncoro et al., 2016; Zhou and Zhao, 2019).

In the following, we outline our proposals for using G2GT for syntactic parsing tasks.

4.1.1 Transition-based Dependency Parsing

In (Mohammadshahi and Henderson, 2020), we integrate the G2GT model with two baselines, named StateTransformer (StateTr) and SentenceTransformer (SentTr). In the former model, we directly input the parser state into the G2GT model, while the latter takes the initial sentence as the input. For better efficiency of our transition-based model, we used an alternative version of G2GT, introduced in Section 3, where the interaction of graph relations with key matrices in Equation 1 is removed. Each parser decision is conditioned on the history of previous decisions by inputting an unlabelled partially constructed dependency graph to the G2GT model. Mohammadshahi and Henderson (2020) evaluate the integrated models on the English Penn Treebank (Marcus et al., 1993), and 13 languages of Universal Dependencies Treebanks (Nivre et al., 2018).

Model	UAS	LAS
Andor et al. (2016)	94.61	92.79
StateTr	92.32	89.69
StateTr+G2GT	93.07	91.08
BERT StateTr	95.18	92.73
BERT StateTr+G2GT	**95.58**	**93.74**
BERT SentTr	95.65	93.85
BERT SentTr+G2GT	**96.06**	**94.26**

Table 1: Comparisons to the previous comparable models, including transition-based and sequence-to-sequence approaches (according to Mohammadshahi and Henderson (2020)) on English WSJ Treebank Stanford dependencies. Labelled and Unlabelled Attachment Scores (LAS,UAS) are used as evaluation metrics.

Results of our models on the Penn Treebank are shown in Table 1 (see (Mohammadshahi and Henderson, 2020) for further results on UD Treebanks). Integrating the G2GT model with the StateTr baseline achieves 9.97% LAS Relative Error Reduction (RER) improvement, which confirms the effectiveness of modelling the graph information in the attention mechanism. Furthermore, initialising our model weights with the BERT model (Devlin et al., 2019), provides significant improvement (27.65% LAS RER), which shows the compatibility of our modified attention mechanism with the latent representations learned by BERT pretraining. Integrating the G2GT model with the SentTr baseline results in a similar significant improvement (4.62% LAS RER).

4.1.2 Graph-based Dependency Parsing

The StateTr and SentTr models generate the dependency graph in an autoregressive manner, predicting each parser action conditioned on the history of parser actions. Many previous models have achieved better results with graph-based parsing methods, which use non-autoregressive computation of scores for all individual candidate dependency relations and then use a decoding method to reach the maximum scoring structure (McDonald et al., 2005; Koo and Collins, 2010; Ballesteros et al., 2016; Wang and Chang, 2016; Kuncoro et al., 2016; Zhou and Zhao, 2019). However, these models usually ignore correlations between edges while predicting the complete graph. In (Mohammadshahi and Henderson, 2021), we propose the **R**ecursive **N**on-autoregressive **G**raph-to-Graph **Tr**ansformer (RNGT) architecture, as discussed in Section 3. The RNGT architecture can be applied to any task with a sequence or graph as input and a graph over the same set of nodes as output. Here, we apply it for the syntactic dependency parsing task, and preliminary experiments showed that removing the interaction of graph relations with key vectors, in Equation 1, results in better performance and a more efficient attention mechanism. Mohammadshahi and Henderson (2021) evaluate this RNGT model on Universal Dependency (UD) Treebanks (Nivre et al., 2018), Penn Treebanks (Marcus et al., 1993), and the German CoNLL 2009 Treebank (Hajič et al., 2009) for the syntactic dependency parsing task.

Table 2 shows the results on 13 languages of UD Treebanks. First, we use UDify (Kondratyuk and Straka, 2019), the previous state-of-the-art multilingual dependency parser, as the initial parser for the RNGT model. The integrated model achieves significantly better LAS performance than the UDify model in all languages, which demonstrates the effectiveness of the RNGT model at refining a dependency graph. Then, we combine RNGT with Syntactic Transformer (SynTr), a stronger monolingual dependency parser, which has the same architecture as the RNGT model except without the graph input mechanism. The SynTr+RNGT model reaches further improvement over the strong SynTr baseline (four languages are significant), which is stronger evidence for the effectiveness of the graph refinement method. Interestingly, there is little difference between the performance with different initial parsers, implying that the RNGT model is effective enough to refine any initial graphs. In fact, even when we initialise with an empty parse, the Empty+RNGT model achieves competitive results with the other RNGT models, again confirming our powerful method of graph refinement.

4.2 Semantic Role Labelling

The semantic role labelling (SRL) task provides a shallow semantic representation of a sentence and builds event properties and relations among relevant words, and is defined in both dependency-based (Surdeanu et al., 2008) and span-based (Carreras and Màrquez, 2005; Pradhan et al., 2012) styles. Previous work (Marcheggiani and Titov, 2017; Strubell et al., 2018; Cai and Lapata, 2019; Fei et al., 2021; Zhou et al., 2020) showed that the syntactic graph helps SRL models to predict better output graphs, but finding the most effective way to incorporate the auxiliary syntactic information into SRL models was still an open question. In (Mohammadshahi and Henderson, 2023), we introduce the Syntax-aware Graph-to-Graph Transformer (SynG2G-Tr) architecture. The model conditions on the sentence's dependency structure and jointly predicts both span-based (Carreras and Màrquez, 2005) and dependency-based (Hajič et al., 2009) SRL structures. Regarding the self-attention mechanism, we remove the interaction of graph embeddings with value vectors in Equation 2, as it reaches better performance in this particular task (Mohammadshahi and Henderson, 2023).

Results for span-based SRL are shown in Table 3. Without initialising the models with BERT (Devlin et al., 2019), the SynG2G-Tr model outperforms a previous comparable state-of-the-art model (Strubell et al., 2018) in both *end-to-end* and *given-predicate* scenarios. The improvement indicates the benefit of encoding the graph information in the self-attention mechanism of Transformer with a soft bias, instead of hard-coding the graph structure into deep learning models (Marcheggiani and Titov, 2017; Strubell et al., 2018; Xia et al., 2019), as the model can still learn other attention patterns in combination with this graph knowledge. BERT (Devlin et al., 2019) initialisation results in further significant improvement in both settings, which again shows the compatibility of the G2GT modified self-attention mechanism with the latent structures learned by BERT pretraining.

4.3 Coreference Resolution

Coreference resolution (CR) is an important and complex task which is necessary for higher-level semantic representations. We show that it benefits from a graph-based global optimisation of all the coreference chains in a document.

Language	Multi UDify	Multi+Mono UDify+RNGT	Mono SynTr	Mono SynTr+RNGT	Mono Empty+RNGT
Arabic	82.88	**85.93** (+17.81%)	**86.23**	**86.31** (+0.58%)	**86.05**
Basque	80.97	87.55 (+34.57%)	87.49	**88.2** (+5.68%)	**87.96**
Chinese	83.75	89.05 (+32.62%)	89.53	**90.48** (+9.08%)	89.82
English	88.5	91.23 (+23.74%)	**91.41**	**91.52** (+1.28%)	91.23
Finnish	82.03	**91.87** (+54.76%)	**91.80**	**91.92** (+1.46%)	**91.78**
Hebrew	88.11	90.80 (+22.62%)	**91.07**	**91.32** (+2.79%)	90.56
Hindi	91.46	93.94 (+29.04%)	93.95	**94.21** (+4.3%)	93.97
Italian	93.69	94.65 (+15.21%)	**95.08**	**95.16** (+1.62%)	**94.96**
Japanese	92.08	**95.41** (+42.06%)	**95.66**	**95.71** (+1.16%)	**95.56**
Korean	74.26	**89.12** (+57.73%)	**89.29**	**89.45** (+1.5%)	**89.1**
Russian	93.13	**94.51** (+20.09%)	**94.60**	**94.47** (-2.4%)	94.31
Swedish	89.03	92.02 (+27.26%)	92.03	**92.46** (+5.4%)	**92.40**
Turkish	67.44	72.07 (+14.22%)	**72.52**	**73.08** (+2.04%)	71.99
Average	85.18	89.86	90.05	90.33	89.98

Table 2: Labelled attachment scores of monolingual (SynTr) and multilingual (UDify (Kondratyuk and Straka, 2019)) baselines, and the refined models (+RNGT) pre-trained with BERT (Devlin et al., 2019) on 13 languages of UD Treebanks. The relative error reduction after the integration is illustrated in parentheses. Bold scores are not significantly different from the best score in that row (with $\alpha=0.01$).

Model	in-domain	out-of-domain
end-to-end		
Strubell et al. (2018)	84.99	74.66
SynG2G-Tr (w/o BERT)	**85.45**	**75.26**
+pre-training		
Strubell et al. (2018)	86.9	78.25
SynG2G-Tr	**87.57**	**80.53**
given predicate		
Strubell et al. (2018)	86.04	76.54
SynG2G-Tr (w/o BERT)	**86.50**	**77.45**
+pre-training		
Jia et al. (2022)	88.25	81.90
SynG2G-Tr	**88.93**	**83.21**

Table 3: Comparing our SynG2G-Tr with previous comparable SoTA model on CoNLL 2005 test sets for both in-domain (WSJ), and out-of-domain (Brown) sets. Scores being boldfaced means that they are significantly better.

Figure 2: Example of a graph structure for coreference. Mention spans are shown in bold, and colours represent entity clusters. The mention heads are underlined.

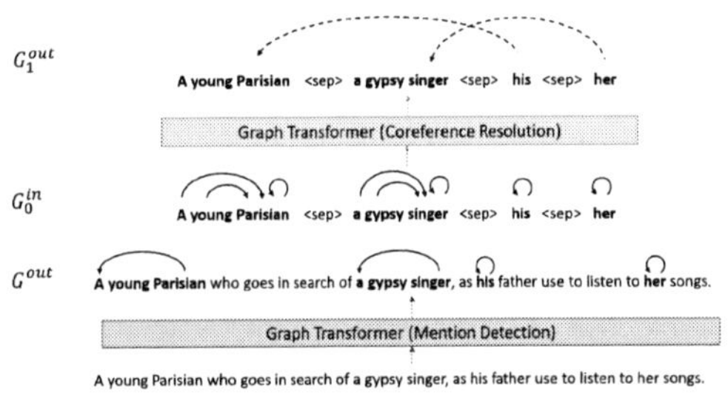

Figure 3: Example of iterations with G2GT in two stages.

4.3.1 CR Task Definition and Background

Coreference resolution is the task of linking all linguistic expressions in a text that refer to the same entity. Solutions for this task involve three parts: mention-detection (Yu et al., 2020; Miculicich and Henderson, 2020), classification or ranking of mentions, and finally reconciling the decisions to create entity chains. These approaches fall within three principal categories: mention-pair models which perform binary decisions (McCarthy and Lehnert, 1995; Aone and William, 1995; Soon et al., 2001), entity-based models which focus on maintaining single underlying entity representation, contrasting the independent pair-wise decisions of mention-pair approaches (Clark and Manning, 2015, 2016), and ranking models which aim at ranking the possible antecedents of each mention instead of making binary decisions (Wiseman et al., 2016). A limitation of these methods lies in their bottom-up construction, resulting in an underutilisation of comprehensive global information regarding coreference links among all mentions in individual decisions. Furthermore, these methods tend to exhibit significant complexity. Modelling of coreference resolution as a graph-based approach offer an alternative to deal with these limitations.

4.3.2 Iterative Graph-based CR

Miculicich and Henderson (2022) proposed a novel approach to modelling coreference resolution, treating it as a graph problem. In this framework, the tokens within the text serve as nodes, and the connections between them signify coreference links (see Figure 2). Given a document $D=[x_1,...,x_N]$ with length N, the coreference graph is formally defined as the matrix $G\subset\mathbb{N}^{N\times N}$, which represents the relationships between tokens. Specifically, the relationship type between any two tokens, x_i and x_j, is labelled as $g_{i,j}\in\{0,1,2\}$ for the three distinct relation types: (0) no link, (1) mention link, and (2) coreference link.

The primary objective of this approach is to learn the conditional probability distribution $p(G|D)$. To achieve this, an iterative refinement strategy is employed, which captures interdependencies among relations. The model iterates over the same document D for a total of T iterations. In each iteration t, the predicted coreference graph G_t is conditioned on the previous prediction, denoted as G_{t-1}. Thus, the conditional probability distribution of the model is defined as follows:

$$p(G^t|D,G^{t-1})=\prod_{i=1}^{N}\prod_{j=1}^{i}p(g_{i,j}|D,G^{t-1}) \quad (4)$$

The proposed model operates on two levels of representation. In each iteration, it predicts the entire graph. However, during the first iteration, the model focuses on predicting edges that pinpoint mention spans, given that coreferent links only have relevance when mentions are detected. From the second iteration, both mention links, and coreference links are refined. This iterative strategy permits the model to enhance mention-related decisions based on coreference resolutions, and vice versa. This framework utilises iterative graph refinement as a substitute for conventional pipeline architectures in multi-level deep learning models. The iterative process concludes either when the graph no longer undergoes changes or when a predetermined maximum iteration count is attained (see Figure 3).

Ideally, encoding the entirety of the document in a single pass would be optimal. However, in practical scenarios, a constraint on maximum length arises due to limitations in hardware memory capacity. To address this challenge, Miculicich and Henderson (2022) introduce two strategies: overlapping windows and reduced document approach. In the latter strategy, mentions are identified during an initial iteration with a focus on optimising recall, as previously suggested in (Miculicich and Henderson, 2020). Only the representations of these identified spans are subsequently used as inputs for the following iterations.

Miculicich and Henderson (2022) conducted experiments on the CoNLL 2012 corpus (Pradhan et al., 2012) and showed improvements over relevant baselines and previous state-of-the-art methods, summarised in Table 4. We compare our model with three baselines: Lee et al. (2017) proposed the first end-to-end model for coreference resolution; Lee et al. (2018) extended the previous model by introducing higher order inference; and Xu and Choi (2020) used the span based pretrained model SpanBERT (Joshi et al., 2020). The 'Baseline' of Lee et al. (2018) uses ELMo (Peters et al., 2018) to obtain token representations, so versions of this Baseline which use 'BERT-large' (Joshi et al., 2019) and 'SpanBERT-large' (Joshi et al., 2020) as their pretrained models, are directly comparable to our 'G2GT BERT-large' and 'G2GT SpanBERT-large' models, respectively.

These results show that coreference resolution benefits from making global coreference decisions using document-level information, as supported by the G2GT architecture. Our model achieves its optimal solution within a maximum of three iterations. Notably, due to the model's ability to predict the entire graph in a single iteration, its computational complexity is lower compared to that of the baseline approaches.

5 Discussion

The empirical success of Graph-to-Graph Transformers on modelling these various graph structures helps us understand how Transformers model language. This success demonstrates that Transformers are computationally adequate for modelling linguistic structures, which are central to the nature of language. The reliance of these G2GT models on using self-attention mechanisms to extract and encode these graph relations shows that self-attention is crucial to how Transformers can do this modelling. The large improvements gained by initialising with pretrained models indicates that pretrained Transformers are in fact using the same mechanisms to learn about this linguistic structure, but in an unsupervised fashion.

These insights into pretrained Transformers give us a better understanding of the current generation of Large Language Models (LLMs). It is not that these models do not need linguistic structure (since their attention mechanisms do learn it); it is that these models do not need supervised learning of linguistic structure. But perhaps in a

Model	MUC P	MUC R	MUC F1	B^3 P	B^3 R	B^3 F1	$CEAF_{\phi_4}$ P	$CEAF_{\phi_4}$ R	$CEAF_{\phi_4}$ F1	Avg. F1
Lee et al. (2017)	78.4	73.4	75.8	68.6	61.8	65.0	62.7	59.0	60.8	67.2
Xu and Choi (2020)	**85.9**	85.5	85.7	79.0	78.9	79.0	**76.7**	75.2	75.9	80.2
Baseline (Lee et al., 2018)	81.4	79.5	80.4	72.2	69.5	70.8	68.2	67.1	67.6	73.0
+ BERT-large (Joshi et al., 2019)	84.7	82.4	83.5	76.5	74.0	75.3	74.1	69.8	71.9	76.9
+ SpanBERT-large (Joshi et al., 2020)	85.8	84.8	85.3	78.3	77.9	78.1	76.4	74.2	75.3	79.6
G2GT BERT-large *reduced*	84.7	83.1	83.9	76.8	74.0	75.4	75.3	70.1	72.6	77.3
G2GT SpanBERT-large *reduced*	**85.9**	**86.0***†	**85.9***	**79.3***	**79.4***†	**79.3***	76.4	**75.9***	**76.1***	**80.5***

Table 4: Evaluation of CR on the test set (CoNLL 2012) in terms of precision (P), recall (R) and F1 score for three metrics, as well as the average F1 over metrics. $*$ significant at $p < 0.01$ compared to (Joshi et al., 2020), $\dagger$ significant at $p < 0.05$ compared to (Xu and Choi, 2020).

low-resource scenario LLMs would benefit from the inductive bias provided by supervised learning of linguistic structures, such as for many of the world's languages other than English. And these insights are potentially relevant to the issues of interpretability and controllability of LLMs.

These insights are also relevant for any applications which could benefit from integrating text with structured representations. Our current work investigates jointly embedding text and parts of a knowledge base in a single G2GT model, providing a way to integrate interpretable structured knowledge with knowledge in text. Such representations would be useful for information extraction, question answering and information retrieval, amongst many other applications. Other graphs we might want to model with a Transformer and integrate with text include hyperlink graphs, citation graphs, and social networks. An important open problem with such models is the scale of the resulting Transformer embedding.

6 Conclusion and Future Work

The Graph-to-Graph Transformer architecture makes explicit the implicit graph processing abilities of Transformers, but further research is needed to fully leverage the potential of G2GT.

6.1 Conclusions

The success of the above models of a variety linguistic structures shows that Transformers are underlyingly graph-to-graph models, not limited to sequence-to-sequence tasks. The G2GT architecture with its RNGT method provides an effective way to exploit this underlying ability when modelling explicit graphs, effectively integrating them with the implicit graphs learned by pre-trained Transformers. Inputting graph relations as features to the self-attention mechanism enables the information input to the model to be steered by domain-specific knowledge or desired outcomes but still learned by the Transformer, opening up the possibility for a more tailored and customised encoding process. Predicting graph relations with attention-like functions and then re-inputting them for iterative refinement, encodes the input, predicted and latent graphs in a single joint Transformer embedding which is effective for making global decisions about structure in a text.

6.2 Future Work

One topic of research where explicit graphs are indispensable is knowledge graphs. Knowledge needs to be interpretable, so that it can be audited, edited, and learned by people. And it needs to be integrated with existing knowledge graphs. Our current work uses G2GT to integrate knowledge graphs with knowledge conveyed by text.

One of the limitations of the models discussed in this paper is that the set of nodes in the output graph needs to be (a subset of) the nodes in the input graph. General purpose graph-to-graph mappings would require also predicting a set of new nodes in the output graph. One natural solution would be autoregressive prediction of one node at a time, as is done for text generation, but an exciting alternative would be to use methods from non-autoregressive text generation in combination with our iterative refinement method RNGT.

The excellent performance of the models presented in this paper suggest that many more problems can be successfully formulated as graph-to-graph problems and modelled with G2GT, in NLP and beyond. The code for G2GT and RNGT is open-source and publicly available at `https://github.com/idiap/g2g-transformer`.

Acknowledgement

We would like to especially thank the Swiss National Science Foundation for funding this work, under grants 200021E_189458, CRSII5_180320, and 200021_178862. We would also like to thank other members of the the Natural Language Understanding group at Idiap Research Institute for useful discussion and feedback, including Florian Mai, Rabeeh Karimi, Andreas Marfurt, Melika Behjati, and Fabio Fehr.

References

Uri Alon and Eran Yahav. 2021. On the bottleneck of graph neural networks and its practical implications. In *International Conference on Learning Representations*.

Daniel Andor, Chris Alberti, David Weiss, Aliaksei Severyn, Alessandro Presta, Kuzman Ganchev, Slav Petrov, and Michael Collins. 2016. Globally normalized transition-based neural networks. In *Proceedings of the 54th Annual Meeting of the Association for Computational Linguistics (Volume 1: Long Papers)*, pages 2442–2452, Berlin, Germany. Association for Computational Linguistics.

Chinatsu Aone and Scott William. 1995. Evaluating automated and manual acquisition of anaphora resolution strategies. In *33rd Annual Meeting of the Association for Computational Linguistics*, pages 122–129, Cambridge, Massachusetts, USA. Association for Computational Linguistics.

Miguel Ballesteros, Yoav Goldberg, Chris Dyer, and Noah A. Smith. 2016. Training with exploration improves a greedy stack LSTM parser. In *Proceedings of the 2016 Conference on Empirical Methods in Natural Language Processing*, pages 2005–2010, Austin, Texas. Association for Computational Linguistics.

Joan Bruna, Wojciech Zaremba, Arthur Szlam, and Yann LeCun. 2013. Spectral networks and locally connected networks on graphs. *CoRR*, abs/1312.6203.

Rui Cai and Mirella Lapata. 2019. Semi-supervised semantic role labeling with cross-view training. In *Proceedings of the 2019 Conference on Empirical Methods in Natural Language Processing and the 9th International Joint Conference on Natural Language Processing (EMNLP-IJCNLP)*, pages 1018–1027, Hong Kong, China. Association for Computational Linguistics.

Xavier Carreras. 2007. Experiments with a higher-order projective dependency parser. In *Proceedings of the 2007 Joint Conference on Empirical Methods in Natural Language Processing and Computational Natural Language Learning (EMNLP-CoNLL)*, pages 957–961, Prague, Czech Republic. Association for Computational Linguistics.

Xavier Carreras and Lluís Màrquez. 2005. Introduction to the CoNLL-2005 shared task: Semantic role labeling. In *Proceedings of the Ninth Conference on Computational Natural Language Learning (CoNLL-2005)*, pages 152–164, Ann Arbor, Michigan. Association for Computational Linguistics.

Huadong Chen, Shujian Huang, David Chiang, and Jiajun Chen. 2017. Improved neural machine translation with a syntax-aware encoder and decoder. *Proceedings of the 55th Annual Meeting of the Association for Computational Linguistics (Volume 1: Long Papers)*.

Peng Chen. 2021. PermuteFormer: Efficient relative position encoding for long sequences. In *Proceedings of the 2021 Conference on Empirical Methods in Natural Language Processing*, pages 10606–10618, Online and Punta Cana, Dominican Republic. Association for Computational Linguistics.

Krzysztof Choromanski, Valerii Likhosherstov, David Dohan, Xingyou Song, Andreea Gane, Tamás Sarlós, Peter Hawkins, Jared Davis, Afroz Mohiuddin, Lukasz Kaiser, David Belanger, Lucy J. Colwell, and Adrian Weller. 2020. Rethinking attention with performers. *ArXiv*, abs/2009.14794.

Kevin Clark and Christopher D. Manning. 2015. Entity-centric coreference resolution with model stacking. In *Proceedings of the 53rd Annual Meeting of the Association for Computational Linguistics and the 7th International Joint Conference on Natural Language Processing (Volume 1: Long Papers)*, pages 1405–1415, Beijing, China. Association for Computational Linguistics.

Kevin Clark and Christopher D. Manning. 2016. Improving coreference resolution by learning entity-level distributed representations. In *Proceedings of the 54th Annual Meeting of the Association for Computational Linguistics (Volume 1: Long Papers)*, pages 643–653, Berlin, Germany. Association for Computational Linguistics.

Zihang Dai, Zhilin Yang, Yiming Yang, Jaime Carbonell, Quoc Le, and Ruslan Salakhutdinov. 2019. Transformer-XL: Attentive language models beyond a fixed-length context. In *Proceedings of the 57th Annual Meeting of the Association for Computational Linguistics*, pages 2978–2988, Florence, Italy. Association for Computational Linguistics.

Jacob Devlin, Ming-Wei Chang, Kenton Lee, and Kristina Toutanova. 2019. BERT: Pre-training of deep bidirectional transformers for language understanding. In *Proceedings of the 2019 Conference of the North American Chapter of the Association for Computational Linguistics: Human Language Technologies, Volume 1 (Long and Short Papers)*, pages 4171–4186, Minneapolis, Minnesota. Association for Computational Linguistics.

Cameron Diao and Ricky Loynd. 2022. Relational attention: Generalizing transformers for graph-structured tasks. *ArXiv*, abs/2210.05062.

Philipp Dufter, Martin Schmitt, and Hinrich Schütze. 2022. Position information in transformers: An overview. *Computational Linguistics*, 48(3):733–763.

Chris Dyer, Miguel Ballesteros, Wang Ling, Austin Matthews, and Noah A. Smith. 2015. Transition-based dependency parsing with stack long short-term memory. In *Proceedings of the 53rd Annual Meeting of the Association for Computational Linguistics and the 7th International Joint Conference on Natural Language Processing (Volume 1: Long Papers)*, pages 334–343, Beijing, China. Association for Computational Linguistics.

Luis Espinosa Anke, Alexander Shvets, Alireza Mohammadshahi, James Henderson, and Leo Wanner. 2022. Multilingual extraction and categorization of lexical collocations with graph-aware transformers. In *Proceedings of the 11th Joint Conference on Lexical and Computational Semantics*, pages 89–100, Seattle, Washington. Association for Computational Linguistics.

Hao Fei, Fei Li, Bobo Li, and Donghong Ji. 2021. Encoder-decoder based unified semantic role labeling with label-aware syntax. *Proceedings of the AAAI Conference on Artificial Intelligence*, 35(14):12794–12802.

Justin Gilmer, Samuel S Schoenholz, Patrick F Riley, Oriol Vinyals, and George E Dahl. 2017. Neural message passing for quantum chemistry. In *International conference on machine learning*, pages 1263–1272. PMLR.

Marco Gori, Gabriele Monfardini, and Franco Scarselli. 2005. A new model for learning in graph domains. In *Proceedings. 2005 IEEE International Joint Conference on Neural Networks, 2005.*, volume 2, pages 729–734. IEEE.

Jan Hajič, Massimiliano Ciaramita, Richard Johansson, Daisuke Kawahara, Maria Antònia Martí, Lluís Màrquez, Adam Meyers, Joakim Nivre, Sebastian Padó, Jan Štěpánek, Pavel Straňák, Mihai Surdeanu, Nianwen Xue, and Yi Zhang. 2009. The CoNLL-2009 shared task: Syntactic and semantic dependencies in multiple languages. In *Proceedings of the Thirteenth Conference on Computational Natural Language Learning (CoNLL 2009): Shared Task*, pages 1–18, Boulder, Colorado. Association for Computational Linguistics.

James Henderson. 2003. Inducing history representations for broad coverage statistical parsing. In *Proceedings of the 2003 Human Language Technology Conference of the North American Chapter of the Association for Computational Linguistics*, pages 103–110.

James Henderson. 2004. Discriminative training of a neural network statistical parser. In *Proceedings of the 42nd Annual Meeting of the Association for Computational Linguistics (ACL-04)*, pages 95–102, Barcelona, Spain.

James Henderson. 2020. The unstoppable rise of computational linguistics in deep learning. In *Proceedings of the 58th Annual Meeting of the Association for Computational Linguistics*, pages 6294–6306, Online. Association for Computational Linguistics.

James Henderson, Paola Merlo, Ivan Titov, and Gabriele Musillo. 2013. Multilingual joint parsing of syntactic and semantic dependencies with a latent variable model. *Computational Linguistics*, 39(4):949–998.

John Hewitt, Kawin Ethayarajh, Percy Liang, and Christopher Manning. 2021. Conditional probing: measuring usable information beyond a baseline. In *Proceedings of the 2021 Conference on Empirical Methods in Natural Language Processing*, pages 1626–1639, Online and Punta Cana, Dominican Republic. Association for Computational Linguistics.

John J Hopfield. 1982. Neural networks and physical systems with emergent collective computational abilities. *Proceedings of the national academy of sciences*, 79(8):2554–2558.

Zhiheng Huang, Davis Liang, Peng Xu, and Bing Xiang. 2020. Improve transformer models with better relative position embeddings. In *Findings of the Association for Computational Linguistics: EMNLP 2020*, pages 3327–3335, Online. Association for Computational Linguistics.

Zixia Jia, Zhaohui Yan, Haoyi Wu, and Kewei Tu. 2022. Span-based semantic role labeling with argument pruning and second-order inference. *Proceedings of the AAAI Conference on Artificial Intelligence*, 36(10):10822–10830.

Mandar Joshi, Danqi Chen, Yinhan Liu, Daniel S. Weld, Luke Zettlemoyer, and Omer Levy. 2020. SpanBERT: Improving pre-training by representing and predicting spans. *Transactions of the Association for Computational Linguistics*, 8:64–77.

Mandar Joshi, Omer Levy, Luke Zettlemoyer, and Daniel Weld. 2019. BERT for coreference resolution: Baselines and analysis. In *Proceedings of the 2019 Conference on Empirical Methods in Natural Language Processing and the 9th International Joint Conference on Natural Language Processing (EMNLP-IJCNLP)*, pages 5803–5808, Hong Kong, China. Association for Computational Linguistics.

Pei Ke, Haozhe Ji, Yu Ran, Xin Cui, Liwei Wang, Linfeng Song, Xiaoyan Zhu, and Minlie Huang. 2021. JointGT: Graph-text joint representation learning for text generation from knowledge graphs. In *Findings of the Association for Computational Linguistics: ACL-IJCNLP 2021*, pages 2526–2538, Online. Association for Computational Linguistics.

Thomas N. Kipf and Max Welling. 2017. Semi-supervised classification with graph convolutional networks. In *International Conference on Learning Representations*.

Dan Kondratyuk and Milan Straka. 2019. 75 languages, 1 model: Parsing Universal Dependencies universally. In *Proceedings of the 2019 Conference on Empirical Methods in Natural Language Processing and the 9th International Joint Conference on Natural Language Processing (EMNLP-IJCNLP)*, pages 2779–2795, Hong Kong, China. Association for Computational Linguistics.

Terry Koo and Michael Collins. 2010. Efficient third-order dependency parsers. In *Proceedings of the 48th Annual Meeting of the Association for Computational Linguistics*, pages 1–11.

Adhiguna Kuncoro, Miguel Ballesteros, Lingpeng Kong, Chris Dyer, and Noah A. Smith. 2016. Distilling an ensemble of greedy dependency parsers into one MST parser. In *Proceedings of the 2016 Conference on Empirical Methods in Natural Language Processing*, pages 1744–1753, Austin, Texas. Association for Computational Linguistics.

Kenton Lee, Luheng He, Mike Lewis, and Luke Zettlemoyer. 2017. End-to-end neural coreference resolution. In *Proceedings of the 2017 Conference on Empirical Methods in Natural Language Processing*, pages 188–197, Copenhagen, Denmark. Association for Computational Linguistics.

Kenton Lee, Luheng He, and Luke Zettlemoyer. 2018. Higher-order coreference resolution with coarse-to-fine inference. In *Proceedings of the 2018 Conference of the North American Chapter of the Association for Computational Linguistics: Human Language Technologies, Volume 2 (Short Papers)*, pages 687–692, New Orleans, Louisiana. Association for Computational Linguistics.

Yujia Li, Daniel Tarlow, Marc Brockschmidt, and Richard S. Zemel. 2015. Gated graph sequence neural networks. *CoRR*, abs/1511.05493.

Antoine Liutkus, Ondřej Cífka, Shih-Lun Wu, Umut Simsekli, Yi-Hsuan Yang, and Gaël Richard. 2021. Relative positional encoding for transformers with linear complexity. In *International Conference on Machine Learning*.

Christopher Manning and Hinrich Schutze. 1999. *Foundations of statistical natural language processing*. MIT press.

Diego Marcheggiani and Ivan Titov. 2017. Encoding sentences with graph convolutional networks for semantic role labeling. In *Proceedings of the 2017 Conference on Empirical Methods in Natural Language Processing*, pages 1506–1515, Copenhagen, Denmark. Association for Computational Linguistics.

Diego Marcheggiani and Ivan Titov. 2020. Graph convolutions over constituent trees for syntax-aware semantic role labeling. In *Proceedings of the 2020 Conference on Empirical Methods in Natural Language Processing (EMNLP)*, pages 3915–3928, Online. Association for Computational Linguistics.

Mitchell P. Marcus, Beatrice Santorini, and Mary Ann Marcinkiewicz. 1993. Building a large annotated corpus of English: The Penn Treebank. *Computational Linguistics*, 19(2):313–330.

Joseph F. McCarthy and Wendy G. Lehnert. 1995. Using decision trees for coreference resolution. In *International Joint Conference on Artificial Intelligence*.

Ryan McDonald, Koby Crammer, and Fernando Pereira. 2005. Online large-margin training of dependency parsers. In *Proceedings of the 43rd Annual Meeting of the Association for Computational Linguistics (ACL'05)*, pages 91–98, Ann Arbor, Michigan. Association for Computational Linguistics.

Julian Michael, Jan A. Botha, and Ian Tenney. 2020. Asking without telling: Exploring latent ontologies in contextual representations. In *Proceedings of the 2020 Conference on Empirical Methods in Natural Language Processing (EMNLP)*, pages 6792–6812, Online. Association for Computational Linguistics.

Lesly Miculicich and James Henderson. 2020. Partially-supervised mention detection. In *Proceedings of the Third Workshop on Computational Models of Reference, Anaphora and Coreference*, pages 91–98, Barcelona, Spain (online). Association for Computational Linguistics.

Lesly Miculicich and James Henderson. 2022. Graph refinement for coreference resolution. In *Findings of the Association for Computational Linguistics: ACL 2022*, pages 2732–2742, Dublin, Ireland. Association for Computational Linguistics.

Alireza Mohammadshahi and James Henderson. 2020. Graph-to-graph transformer for transition-based dependency parsing. In *Findings of the Association for Computational Linguistics: EMNLP 2020*, pages 3278–3289, Online. Association for Computational Linguistics.

Alireza Mohammadshahi and James Henderson. 2021. Recursive Non-Autoregressive Graph-to-Graph Transformer for Dependency Parsing with Iterative Refinement. *Transactions of the Association for Computational Linguistics*, 9:120–138.

Alireza Mohammadshahi and James Henderson. 2023. Syntax-aware graph-to-graph transformer for semantic role labelling. In *Proceedings of the 8th Workshop on Representation Learning for NLP (RepL4NLP 2023)*, pages 174–186, Toronto, Canada. Association for Computational Linguistics.

Joakim Nivre. 2003. An efficient algorithm for projective dependency parsing. In *Proceedings of the Eighth International Conference on Parsing Technologies*, pages 149–160, Nancy, France.

Joakim Nivre, Mitchell Abrams, Željko Agić, Lars Ahrenberg, Lene Antonsen, Katya Aplonova, Maria Jesus Aranzabe, Gashaw Arutie, Masayuki Asahara, Luma Ateyah, Mohammed Attia, Aitziber Atutxa, Liesbeth Augustinus, Elena Badmaeva,

Miguel Ballesteros, Esha Banerjee, Sebastian Bank, Verginica Barbu Mititelu, Victoria Basmov, John Bauer, Sandra Bellato, Kepa Bengoetxea, Yevgeni Berzak, Irshad Ahmad Bhat, Riyaz Ahmad Bhat, Erica Biagetti, Eckhard Bick, Rogier Blokland, Victoria Bobicev, Carl Börstell, Cristina Bosco, Gosse Bouma, Sam Bowman, Adriane Boyd, Aljoscha Burchardt, Marie Candito, Bernard Caron, Gauthier Caron, Gülşen Cebiroğlu Eryiğit, Flavio Massimiliano Cecchini, Giuseppe G. A. Celano, Slavomír Čéplö, Savas Cetin, Fabricio Chalub, Jinho Choi, Yongseok Cho, Jayeol Chun, Silvie Cinková, Aurélie Collomb, Çağrı Çöltekin, Miriam Connor, Marine Courtin, Elizabeth Davidson, Marie-Catherine de Marneffe, Valeria de Paiva, Arantza Diaz de Ilarraza, Carly Dickerson, Peter Dirix, Kaja Dobrovoljc, Timothy Dozat, Kira Droganova, Puneet Dwivedi, Marhaba Eli, Ali Elkahky, Binyam Ephrem, Tomaž Erjavec, Aline Etienne, Richárd Farkas, Hector Fernandez Alcalde, Jennifer Foster, Cláudia Freitas, Katarína Gajdošová, Daniel Galbraith, Marcos Garcia, Moa Gärdenfors, Sebastian Garza, Kim Gerdes, Filip Ginter, Iakes Goenaga, Koldo Gojenola, Memduh Gökırmak, Yoav Goldberg, Xavier Gómez Guinovart, Berta Gonzáles Saavedra, Matias Grioni, Normunds Grūzītis, Bruno Guillaume, Céline Guillot-Barbance, Nizar Habash, Jan Hajič, Jan Hajič jr., Linh Hà Mỹ, Na-Rae Han, Kim Harris, Dag Haug, Barbora Hladká, Jaroslava Hlaváčová, Florinel Hociung, Petter Hohle, Jena Hwang, Radu Ion, Elena Irimia, Ọlájídé Ishola, Tomáš Jelínek, Anders Johannsen, Fredrik Jørgensen, Hüner Kaşıkara, Sylvain Kahane, Hiroshi Kanayama, Jenna Kanerva, Boris Katz, Tolga Kayadelen, Jessica Kenney, Václava Kettnerová, Jesse Kirchner, Kamil Kopacewicz, Natalia Kotsyba, Simon Krek, Sookyoung Kwak, Veronika Laippala, Lorenzo Lambertino, Lucia Lam, Tatiana Lando, Septina Dian Larasati, Alexei Lavrentiev, John Lee, Phùòng Lê Hồng, Alessandro Lenci, Saran Lertpradit, Herman Leung, Cheuk Ying Li, Josie Li, Keying Li, Kyung-Tae Lim, Nikola Ljubešić, Olga Loginova, Olga Lyashevskaya, Teresa Lynn, Vivien Macketanz, Aibek Makazhanov, Michael Mandl, Christopher Manning, Ruli Manurung, Cătălina Mărănduc, David Mareček, Katrin Marheinecke, Héctor Martínez Alonso, André Martins, Jan Mašek, Yuji Matsumoto, Ryan McDonald, Gustavo Mendonça, Niko Miekka, Margarita Misirpashayeva, Anna Missilä, Cătălin Mititelu, Yusuke Miyao, Simonetta Montemagni, Amir More, Laura Moreno Romero, Keiko Sophie Mori, Shinsuke Mori, Bjartur Mortensen, Bohdan Moskalevskyi, Kadri Muischnek, Yugo Murawaki, Kaili Müürisep, Pinkey Nainwani, Juan Ignacio Navarro Horñiacek, Anna Nedoluzhko, Gunta Nešpore-Bērzkalne, Lùòng Nguyễn Thị, Huyền Nguyễn Thị Minh, Vitaly Nikolaev, Rattima Nitisaroj, Hanna Nurmi, Stina Ojala, Adédayọ̀ Olúòkun, Mai Omura, Petya Osenova, Robert Östling, Lilja Øvrelid, Niko Partanen, Elena Pascual, Marco Passarotti, Agnieszka Patejuk, Guilherme Paulino-Passos, Siyao Peng, Cenel-Augusto Perez, Guy Perrier, Slav Petrov, Jussi Piitulainen, Emily Pitler, Barbara Plank, Thierry Poibeau, Martin Popel, Lauma Pretkalniņa, Sophie Prévost, Prokopis Prokopidis, Adam Przepiórkowski, Tiina Puolakainen, Sampo Pyysalo, Andriela Rääbis, Alexandre Rademaker, Loganathan Ramasamy, Taraka Rama, Carlos Ramisch, Vinit Ravishankar, Livy Real, Siva Reddy, Georg Rehm, Michael Rießler, Larissa Rinaldi, Laura Rituma, Luisa Rocha, Mykhailo Romanenko, Rudolf Rosa, Davide Rovati, Valentin Roșca, Olga Rudina, Jack Rueter, Shoval Sadde, Benoît Sagot, Shadi Saleh, Tanja Samardžić, Stephanie Samson, Manuela Sanguinetti, Baiba Saulīte, Yanin Sawanakunanon, Nathan Schneider, Sebastian Schuster, Djamé Seddah, Wolfgang Seeker, Mojgan Seraji, Mo Shen, Atsuko Shimada, Muh Shohibussirri, Dmitry Sichinava, Natalia Silveira, Maria Simi, Radu Simionescu, Katalin Simkó, Mária Šimková, Kiril Simov, Aaron Smith, Isabela Soares-Bastos, Carolyn Spadine, Antonio Stella, Milan Straka, Jana Strnadová, Alane Suhr, Umut Sulubacak, Zsolt Szántó, Dima Taji, Yuta Takahashi, Takaaki Tanaka, Isabelle Tellier, Trond Trosterud, Anna Trukhina, Reut Tsarfaty, Francis Tyers, Sumire Uematsu, Zdeňka Urešová, Larraitz Uria, Hans Uszkoreit, Sowmya Vajjala, Daniel van Niekerk, Gertjan van Noord, Viktor Varga, Eric Villemonte de la Clergerie, Veronika Vincze, Lars Wallin, Jing Xian Wang, Jonathan North Washington, Seyi Williams, Mats Wirén, Tsegay Woldemariam, Taksum Wong, Chunxiao Yan, Marat M. Yavrumyan, Zhuoran Yu, Zdeněk Žabokrtský, Amir Zeldes, Daniel Zeman, Manying Zhang, and Hanzhi Zhu. 2018. Universal dependencies 2.3. LINDAT/CLARIAH-CZ digital library at the Institute of Formal and Applied Linguistics (ÚFAL), Faculty of Mathematics and Physics, Charles University.

Joakim Nivre and Ryan McDonald. 2008. Integrating graph-based and transition-based dependency parsers. In *Proceedings of ACL-08: HLT*, pages 950–958, Columbus, Ohio. Association for Computational Linguistics.

Joakim Nivre and Mario Scholz. 2004. Deterministic dependency parsing of English text. In *COLING 2004: Proceedings of the 20th International Conference on Computational Linguistics*, pages 64–70, Geneva, Switzerland. COLING.

Kenta Oono and Taiji Suzuki. 2020. Graph neural networks exponentially lose expressive power for node classification. In *International Conference on Learning Representations*.

Deric Pang, Lucy H. Lin, and Noah A. Smith. 2019. Improving natural language inference with a pretrained parser.

Jinyoung Park, Hyeong Kyu Choi, Juyeon Ko, Hyeon ju Park, Ji-Hoon Kim, Jisu Jeong, Kyungmin Kim, and Hyunwoo J. Kim. 2022. Relation-aware language-graph transformer for question answering. *ArXiv*, abs/2212.00975.

Matthew E. Peters, Mark Neumann, Mohit Iyyer, Matt Gardner, Christopher Clark, Kenton Lee, and Luke Zettlemoyer. 2018. Deep contextualized word representations. In *Proceedings of the 2018*

Conference of the North American Chapter of the Association for Computational Linguistics: Human Language Technologies, Volume 1 (Long Papers)*, pages 2227–2237, New Orleans, Louisiana. Association for Computational Linguistics.

Sameer Pradhan, Alessandro Moschitti, Nianwen Xue, Olga Uryupina, and Yuchen Zhang. 2012. CoNLL-2012 shared task: Modeling multilingual unrestricted coreference in OntoNotes. In *Joint Conference on EMNLP and CoNLL - Shared Task*, pages 1–40, Jeju Island, Korea. Association for Computational Linguistics.

Franco Scarselli, Marco Gori, Ah Chung Tsoi, Markus Hagenbuchner, and Gabriele Monfardini. 2008. The graph neural network model. *IEEE transactions on neural networks*, 20(1):61–80.

Peter Shaw, Jakob Uszkoreit, and Ashish Vaswani. 2018. Self-attention with relative position representations. In *Proceedings of the 2018 Conference of the North American Chapter of the Association for Computational Linguistics: Human Language Technologies, Volume 2 (Short Papers)*, pages 464–468, New Orleans, Louisiana. Association for Computational Linguistics.

Wee Meng Soon, Hwee Tou Ng, and Daniel Chung Yong Lim. 2001. A machine learning approach to coreference resolution of noun phrases. *Computational Linguistics*, 27(4):521–544.

Emma Strubell, Patrick Verga, Daniel Andor, David Weiss, and Andrew McCallum. 2018. Linguistically-informed self-attention for semantic role labeling. In *Proceedings of the 2018 Conference on Empirical Methods in Natural Language Processing*, pages 5027–5038, Brussels, Belgium. Association for Computational Linguistics.

Jianlin Su, Yu Lu, Shengfeng Pan, Bo Wen, and Yunfeng Liu. 2021. Roformer: Enhanced transformer with rotary position embedding. *ArXiv*, abs/2104.09864.

Mihai Surdeanu, Richard Johansson, Adam Meyers, Lluís Màrquez, and Joakim Nivre. 2008. The CoNLL 2008 shared task on joint parsing of syntactic and semantic dependencies. In *CoNLL 2008: Proceedings of the Twelfth Conference on Computational Natural Language Learning*, pages 159–177, Manchester, England. Coling 2008 Organizing Committee.

Ivan Titov and James Henderson. 2007a. Constituent parsing with incremental sigmoid belief networks. In *Proceedings of the 45th Annual Meeting of the Association of Computational Linguistics*, pages 632–639, Prague, Czech Republic. Association for Computational Linguistics.

Ivan Titov and James Henderson. 2007b. A latent variable model for generative dependency parsing. In *Proceedings of the Tenth International Conference on Parsing Technologies*, pages 144–155, Prague, Czech Republic. Association for Computational Linguistics.

Jake Topping, Francesco Di Giovanni, Benjamin Paul Chamberlain, Xiaowen Dong, and Michael M. Bronstein. 2021. Understanding over-squashing and bottlenecks on graphs via curvature. *ArXiv*, abs/2111.14522.

Hugo Touvron, Thibaut Lavril, Gautier Izacard, Xavier Martinet, Marie-Anne Lachaux, Timothée Lacroix, Baptiste Rozière, Naman Goyal, Eric Hambro, Faisal Azhar, Aurelien Rodriguez, Armand Joulin, Edouard Grave, and Guillaume Lample. 2023a. Llama: Open and efficient foundation language models.

Hugo Touvron, Louis Martin, Kevin Stone, Peter Albert, Amjad Almahairi, Yasmine Babaei, Nikolay Bashlykov, Soumya Batra, Prajjwal Bhargava, Shruti Bhosale, Dan Bikel, Lukas Blecher, Cristian Canton Ferrer, Moya Chen, Guillem Cucurull, David Esiobu, Jude Fernandes, Jeremy Fu, Wenyin Fu, Brian Fuller, Cynthia Gao, Vedanuj Goswami, Naman Goyal, Anthony Hartshorn, Saghar Hosseini, Rui Hou, Hakan Inan, Marcin Kardas, Viktor Kerkez, Madian Khabsa, Isabel Kloumann, Artem Korenev, Punit Singh Koura, Marie-Anne Lachaux, Thibaut Lavril, Jenya Lee, Diana Liskovich, Yinghai Lu, Yuning Mao, Xavier Martinet, Todor Mihaylov, Pushkar Mishra, Igor Molybog, Yixin Nie, Andrew Poulton, Jeremy Reizenstein, Rashi Rungta, Kalyan Saladi, Alan Schelten, Ruan Silva, Eric Michael Smith, Ranjan Subramanian, Xiaoqing Ellen Tan, Binh Tang, Ross Taylor, Adina Williams, Jian Xiang Kuan, Puxin Xu, Zheng Yan, Iliyan Zarov, Yuchen Zhang, Angela Fan, Melanie Kambadur, Sharan Narang, Aurelien Rodriguez, Robert Stojnic, Sergey Edunov, and Thomas Scialom. 2023b. Llama 2: Open foundation and fine-tuned chat models.

Ashish Vaswani, Noam Shazeer, Niki Parmar, Jakob Uszkoreit, Llion Jones, Aidan N Gomez, Ł ukasz Kaiser, and Illia Polosukhin. 2017. Attention is all you need. In *Advances in Neural Information Processing Systems*, volume 30. Curran Associates, Inc.

Petar Veličković, Guillem Cucurull, Arantxa Casanova, Adriana Romero, Pietro Liò, and Yoshua Bengio. 2018. Graph Attention Networks. *International Conference on Learning Representations*. Accepted as poster.

Wenhui Wang and Baobao Chang. 2016. Graph-based dependency parsing with bidirectional LSTM. In *Proceedings of the 54th Annual Meeting of the Association for Computational Linguistics (Volume 1: Long Papers)*, pages 2306–2315, Berlin, Germany. Association for Computational Linguistics.

Boris Weisfeiler and Andrei Leman. 1968. The reduction of a graph to canonical form and the algebra which appears therein. *nti, Series*, 2(9):12–16.

David Weiss, Chris Alberti, Michael Collins, and Slav Petrov. 2015. Structured training for neural network transition-based parsing. In *Proceedings of the 53rd Annual Meeting of the Association for Computational Linguistics and the 7th International Joint Conference on Natural Language Processing (Volume 1: Long Papers)*, pages 323–333, Beijing, China. Association for Computational Linguistics.

Sam Wiseman, Alexander M. Rush, and Stuart M. Shieber. 2016. Learning global features for coreference resolution. In *Proceedings of the 2016 Conference of the North American Chapter of the Association for Computational Linguistics: Human Language Technologies*, pages 994–1004, San Diego, California. Association for Computational Linguistics.

Zhiyong Wu, Yun Chen, Ben Kao, and Qun Liu. 2020. Perturbed masking: Parameter-free probing for analyzing and interpreting BERT. In *Proceedings of the 58th Annual Meeting of the Association for Computational Linguistics*, pages 4166–4176, Online. Association for Computational Linguistics.

Qingrong Xia, Zhenghua Li, Min Zhang, Meishan Zhang, Guohong Fu, Rui Wang, and Luo Si. 2019. Syntax-aware neural semantic role labeling. *Proceedings of the AAAI Conference on Artificial Intelligence*, 33(01):7305–7313.

Benfeng Xu, Quan Wang, Yajuan Lyu, Yong Zhu, and Zhendong Mao. 2021. Entity structure within and throughout: Modeling mention dependencies for document-level relation extraction. In *AAAI Conference on Artificial Intelligence*.

Liyan Xu and Jinho D. Choi. 2020. Revealing the myth of higher-order inference in coreference resolution. In *Proceedings of the 2020 Conference on Empirical Methods in Natural Language Processing (EMNLP)*, pages 8527–8533, Online. Association for Computational Linguistics.

Hiroyasu Yamada and Yuji Matsumoto. 2003. Statistical dependency analysis with support vector machines. In *Proceedings of the Eighth International Conference on Parsing Technologies*, pages 195–206, Nancy, France.

Jingfeng Yang, Aditya Gupta, Shyam Upadhyay, Luheng He, Rahul Goel, and Shachi Paul. 2022. TableFormer: Robust transformer modeling for table-text encoding. In *Proceedings of the 60th Annual Meeting of the Association for Computational Linguistics (Volume 1: Long Papers)*, pages 528–537, Dublin, Ireland. Association for Computational Linguistics.

Majid Yazdani and James Henderson. 2015. Incremental recurrent neural network dependency parser with search-based discriminative training. In *Proceedings of the Nineteenth Conference on Computational Natural Language Learning*, pages 142–152, Beijing, China. Association for Computational Linguistics.

Chengxuan Ying, Tianle Cai, Shengjie Luo, Shuxin Zheng, Guolin Ke, Di He, Yanming Shen, and Tie-Yan Liu. 2021. Do transformers really perform bad for graph representation? In *Neural Information Processing Systems*.

Juntao Yu, Bernd Bohnet, and Massimo Poesio. 2020. Neural mention detection. In *Proceedings of the Twelfth Language Resources and Evaluation Conference*, pages 1–10, Marseille, France. European Language Resources Association.

Susan Zhang, Stephen Roller, Naman Goyal, Mikel Artetxe, Moya Chen, Shuohui Chen, Christopher Dewan, Mona Diab, Xian Li, Xi Victoria Lin, Todor Mihaylov, Myle Ott, Sam Shleifer, Kurt Shuster, Daniel Simig, Punit Singh Koura, Anjali Sridhar, Tianlu Wang, and Luke Zettlemoyer. 2022. Opt: Open pre-trained transformer language models.

Yue Zhang and Joakim Nivre. 2011. Transition-based dependency parsing with rich non-local features. In *Proceedings of the 49th Annual Meeting of the Association for Computational Linguistics: Human Language Technologies*, pages 188–193, Portland, Oregon, USA. Association for Computational Linguistics.

Yuhao Zhang, Peng Qi, and Christopher D. Manning. 2018. Graph convolution over pruned dependency trees improves relation extraction. In *Proceedings of the 2018 Conference on Empirical Methods in Natural Language Processing*, pages 2205–2215, Brussels, Belgium. Association for Computational Linguistics.

Junru Zhou, Zuchao Li, and Hai Zhao. 2020. Parsing all: Syntax and semantics, dependencies and spans. In *Findings of the Association for Computational Linguistics: EMNLP 2020*, pages 4438–4449, Online. Association for Computational Linguistics.

Junru Zhou and Hai Zhao. 2019. Head-Driven Phrase Structure Grammar parsing on Penn Treebank. In *Proceedings of the 57th Annual Meeting of the Association for Computational Linguistics*, pages 2396–2408, Florence, Italy. Association for Computational Linguistics.

It's MBR All the Way Down: Modern Generation Techniques Through the Lens of Minimum Bayes Risk

Amanda Bertsch* and **Alex Xie*** and **Graham Neubig** and **Matthew R. Gormley**
Carnegie Mellon University
[abertsch, alexx]@cs.cmu.edu

Abstract

Minimum Bayes Risk (MBR) decoding is a method for choosing the outputs of a machine learning system based not on the output with the highest probability, but the output with the lowest risk (expected error) among multiple candidates. It is a simple but powerful method: for an additional cost at inference time, MBR provides reliable several-point improvements across metrics for a wide variety of tasks without any additional data or training. Despite this, MBR is not frequently applied in NLP works, and knowledge of the method itself is limited. We first provide an introduction to the method and the recent literature. We show that several recent methods that do not reference MBR can be written as special cases of MBR; this reformulation provides additional theoretical justification for the performance of these methods, explaining some results that were previously only empirical. We provide theoretical and empirical results about the effectiveness of various MBR variants and make concrete recommendations for the application of MBR in NLP models, including future directions in this area.

1 Introduction

> "Sometimes innovation is only old ideas reappearing in new guises ... [b]ut the new costumes are better made, of better materials, as well as more becoming: so research is not so much going round in circles as ascending a spiral."
>
> (Jones, 1994)

Minimum Bayes Risk (MBR) decoding (Bickel and Doksum (1977); §2) is a decoding method following a simple intuition: when choosing a best output from a set of candidates, the desirable output should be both 1) high probability and 2) relatively consistent with the rest of the outputs (i.e., outputs that are not consistent with the other outputs are high *risk*– they may be dramatically better or worse than the consensus). MBR thus provides an alternative to the more standard maximum-likelihood decoding; when a sample of sufficient size is taken, MBR almost uniformly outperforms beam search and single-output sampling across tasks, metrics, and datasets (see §6). It is also notable in its flexibility; in §3 we organize and discuss several different design decisions that go into the use of MBR and how they affect the efficacy of the method.

While MBR is rarely applied by name in modern NLP, a number of methods with similar intuitions have gained popularity. In §4, we demonstrate that a number of generation techniques widely used with modern language models can be viewed as special instances of MBR: **self-consistency** (Wang et al., 2023) and its extensions, **range voting** (Borgeaud and Emerson, 2020), **output ensembling** (DeNero et al., 2010; Martínez Lorenzo et al., 2023), and some types of **density estimation** (Kobayashi, 2018). This view exposes connections between seemingly disparate methods and presents theoretical justifications for existing empirical results using these methods. We also discuss how insights from the MBR literature can inform the use of these other MBR-like methods.

With the framing of MBR, the theoretical justification for the empirical performance of several methods becomes clear; the extension of self-consistency to open-ended generations becomes trivial; and several promising modifications to self-consistency and output ensembling are exposed. In particular, modern MBR-like methods often do not apply the insights from research on MBR, suggesting that these methods could be further improved. In §5, we show that some design choices, though seemingly intuitive to a practitioner accustomed to search-based decoding methods, should be avoided when applying MBR.

2 Formalization

We begin with the basics of decoding and MBR.

*Denotes equal contribution.

Proceedings of the the Big Picture Workshop, pages 108–122
December 7, 2023 ©2023 Association for Computational Linguistics

2.1 Standard decoding

Decoding from an autoregressive model (such as a transformer decoder) is performed tokenwise. The distribution at each decoding step is conditioned on the prior tokens and the input text:

$$p(y_i|y_{<i}, x) \tag{1}$$

The model is *locally normalized*; the probabilities of next tokens sum to 1. The probability of a sequence under this global model distribution is

$$p(y|x) = \prod_{i=1}^{T} p(y_i|y_{<i}, x) \tag{2}$$

Given this distribution, there are several ways of extracting an output: by sampling at each decoding step from the distribution over next tokens (often with some modification to the distribution, e.g. temperature, nucleus, or epsilon sampling; Holtzman et al. (2019)); by always choosing the most probable next token (i.e. greedy decoding); or by performing a search over some subset of the output space, guided by the distribution (e.g. beam search, best-first search). These methods generally return a single output; if multiple output candidates are present, the one with the *maximum likelihood* under the model distribution is returned.

2.2 Minimum Bayes Risk decoding

The traditional formulation of MBR is as a minimization objective. Given a *output space* $\mathscr{Y}$ and a probability distribution over this space $p(y|x)$, we compute the risk $R(y')$ of a candidate decoding y' as the expected error (also called *loss*) under this distribution (Bickel and Doksum, 1977; Kumar and Byrne, 2004; Tromble et al., 2008). The MBR decoding is then the y' within $\mathscr{Y}$ that minimizes risk:

$$\hat{y} = \operatorname*{argmin}_{y' \in \mathscr{Y}} R(y') \tag{3}$$

$$= \operatorname*{argmin}_{y' \in \mathscr{Y}} \mathbb{E}_{y|x}[L(y, y')] \tag{4}$$

$$= \operatorname*{argmin}_{y' \in \mathscr{Y}} \sum_{y \in \mathscr{Y}} L(y, y')p(y|x) \tag{5}$$

We can trivially rewrite the risk as a maximization of gain (also called *utility*) rather than a minimization of error, where $G(y, y') = -L(y, y')$. Gain or loss functions are any function (e.g. a metric) that compares two sequences $G : \mathscr{Y} \times \mathscr{Y} \rightarrow \mathbb{R}$.

Approximating risk Computing this sum over the space of all possible outputs $\mathscr{Y}$ is intractable for most models.[1] In these cases, we approximate the risk $R(y')$ by using a subset of the full space $\mathcal{Y} \subset \mathscr{Y}$; that is, instead of exact computation of the expectation, we approximate it with a sum over independent samples from $p(y|x)$. Generally, this is performed by sampling repeatedly from a model (or several models) and estimating the probability of each individual output as proportional to the relative frequency that the output occurs.[2] For an unbiased sampling method[3] (e.g. ancestral sampling), as the number of outputs drawn goes to infinity, this recovers the model's true distribution of probability over sequences. Thus, we approximate risk using this sample:

$$R(y') \approx \frac{1}{|\mathcal{Y}|} \sum_{y \in \mathcal{Y}} L(y, y') \tag{6}$$

$$= -\frac{1}{|\mathcal{Y}|} \sum_{y \in \mathcal{Y}} G(y, y') \tag{7}$$

Thus, given a sample (which may include duplicates) $\mathcal{Y}$ and a gain function, we approximate the true MBR decoding rule as:

$$\hat{y} = \operatorname*{argmax}_{y' \in \mathcal{Y}} \frac{1}{|\mathcal{Y}|} \sum_{y \in \mathcal{Y}_e} G(y, y') \tag{8}$$

Separation of evidence and hypothesis sets In many cases, the same subset of the output space is used for both the risk estimate and the candidate outputs. However, when the sample is substantially smaller than the full output space, it is often beneficial to use separate sets (Eikema and Aziz, 2022; Yan et al., 2023). Following prior work (§2.2), we refer to these as the *evidence set* ($\mathcal{Y}_e$) and *hypothesis set* ($\mathcal{Y}_h$).

This separation is beneficial because there are distinct and potentially contradictory desiderata for the two sets. We wish for our evidence set to cover a large, representative portion of the search space to obtain a more accurate estimate of risk. However, we want our hypothesis set to only cover the narrower, high-quality region of the space, as we do not want to consider candidate hypotheses that are low-quality. Applying the separation of evidence and hypothesis sets yields the equation for MBR over two subsets of the output space:

[1]This is the case for many deep generative models, such as a transformer language model and other autoregressive models without conditional independence assumptions.

[2]This is called a Monte Carlo approximation.

[3]We discuss the use of biased samplers in §3.2 and §3.1.

$$\hat{y} = \underset{y' \in \mathcal{Y}_h}{\text{argmax}} \sum_{y \in \mathcal{Y}_e} G(y, y') \quad (9)$$

Note that this implicitly encodes the distribution of the evidence set samples in the sum. That is, by averaging over the gain on evidence set examples, we are estimating the expected gain *under this evidence set's distribution over sequences*.

3 Taxonomy of MBR

Equation 9 demonstrates four major axes along which an MBR method may vary:

1. Choice of hypothesis set $\mathcal{Y}_h$
2. Choice of evidence set $\mathcal{Y}_e$
3. Choice of gain (or error) function $G(y, y')$
4. Choice of evidence distribution $p(y|x)$

In this section, we examine how these four factors affect the efficacy of MBR and give recommendations for each; in Section 4, we discuss how these apply to other MBR-like methods.

3.1 Sampling a hypothesis set

Several recent works show benefits from improving the quality of the hypothesis space. Fernandes et al. (2022) apply a two-stage approach where they first apply an N-best (referenceless) reranker and then do MBR over only the most highly ranked hypotheses, which they also use as the evidence set. Eikema and Aziz (2022) introduce a method, Coarse-to-Fine MBR, that first uses MBR with a cheap-to-compute metric to filter a large hypothesis space to a smaller set, then uses MBR with a better but more expensive to compute metric over the smaller set; they separate evidence and hypothesis sets. Freitag et al. (2023) further investigates sampling strategies for MBR, finding that epsilon sampling (Hewitt et al., 2022) outperforms other strategies in automated and human evaluations.

Another earlier line of work has considered growing *post hoc* the hypothesis set in order to obtain hypotheses with higher expected gain (González-Rubio et al., 2011; González-Rubio and Casacuberta, 2013; Hoang et al., 2021).

3.2 Sampling an evidence set

Comparatively less work has studied strategies for sampling the evidence set. Most recent work has adopted the unbiased sampling strategy of Eikema and Aziz (2020), i.e. drawing i.i.d. samples from the model distribution $p(y|x)$ (equation 2). This strategy is motivated by their observation that unbiased sampling is reasonably reflective of the data distribution, much more so than beam search. However, their approach is incompatible with models trained via label smoothing (Szegedy et al., 2016). Yan et al. (2023) attempt to remedy this by sampling the evidence set with temperature $\tau < 1$, sharpening the model distribution.

3.3 What metric do we want to maximize?

The gain G (alternatively, error L) may be an arbitrary function $\mathcal{Y}_e \times \mathcal{Y}_h \rightarrow \mathbb{R}$. Early work focused on simple, token-level metrics like word error rate and BLEU (Kumar and Byrne, 2004; Ehling et al., 2007), but more recent work has explored the use of neural metrics (Amrhein and Sennrich, 2022; Freitag et al., 2022), as well as executing outputs in code generation (Shi et al., 2022; Li et al., 2022).

Generally, for both neural and non-neural metrics, MBR with metric G as a gain function will yield the largest downstream improvements on G (Müller and Sennrich, 2021; Freitag et al., 2022; Fernandes et al., 2022). In other words, if one aims to optimize system performance on metric M, one should perform MBR with M as gain. Although MBR uses pseudoreferences, using a metric M to score candidates against these pseudoreferences generally produces a candidate that also scores quite highly on M against the gold reference.

However, MBR also inherits the weaknesses and biases of the gain metric used. MBR has been shown to suffer from length and token frequency biases brought on by the metric, i.e. MBR with BLEU prefers shorter sentences (Nakov et al., 2012; Müller and Sennrich, 2021). Similarly, Amrhein and Sennrich (2022) find that MBR using the metric COMET (Rei et al., 2020) causes higher rates of errors for named entities and numbers due to a lack of sensitivity in the metric. Moreover, MBR is susceptible to overfitting to the metric; Freitag et al. (2023) show that the MBR setting that maximizes the metric is not the one that humans prefer. Thus, if the same metric is used for both MBR and evaluation of the output, *not all of the improvement in that metric can be attributed to higher quality*: it is possible that some of the improvement comes from gaming the metric. This provides an additional reason to evaluate across multiple, diverse metrics.

Note that in the most trivial case, where the met-

Method	Evidence Gen.	Hypothesis Gen.	Metric	$p(y\|x)$
Lattice MBR (Tromble et al., 2008)	N-best list	N-best list	BLEU	translation lattice
Coarse-to-fine MBR (Eikema and Aziz, 2022)	ancestral sampling	`filter`(sample)	BEER	single model
Wiher et al. (2022)	ancestral sampling	evidence + more decodings	BEER	single model
MBR-DC (Yan et al., 2023)	temperature sampling[1]	temperature sampling[1]	BLEURT	single model
Ours (§ 3.3)	ancestral sampling	temperature sampling	BERTScore	single model
Ours (§ 3.4)	ancestral sampling	temperature sampling	BERTScore	length-corrected scores
Freitag et al. (2023)	epsilon sampling		BLEURT	single model
Crowd sampling[2] (Suzgun et al., 2023)	temperature sampling		neural score metric	single model
MBR-Exec (Shi et al., 2022)	temperature sampling		execution match	single model
Self-consistency (SC) (Wang et al., 2023)	temperature sampling		exact answer match	single model
Complex SC (Fu et al., 2022)	`filter`(temperature sample)		exact answer match	single model
SC for open-ended gen (Jain et al., 2023)	temperature sampling		n-gram overlap	single model
Range voting (Borgeaud and Emerson, 2020)	beam search		n-gram overlap	single model
Post-Ensemble (Kobayashi, 2018)	beam search for each model in ensemble		cosine similarity	model set
AMRs Assemble! (Martínez Lorenzo et al., 2023)	model set	beam search	perplexity	model set

Table 1: Recent work under our taxonomy. The line separates methods that are explicitly MBR (above) from those that we identify as MBR-like (below).
[1] Different temperatures used for evidence and hypothesis.
[2] While Suzgun et al. (2023) coin the new term *crowd sampling*, they also explicitly refer to their method as MBR.

ric is $G(y, y') = \mathbb{1}[y = y']$, MBR recovers mode-seeking methods like beam search– i.e. MBR under this metric, in expectation, yields the maximum likelihood decoding. This is because, as the size of the sampled evidence set grows to infinity, the most frequent evidence set sequence (and thus the sequence with the highest gain) becomes the one with the highest probability under the sampling distribution.

3.4 What probability distribution should we use to estimate risk?

Most MBR decoding methods use the model's score distribution over outputs, s, as the (unnormalized) evidence distribution. Alternately, this distribution may be normalized by a temperature (during minimum risk training (Smith and Eisner, 2006) or decoding (Yan et al., 2023)). Some work (e.g Suzgun et al. (2023)) interprets this as a weak proxy for the human or true distribution, arguing that the true objective is to minimize error under the human distribution:

$$\underset{y' \in \mathcal{Y}_h}{\operatorname{argmin}}\, \mathbb{E}_{y \sim p_{\text{human}}}[L(y, y')]$$

Note that this is not the only reasonable choice of $p(y|x)$; other possible distributions include a distribution over outputs from multiple models (§4.2) or the length-penalized distribution over a single model's outputs $p_l(y|x)$ (§5.3).

4 MBR as a frame for other methods

Self-consistency, output ensembling, density estimation, and range voting can all be viewed through the framing of MBR. This exposes unstated connections between the methods and provides some theoretical backing to the empirical success of these methods. We discuss each in turn.

4.1 Self-consistency as MBR

Self-consistency (Wang et al., 2023) is a method for choosing outputs from language models. In self-consistency, the model is prompted to generate an explanation and then an answer. Multiple outputs $\mathcal{O} = \{y_1, \ldots, y_m\}$ are sampled from the model, the answers $\mathcal{A} = \{a_1, \ldots, a_m\}$ are extracted $a_i = \text{ans}(y_i)$, and the most frequent answer is returned:

$$\underset{a}{\operatorname{argmax}} \sum_{i=1}^{m} \mathbb{1}(a_i = a) \tag{10}$$

Self-consistency only computes exact match over the *answer*, not the reasoning chain. It is possible to recover MBR from this method by either taking the hypothesis/evidence sets to be the set of resulting answers $\mathcal{Y}_h = \mathcal{Y}_e = \mathcal{A}$ discarding the reasoning chain, or by defining a gain function $G(y, y') = \mathbb{1}(\text{ans}(y) = \text{ans}(y'))$ over full outputs $\mathcal{O}$; though notationally different, they are mathematically equivalent.

Thus, self-consistency is a type of MBR decoding in which we approximate the risk with a Monte Carlo estimate (cf. Eq. 6), the answers are sampled from the model (conditioned on the prompt), and the metric is exact match of the "final answer."

This framing additionally explains some results from the self-consistency paper. Wang et al. (2023) compare the performance of self-consistency across sampling strategies, finding that the best of the strategies they tried are those that are closest to ancestral sampling (nucleus sampling with $p = 0.95$ and $\tau = 0.7$ without top-k sampling). They also find that self-consistency works better with a sampled output rather than outputs from beam search (their Table 6). Through the lens of MBR, this empirical result has a clear theoretical justification: ancestral sampling of evidence sets generally yields the best performance for MBR because this provides an unbiased estimator of the probabilities of the sampled sequences. This also presents an opportunity for improvement: while Wang et al. (2023) do not evaluate on ancestral sampling, it is possible that this would outperform their best results.

Self-consistency is a special case of MBR. Proposed extensions to self-consistency have recovered aspects of generalized MBR decoding, including filtering to smaller hypothesis/evidence sets (Fu et al., 2022) and the use of alternative gain metrics (Jain et al., 2023). As a result, the term *self-consistency* has widened in definition from a specific type of MBR to a catch-all for MBR-based decoding methods on large language models.

4.2 Output Ensembling as MBR

Model ensembling techniques that operate on *completed outputs* of models may also be cast in MBR terms. Note that this does not include methods that operate on model weights or partial outputs. Common ensembling methods such as averaging model weights (Izmailov et al., 2018) or averaging token-level probabilities (Sennrich et al., 2016; Manakul et al., 2023) cannot be explicitly formulated as MBR.

The connection to MBR is most straightforward in methods that perform MBR decoding over the outputs of multiple models (DeNero et al., 2010; Duh et al., 2011; Barzdins and Gosko, 2016; Lee et al., 2022, *inter alia*). Representative of this family of methods is Post-Ensemble (Kobayashi, 2018), which ensembles multiple text generation models $\theta_1, \theta_2, \ldots, \theta_n$ by separately decoding from each model, computing pairwise sentence embedding similarity between all pairs of outputs, and yielding the output with greatest average similarity. Observe that this may be framed as MBR minimizing the expected risk over the mixture distribution

$$p_{\text{ensemble}}(y|x) = \begin{cases} p_{\theta_1}(y|x) & \text{with probability } \pi_1 \\ \cdots & \\ p_{\theta_n}(y|x) & \text{with probability } \pi_n \end{cases}$$

where $\sum_{i=1}^{n} \pi_i = 1$. While π_i is usually taken to be uniform over the ensemble, this need not always be the case (Duan et al., 2010).

Other methods may be viewed as relaxations of MBR decoding. Assemble! (Martínez Lorenzo et al., 2023) ensembles Abstract Meaning Representation (AMR) graph parsers by computing the pairwise perplexities of each output under *each parser*. While this is not precisely MBR, it may be viewed as a variation where the evidence set is *a set of models*, not a set of model outputs.

$$\hat{y} = \underset{y' \in \mathcal{Y}_h}{\operatorname{argmin}} \, \mathbb{E}_{\theta \sim \pi(\cdot)}[L(\theta, y')]$$

In this case, the error $L(\theta, y')$ is the perplexity of y' under model θ, i.e. $\exp(-\log p_\theta(y')) = \frac{1}{p_\theta(y')}$, and $\pi(\cdot)$ is the distribution over models.

4.3 MBR as Density Estimation

Interestingly, Post-Ensemble (Kobayashi, 2018) (§4.2) was not formulated as MBR (and in fact never referred to by name as MBR), but rather as kernel density estimation. Kernel density estimation is a non-parametric method for estimating the probability density function p of an unknown distribution, given samples $(x_1, x_2, \cdots, x_n)$ from that distribution (Rosenblatt, 1956; Parzen, 1962).

$$\hat{p}(x) = \frac{1}{n} \sum_{i=1}^{n} K(x, x_i) \tag{11}$$

Indeed, Equation 11 very closely resembles the Monte Carlo estimator of expected loss in Equation 6. This connection allowed (Kobayashi, 2018) to propose approximation error bounds on MBR, drawing from the density estimation literature.[4]

Note that the kernel function $K(x, x_i)$ is more commonly written as $K(x - x_i)$, or $K(x^T x_i)$ for directional statistics. While this may seem limiting, we can rewrite commonly used MBR metrics in this form; we show this for ROUGE-n as an example. For a sequence y, define $T_n(y)$ to be a vector of size $|V|^n$, where $|V|$ is the size of the vocabulary, containing the number of times every possible n-gram appears in y. Then we can rewrite ROUGE-n as the following:

$$\begin{aligned} & K_{\text{R}}(T_n(y) - T_n(y')) \\ & = 1 - \frac{|T_n(y) - T_n(y')|_1}{|T_n(y)|_1 + |T_n(y')|_1} \end{aligned} \tag{12}$$

[4]We do not reproduce their bounds here; we direct interested readers to the original paper.

where $|\cdot|_1$ is the $L1$ norm.

The similarity between density estimation and MBR yields an alternative interpretation of MBR as a mode-seeking search. However, we are not seeking the mode of the model's distribution over outputs, $p(y|x)$, but rather that of a distribution over some features $\phi(y)$ of our output, $p'(\phi(y)|x)$. For instance, in the case of ROUGE-n MBR,

$$\hat{y} = \underset{y' \in \mathcal{Y}_h}{\operatorname{argmax}} \sum_{y \in \mathcal{Y}_e} K_{\mathrm{R}}(T_n(y') - T_n(y)) \quad (13)$$

$$\approx \underset{y' \in \mathcal{Y}_h}{\operatorname{argmax}}\, p'(T_n(y')|x) \quad (14)$$

We posit that this alternative distribution $p'(T_n(y')|x)$ may be better correlated with performance on specific downstream metrics than the original model distribution, potentially adding an additional justification for MBR's effectiveness. We hope this may inspire future work investigating the theoretical underpinnings of MBR.

4.4 Range Voting as MBR

Methods that take inspiration from outside of NLP may also be MBR-like; in particular, some MBR-like algorithms in the literature are formulated from a voting theory perspective where candidate hypotheses are assigned votes based on similarity to some set of voters (Wang et al., 2023; Jain et al., 2023; Suzgun et al., 2023; Hoang et al., 2021). We show here that range voting (Borgeaud and Emerson, 2020), which broadly encapsulates these proposed voting methods, reduces to MBR.

Range voting describes a family of voting systems in which each voter assigns each candidate a score and the candidate with the greatest total or average score is elected. Observe that the set of candidates C corresponds to the hypothesis set $\mathcal{Y}_h$ and the set of voters V corresponds to the evidence set $\mathcal{Y}_e$. Then, if voter v's score for candidate c is taken to be a gain $G(v, c)$ and each voter is assigned uniform weight, range voting is equivalent to the MBR decision rule in Equation 8:

$$c_{\text{elected}} = \underset{c \in C}{\operatorname{argmax}} \frac{1}{|V|} \sum_{v \in V} G(v, c) \quad (15)$$

Other range-voting methods can similarly be cast as MBR variants.

5 Design Decisions Impact MBR Performance

Although all the methods in Section 4 are MBR-like, they make very different decisions about the four design choices in our MBR taxonomy. To demonstrate the importance of the method design, we consider empirically two cases where changing design impacts the performance of the method.

5.1 Experimental Details

We run MBR experiments for abstractive summarization on CNN/DM (Nallapati et al., 2016) with a fine-tuned BART-Large[5] released by the BART authors (Lewis et al., 2020) as our base model. In §5.3, we additionally report results for translation on WMT'16 Romanian-English (Ro-En) (Bojar et al., 2016) using mBART-50 (Liu et al., 2020).[6]

We draw n_e ancestral samples for our evidence set and n_t temperature samples ($\tau = 0.5$ for CNN/DM, $\tau = 0.3$ for WMT'16 Ro-En) for our hypothesis set. We set $n_e = n_t = 30$ in §5.2 and $n_e = n_t = 50$ in §5.3. Unless otherwise specified, we take ROUGE-1 (Lin, 2004) as our gain metric for summarization and BLEU-4 (Papineni et al., 2002)[7] as our gain metric for translation.

Our code is available at `https://github.com/abertsch72/minimum-bayes-risk`.

5.2 The MBR metric matters – but perhaps not as much as the hypothesis set

We find that using MBR with the summarization n-gram metric ROUGE-1 (Lin, 2004) improves abstractive summarization performance over beam search on CNN/DM, even when evaluating performance with neural metrics; using the general-purpose neural metric BERTScore (Zhang et al., 2020) as the MBR metric yields highest BERTScore but smaller gains on non-neural metrics, a finding consistent with past work; and even BEER (Stanojević and Sima'an, 2014), a translation metric, works as an MBR metric for this task.

However, prior work using the same dataset and model (Wiher et al., 2022) found that BEER (Stanojević and Sima'an, 2014) underperforms beam search. This divergence in results is likely due to our different choices in hypothesis set – Wiher et al. (2022) use the evidence set plus additional

[5] `facebook/bart-large-cnn` on HuggingFace (Wolf et al., 2020)

[6] `facebook/mbart-large-50-many-to-many-mmt`

[7] We use the implementation from `sacrebleu` (Post, 2018) with signature `nrefs:1|case:mixed|eff:yes|tok:13a|smooth:exp|version:2.3.1`

Method	R1	R2	RL	BS
Greedy	43.98	20.88	30.88	88.04
BS ($k = 5$)	43.16	20.63	30.53	87.82
BS ($k = 10$)	42.62	20.23	30.02	87.71
DBS ($k = g = 5$)	43.77	20.85	30.77	87.97
MBR ROUGE-1	**46.89**	22.29	32.01	88.41
MBR BEER	46.31	**22.36**	32.02	88.38
MBR BERTScore	46.04	22.09	**32.09**	**88.68**

Table 2: MBR results on CNN/DM for various gain functions. We additionally test the same non-MBR, (approximate) mode-seeking baselines as Wiher et al. (2022). All MBR methods outperform all non-MBR methods tested.

outputs from other decoding methods as hypotheses, while we use temperature samples at $\tau = 0.5$. While reusing the evidence set is more efficient than sampling a separate set of hypotheses, it leads to performance degregation in this case; this further emphasizes the importance of choosing the hypothesis set in MBR.

5.3 Varying the risk distribution: lessons from beam search don't translate to MBR

By nature, autoregressive text generation models suffer from length bias: sequence probability monotonically decreases with increasing length, causing shorter, potentially less informative sequences to be favored by the model distribution (Koehn and Knowles, 2017; Stahlberg and Byrne, 2019). For non-sampling methods such as beam search, the sequence probabilities are generally modified with a length-dependent term when comparing sequences (Murray and Chiang, 2018; Cho et al., 2014). Hence, it stands to reason that a length-corrected distribution with these biases alleviated may provide a better estimate of the risk $R(y')$.

Vanilla Monte Carlo MBR (as depicted in Equation 6) yields an estimate of the expected risk under the distribution that our evidence samples are drawn from. To modify the distribution used in our estimate, we turn to **importance sampling**, a method for estimating the expected value of a quantity under target distribution p, given samples from proposal distribution q (Kloek and van Dijk, 1978). For a brief tutorial on importance sampling and description of our estimator, see Appendix A.

We take the *score* of a sequence to be the log probability: We then experiment with two of the strategies described in Murray and Chiang (2018) for constructing the length corrected score $s_l(y|x)$:

(a) **Length normalization**: The model distribution is smoothed with temperature T^β, where T is the sequence length and β is the length penalty, a hyperparameter. A larger β more heavily prioritizes longer sequences.

$$s_l(y|x) = s(y|x)/T^\beta \qquad (16)$$

(b) **Length reward** (He et al., 2016): A fixed reward γ is added to the score per token generated.

$$s_l(y|x) = s(y|x) + \gamma T \qquad (17)$$

The length-corrected distribution is then $p_l(y|x) \propto \exp s_l(y|x)$. We apply **normalized importance sampling** (Rubinstein and Kroese, 2016) to estimate the risk under the length corrected distribution, i.e. $R(y') = \mathbb{E}_{y\sim p_l}[L(y, y')]$, given samples drawn from the model distribution $p(y|x)$.

We compare our MBR results against beam search both with and without length normalization. We use the models' default values for length penalty ($\beta = 2$ for BART, $\beta = 1$ for mBART).

Our results are Tables 3 and 4. In line with past work, we find that beam search generally benefits from incorporating a length penalty. However, we find that length-corrected MBR underperforms vanilla MBR. This may be due to a gap between the sampling and length-correction distibutions, leading to a high-variance estimator of risk.

Method	R1	R2	RL	BS	LR
Beam search, no correction	43.88	20.96	30.77	87.79	**108.00**
Beam search	43.95	21.00	30.84	87.81	114.39
MBR, No correction	**47.70**	**23.00**	**32.54**	**88.50**	111.64
MBR, Length norm, $\beta = 0.5$	44.29	19.95	29.99	88.03	110.75
MBR, Length norm, $\beta = 1.0$	44.29	19.98	30.0	88.03	110.77
MBR, Length reward, $\gamma = 0.5$	47.60	22.93	32.48	88.48	112.52
MBR, Length reward, $\gamma = 1.0$	47.41	22.72	32.25	88.43	112.50

Table 3: MBR results for various length correction schemes on CNN/DM. We report ROUGE-1, ROUGE-2, ROUGE-L, BERTScore, and length ratio, respectively.

Method	BLEU	chrF	BLEURT	BS	LR
Beam search, no correction	33.21	59.81	65.50	94.95	99.37
Beam search	33.06	**60.05**	**65.60**	**94.96**	101.58
MBR, No correction	**33.56**	**60.00**	65.53	**94.96**	**100.04**
MBR, Length norm, $\beta = 0.5$	31.14	58.53	64.70	94.71	102.82
MBR, Length norm, $\beta = 1.0$	31.09	58.51	64.68	94.71	102.60
MBR, Length reward, $\gamma = 0.5$	32.09	59.63	65.19	94.82	105.00
MBR, Length reward, $\gamma = 1.0$	31.29	59.17	64.91	94.73	105.63

Table 4: MBR results for various length correction schemes on WMT'16 Romanian-English. We report BLEU, chrF, BLEURT, BERTScore, and length ratio, respectively. We use the chrF (Popović, 2015) implementation from `sacrebleu`. We use the smaller `BLEURT-20-D6` checkpoint for efficiency (Sellam et al., 2020; Pu et al., 2021).

However, our results are also emblematic of a wider trend among minimum-risk techniques. Past work has found that models trained with Minimum Error Rate Training (Och, 2003; Shen et al., 2016), an error-aware training method, do not require length correction in beam search (Neubig, 2016). Similarly, we find that MBR without length correction generates outputs relatively close in length to the references, more so than length-normalized beam search. This suggests that MBR may be to some extent immune from length biases, when they are not introduced by the MBR metric (Müller and Sennrich, 2021).

6 MBR applications in NLP

The use of minimum Bayes risk decoding in NLP predates these MBR-like methods; MBR has been applied by name in NLP since the 1990s.

Historical context Minimum Bayes Risk decoding has roots in Bayesian decision theory, a field of study that dates as far back as the Age of Enlightenment (Bernoulli, 1738; Parmigiani, 2001). Central to Bayesian decision theory is the principle of risk minimization: in the face of uncertainty, an optimal decision maker should choose the option that minimizes the amount of error they can expect to suffer – or, in other terms, maximizes the amount of utility they can expect to enjoy (DeGroot, 1970; Bickel and Doksum, 1977). This is precisely the intuition encoded in MBR (i.e. Equation 3).

Adoption in NLP MBR was adopted by the speech and NLP communities in the 1990s and early 2000s, finding applications in syntactical parsing (Goodman, 1996; Sima'an, 2003), automatic speech recognition (Stolcke et al., 1997; Goel and Byrne, 2000), and statistical machine translation (Kumar and Byrne, 2004; Tromble et al., 2008; Kumar et al., 2009). Many NLP tasks during this time relied upon graph structures as inductive biases (i.e. parse trees or translation lattices/hypergraphs). As such, early MBR works often used these graphical models as hypothesis and evidence spaces. Work on lattice MBR (Tromble et al., 2008), for instance, treated the set of all hypotheses encoded in a word lattice, of which there are exponentially many, as both evidence and hypothesis sets. This is in contrast to most later MBR work, which operates on a relatively small list of text outputs obtained from a neural model. As a result, early work relied on rather involved dynamic programming algorithms

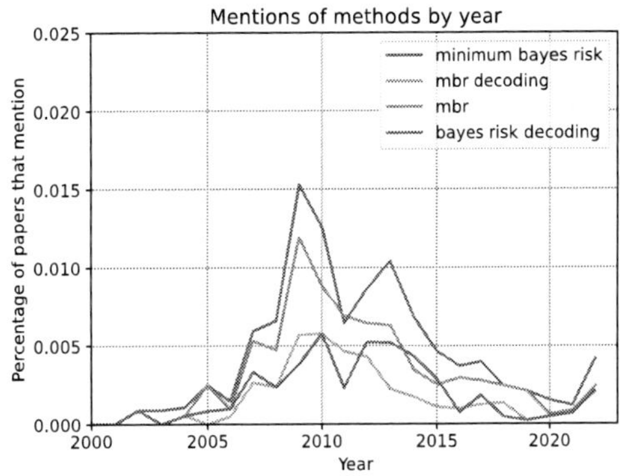

Figure 1: The use of MBR (by name) peaked in the mid-2010s. This graph shows the percentage of ACL Anthology papers that mention several MBR-related phrases by year, from 2000 to 2022.

for exact MBR decoding and were restricted to token-factorizable metrics such as BLEU and edit distance. Later work additionally demonstrated the efficacy of MBR for question answering (Duan, 2013) and for joining statistical and neural approaches to translation (Stahlberg et al., 2017).

Recent usage In an effort to move past beam search, which has well-known pathologies (Stahlberg and Byrne, 2019), MBR has in recent years resurfaced as a decision rule for text-generation models (Eikema and Aziz, 2020). As discussed earlier in §3, several lines of work have sprung up investigating the properties of MBR in modern neural text generation setups. Notably, however, most of these works have focused on applications of the method to neural machine translation, with only a few very recent works studying its applications in other text generation tasks (Shi et al., 2022; Wiher et al., 2022; Suzgun et al., 2023).

Outside of these areas, the method has largely been applied in shared task papers (e.g. Manakul et al. (2023); Yan et al. (2022); Barzdins and Gosko (2016)), as it provides a reliable boost in performance. The fraction of papers in the ACL Anthology that reference MBR (at least by this name) has declined from its peak around 2009 (Figure 1).

7 Conclusion

Minimum Bayes Risk decoding has declined in popularity, but the underlying concept of sampling a set from a distribution and choosing an output to minimize risk according to that set has remained. This concept now takes many surface forms– from self-consistency to range voting to output ensembles– and current research in these areas rarely draws connections to MBR. While rediscovery is a key part of science, so is recontextualizing new methods within a broader research narrative. This can often reveal new insights or cast findings in a different light. For instance, the empirical benefits of self-consistency can be justified through an MBR framing; work on extensions to self-consistency has rediscovered other properties of MBR; and work on ensembling has raised questions about how to weight mixtures of models that can be reasoned about within the framework of noisy estimates of global probability distributions.

The adoption of newer terms for MBR-like methods may be a type of terminology drift. Related phenomena have been studied in the philosophy of science literature, including pressures to coin new terms (Dyke, 1992; Merton, 1957), potential negative consequences of divergent terminology (Calvert, 1956; Samigullina et al., 2020), and decreased citation of older methods in NLP (Singh et al., 2023). For a more involved discussion of the literature on term coining and possible connections, see Appendix B.

Language is not static, so some degree of terminology drift in scientific literature is unavoidable. However, recognizing the connections between modern techniques and older work is crucial to understanding why such methods are effective. We must not forget the lessons of the past as we search for the methods of the future.

Acknowledgments

We would like to thank Jason Eisner, Patrick Fernandes, and Sireesh Gururaja for useful early discussions about this work, and Saujas Vaduguru, Daniel Fried, and Shuyan Zhou for feedback on this draft.

This work was supported in part by grants from the Singapore Defence Science and Technology Agency, 3M — M*Modal, the Air Force Research Laboratory (AFRL), and the National Science Foundation Graduate Research Fellowship Program under Grant No. DGE2140739. Any opinions, findings, and conclusions or recommendations expressed in this material are those of the author(s) and do not necessarily reflect the views of the sponsors.

References

Chantal Amrhein and Rico Sennrich. 2022. Identifying weaknesses in machine translation metrics through minimum Bayes risk decoding: A case study for COMET. In *Proceedings of the 2nd Conference of the Asia-Pacific Chapter of the Association for Computational Linguistics and the 12th International Joint Conference on Natural Language Processing (Volume 1: Long Papers)*, pages 1125–1141, Online only. Association for Computational Linguistics.

Guntis Barzdins and Didzis Gosko. 2016. RIGA at SemEval-2016 task 8: Impact of Smatch extensions and character-level neural translation on AMR parsing accuracy. In *Proceedings of the 10th International Workshop on Semantic Evaluation (SemEval-2016)*, pages 1143–1147, San Diego, California. Association for Computational Linguistics.

Daniel Bernoulli. 1738. Specimen theoriae novae de mensura sortis. *Commentarii academiae scientiarum imperialis Petropolitanae*, 5:175–192.

Peter J. Bickel and Kjell A. Doksum. 1977. *Mathematical Statistic: Basic Ideas and Selected Topics*. Holden-Day Inc., Oakland, CA.

Ondřej Bojar, Rajen Chatterjee, Christian Federmann, Yvette Graham, Barry Haddow, Matthias Huck, Antonio Jimeno Yepes, Philipp Koehn, Varvara Logacheva, Christof Monz, Matteo Negri, Aurélie Névéol, Mariana Neves, Martin Popel, Matt Post, Raphael Rubino, Carolina Scarton, Lucia Specia, Marco Turchi, Karin Verspoor, and Marcos Zampieri. 2016. Findings of the 2016 conference on machine translation. In *Proceedings of the First Conference on Machine Translation: Volume 2, Shared Task Papers*, pages 131–198, Berlin, Germany. Association for Computational Linguistics.

Marcel Bollmann and Desmond Elliott. 2020. On forgetting to cite older papers: An analysis of the ACL Anthology. In *Proceedings of the 58th Annual Meeting of the Association for Computational Linguistics*, pages 7819–7827, Online. Association for Computational Linguistics.

Sebastian Borgeaud and Guy Emerson. 2020. Leveraging sentence similarity in natural language generation: Improving beam search using range voting. In *Proceedings of the Fourth Workshop on Neural Generation and Translation*, pages 97–109, Online. Association for Computational Linguistics.

E. S. Calvert. 1956. Technical terms in science and technology. *The American Journal of Psychology*, 69(3):476–479.

Kyunghyun Cho, Bart van Merriënboer, Dzmitry Bahdanau, and Yoshua Bengio. 2014. On the properties of neural machine translation: Encoder–decoder approaches. In *Proceedings of SSST-8, Eighth Workshop on Syntax, Semantics and Structure in Statistical Translation*, pages 103–111, Doha, Qatar. Association for Computational Linguistics.

Morris H. DeGroot. 1970. *Optimal Statistical Decisions*. McGraw-Hill, Inc., New York.

John DeNero, Shankar Kumar, Ciprian Chelba, and Franz Och. 2010. Model combination for machine translation. In *Human Language Technologies: The 2010 Annual Conference of the North American Chapter of the Association for Computational Linguistics*, pages 975–983, Los Angeles, California. Association for Computational Linguistics.

Nan Duan. 2013. Minimum Bayes risk based answer re-ranking for question answering. In *Proceedings of the 51st Annual Meeting of the Association for Computational Linguistics (Volume 2: Short Papers)*, pages 424–428, Sofia, Bulgaria. Association for Computational Linguistics.

Nan Duan, Mu Li, Dongdong Zhang, and Ming Zhou. 2010. Mixture model-based minimum Bayes risk decoding using multiple machine translation systems. In *Proceedings of the 23rd International Conference on Computational Linguistics (Coling 2010)*, pages 313–321, Beijing, China. Coling 2010 Organizing Committee.

Kevin Duh, Katsuhito Sudoh, Xianchao Wu, Hajime Tsukada, and Masaaki Nagata. 2011. Generalized minimum Bayes risk system combination. In *Proceedings of 5th International Joint Conference on Natural Language Processing*, pages 1356–1360, Chiang Mai, Thailand. Asian Federation of Natural Language Processing.

Carolynn Van Dyke. 1992. Old words for new worlds: Modern scientific and technological word-formation. *American Speech*, 67(4):383–405.

Nicola Ehling, Richard Zens, and Hermann Ney. 2007. Minimum Bayes risk decoding for BLEU. In *Proceedings of the 45th Annual Meeting of the Association for Computational Linguistics Companion Volume Proceedings of the Demo and Poster Sessions*, pages 101–104, Prague, Czech Republic. Association for Computational Linguistics.

Bryan Eikema and Wilker Aziz. 2020. Is MAP decoding all you need? the inadequacy of the mode in neural machine translation. In *Proceedings of the 28th International Conference on Computational Linguistics*, pages 4506–4520, Barcelona, Spain (Online). International Committee on Computational Linguistics.

Bryan Eikema and Wilker Aziz. 2022. Sampling-based approximations to minimum Bayes risk decoding for neural machine translation. In *Proceedings of the 2022 Conference on Empirical Methods in Natural Language Processing*, pages 10978–10993, Abu Dhabi, United Arab Emirates. Association for Computational Linguistics.

Patrick Fernandes, António Farinhas, Ricardo Rei, José G. C. de Souza, Perez Ogayo, Graham Neubig, and Andre Martins. 2022. Quality-aware decoding for neural machine translation. In *Proceedings of the 2022 Conference of the North American Chapter of the Association for Computational Linguistics: Human Language Technologies*, pages 1396–1412, Seattle, United States. Association for Computational Linguistics.

Markus Freitag, Behrooz Ghorbani, and Patrick Fernandes. 2023. Epsilon sampling rocks: Investigating sampling strategies for minimum bayes risk decoding for machine translation.

Markus Freitag, David Grangier, Qijun Tan, and Bowen Liang. 2022. High quality rather than high model probability: Minimum Bayes risk decoding with neural metrics. *Transactions of the Association for Computational Linguistics*, 10:811–825.

Yao Fu, Hao-Chun Peng, Ashish Sabharwal, Peter Clark, and Tushar Khot. 2022. Complexity-based prompting for multi-step reasoning. *ArXiv*, abs/2210.00720.

Vaibhava Goel and William J Byrne. 2000. Minimum bayes-risk automatic speech recognition. *Computer Speech & Language*, 14(2):115–135.

Jesús González-Rubio and Francisco Casacuberta. 2013. Improving the minimum Bayes' risk combination of machine translation systems. In *Proceedings of the 10th International Workshop on Spoken Language Translation: Papers*, Heidelberg, Germany.

Jesús González-Rubio, Alfons Juan, and Francisco Casacuberta. 2011. Minimum Bayes-risk system combination. In *Proceedings of the 49th Annual Meeting of the Association for Computational Linguistics: Human Language Technologies*, pages 1268–1277, Portland, Oregon, USA. Association for Computational Linguistics.

Joshua Goodman. 1996. Efficient algorithms for parsing the DOP model. In *Conference on Empirical Methods in Natural Language Processing*.

Wei He, Zhongjun He, Hua Wu, and Haifeng Wang. 2016. Improved neural machine translation with smt features. In *Proceedings of the Thirtieth AAAI Conference on Artificial Intelligence*, AAAI'16, page 151–157. AAAI Press.

John Hewitt, Christopher Manning, and Percy Liang. 2022. Truncation sampling as language model desmoothing. In *Findings of the Association for Computational Linguistics: EMNLP 2022*, pages 3414–3427, Abu Dhabi, United Arab Emirates. Association for Computational Linguistics.

Thanh Lam Hoang, Gabriele Picco, Yufang Hou, Young-Suk Lee, Lam Nguyen, Dzung Phan, Vanessa Lopez, and Ramon Fernandez Astudillo. 2021. Ensembling graph predictions for amr parsing. In *Advances in Neural Information Processing Systems*, volume 34, pages 8495–8505. Curran Associates, Inc.

Ari Holtzman, Jan Buys, Li Du, Maxwell Forbes, and Yejin Choi. 2019. The curious case of neural text degeneration. *International Conference on Learning Representations*.

Anna Kristina Hultgren. 2013. Lexical borrowing from english into danish in the sciences: An empirical investigation of 'domain loss'. *International Journal of Applied Linguistics*, 23(2):166–182.

Pavel Izmailov, Dmitrii Podoprikhin, T. Garipov, Dmitry P. Vetrov, and Andrew Gordon Wilson. 2018. Averaging weights leads to wider optima and better generalization. In *Conference on Uncertainty in Artificial Intelligence*.

Siddhartha Jain, Xiaofei Ma, Anoop Deoras, and Bing Xiang. 2023. Self-consistency for open-ended generations.

Karen Sparck Jones. 1994. *Natural Language Processing: A Historical Review*, pages 3–16. Springer Netherlands, Dordrecht.

T. Kloek and H. K. van Dijk. 1978. Bayesian estimates of equation system parameters: An application of integration by monte carlo. *Econometrica*, 46(1):1–19.

Hayato Kobayashi. 2018. Frustratingly easy model ensemble for abstractive summarization. In *Proceedings of the 2018 Conference on Empirical Methods in Natural Language Processing*, pages 4165–4176, Brussels, Belgium. Association for Computational Linguistics.

Philipp Koehn and Rebecca Knowles. 2017. Six challenges for neural machine translation. In *Proceedings of the First Workshop on Neural Machine Translation*, pages 28–39, Vancouver. Association for Computational Linguistics.

Shankar Kumar and William Byrne. 2004. Minimum Bayes-risk decoding for statistical machine translation. In *Proceedings of the Human Language Technology Conference of the North American Chapter of the Association for Computational Linguistics: HLT-NAACL 2004*, pages 169–176, Boston, Massachusetts, USA. Association for Computational Linguistics.

Shankar Kumar, Wolfgang Macherey, Chris Dyer, and Franz Och. 2009. Efficient minimum error rate training and minimum Bayes-risk decoding for translation hypergraphs and lattices. In *Proceedings of the Joint Conference of the 47th Annual Meeting of the ACL and the 4th International Joint Conference on Natural Language Processing of the AFNLP*, pages 163–171, Suntec, Singapore. Association for Computational Linguistics.

Young-Suk Lee, Ramón Astudillo, Hoang Thanh Lam, Tahira Naseem, Radu Florian, and Salim Roukos. 2022. Maximum Bayes Smatch ensemble distillation for AMR parsing. In *Proceedings of the 2022 Conference of the North American Chapter of the Association for Computational Linguistics: Human Language Technologies*, pages 5379–5392, Seattle, United States. Association for Computational Linguistics.

Mike Lewis, Yinhan Liu, Naman Goyal, Marjan Ghazvininejad, Abdelrahman Mohamed, Omer Levy, Veselin Stoyanov, and Luke Zettlemoyer. 2020. BART: Denoising sequence-to-sequence pre-training for natural language generation, translation, and comprehension. In *Proceedings of the 58th Annual Meeting of the Association for Computational Linguistics*, pages 7871–7880, Online. Association for Computational Linguistics.

Yujia Li, David Choi, Junyoung Chung, Nate Kushman, Julian Schrittwieser, Rémi Leblond, Tom Eccles, James Keeling, Felix Gimeno, Agustin Dal Lago, Thomas Hubert, Peter Choy, Cyprien de Masson d'Autume, Igor Babuschkin, Xinyun Chen, Po-Sen Huang, Johannes Welbl, Sven Gowal, Alexey Cherepanov, James Molloy, Daniel J. Mankowitz, Esme Sutherland Robson, Pushmeet Kohli, Nando de Freitas, Koray Kavukcuoglu, and Oriol Vinyals. 2022. Competition-level code generation with alphacode. *Science*, 378(6624):1092–1097.

Chin-Yew Lin. 2004. ROUGE: A package for automatic evaluation of summaries. In *Text Summarization Branches Out*, pages 74–81, Barcelona, Spain. Association for Computational Linguistics.

Yinhan Liu, Jiatao Gu, Naman Goyal, Xian Li, Sergey Edunov, Marjan Ghazvininejad, Mike Lewis, and Luke Zettlemoyer. 2020. Multilingual denoising pre-training for neural machine translation. *Transactions of the Association for Computational Linguistics*, 8:726–742.

Potsawee Manakul, Yassir Fathullah, Adian Liusie, Vyas Raina, Vatsal Raina, and Mark Gales. 2023. CUED at ProbSum 2023: Hierarchical ensemble of summarization models. In *The 22nd Workshop on Biomedical Natural Language Processing and BioNLP Shared Tasks*, pages 516–523, Toronto, Canada. Association for Computational Linguistics.

Abelardo Carlos Martínez Lorenzo, Pere Lluís Huguet Cabot, and Roberto Navigli. 2023. AMRs assemble! learning to ensemble with autoregressive models for AMR parsing. In *Proceedings of the 61st Annual Meeting of the Association for Computational Linguistics (Volume 2: Short Papers)*, pages 1595–1605, Toronto, Canada. Association for Computational Linguistics.

Robert K. Merton. 1957. Priorities in scientific discovery: A chapter in the sociology of science. *American Sociological Review*, 22(6):635–659.

Saif M. Mohammad. 2020. Gender gap in natural language processing research: Disparities in authorship and citations. In *Proceedings of the 58th Annual Meeting of the Association for Computational Linguistics*, pages 7860–7870, Online. Association for Computational Linguistics.

Mathias Müller and Rico Sennrich. 2021. Understanding the properties of minimum Bayes risk decoding in neural machine translation. In *Proceedings of the*

59th Annual Meeting of the Association for Computational Linguistics and the 11th International Joint Conference on Natural Language Processing (Volume 1: Long Papers), pages 259–272, Online. Association for Computational Linguistics.

Kenton Murray and David Chiang. 2018. Correcting length bias in neural machine translation. In *Proceedings of the Third Conference on Machine Translation: Research Papers*, pages 212–223, Brussels, Belgium. Association for Computational Linguistics.

Preslav Nakov, Francisco Guzman, and Stephan Vogel. 2012. Optimizing for sentence-level BLEU+1 yields short translations. In *Proceedings of COLING 2012*, pages 1979–1994, Mumbai, India. The COLING 2012 Organizing Committee.

Ramesh Nallapati, Bowen Zhou, Cicero dos Santos, Çağlar Gulçehre, and Bing Xiang. 2016. Abstractive text summarization using sequence-to-sequence RNNs and beyond. In *Proceedings of the 20th SIGNLL Conference on Computational Natural Language Learning*, pages 280–290, Berlin, Germany. Association for Computational Linguistics.

Graham Neubig. 2016. Lexicons and minimum risk training for neural machine translation: NAIST-CMU at WAT2016. In *Proceedings of the 3rd Workshop on Asian Translation (WAT2016)*, pages 119–125, Osaka, Japan. The COLING 2016 Organizing Committee.

Franz Josef Och. 2003. Minimum error rate training in statistical machine translation. In *Proceedings of the 41st Annual Meeting of the Association for Computational Linguistics*, pages 160–167, Sapporo, Japan. Association for Computational Linguistics.

Kishore Papineni, Salim Roukos, Todd Ward, and Wei-Jing Zhu. 2002. Bleu: a method for automatic evaluation of machine translation. In *Proceedings of the 40th Annual Meeting of the Association for Computational Linguistics*, pages 311–318, Philadelphia, Pennsylvania, USA. Association for Computational Linguistics.

G. Parmigiani. 2001. Decision theory: Bayesian. In Neil J. Smelser and Paul B. Baltes, editors, *International Encyclopedia of the Social & Behavioral Sciences*, pages 3327–3334. Pergamon, Oxford.

Emanuel Parzen. 1962. On Estimation of a Probability Density Function and Mode. *The Annals of Mathematical Statistics*, 33(3):1065 – 1076.

Maja Popović. 2015. chrF: character n-gram F-score for automatic MT evaluation. In *Proceedings of the Tenth Workshop on Statistical Machine Translation*, pages 392–395, Lisbon, Portugal. Association for Computational Linguistics.

Matt Post. 2018. A call for clarity in reporting BLEU scores. In *Proceedings of the Third Conference on Machine Translation: Research Papers*, pages 186–191, Brussels, Belgium. Association for Computational Linguistics.

Amy Pu, Hyung Won Chung, Ankur Parikh, Sebastian Gehrmann, and Thibault Sellam. 2021. Learning compact metrics for MT. In *Proceedings of the 2021 Conference on Empirical Methods in Natural Language Processing*, pages 751–762, Online and Punta Cana, Dominican Republic. Association for Computational Linguistics.

B. L. Raad. 1989. Modern trends in scientific terminology: Morphology and metaphor. *American Speech*, 64(2):128–136.

Ricardo Rei, Craig Stewart, Ana C Farinha, and Alon Lavie. 2020. COMET: A neural framework for MT evaluation. In *Proceedings of the 2020 Conference on Empirical Methods in Natural Language Processing (EMNLP)*, pages 2685–2702, Online. Association for Computational Linguistics.

Murray Rosenblatt. 1956. Remarks on Some Nonparametric Estimates of a Density Function. *The Annals of Mathematical Statistics*, 27(3):832 – 837.

Reuven Y. Rubinstein and Dirk P. Kroese. 2016. *Simulation and the Monte Carlo Method*, 3rd edition. Wiley Publishing.

Mukund Rungta, Janvijay Singh, Saif M. Mohammad, and Diyi Yang. 2022. Geographic citation gaps in NLP research. In *Proceedings of the 2022 Conference on Empirical Methods in Natural Language Processing*, pages 1371–1383, Abu Dhabi, United Arab Emirates. Association for Computational Linguistics.

L.Z. Samigullina, E.F. Samigullina, O.V. Danilova, and I.A. Latypova. 2020. Linguistic borrowing as a way to enrich oil and gas terminology. In *Proceedings of the International Session on Factors of Regional Extensive Development (FRED 2019)*, pages 58–61. Atlantis Press.

Thibault Sellam, Dipanjan Das, and Ankur Parikh. 2020. BLEURT: Learning robust metrics for text generation. In *Proceedings of the 58th Annual Meeting of the Association for Computational Linguistics*, pages 7881–7892, Online. Association for Computational Linguistics.

Rico Sennrich, Barry Haddow, and Alexandra Birch. 2016. Improving neural machine translation models with monolingual data. In *Proceedings of the 54th Annual Meeting of the Association for Computational Linguistics (Volume 1: Long Papers)*, pages 86–96, Berlin, Germany. Association for Computational Linguistics.

Shiqi Shen, Yong Cheng, Zhongjun He, Wei He, Hua Wu, Maosong Sun, and Yang Liu. 2016. Minimum risk training for neural machine translation. In *Proceedings of the 54th Annual Meeting of the Association for Computational Linguistics (Volume 1: Long Papers)*, pages 1683–1692, Berlin, Germany. Association for Computational Linguistics.

Freda Shi, Daniel Fried, Marjan Ghazvininejad, Luke Zettlemoyer, and Sida I. Wang. 2022. Natural language to code translation with execution. In *Proceedings of the 2022 Conference on Empirical Methods in Natural Language Processing*, pages 3533–3546, Abu Dhabi, United Arab Emirates. Association for Computational Linguistics.

Khalil Sima'an. 2003. On maximizing metrics for syntactic disambiguation. In *Proceedings of the Eighth International Conference on Parsing Technologies*, pages 183–194, Nancy, France.

Janvijay Singh, Mukund Rungta, Diyi Yang, and Saif Mohammad. 2023. Forgotten knowledge: Examining the citational amnesia in NLP. In *Proceedings of the 61st Annual Meeting of the Association for Computational Linguistics (Volume 1: Long Papers)*, pages 6192–6208, Toronto, Canada. Association for Computational Linguistics.

David A. Smith and Jason Eisner. 2006. Minimum risk annealing for training log-linear models. In *Proceedings of the COLING/ACL 2006 Main Conference Poster Sessions*, pages 787–794, Sydney, Australia. Association for Computational Linguistics.

Felix Stahlberg and Bill Byrne. 2019. On NMT search errors and model errors: Cat got your tongue? In *Proceedings of the 2019 Conference on Empirical Methods in Natural Language Processing and the 9th International Joint Conference on Natural Language Processing (EMNLP-IJCNLP)*, pages 3356–3362, Hong Kong, China. Association for Computational Linguistics.

Felix Stahlberg, Adrià de Gispert, Eva Hasler, and Bill Byrne. 2017. Neural machine translation by minimising the Bayes-risk with respect to syntactic translation lattices. In *Proceedings of the 15th Conference of the European Chapter of the Association for Computational Linguistics: Volume 2, Short Papers*, pages 362–368, Valencia, Spain. Association for Computational Linguistics.

Miloš Stanojević and Khalil Sima'an. 2014. Fitting sentence level translation evaluation with many dense features. In *Proceedings of the 2014 Conference on Empirical Methods in Natural Language Processing (EMNLP)*, pages 202–206, Doha, Qatar. Association for Computational Linguistics.

Andreas Stolcke, Yochai Konig, and Mitchel Weintraub. 1997. Explicit word error minimization in n-best list rescoring.

Mirac Suzgun, Luke Melas-Kyriazi, and Dan Jurafsky. 2023. Follow the wisdom of the crowd: Effective text generation via minimum Bayes risk decoding. In *Findings of the Association for Computational Linguistics: ACL 2023*, pages 4265–4293, Toronto, Canada. Association for Computational Linguistics.

Christian Szegedy, Vincent Vanhoucke, Sergey Ioffe, Jon Shlens, and Zbigniew Wojna. 2016. Rethinking the inception architecture for computer vision. In *Proceedings of the IEEE Conference on Computer Vision and Pattern Recognition (CVPR)*.

Roy Tromble, Shankar Kumar, Franz Och, and Wolfgang Macherey. 2008. Lattice Minimum Bayes-Risk decoding for statistical machine translation. In *Proceedings of the 2008 Conference on Empirical Methods in Natural Language Processing*, pages 620–629, Honolulu, Hawaii. Association for Computational Linguistics.

Xuezhi Wang, Jason Wei, Dale Schuurmans, Quoc V Le, Ed H. Chi, Sharan Narang, Aakanksha Chowdhery, and Denny Zhou. 2023. Self-consistency improves chain of thought reasoning in language models. In *The Eleventh International Conference on Learning Representations*.

Gian Wiher, Clara Meister, and Ryan Cotterell. 2022. On decoding strategies for neural text generators. *Transactions of the Association for Computational Linguistics*, 10:997–1012.

Thomas Wolf, Lysandre Debut, Victor Sanh, Julien Chaumond, Clement Delangue, Anthony Moi, Pierric Cistac, Tim Rault, Remi Louf, Morgan Funtowicz, Joe Davison, Sam Shleifer, Patrick von Platen, Clara Ma, Yacine Jernite, Julien Plu, Canwen Xu, Teven Le Scao, Sylvain Gugger, Mariama Drame, Quentin Lhoest, and Alexander Rush. 2020. Transformers: State-of-the-art natural language processing. In *Proceedings of the 2020 Conference on Empirical Methods in Natural Language Processing: System Demonstrations*, pages 38–45, Online. Association for Computational Linguistics.

Brian Yan, Patrick Fernandes, Siddharth Dalmia, Jiatong Shi, Yifan Peng, Dan Berrebbi, Xinyi Wang, Graham Neubig, and Shinji Watanabe. 2022. CMU's IWSLT 2022 dialect speech translation system. In *Proceedings of the 19th International Conference on Spoken Language Translation (IWSLT 2022)*, pages 298–307, Dublin, Ireland (in-person and online). Association for Computational Linguistics.

Jianhao Yan, Jin Xu, Fandong Meng, Jie Zhou, and Yue Zhang. 2023. Dc-mbr: Distributional cooling for minimum bayesian risk decoding.

Tianyi Zhang, Varsha Kishore, Felix Wu, Kilian Q. Weinberger, and Yoav Artzi. 2020. Bertscore: Evaluating text generation with bert.

A More details on importance sampling for MBR

We present in this section the normalized importance sampling estimator of risk used in our experiments in §5.3.

The core insight of importance sampling is that we can rewrite the expected value of a random variable $f(x)$ under target distribution p as another expectation under some proposal distribution q:

$$\begin{aligned}\mathbb{E}_p[f(x)] &= \sum_x f(x)p(x) \\ &= \sum_x f(x)\frac{p(x)}{q(x)}q(x) \\ &= \mathbb{E}_q\left[f(x)\frac{p(x)}{q(x)}\right]\end{aligned}$$

Importance sampling can be particularly useful when sampling from the proposal distribution is easy, but sampling from the target distribution is costly or intractable; this is indeed the case for MBR, as sampling from the length-corrected distribution $p_l(y|x)$ requires computation of its partition function, which has exponential complexity.

Hence, for MBR, if we draw evidence samples $\mathcal{Y}_e$ according to model distribution $p(y|x)$ but wish to compute the risk under some length-corrected distribution $p_l(y|x)$, we may compute

$$\begin{aligned}R(y') &= \mathbb{E}_{y\sim p_l}[L(y, y')] \\ &= \mathbb{E}_{y\sim p}\left[L(y, y')\frac{p_l(y|x)}{p(y|x)}\right] \\ &= \sum_{y\in\mathcal{Y}_e} L(y, y')\frac{p_l(y|x)}{p(y|x)} \\ &= \sum_{y\in\mathcal{Y}_e} L(y, y')w(y)\end{aligned}$$

where we let $w(y) = p_l(y|x)/p(y|x)$, commonly referred to as the importance weight.

Note, however, that importance sampling requires us to be able to exactly compute the probabilities $p(y|x)$ and $p_l(y|x)$; while the former can be computed efficiently (Equation 2), the latter is intractable, again because it requires the partition function. What we can efficiently compute is the unnormalized probability $\tilde{p}_l(y|x) = \exp s_l(y|x)$, where s_l is the length-corrected score given by either Equation 16 or 17.

Fortunately, we can use **normalized importance sampling** to obtain a consistent estimator of the risk by adjusting importance weights (Rubinstein and Kroese, 2016):

$$R(y') = \mathbb{E}_{y\sim p_l}[L(y, y')] \tag{18}$$

$$= \frac{\mathbb{E}_{y\sim p}[L(y, y')\tilde{w}(y)]}{\mathbb{E}_{y\sim p}[\tilde{w}(y)]} \tag{19}$$

$$= \sum_{y\in\mathcal{Y}_e} L(y, y') \cdot \frac{\tilde{w}(y)}{\sum_{y\in\mathcal{Y}_e}\tilde{w}(y)} \tag{20}$$

where $\tilde{w}(y) = \tilde{p}_l(y|x)/p(y|x)$. As it is the ratio of two estimates, the normalized importance sampling estimator is *biased* for finite sample sizes.

B Contextualizing this work within philosophy of science

In this section, we contextualize our work in the broader framings of meta-analysis of scientific research.

Patterns of citation in NLP Several factors have been shown to correlate with citation rate in NLP, including author geographic location (Rungta et al., 2022), author gender (Mohammad, 2020), and publication date (Bollmann and Elliott, 2020; Singh et al., 2023). Bollmann and Elliott (2020) conduct a bibliometric anaylsis of the ACL Anthology, finding that the mean age of papers cited decreased significantly from 2010 to 2019. Singh et al. (2023) expand this analysis to the full anthology, finding that, while citations of older papers rose briefly in the mid-2010s, it has since declined, with 2021 marking a historic low for the percentage of citations that went to older papers[8]. They term this *citational amnesia* and discuss several possible reasons for the result, including the shift to neural methods and the rise of new areas of NLP.

Our work raises another potential explanation: some citational amnesia is due to *terminology drift* over time, as old methods begin to be referred to by newer names.

Term coining in science Work in science and technology studies has examined the broader phenomenon of term coining in science. Dyke (1992) argues that neologisms emerge more frequently in fields that prize novelty and see science as fundamentally about leaps of discovery, and fields that are perceived as synthesizing findings from multiple fields are most likely to recycle terms from other disciplines. She cites computer science as an example of a field where most new terms of art emerge from recycling common words, often those that draw a metaphor to some basic physical or human concept; this is reflected in the adoption of the humanizing "self-consistency" and the political-science-inspired "range voting" in decoding. Raad (1989) suggests that evocative, metaphor-laden names are more likely to emerge as a scientific field grows more public-facing and in times where many new terms are being coined; both of these descriptors apply to modern NLP. While several works in linguistics and STS have considered the coining of new terms for new phenomena, relatively little work has focused on the divergence of terminology for previously observed phenomena.

The consequences of divergent or distinct terminology have also been studied, with differences in terminology across fields blamed for slow adaptation of research to practical applications (e.g. in studying visual distortions during plane take-off (Calvert, 1956)). Borrowing terminology from another language (often Latin or Greek) or from another field has been described as a method to build common ground between researchers (Samigullina et al., 2020) and as a possibly concerning pressure against developing language-specific scientific terminology in lower-resourced languages (Hultgren, 2013). However, most work on lexical divides in science has focused on divides across language or field rather than divides across time in the same field.

[8]They define an "older paper" as one that is more than 10 years older than the paper that is citing it.

Analyzing Pre-trained and Fine-tuned Language Models

Marius Mosbach
Department of Language Science and Technology
Saarland University
mmosbach@lsv.uni-saarland.de

Abstract

Since the introduction of transformer-based language models in 2018, the current generation of natural language processing (NLP) models continues to demonstrate impressive capabilities on a variety of academic benchmarks and real-world applications. This progress is based on a simple but general pipeline which consists of pre-training neural language models on large quantities of text, followed by an adaptation step that fine-tunes the pre-trained model to perform a specific NLP task of interest. However, despite the impressive progress on academic benchmarks and the widespread deployment of pre-trained and fine-tuned language models in industry we still lack a fundamental understanding of how and why pre-trained and fine-tuned language models work, as well as they do. We make several contributions towards improving our understanding of pre-trained and fine-tuned language models, ranging from analyzing the linguistic knowledge of pre-trained language models and how it is affected by fine-tuning, to a rigorous analysis of the fine-tuning process itself and how the choice of adaptation technique affects the generalization of models. We thereby provide new insights about previously unexplained phenomena and the capabilities of pre-trained and fine-tuned language models.

1 Introduction

Since the introduction of transformer-based pre-trained neural language models in 2018 (Devlin et al., 2019; Liu et al., 2019b), the field of natural language processing (NLP) has witnessed a paradigm shift. Instead of designing and training highly task-specific models from scratch, the current default approach for most NLP tasks consists of adapting general-purpose pre-trained language models, a process which typically requires only very few task-specific changes to the model architecture, and therefore allows us to easily apply the same pre-trained model to different tasks. Over the last five years (2019 – 2023), this paradigm shift has led to impressive progress on a large variety of downstream NLP tasks, ranging from traditional computational linguistics tasks such as part-of-speech tagging and more challenging tasks like natural language inference, to text-based dialogue and assistant systems (Wang et al., 2018, 2019; OpenAI, 2023, *inter alia*).

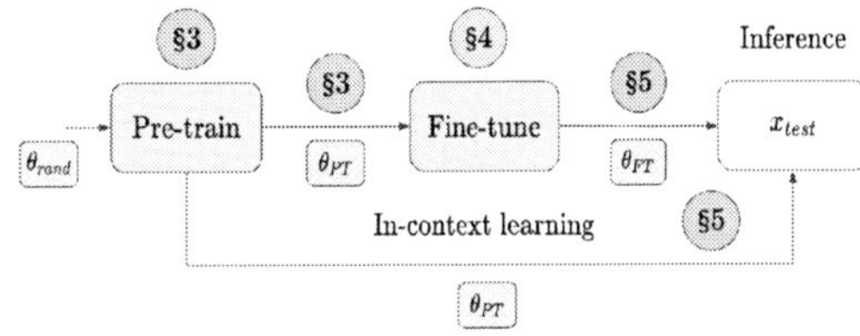

Figure 1: Our contributions positioned along the *pre-train then adapt pipeline* which is prevalent in modern-day NLP. §3 is concerned with how fine-tuning affects the linguistic knowledge of a model, §4 focuses on a better understanding of the fine-tuning process, and §5 is concerned with the generalization of models adapted via fine-tuning and in-context learning during inference.

At the core of this impressive progress lies a very simple but general pipeline which is illustrated in Figure 1 together with our contributions. The first step of this pipeline, which we will refer to as the *pre-train then adapt pipeline*, consists of pre-training a (large) neural language model on large quantities of text using self-supervised training. Due to the discrepancy between the pre-training objective (e.g., masked language modeling) and the downstream task (e.g., classification), the pre-training step is followed by an adaptation step which fine-tunes the pre-trained model to perform a specific task of interest. During fine-tuning, we either update all of the pre-trained parameters or update only a small fraction of them by leveraging parameter-efficient fine-tuning techniques. In both cases, however, fine-tuning results in a task-specific model which can be used for a single task. An alternative task-adaptation technique which was popularized by the most recent advances in training

Proceedings of the the Big Picture Workshop, pages 123–134
December 7, 2023 ©2023 Association for Computational Linguistics

pre-trained language models (Brown et al., 2020; OpenAI, 2023), allows us to bypass the fine-tuning step by treating the downstream task as a language modeling problem. This process, known as in-context learning, enables adapting a pre-trained model without updating any parameters and allows even non-expert users to easily leverage pre-trained language models.

Recent advancements in in-context learning have led to impressive progress on challenging reasoning benchmarks, surpassing the capabilities of fine-tuned language models by large margins (Wei et al., 2022a), a development which has resulted in unprecedented interest from the general public in the promises and potential risks associated with the use of large language models.

2 Research objectives

The previously described pipeline is ubiquitous in modern-day NLP and pre-trained and fine-tuned language models are now dominating research in academia as well as in industry. However, regardless of their impressive capabilities, pre-trained and fine-tuned language models are not without shortcomings. Our contributions center around three major shortcomings of pre-trained and fine-tuned language models. Each of the shortcomings concerns a specific component (or the interaction between two components) of the pre-train then align pipeline (see Figure 1).

2.1 Interplay between fine-tuning and probing

It is well established that fine-tuned language models are often right for the wrong reasons and their good performance on downstream tasks can at least in part be explained by the tendency to pick up spurious correlations during the adaptation process (Jia and Liang, 2017; McCoy et al., 2019; Niven and Kao, 2019; Warstadt et al., 2020, *inter alia*). These results stand in contrast to a large body of evidence that pre-trained language models encode various forms of linguistic and factual knowledge (Liu et al., 2019a; Tenney et al., 2019a; Petroni et al., 2019; Goldberg, 2019; Hewitt and Manning, 2019, *inter alia*).

When combined, these findings require taking a nuanced perspective on the connection between the strong capabilities of language models, as shown by their impressive results on common NLP tasks, and their encoding of linguistic and factual knowledge. These findings also demonstrate the need for investigating the interplay between the linguistic capabilities of pre-trained language models and their downstream performance.

2.2 Investigating fine-tuning stability

Fine-tuned language models often exhibit striking variation in downstream task performance when performing small changes to the adaptation process such as changing the random seed used for initializing model weights, the order of training examples, or the format of a task instruction (Dodge et al., 2020; Webson and Pavlick, 2022; Lu et al., 2022). Large variations in fine-tuning performance are undesirable for several reasons such as hindering reproducible research and complicating the distinction between actual improvements due to modeling or algorithmic advances and comparisons against weak baselines.

Given the ubiquity of fine-tuned language models, it is therefore critical to gain a better understanding of the fine-tuning algorithms that are commonly applied to adapt language models to downstream tasks.

2.3 Generalization of task-adapted models

As mentioned in the previous section, the rapid progress in training ever larger language models has resulted in novel ways to adapt pre-trained language models to downstream tasks by simply instructing them to perform a task of interest via in-context learning. Instead of adapting a model via gradient based fine-tuning, in-context learning allows task adaptation via mere textual interaction and has lead to impressive progress on challenging reasoning benchmarks (Wei et al., 2022b,a). At the same time, there is growing evidence that in-context learning suffers from similar shortcomings to fine-tuning such as their sensitivity to changes in the data order (Min et al., 2022; Lu et al., 2022) and difficulties with generalizing to out-of-distribution inputs (Si et al., 2023).

Given the prevalence of task adaptation via fine-tuning and in-context learning in modern NLP, it is necessary to investigate their respective benefits and downsides and provide a fair comparison of task adaptation approaches.

3 Interplay between fine-tuning and probing (Mosbach et al., 2020)

Our first contribution focuses on the connection between high performance on downstream tasks and

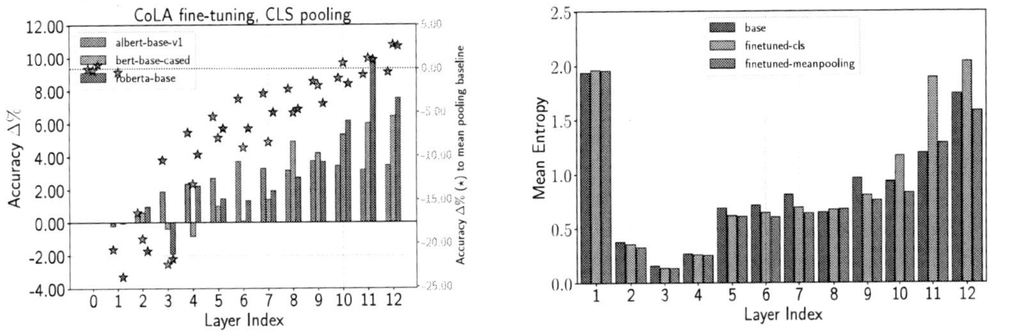

(a) Difference in probing accuracy before and after fine-tuning on CoLA using different models and pooling strategies.

(b) Entropy of the attention distribution for the cls-token of the RoBERTa model on the bigram-shift dataset.

Figure 2: A selection of our findings. (a) shows that when comparing to a stronger pooling baseline, fine-tuning has a negligible impact on probing performance. (b) shows that fine-tuning results in a more uniform attention which offers an alternative explanation for improved sentence-level probing performance.

the linguistic information encoded by a pre-trained model. Specifically, we investigate the hypothesis that the strong capabilities of fine-tuned language models can at least implicitly be attributed to the vast amount of linguistic knowledge which they encode (Pruksachatkun et al., 2020).

3.1 Previous work

A large body of previous work focused on analyzing the internal representations of neural models and the linguistic knowledge they encode via probing (Shi et al., 2016; Ettinger et al., 2016; Adi et al., 2016; Belinkov et al., 2017; Hupkes et al., 2018; Conneau et al., 2018; Krasnowska-Kieraś and Wróblewska, 2019). In a similar spirit to these first works on probing, Conneau et al. (2018) were the first to compare different sentence embedding methods based on the linguistic knowledge they encode. Krasnowska-Kieraś and Wróblewska (2019) extended this approach to study sentence-level probing tasks on English and Polish sentences.

Alongside sentence-level probing, a lot of recent work (Peters et al., 2018; Liu et al., 2019a; Tenney et al., 2019b; Lin et al., 2019; Hewitt and Manning, 2019) has focused on token-level probing tasks investigating more recent contextualized embedding models such as ELMo (Peters et al., 2018), GPT (rad), and BERT (Devlin et al., 2019). Two of the most prominent works following this methodology are Liu et al. (2019a) and Tenney et al. (2019b).

Limitations In contrast to our work, most studies that investigate pre-trained contextualized embedding models focus on pre-trained models and not fine-tuned ones. Therefore, little is known about the interaction between fine-tuning and probing. In our work, we aim to assess how probing performance changes with fine-tuning and how these changes differ based on the model architecture, as well as probing and fine-tuning task combination.

3.2 Our contributions

Setup We study three different pre-trained language models: BERT (Devlin et al., 2019), RoBERTa (Liu et al., 2019b), and ALBERT (Lan et al., 2020), and investigate via sentence-level probing (Conneau et al., 2018) how fine-tuning them on downstream tasks affects the linguistic information encoded in their representations.

We fine-tune on four datasets: CoLA (Warstadt et al., 2018), SST-2 (Socher et al., 2013), RTE (Dagan et al., 2005), SQuAD (Rajpurkar et al., 2016), and perform sentence-level probing experiments on three tasks from the SentEval probing suite (Conneau et al., 2018), each of which targets a different level of linguistic competence: bigram-shift, semantic-odd-man-out, and coordination inversion.

To evaluate the impact of fine-tuning on the linguistic information encoded by a model, we compare probing results before and after fine-tuning.

Fine-tuning mostly affects upper layers Comparing differences in probing performance before and after fine-tuning, we observe that fine-tuning mostly interacts with the upper layers of the pre-trained model. Changes in probing performance are typically larger for higher layers and this finding is consistent across all models and tasks we experiment with.

Positive effect on probing performance is marginal When following the default strategy for sentence-level probing, i.e., constructing sentence representations based on the cls-token of the last hidden layer, we indeed observe large positive changes in probing performance due to fine-tuning, suggesting the encoding of new linguistic information during fine-tuning. However, when we change the pooling approach during probing to mean-pooling, the positive impact of fine-tuning on probing becomes negligible. This effect is illustrated in Figure 2a. For all models, we observe a large increase in probing performance when using cls-pooling to construct sentence representations. However, with mean-pooling, the difference in probing accuracy between the pre-trained and fine-tuned models becomes marginal and fine-tuning even hurts probing performance in lower layers.

Fine-tuning affects attention distribution To better understand the origin of the positive improvements in probing accuracy for cls-pooling, we investigate the attention distribution of the cls-token at every layer. We observe a large increase in entropy in the last three layers when fine-tuning on the cls-token (orange bars in Figure 2b). This is consistent with our hypothesis that during fine-tuning, the cls-token learns to take more sentence-level information into account, thus spreading its attention over more tokens, which offers an alternative explanation to why fine-tuning has a positive impact on probing performance.

3.3 Discussion

Our work provides novel insight into how to perform a fine-grained evaluation of the linguistic knowledge of pre-trained language models and on the interaction between probing performance and fine-tuning. Our findings demonstrate that there is no straightforward causal relationship between the linguistic information encoded by a model and its performance on NLP downstream tasks, which calls for a careful interpretation of changes in probing performance as a result of fine-tuning.

4 Investigating fine-tuning stability (Mosbach et al., 2021)

Our next contribution focuses on the second step of the pre-train then adapt pipeline. We analyze the fine-tuning process itself and study the intriguing finding that fine-tuned models tend to exhibit a large variance in performance, a phenomenon commonly referred to as fine-tuning instability.

4.1 Previous work

Previous work (Devlin et al., 2019; Lee et al., 2020; Dodge et al., 2020) has observed large differences in downstream task performance simply when fine-tuning models with different random seeds. Devlin et al. (2019) report instabilities when fine-tuning BERT-large on small datasets and resort to performing multiple restarts of fine-tuning and selecting the model that performs best on the development set. Dodge et al. (2020) performed a large-scale empirical investigation of the fine-tuning instability of BERT and found dramatic variations in fine-tuning accuracy across multiple restarts and argue how it might be related to the choice of random seed and the dataset size. Few approaches have been proposed to address the observed fine-tuning instability. Phang et al. (2018) study intermediate task training before fine-tuning with the goal of improving performance on the GLUE benchmark and find that their proposed method leads to improved fine-tuning stability. Lee et al. (2020) propose a new regularization technique termed Mixout which improves stability during fine-tuning.

Limitations While previous work on fine-tuning instability commonly states two hypotheses for the observed instability: catastrophic forgetting (Lee et al., 2020) and the small size of the training data (Dodge et al., 2020), there is no previous work that provides a sufficient understanding of why fine-tuning is prone to instability in the first place.

4.2 Our contributions

Motivated by the anecdotal observations stated in previous work, we perform a rigorous investigation of fine-tuning instability in order to determine its root cause.

Setup We analyze three different pre-trained language models: BERT (Devlin et al., 2019), RoBERTa (Liu et al., 2019b), and ALBERT (Lan et al., 2020) and fine-tune them on widely used

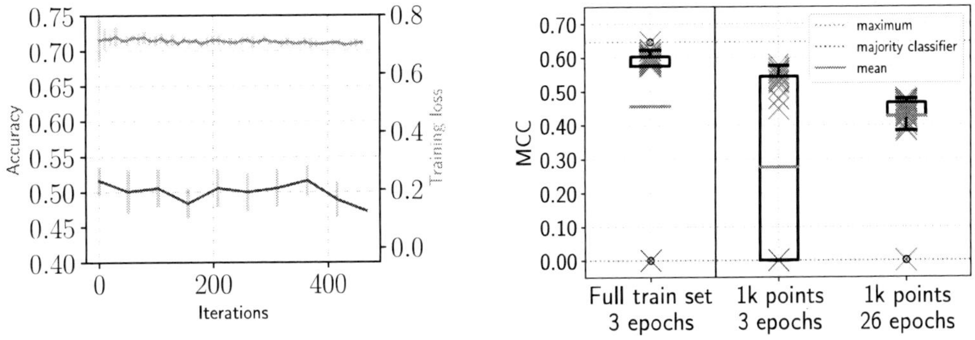

(a) Training of failed models (b) Results on down-sampled CoLA

Figure 3: Previous hypotheses fail to explain fine-tuning stability. (a) shows average training loss and validation accuracy across 3 failed fine-tuning runs on RTE. (b) shows validation performance of models fine-tuned on down-sampled CoLA.

datasets from the GLUE benchmark (Wang et al., 2018). We summarize our contributions below.

Previous hypotheses fail to explain instability First, we show that both catastrophic forgetting and the small size of the training data fail to explain the observed instability phenomenon. As shown in Figure 3a, failed fine-tuning runs in fact do not learn at all, violating the core assumption of catastrophic forgetting that the model performs well on the new task.

Regarding the small size of the training data, Figure 3b shows that fine-tuning on a down-sampled dataset for a small number of epochs does increase variance on the downstream task, however simply training for more iterations fully recovers the original variance in fine-tuning performance. This suggests that the observed instability on small datasets is connected to the number of training steps and not the size of the training set.

Optimization difficulties cause instability Next, we demonstrate that the observed instability is caused by optimization difficulties during fine-tuning that lead to vanishing gradients and models converging to sub-optimal local minima (illustrated in Figure 4). As we show in our work, this behavior is further amplified by choosing too large step sizes, fixing the number of epochs, and not warming up learning rates during the initial phase of fine-tuning.

A strong baseline for fine-tuning Based on our analysis, we present recommendations and a simple but strong baseline approach for fine-tuning. We recommend using small learning rates combined with warmup to avoid vanishing gradients during the initial fine-tuning phase. Additionally, when fine-tuning on small datasets, we suggest not fixing the number of epochs a priori (as was common practice) but rather fix the number of training steps.

Approach	RTE			MRPC			CoLA		
	std	mean	max	std	mean	max	std	mean	max
Devlin	4.5	50.9	67.5	3.9	84.0	91.2	25.6	45.6	64.6
Lee	7.9	65.3	**74.4**	3.8	87.8	**91.8**	20.9	51.9	64.0
Ours	**2.7***	**67.3**	71.1	**0.8***	**90.3**	91.7	**1.8***	**62.1**	**65.3**

Table 1: Standard deviation, mean, and maximum performance on the development set of RTE, MRPC, and CoLA when fine-tuning BERT over 25 random seeds. Standard deviation: lower is better, i.e., fine-tuning is more stable. * denotes significant difference ($p < 0.001$) when compared to the second smallest standard deviation.

As can be seen in Table 1, our baseline makes fine-tuning pre-trained language models significantly more stable than previously proposed approaches while at the same time maintaining or even improving performance.

4.3 Discussion

Our work answers an open question about the instability of fine-tuning and shows that neither catastrophic forgetting nor small dataset sizes sufficiently explain fine-tuning instability. Instead, our analysis reveals that fine-tuning instability can be characterized by two distinct problems: (1) optimization difficulties early in training, characterized by vanishing gradients, and (2) differences in generalization, characterized by a large variance of de-

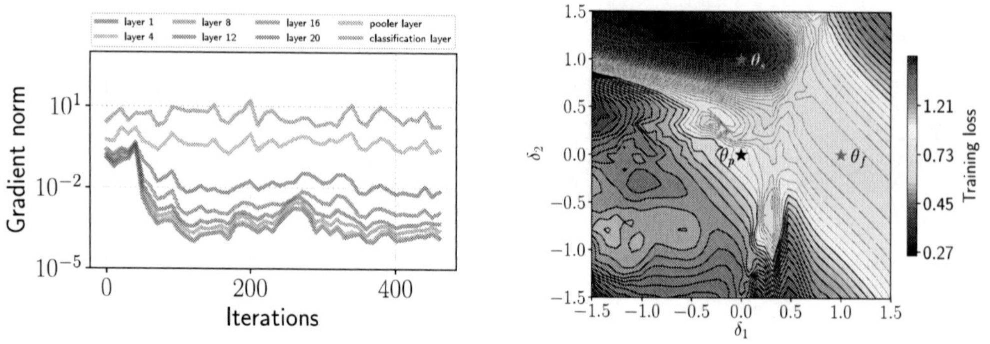

(a) Vanishing gradients during fine-tuning of BERT-large.

(b) 2D loss surface.

Figure 4: Fine-tuning instabilities are characterized by vanishing gradients (a) and convergence to sub-optimal local minima. The 2D loss surface in (b) is spanned by $\delta_1 = \boldsymbol{\theta}_f - \boldsymbol{\theta}_p$ and $\delta_2 = \boldsymbol{\theta}_s - \boldsymbol{\theta}_p$ on RTE.

velopment set accuracy for runs with almost equivalent training performance. Based on our analysis, we propose a simple but strong baseline strategy for fine-tuning BERT which outperforms previous works in terms of fine-tuning stability while maintaining or even increasing overall performance.

5 Generalization of task-adapted models (Mosbach et al., 2023)

Our final contribution is concerned with the last step of the NLP pipeline, namely, inference. We compare the generalization behavior of task-adaptation via few-shot fine-tuning and in-context learning (ICL), which has recently gained popularity over fine-tuning due to its simplicity and strong performance on challenging reasoning tasks.

5.1 Previous work

Brown et al. (2020) compared GPT-3's few-shot in-context learning performance with fine-tuned language models trained in the fully supervised setting and found that both approaches lead to similar results in question answering. More recently, Liu et al. (2022) compared parameter-efficient few-shot FT of T0 (Sanh et al., 2022) to in-context learning with GPT-3, finding that their parameter-efficient fine-tuning approach outperforms in-context learning when evaluated on in-domain data. Focusing on out-of-domain (OOD) performance, Si et al. (2023) investigated the generalization of GPT-3 along various axes, including generalization under covariate shift. They observed much better OOD performance for in-context learning than fine-tuning, concluding that in-context learning with GPT-3 is more robust than fine-tuning using BERT or RoBERTa. Another work that compares the OOD generalization of different adaptation approaches is Awadalla et al. (2022). They investigate the robustness of question answering models under various types of distribution shifts and find that in-context learning is more robust to distribution shifts than fine-tuning. Moreover, they argue that for fine-tuning, increasing model size does not have a strong impact on generalization.

Utama et al. (2021) investigate the OOD generalization of encoder-only models adapted via pattern-based few-shot fine-tuning. For MNLI and HANS, they find that these models adopt similar inference heuristics to those trained with vanilla fine-tuning and hence perform poorly OOD. They observe that models rely even more on heuristics when fine-tuned on more data. Lastly, Bandel et al. (2022) show that masked language models can generalize well on HANS if fine-tuned for a sufficient number of steps.

Limitations A common limitation in the previous literature is the comparisons of generalization abilities under unequal conditions. Most studies either compare the in-context learning abilities of large models (e.g., GPT-3, 175B; Brown et al., 2020) to the fine-tuning abilities of much smaller models (e.g., RoBERTa-large, 350M; Liu et al., 2019b), or compare models fine-tuned on large datasets to few-shot in-context learning (Si et al., 2023). These comparisons raise the question of whether fine-tuning leads to weaker OOD generalization than in-context learning, or whether this is

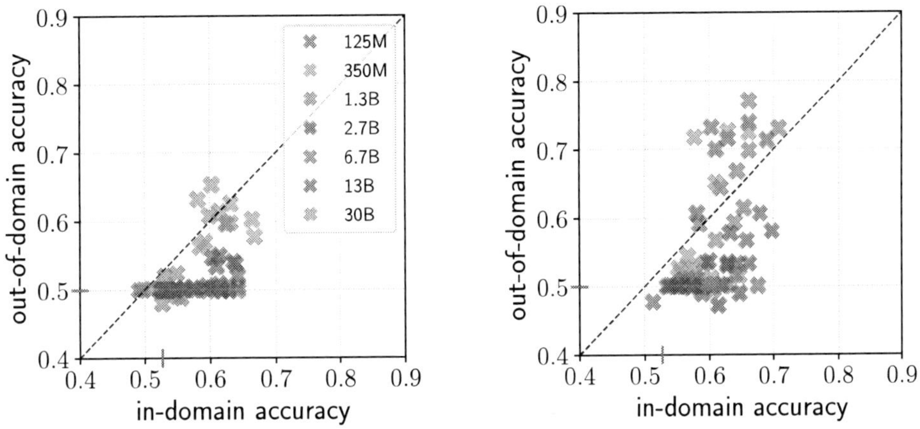

(a) In-context learning

(b) Fine-tuning

Figure 5: In-domain (RTE) and out-of-domain performance (HANS) for in-context learning and fine-tuning with OPT models of various sizes. We fine-tune models using pattern-based fine-tuning. We report results using 10 different data seeds. When using 16 samples, in-context learning's performance with a 30B model is comparable to that of fine-tuning with smaller models (6.7B) and for most model sizes, fine-tuning outperforms in-context learning. — in the x- and y-axes indicates majority class accuracy.

just a byproduct of the experimental setup.

5.2 Our contributions

In our work, we investigate whether the observed weaker out-of-domain generalization of fine-tuned models by previous work is an inherent property of fine-tuning or an artifact of their experimental setup and provide a fair comparison between the generalization of fine-tuning and in-context learning.

Setup For our experiments, we consider few-shot pattern-based fine-tuning (Schick and Schütze, 2021; Gao et al., 2021, *inter alia*) and in-context learning (Brown et al., 2020). We perform a fair comparison of task adaptation focusing on in-domain and OOD generalization under *covariate shift* (Hupkes et al., 2022). We run all experiments using 7 different OPT models (Zhang et al., 2022) ranging from 125 million to 30 billion parameters. During fine-tuning, we update all model parameters if not stated otherwise.

Fine-tuned models can generalize well OOD For our first experiment, we compare fine-tuning and in-context learning using 16 examples for each. We plot the results of this experiment in Figure 5. For in-context learning, we observe an increase in in-domain performance with model size and non-trivial OOD performance only for the largest model (30B). For fine-tuning, we similarly observe that

		PBFT						
		125M	350M	1.3B	2.7B	6.7B	13B	30B
ICL	125M	−0.00	0.01	0.02	0.03	0.12	0.14	0.09
	350M	−0.00	0.01	0.02	0.03	0.12	0.14	0.09
	1.3B	−0.00	0.01	0.02	0.03	0.12	0.14	0.09
	2.7B	−0.00	0.01	0.02	0.03	0.12	0.14	0.09
	6.7B	−0.00	0.01	0.02	0.03	0.12	0.14	0.09
	13B	−0.04	−0.02	−0.01	−0.00	0.09	0.11	0.05
	30B	−0.11	−0.09	−0.08	−0.08	0.02	0.03	−0.02

Table 2: Difference between average **out-of-domain performance** of ICL and FT on RTE across model sizes. We use 16 examples and 10 random seeds for both approaches. We perform a Welch's t-test and color cells according to whether: ICL performs significantly better than FT, FT performs significantly better than ICL. For cells without color, there is no significant difference.

in-domain performance increases with model size. However, as model size increases, OOD performance increases as well, demonstrating that even in the challenging few-shot setting, fine-tuned models can generalize OOD. In Table 2 we provide significance tests that further support our findings. In-context learning only outperforms fine-tuning when comparing large models adapted via in-context learning to small fine-tuned models, which is unfair. Comparing models of the same size however, reveals that fine-tuned models either perform significantly better or similarly to models adapted via in-context learning.

Generalization improves with more data In contrast to in-context learning, where the maximum number of demonstrations is limited by the context size of a model, fine-tuning allows us to perform task adaptation using arbitrary amounts of training data. Therefore, we analyze how the relationship between in-domain and OOD performance is impacted by training on more data. For the smallest models, we find that while in-domain performance increases with more training data, OOD performance remains low, which is consistent with previous work (Utama et al., 2021). However, for larger models, OOD performance improves as the amount of training data increases.

Findings generalize beyond OPT To test the generality of our findings beyond the OPT models, we run the same experiments using Pythia models of different sizes (Biderman et al., 2023). Similarly to OPT, we observe a clear effect of model size on both in-domain and OOD performance. For most model sizes, fine-tuning leads to significantly better OOD performance than in-context learning. Additionally, both the in-domain and OOD performance of Pythia models improve drastically as we fine-tune on more data.

Findings generalize to parameter-efficient fine-tuning We additionally experiment with parameter-efficient fine-tuning via LoRA (Hu et al., 2022) to demonstrate the generality of our findings beyond full fine-tuning. Using LoRA makes adaptation via fine-tuning more similar to adaptation via in-context learning as it allows the re-use of a large fraction of the weights of a pre-trained language model across tasks. Figure 6 shows that fine-tuning via LoRA leads to similar performance as training all parameters (shown in Figure 5b) which demonstrates the generality of our findings beyond a specific fine-tuning method.

5.3 Discussion

Our findings are an important first step towards a better understanding of the fundamental differences in model behavior between different task adaptation approaches. We demonstrate that fine-tuned language models can generalize well both in and out-of-domain. In fact, we find that the generalization of fine-tuning and in-context learning is highly similar as both approaches exhibit large variation in performance and strongly depend on properties such as model size and the number of examples. Hence, our work provides evidence that the poor out-of-domain generalization of fine-tuned models observed in previous work is not a fundamental flaw of fine-tuning but rather a result of their experimental setup, highlighting that truly robust task adaptation remains a challenge.

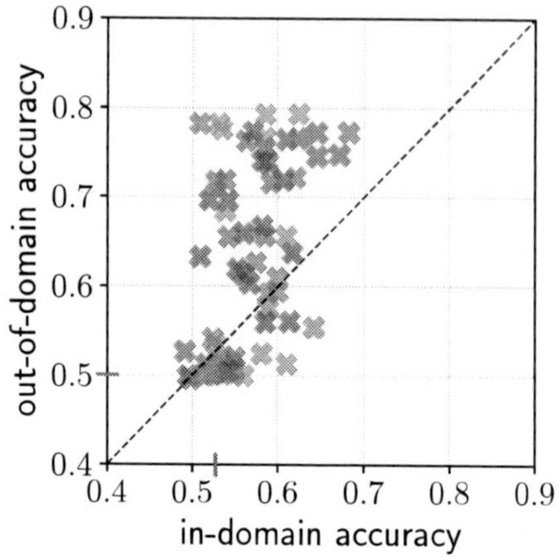

Figure 6: In-domain and OOD performance of parameter-efficient fine-tuning via LoRA on RTE. — in the x- and y-axes indicates the accuracy of the majority class label.

6 The bigger picture

Adapting pre-trained language models via fine-tuning or in-context learning is an integral part of modern-day NLP. While from late 2018 to mid-2020, fine-tuning was the dominating strategy for task adaptation, i.e., converting a pre-trained (masked) language model into a classifier, the introduction of GPT-3 (Brown et al., 2020) in 2020 and the demonstration of its in-context learning abilities resulted in an increasing interest in in-context learning as a new promising paradigm for task adaptation. Recently however, driven by work on instruction fine-tuning (Sanh et al., 2022; Wang et al., 2022, *inter alia*) and alignment to human preferences (Ouyang et al., 2022; Zhou et al., 2023, *inter alia*), fine-tuning[1] is again gaining significant interest from the NLP research community.

Given the ubiquity of language model adaptation in modern-day NLP and machine learning research, it is crucial to make progress towards a better understanding of the inner workings of commonly used

[1]Due to the dominance of decoder-only language models fine-tuning is however no longer used to explicitly adapt language models into classifiers but is instead used to adapt language models to assign higher probability to specific distributions, e.g., instructions and information seeking questions.

adaptation techniques as well as their limitations. The work presented in this paper demonstrates how empirical research can help to achieve this goal and hopefully serves as an inspiration for future research that critically investigates the rapid progress made along the pre-train then adapt pipeline.

7 Summary

Our work makes several contributions towards improving our understanding of pre-trained and fine-tuned language models by carrying out a detailed analysis of various parts of the pre-train then adapt pipeline. Our contributions range from analyzing the linguistic knowledge of pre-trained language models and how it is affected by fine-tuning, to a rigorous analysis of the fine-tuning process itself and how the choice of adaptation technique affects the generalization of models. We provide new insights about previously unexplained phenomena and the capabilities of pre-trained and fine-tuned language models and overall a better understanding of a crucial component of the modern NLP toolbox. Beyond our empirical contributions, we hope that our work demonstrates the importance of taking a critical perspective on previous work and shows that despite the rapid progress in our field, there is a need for work that critically analyzes this progress.

Acknowledgements

Marius Mosbach acknowledges funding from the Deutsche Forschungsgemeinschaft (DFG, German Research Foundation) – Project-ID 232722074 – SFB 1102.

References

Yossi Adi, Einat Kermany, Yonatan Belinkov, Ofer Lavi, and Yoav Goldberg. 2016. Fine-grained analysis of sentence embeddings using auxiliary prediction tasks. *arXiv preprint arXiv:1608.04207*.

Anas Awadalla, Mitchell Wortsman, Gabriel Ilharco, Sewon Min, Ian Magnusson, Hannaneh Hajishirzi, and Ludwig Schmidt. 2022. Exploring the landscape of distributional robustness for question answering models. In *Findings of the Association for Computational Linguistics: EMNLP 2022*, pages 5971–5987, Abu Dhabi, United Arab Emirates. Association for Computational Linguistics.

Elron Bandel, Yoav Goldberg, and Yanai Elazar. 2022. Lexical generalization improves with larger models and longer training. In *Findings of the Association for Computational Linguistics: EMNLP 2022*, pages 4398–4410, Abu Dhabi, United Arab Emirates. Association for Computational Linguistics.

Yonatan Belinkov, Nadir Durrani, Fahim Dalvi, Hassan Sajjad, and James Glass. 2017. What do neural machine translation models learn about morphology? In *Proceedings of the 55th Annual Meeting of the Association for Computational Linguistics (Volume 1: Long Papers)*, pages 861–872, Vancouver, Canada. Association for Computational Linguistics.

Stella Biderman, Hailey Schoelkopf, Quentin Anthony, Herbie Bradley, Kyle O'Brien, Eric Hallahan, Mohammad Aflah Khan, Shivanshu Purohit, USVSN Sai Prashanth, Edward Raff, Aviya Skowron, Lintang Sutawika, and Oskar van der Wal. 2023. Pythia: A suite for analyzing large language models across training and scaling.

Tom Brown, Benjamin Mann, Nick Ryder, Melanie Subbiah, Jared D Kaplan, Prafulla Dhariwal, Arvind Neelakantan, Pranav Shyam, Girish Sastry, Amanda Askell, Sandhini Agarwal, Ariel Herbert-Voss, Gretchen Krueger, Tom Henighan, Rewon Child, Aditya Ramesh, Daniel Ziegler, Jeffrey Wu, Clemens Winter, Chris Hesse, Mark Chen, Eric Sigler, Mateusz Litwin, Scott Gray, Benjamin Chess, Jack Clark, Christopher Berner, Sam McCandlish, Alec Radford, Ilya Sutskever, and Dario Amodei. 2020. Language models are few-shot learners. In *Advances in Neural Information Processing Systems*, volume 33, pages 1877–1901. Curran Associates, Inc.

Alexis Conneau, German Kruszewski, Guillaume Lample, Loïc Barrault, and Marco Baroni. 2018. What you can cram into a single $&!#* vector: Probing sentence embeddings for linguistic properties. In *Proceedings of the 56th Annual Meeting of the Association for Computational Linguistics (Volume 1: Long Papers)*, pages 2126–2136, Melbourne, Australia. Association for Computational Linguistics.

Ido Dagan, Oren Glickman, and Bernardo Magnini. 2005. The pascal recognising textual entailment challenge. In *Proceedings of the First International Conference on Machine Learning Challenges: Evaluating Predictive Uncertainty Visual Object Classification, and Recognizing Textual Entailment*, MLCW'05, page 177–190, Berlin, Heidelberg. Springer-Verlag.

Jacob Devlin, Ming-Wei Chang, Kenton Lee, and Kristina Toutanova. 2019. BERT: Pre-training of deep bidirectional transformers for language understanding. In *Proceedings of the 2019 Conference of the North American Chapter of the Association for Computational Linguistics: Human Language Technologies, Volume 1 (Long and Short Papers)*, pages 4171–4186, Minneapolis, Minnesota. Association for Computational Linguistics.

Jesse Dodge, Gabriel Ilharco, Roy Schwartz, Ali Farhadi, Hannaneh Hajishirzi, and Noah Smith. 2020.

Fine-tuning pretrained language models: Weight initializations, data orders, and early stopping. *arXiv preprint arXiv:2002.06305*.

Allyson Ettinger, Ahmed Elgohary, and Philip Resnik. 2016. Probing for semantic evidence of composition by means of simple classification tasks. In *Proceedings of the 1st Workshop on Evaluating Vector-Space Representations for NLP*, pages 134–139, Berlin, Germany. Association for Computational Linguistics.

Tianyu Gao, Adam Fisch, and Danqi Chen. 2021. Making pre-trained language models better few-shot learners. In *Proceedings of the 59th Annual Meeting of the Association for Computational Linguistics and the 11th International Joint Conference on Natural Language Processing (Volume 1: Long Papers)*, pages 3816–3830, Online. Association for Computational Linguistics.

Yoav Goldberg. 2019. Assessing BERT's syntactic abilities. *arXiv preprint arXiv:1901.05287*.

John Hewitt and Christopher D. Manning. 2019. A structural probe for finding syntax in word representations. In *Proceedings of the 2019 Conference of the North American Chapter of the Association for Computational Linguistics: Human Language Technologies, Volume 1 (Long and Short Papers)*, pages 4129–4138, Minneapolis, Minnesota. Association for Computational Linguistics.

Edward J Hu, yelong shen, Phillip Wallis, Zeyuan Allen-Zhu, Yuanzhi Li, Shean Wang, Lu Wang, and Weizhu Chen. 2022. LoRA: Low-rank adaptation of large language models. In *International Conference on Learning Representations*.

Dieuwke Hupkes, Mario Giulianelli, Verna Dankers, Mikel Artetxe, Yanai Elazar, Tiago Pimentel, Christos Christodoulopoulos, Karim Lasri, Naomi Saphra, Arabella Sinclair, Dennis Ulmer, Florian Schottmann, Khuyagbaatar Batsuren, Kaiser Sun, Koustuv Sinha, Leila Khalatbari, Maria Ryskina, Rita Frieske, Ryan Cotterell, and Zhijing Jin. 2022. State-of-the-art generalisation research in nlp: a taxonomy and review. In *arXiv*.

Dieuwke Hupkes, Sara Veldhoen, and Willem Zuidema. 2018. Visualisation and'diagnostic classifiers' reveal how recurrent and recursive neural networks process hierarchical structure. *Journal of Artificial Intelligence Research*, 61:907–926.

Robin Jia and Percy Liang. 2017. Adversarial examples for evaluating reading comprehension systems. In *Proceedings of the 2017 Conference on Empirical Methods in Natural Language Processing*, pages 2021–2031, Copenhagen, Denmark. Association for Computational Linguistics.

Katarzyna Krasnowska-Kieraś and Alina Wróblewska. 2019. Empirical linguistic study of sentence embeddings. In *Proceedings of the 57th Annual Meeting of the Association for Computational Linguistics*, pages 5729–5739, Florence, Italy. Association for Computational Linguistics.

Zhenzhong Lan, Mingda Chen, Sebastian Goodman, Kevin Gimpel, Piyush Sharma, and Radu Soricut. 2020. ALBERT: A lite BERT for self-supervised learning of language representations. In *International Conference on Learning Representations*.

Cheolhyoung Lee, Kyunghyun Cho, and Wanmo Kang. 2020. Mixout: Effective regularization to finetune large-scale pretrained language models. In *International Conference on Learning Representations*.

Yongjie Lin, Yi Chern Tan, and Robert Frank. 2019. Open sesame: Getting inside BERT's linguistic knowledge. In *Proceedings of the 2019 ACL Workshop BlackboxNLP: Analyzing and Interpreting Neural Networks for NLP*, pages 241–253, Florence, Italy. Association for Computational Linguistics.

Haokun Liu, Derek Tam, Muqeeth Mohammed, Jay Mohta, Tenghao Huang, Mohit Bansal, and Colin Raffel. 2022. Few-shot parameter-efficient fine-tuning is better and cheaper than in-context learning. In *Advances in Neural Information Processing Systems*.

Nelson F. Liu, Matt Gardner, Yonatan Belinkov, Matthew E. Peters, and Noah A. Smith. 2019a. Linguistic knowledge and transferability of contextual representations. In *Proceedings of the 2019 Conference of the North American Chapter of the Association for Computational Linguistics: Human Language Technologies, Volume 1 (Long and Short Papers)*, pages 1073–1094, Minneapolis, Minnesota. Association for Computational Linguistics.

Yinhan Liu, Myle Ott, Naman Goyal, Jingfei Du, Mandar Joshi, Danqi Chen, Omer Levy, Mike Lewis, Luke Zettlemoyer, and Veselin Stoyanov. 2019b. RoBERTa: A robustly optimized BERT pretraining approach. *CoRR*, abs/1907.11692.

Yao Lu, Max Bartolo, Alastair Moore, Sebastian Riedel, and Pontus Stenetorp. 2022. Fantastically ordered prompts and where to find them: Overcoming few-shot prompt order sensitivity. In *Proceedings of the 60th Annual Meeting of the Association for Computational Linguistics (Volume 1: Long Papers)*, pages 8086–8098, Dublin, Ireland. Association for Computational Linguistics.

Tom McCoy, Ellie Pavlick, and Tal Linzen. 2019. Right for the wrong reasons: Diagnosing syntactic heuristics in natural language inference. In *Proceedings of the 57th Annual Meeting of the Association for Computational Linguistics*, pages 3428–3448, Florence, Italy. Association for Computational Linguistics.

Sewon Min, Xinxi Lyu, Ari Holtzman, Mikel Artetxe, Mike Lewis, Hannaneh Hajishirzi, and Luke Zettlemoyer. 2022. Rethinking the role of demonstrations: What makes in-context learning work? In *Proceedings of the 2022 Conference on Empirical Methods in Natural Language Processing*, pages 11048–11064,

Abu Dhabi, United Arab Emirates. Association for Computational Linguistics.

Marius Mosbach, Maksym Andriushchenko, and Dietrich Klakow. 2021. On the stability of fine-tuning BERT: Misconceptions, explanations, and strong baselines. In *International Conference on Learning Representations*.

Marius Mosbach, Anna Khokhlova, Michael A. Hedderich, and Dietrich Klakow. 2020. On the Interplay Between Fine-tuning and Sentence-level Probing for Linguistic Knowledge in Pre-trained Transformers. In *Findings of the Association for Computational Linguistics: EMNLP 2020*, pages 2502–2516, Online. Association for Computational Linguistics.

Marius Mosbach, Tiago Pimentel, Shauli Ravfogel, Dietrich Klakow, and Yanai Elazar. 2023. Few-shot fine-tuning vs. in-context learning: A fair comparison and evaluation. In *Findings of the Association for Computational Linguistics: ACL 2023*, pages 12284–12314, Toronto, Canada. Association for Computational Linguistics.

Timothy Niven and Hung-Yu Kao. 2019. Probing neural network comprehension of natural language arguments. In *Proceedings of the 57th Annual Meeting of the Association for Computational Linguistics*, pages 4658–4664, Florence, Italy. Association for Computational Linguistics.

OpenAI. 2023. GPT-4 technical report. *arXiv preprint arXiv:2303.08774*.

Long Ouyang, Jeff Wu, Xu Jiang, Diogo Almeida, Carroll L. Wainwright, Pamela Mishkin, Chong Zhang, Sandhini Agarwal, Katarina Slama, Alex Ray, John Schulman, Jacob Hilton, Fraser Kelton, Luke Miller, Maddie Simens, Amanda Askell, Peter Welinder, Paul Christiano, Jan Leike, and Ryan Lowe. 2022. Training language models to follow instructions with human feedback.

Matthew E. Peters, Mark Neumann, Mohit Iyyer, Matt Gardner, Christopher Clark, Kenton Lee, and Luke Zettlemoyer. 2018. Deep contextualized word representations. In *Proceedings of the 2018 Conference of the North American Chapter of the Association for Computational Linguistics: Human Language Technologies, Volume 1 (Long Papers)*, pages 2227–2237, New Orleans, Louisiana. Association for Computational Linguistics.

Fabio Petroni, Tim Rocktäschel, Sebastian Riedel, Patrick Lewis, Anton Bakhtin, Yuxiang Wu, and Alexander Miller. 2019. Language models as knowledge bases? In *Proceedings of the 2019 Conference on Empirical Methods in Natural Language Processing and the 9th International Joint Conference on Natural Language Processing (EMNLP-IJCNLP)*, pages 2463–2473, Hong Kong, China. Association for Computational Linguistics.

Jason Phang, Thibault Févry, and Samuel R Bowman. 2018. Sentence encoders on STILTS: Supplementary training on intermediate labeled-data tasks. *arXiv preprint arXiv:1811.01088*.

Yada Pruksachatkun, Jason Phang, Haokun Liu, Phu Mon Htut, Xiaoyi Zhang, Richard Yuanzhe Pang, Clara Vania, Katharina Kann, and Samuel R. Bowman. 2020. Intermediate-task transfer learning with pretrained language models: When and why does it work? In *Proceedings of the 58th Annual Meeting of the Association for Computational Linguistics*, pages 5231–5247, Online. Association for Computational Linguistics.

Pranav Rajpurkar, Jian Zhang, Konstantin Lopyrev, and Percy Liang. 2016. SQuAD: 100,000+ questions for machine comprehension of text. In *Proceedings of the 2016 Conference on Empirical Methods in Natural Language Processing*, pages 2383–2392, Austin, Texas. Association for Computational Linguistics.

Victor Sanh, Albert Webson, Colin Raffel, Stephen Bach, Lintang Sutawika, Zaid Alyafeai, Antoine Chaffin, Arnaud Stiegler, Arun Raja, Manan Dey, M Saiful Bari, Canwen Xu, Urmish Thakker, Shanya Sharma Sharma, Eliza Szczechla, Taewoon Kim, Gunjan Chhablani, Nihal Nayak, Debajyoti Datta, Jonathan Chang, Mike Tian-Jian Jiang, Han Wang, Matteo Manica, Sheng Shen, Zheng Xin Yong, Harshit Pandey, Rachel Bawden, Thomas Wang, Trishala Neeraj, Jos Rozen, Abheesht Sharma, Andrea Santilli, Thibault Fevry, Jason Alan Fries, Ryan Teehan, Teven Le Scao, Stella Biderman, Leo Gao, Thomas Wolf, and Alexander M Rush. 2022. Multitask prompted training enables zero-shot task generalization. In *International Conference on Learning Representations*.

Timo Schick and Hinrich Schütze. 2021. Exploiting cloze-questions for few-shot text classification and natural language inference. In *Proceedings of the 16th Conference of the European Chapter of the Association for Computational Linguistics: Main Volume*, pages 255–269, Online. Association for Computational Linguistics.

Xing Shi, Inkit Padhi, and Kevin Knight. 2016. Does string-based neural MT learn source syntax? In *Proceedings of the 2016 Conference on Empirical Methods in Natural Language Processing*, pages 1526–1534, Austin, Texas. Association for Computational Linguistics.

Chenglei Si, Zhe Gan, Zhengyuan Yang, Shuohang Wang, Jianfeng Wang, Jordan Lee Boyd-Graber, and Lijuan Wang. 2023. Prompting GPT-3 to be reliable. In *The Eleventh International Conference on Learning Representations*.

Richard Socher, Alex Perelygin, Jean Wu, Jason Chuang, Christopher D. Manning, Andrew Ng, and Christopher Potts. 2013. Recursive deep models for semantic compositionality over a sentiment treebank.

In *Proceedings of the 2013 Conference on Empirical Methods in Natural Language Processing*, pages 1631–1642, Seattle, Washington, USA. Association for Computational Linguistics.

Ian Tenney, Dipanjan Das, and Ellie Pavlick. 2019a. BERT rediscovers the classical NLP pipeline. In *Proceedings of the 57th Annual Meeting of the Association for Computational Linguistics*, pages 4593–4601, Florence, Italy. Association for Computational Linguistics.

Ian Tenney, Patrick Xia, Berlin Chen, Alex Wang, Adam Poliak, R Thomas McCoy, Najoung Kim, Benjamin Van Durme, Sam Bowman, Dipanjan Das, and Ellie Pavlick. 2019b. What do you learn from context? probing for sentence structure in contextualized word representations. In *International Conference on Learning Representations*.

Prasetya Utama, Nafise Sadat Moosavi, Victor Sanh, and Iryna Gurevych. 2021. Avoiding inference heuristics in few-shot prompt-based finetuning. In *Proceedings of the 2021 Conference on Empirical Methods in Natural Language Processing*, pages 9063–9074, Online and Punta Cana, Dominican Republic. Association for Computational Linguistics.

Alex Wang, Yada Pruksachatkun, Nikita Nangia, Amanpreet Singh, Julian Michael, Felix Hill, Omer Levy, and Samuel Bowman. 2019. SuperGLUE: A stickier benchmark for general-purpose language understanding systems. In *Advances in Neural Information Processing Systems*, volume 32. Curran Associates, Inc.

Alex Wang, Amanpreet Singh, Julian Michael, Felix Hill, Omer Levy, and Samuel Bowman. 2018. GLUE: A multi-task benchmark and analysis platform for natural language understanding. In *Proceedings of the 2018 EMNLP Workshop BlackboxNLP: Analyzing and Interpreting Neural Networks for NLP*, pages 353–355, Brussels, Belgium. Association for Computational Linguistics.

Yizhong Wang, Swaroop Mishra, Pegah Alipoormolabashi, Yeganeh Kordi, Amirreza Mirzaei, Atharva Naik, Arjun Ashok, Arut Selvan Dhanasekaran, Anjana Arunkumar, David Stap, Eshaan Pathak, Giannis Karamanolakis, Haizhi Lai, Ishan Purohit, Ishani Mondal, Jacob Anderson, Kirby Kuznia, Krima Doshi, Kuntal Kumar Pal, Maitreya Patel, Mehrad Moradshahi, Mihir Parmar, Mirali Purohit, Neeraj Varshney, Phani Rohitha Kaza, Pulkit Verma, Ravsehaj Singh Puri, Rushang Karia, Savan Doshi, Shailaja Keyur Sampat, Siddhartha Mishra, Sujan Reddy A, Sumanta Patro, Tanay Dixit, and Xudong Shen. 2022. Super-NaturalInstructions: Generalization via declarative instructions on 1600+ NLP tasks. In *Proceedings of the 2022 Conference on Empirical Methods in Natural Language Processing*, pages 5085–5109, Abu Dhabi, United Arab Emirates. Association for Computational Linguistics.

Alex Warstadt, Amanpreet Singh, and Samuel R Bowman. 2018. Neural network acceptability judgments. *arXiv preprint arXiv:1805.12471*.

Alex Warstadt, Yian Zhang, Xiaocheng Li, Haokun Liu, and Samuel R. Bowman. 2020. Learning which features matter: RoBERTa acquires a preference for linguistic generalizations (eventually). In *Proceedings of the 2020 Conference on Empirical Methods in Natural Language Processing (EMNLP)*, pages 217–235, Online. Association for Computational Linguistics.

Albert Webson and Ellie Pavlick. 2022. Do prompt-based models really understand the meaning of their prompts? In *Proceedings of the 2022 Conference of the North American Chapter of the Association for Computational Linguistics: Human Language Technologies*, pages 2300–2344, Seattle, United States. Association for Computational Linguistics.

Jason Wei, Yi Tay, Rishi Bommasani, Colin Raffel, Barret Zoph, Sebastian Borgeaud, Dani Yogatama, Maarten Bosma, Denny Zhou, Donald Metzler, Ed H. Chi, Tatsunori Hashimoto, Oriol Vinyals, Percy Liang, Jeff Dean, and William Fedus. 2022a. Emergent abilities of large language models. *Transactions on Machine Learning Research*. Survey Certification.

Jason Wei, Xuezhi Wang, Dale Schuurmans, Maarten Bosma, brian ichter, Fei Xia, Ed H. Chi, Quoc V Le, and Denny Zhou. 2022b. Chain of thought prompting elicits reasoning in large language models. In *Advances in Neural Information Processing Systems*.

Susan Zhang, Stephen Roller, Naman Goyal, Mikel Artetxe, Moya Chen, Shuohui Chen, Christopher Dewan, Mona Diab, Xian Li, Xi Victoria Lin, Todor Mihaylov, Myle Ott, Sam Shleifer, Kurt Shuster, Daniel Simig, Punit Singh Koura, Anjali Sridhar, Tianlu Wang, and Luke Zettlemoyer. 2022. Opt: Open pre-trained transformer language models.

Chunting Zhou, Pengfei Liu, Puxin Xu, Srini Iyer, Jiao Sun, Yuning Mao, Xuezhe Ma, Avia Efrat, Ping Yu, Lili Yu, Susan Zhang, Gargi Ghosh, Mike Lewis, Luke Zettlemoyer, and Omer Levy. 2023. Lima: Less is more for alignment.

Author Index